OXFORD CLASS

Published under the supervision of a Committee of the
Faculty of Classics in the University of Oxford

The aim of the Oxford Classical Monographs series (which replaces the Oxford Classical and Philosophical Monographs) is to publish books based on the best theses on Greek and Latin literature, ancient history, and ancient philosophy examined by the Faculty Board of Classics.

Emperor Worship and Roman Religion

ITTAI GRADEL

CLARENDON PRESS · OXFORD

This book has been printed digitally and produced in a standard specification in order to ensure its continuing availability

OXFORD
UNIVERSITY PRESS

Great Clarendon Street, Oxford OX2 6DP

Oxford University Press is a department of the University of Oxford.
It furthers the University's objective of excellence in research, scholarship,
and education by publishing worldwide in

Oxford New York

Auckland Cape Town Dar es Salaam Hong Kong Karachi
Kuala Lumpur Madrid Melbourne Mexico City Nairobi
New Delhi Shanghai Taipei Toronto
With offices in
Argentina Austria Brazil Chile Czech Republic France Greece
Guatemala Hungary Italy Japan South Korea Poland Portugal
Singapore Switzerland Thailand Turkey Ukraine Vietnam

Oxford is a registered trade mark of Oxford University Press
in the UK and in certain other countries

Published in the United States
by Oxford University Press Inc., New York

Reprinted 2009

ISBN 978-0-19-927548-9

CONTENTS

PREFACE

The substantial revision and expansion to turn my 1995 thesis into a book was in the main finished in early 1998. Later literature has only been taken into account in instances where it affected my argument. As it happened, 1998 was a golden year in the field of Roman religion, with the appearance of two truly substantial works in the area: *Religions of Rome I–II* by S. Price, M. Beard, and J. North, a treasure trove for anybody interested in the subject; and a superb re-publication, by John Scheid, of the *Arval Acta* (see Bibliography). Though Scheid's splendid tome has superseded the earlier publications of Henzen and others, I have refrained from revising my references to the Arval corpus for two reasons: the high cost of the volume may prevent it from being accessible everywhere; and readers with access to Scheid's book will have no difficulty in converting my references by use of its excellent indices and concordances.

A practical note on my use of parentheses in quotes should clarify matters for non-initiates in epigraphical conventions. In source quotes, Greek or Latin, parenthetical text in the same type (roman or italic) as the surrounding text marks either: (...): expansion of abbreviated text in the original; or: [...]: restoration of text which has not been preserved in the original; or: <...>: letters inadvertently left out by the ancient scribe or stonecutter in the original. Parenthetical text in different type (roman or italic) from the surrounding text is my explanatory interjection.

In English translations of sources in Greek or Latin, however, abbreviations in, or restorations of, the original text are not noted, and [...] marks my explanatory interjection or paraphrase. The sole exception is the Mamia inscription (p. 80), where the translated restoration of a lacuna has similarly been marked with [...]. Translations are my own unless otherwise noted.

I owe great debts to more people than I can possibly enumerate here. My supervisor Simon Price, whose book *Rituals and Power* was the main reason I wanted to go to Oxford in the first place, gave constant support and encouragement far beyond the call of duty. Barbara Levick aided me tremendously with her critical acumen, great kindness and infectious energy. In the revision stage, I was also most fortunate in having the learned and downright enjoyable assistance of John North. Warm thanks are also due to Greg Rowe for inspiring criticism and steadfast friendship throughout, and to Peter Brown of Trinity College for much-appreciated help with Plautus and my Chapter 2. I also benefited much and pleasurably from the learning of the friendly staff at the Heberden Coin Room, in particular Chris Howgego. My editors at OUP have kindly guided me through the tortuous path of publication with diligence and professionalism.

My teachers in archaeology at Aarhus, Niels Hannestad (to whom I originally owe my interest in divine emperors) and Lise Hannestad, have generously aided me throughout my studies, professionally as well as personally. Per Bilde and his wife, Pia Guldager Bilde, gave me kind encouragement at various stages. I also owe a debt of gratitude to Kristian Jeppesen, who first showed me how to use my eyes.

My work was made possible by financial assistance from Aarhus University, who gave me a scholarship, by Forskerakademiet, who paid my Oxford fees, and by Statens Humanistiske Forskningsråd, who enabled me to undertake the substantial expansion of the thesis, which I judged necessary for book publication to make sense. The Faculty of Literae Humaniores kindly supplied a grant to cover the cost of the illustrations.

I also extend my warm thanks to my parents for solid encouragement and occasional peptalks. And lastly, my debt to my wife Hanne is more than words can express: as a small token of my appreciation I dedicate this book to her.

Ittai Gradel
Department of History
University of Copenhagen
April 2002

PREFACE TO THE PAPERBACK EDITION

The appearance in paperback has given me the opportunity to correct various typos, minor errors, and some (though far from all) infelicities of language and expression. I have also, on reflection, concluded that an *Index Locorum* should be helpful in a work so source-fixated as mine pretends to be. In compiling and adding this, the continued Arvalian references to Henzen (1874) and other older publications rather than to Scheid (1998)—for which I refer to the Preface to the original edition—began to look increasingly odd, and I have therefore updated them and finally given Scheid's publication its deserved due as the standard work of reference for this group of inscriptions, the more so since Henzen, with Latin commentary, is in any case becoming increasingly inaccessible to students, and Scheid supplies translations (in French).

My book is a *fin de siècle* product, and it would be both fraudulent and silly to camouflage this fact. I have limited myself to correcting errors and non-deliberate omissions, and therefore not updated the bibliography (with the exception, as mentioned, of the Arval references). Still, given the opportunity, two important books should, on reflection and in hindsight, receive mention here. J. E. Lendon's *Empire of Honour* (Oxford University Press, 1997) I ought, perhaps, to have spotted and read before closing my bibliography, but I got hold of it far too late. It is an eloquent exposition of the concept of honour and its all-pervasive importance in the workings of the Empire; the theme is vitally relevant to my own book, and I have learned much from him. Indeed, while I attempt to describe how and why subjects honoured their emperor with divine worship, Lendon's work addresses the more fundamental question: why were they in the first place so keenly attentive to this figure, whose ability to materially affect their lives was, in actual fact, extremely limited?

In the field specifically of emperor worship, M. Clauss's monumental *Kaiser und Gott* (1999) represents an approach to the problem radically different from my own, so different, in fact, that I found it both impossible and pointless to even attempt incorporating his preliminary study (in *Klio* 78 (1996), 400-33) into my book at the late stage when it came to my attention. Professor Clauss tackles head-on the theological question whether the emperor was viewed as a man or as a god, arguing forcefully for the latter, as well as for the view that emperor worship was indeed a religious rather than a political phenomenon. I do not believe these categories reflect contemporary concerns, but whether or not a reader will be more convinced by my interpretation or by that of Professor Clauss, his book is immensely useful and indeed a veritable goldmine for the quarrying of juicy source bits.

Much else has been written before and after 1998. I have neither claimed nor aimed at completeness in my bibliography, and make no apologies in this regard: it was never my intention to write an annotated *Forschungsbericht*, useful as such an exercise might be. I have rather attempted to keep the sources in focus, hoping—perhaps naively—that this would prolong the book's usefulness. This approach has been deliberate, resulting from what I saw as an increasing imbalance in the field: the tendency for the vast amounts of secondary literature and argument to overshadow and in some cases to utterly submerge the ancient evidence. *Ad fontes*, in short. It is the confrontation with the sources which makes history fun. And it is exactly this confrontation that makes theory too come alive.

Last, but far from least, a note of thanks is overdue to my assistant editor Lavinia Porter, who has always come up with solutions rather than problems, and who salvaged this book when it had almost floundered in the process.

Ittai Gradel
Wolfson College
Oxford
February 2004

LIST OF FIGURES

LIST OF ABBREVIATIONS

AA	*Archäologischer Anzeiger*
Abb.	Abbildung/Figure
AE	*L'Année Épigraphique*
AEHE	*Annuaire de l'École pratique des Hautes Études*
AJA	*American Journal of Archaeology*
AJP	*American Journal of Philology*
ANRW	*Aufstieg und Niedergang der Römischen Welt*
Anth. Graec.	*Anthologia Graeca*
App. *BC*	Appian, *Bella civilia*
ARID	*Analecta Romana Instituti Danici*
Aristoph. *Av.*	Aristophanes, *Aves*
Aristoph. *Eq.*	Aristophanes, *Equites*
Arnob. *Adv. Nat.*	Arnobius, *Adversus Nationes*
Artemidorus, *On.*	Artemidorus Daldianus, *Onirocriticus*
Ascon.	Asconius (ed. A. C. Clark (1907): C)
Aur. Victor, *Caes.*	Aurelius Victor, *Caesares*
BCAR	*Bollettino della Commissione Archeologica Communale in Roma*
BdA	*Bollettino d'arte del Ministero per i beni culturali ed ambientali*
BICS	*Bulletin of the Institute of Classical Studies of the University of London*
BJb	*Bonner Jahrbücher*
BMC	Mattingly and Carson, *British Museum Catalogue of Coins of the Roman Empire (1923–)*
BMC Grueber	*British Museum Catalogue of Republican Coins* (1910)
BMGP	*Bolletino dei monumenti, musei e gallerie pontificie*
C	see Ascon.

CAH	*The Cambridge Ancient History* (1st edn., 1923–39, 2nd edn. 1961–)
Censorinus, *De Die Nat.*	Censorinus, *De Die Natali*
Cic. *Ad Att.*	Cicero, *Epistulae ad Atticum*
Cic. *Caec.*	Cicero, *Pro Caecina*
Cic. *Inv. Rhet.*	Cicero, *De Inventione Rhetorica*
Cic. *Leg.*	Cicero, *De legibus*
Cic. *Nat. Deor.*	Cicero, *De natura deorum*
Cic. *Off.*	Cicero, *De officiis*
Cic. *Phil.*	Cicero, *Orationes Philippicae*
Cic. *Planc.*	Cicero, *Pro Plancio*
Cic. *Rep.*	Cicero, *De Republica*
CIL	*Corpus Inscriptionum Latinarum*
Cod. Iust.	*Codex Iustinianus*
Cons. ad Liviam	see Ps.-Ov.
cos.	consul
CQ	*Classical Quarterly*
CR	*Classical Review*
CRAI	*Comptes rendus de l'Académie des Inscriptions et Belles-Lettres*
Dig.	*Digesta*
Dio (Xiph.)	Xiphilinus' epitome of Dio Cassius
Dion. Hal. *Ant.*	Dionysius of Halicarnassus, *Antiquitates Romanae*
DNMQE	*devotus/-i/-a numini maiestatique eius/eorum*
Ep. Corneliae	*Epistula Corneliae Matris Gracchorum*
Eph. Epigr.	*Ephemeris Epigraphica*
EPRO	*Études préliminaires aux religions orientales dans l'empire romain*
Expl. Arch. de Delos	*Exploration archéologique de Délos*
Fasti Ant. Mai.	*Fasti Antiates maiores*
Fasti Praen.	*Fasti Praenestini*
Fest.	Sextus Pompeius Festus (ed. W. M. Lindsay (1913): L)
Flor. *Epit.*	Florus, *Epitome bellorum*
fr.	fragment
Front. *Ep. ad M. Caes.*	Fronto, *Epistulae ad Marcum Caesarem*

Gaius, *Inst.*	Gaius, *Institutiones*
Gell.	Gellius, *Noctes Atticae*
Germ. *Arat.*	Germanicus, *Aratea*
HA *Ant. Pius*	Historia Augusta, *Antoninus Pius*
HA *Carac.*	Historia Augusta, *Caracalla*
HA *Com.*	Historia Augusta, *Commodus*
HA *Elag.*	Historia Augusta, *Elagabalus*
HA *Get.*	Historia Augusta, *Geta*
HA *Hadr.*	Historia Augusta, *Hadrian*
HA *M. Ant. Phil.*	Historia Augusta, *M. Antoninus Philosophus* (= Marcus Aurelius)
HA *Sev. Al.*	Historia Augusta, *Severus Alexander*
HA *Tac.*	Historia Augusta, *Tacitus*
Herod.	Herodian
Hesiod, *Op.*	Hesiod, *Opera et Dies*
Hor. *Carm.*	Horace, *Carmina*
Hor. *Epist.*	Horace, *Epistulae*
HTR	*Harvard Theological Review*
ILLRP	*Inscriptiones Latinae Liberae Rei Publicae*, ed. A. Degrassi
ILS	H. Dessau, *Inscriptiones Latinae Selectae*
IRT	Reynolds, J. M., and Ward Perkins, J. B., *The Inscriptions of Roman Tripolitania* (1952)
JHS	*Journal of Hellenic Studies*
JRA	*Journal of Roman Archaeology*
JRS	*Journal of Roman Studies*
Justin Mart. *Ap.*	Justin Martyr, *Apologiae*
Juv.	Juvenal
L	see *Fest.*
l.	line
ll.	lines
Lact. *Div. Inst.*	Lactantius, *Divinae Institutiones*
Ling. Lat.	*De Lingua Latina*
Liv.	Livy
MAAR	*Memoirs of the American Academy in Rome*
Manil. *Astr.*	Manilius, *Astronomica*

Mart.	Martial
Mart. Pion.	*Martyrium Pionii*
MEFR	*Mélanges d'archéologie et d'histoire de l'École française de Rome*
Min. Fel.	Minucius Felix
NC	*The Numismatic Chronicle*
NSc	*Notizie degli scavi di antichità*
Ov. *Ex Ponto*	Ovid, *Epistulae ex Ponto*
Ov. *Fast.*	Ovid, *Fasti*
Ov. *Met.*	Ovid, *Metamorphoses*
Ov. *Trist.*	Ovid, *Tristia*
PBSR	*Papers of the British School at Rome*
Pers.	Persius
Phaed.	Phaedrus
Philo, *Leg.*	Philo Judaeus, *Legatio ad Gaium*
PIR	*Prosopographia Imperii Romani*
Plaut. *Asin.*	Plautus, *Asinaria*
Plaut. *Capt.*	Plautus, *Captivi*
Plaut. *Pers.*	Plautus, *Persa*
Plaut. *Pseud.*	Plautus, *Pseudolus*
Plaut. *Rud.*	Plautus, *Rudens*
Plin. *Ep.*	Pliny, *Epistulae*
Plin. *Nat. Hist.*	Pliny, *Naturalis Historia*
Plin. *Pan.*	Pliny, *Panegyricus*
Plut. *Ant.*	Plutarch, *Vitae Parallelae: Antonius*
Plut. *Mar.*	Plutarch, *Vitae Parallelae: Marius*
Plut. *Quaest. Rom.*	Plutarch, *Quaestiones Romanae*
Plut. *Rom.*	Plutarch, *Vitae Parallelae: Romulus*
Plut. *Sulla*	Plutarch, *Vitae Parallelae: Sulla*
Polyb.	Polybius
p. R.	*populi Romani*
P. Red. Quir.	*post reditum Quiritibus* or *ad populum*
Ps.-Ov. *Cons. ad Liviam*	Pseudo-Ovid, *Consolatio ad Liviam* or *Epicedium Drusi*
Quint.	Quintilian
RAL	*Rendiconti della Classe di Scienze morali, storiche e filologiche*

	dell'Academia dei Lincei
RE	Pauly, Wissowa, and Kroll, *Real-Encyclopädie der klassischen Altertumswissenschaft (1893–)*
REA	*Revue des études anciennes*
reg.	region/*regio*
REL	*Revue des Études Latines*
Rhein. Mus.	*Rheinisches Museum*
RIC	Mattingly, Sydenham *et al.*, *Roman Imperial Coinage* (1923–67)
RG	Augustus, *Res Gestae*
RM	*Mitteilungen des deutschen archäologischen Instituts: Römische Abteilung*
SC de Cn. Pisone patre	*Senatusconsultum de Gnaeo Pisone Patre*
Schol. Pers.	*Scholia ad Persium*
Schweiz. Münzbl.	*Schweizische Münzblätter*
SEG	*Supplementum epigraphicum Graecum* (1923–)
Sen. *Ap.*	Seneca, *Apocolocyntosis*
Sen. *Clem.*	Seneca, *De Clementia*
Sen. *De Const. Sap.*	Seneca, *De Constantia Sapientis*
Sen. *De Ira*	Seneca, *De Ira*
Sen. *Tranq.*	Seneca, *De Tranquillitate Animi*
Serv. *Ad Aen.*	Servius, *Ad Aeneidem*
Serv. *Ad Buc.*	Servius, *Ad Bucolica/Eclogas*
Stat. *Silv.*	Statius, *Silvae*
Suet. *Aug.*	Suetonius, *Augustus*
Suct. *Caes.*	Suetonius, *Caesar*
Suet. *Cal.*	Suetonius, *Caligula*
Suet. *Claud.*	Suetonius, *Claudius*
Suet. *Dom.*	Suetonius, *Domitianus*
Suet. *Galb.*	Suetonius, *Galba*
Suet. *Gramm.*	Suetonius, *De Grammaticis*
Suet. *Ner.*	Suetonius, *Nero*
Suet. *Tib.*	Suetonius, *Tiberius*
Suet. *Vesp.*	Suetonius, *Vespasianus*
Suet *Vit.*	Suetonius, *Vitellius*

Tab. Heb.	*Tabula Hebana*
Tab. Siar.	*Tabula Siarensis*
Tac. *Ann.*	Tacitus, *Annales*
Tac. *Hist.*	Tacitus, *Historiae*
TAPA	*Transactions of the American Philological Association*
Tert. *Ap.*	Tertullian, *Apologeticus*
Val. Max.	Valerius Maximus
Varro *ARD*	Varro, *Antiquitates Rerum Divinarum* (fragments, ed. B. Cardauns (1976))
Varro, *Ling. Lat.*	Varro, *De Lingua Latina*
Varro, *Rust.*	Varro, *De Re Rustica*
Vell.	Velleius Paterculus
Villa dei Mist.	Villa dei Misteri
Vitr.	Vitruvius
YCS	*Yale Classical Studies*
ZPE	*Zeitschrift für Papyrologie und Epigraphik*

ACKNOWLEDGEMENTS

Illustration sources (unless noted in captions): Cover, 5.4: Royal Coin Collection, National Museum, Copenhagen; 1.1, 12.2, 12.5, 12.7: Dept. of Classical Archaeology, University of Aarhus; 2.1, 2.2: Dept. of History, University of Copenhagen; 4.1–2, 5.1, 5.3, 7.1.2–7, 11.1: DAI, Rome; 7.1.1: drawing by Anders J. B. Jørgensen; 7.2–3, 12.1, 12.3: Heberden Coin Room, Ashmolean Museum; 12.4: photographer Niels Hannestad; 12.6: Dept. of Classical Antiquities, National Museum, Copenhagen.

I
Introduction

> The proconsul [Quintilian] said: 'Offer sacrifice.' 'No', [Pionius] answered. 'My prayers only must be offered to God.' But [Quintilian] said: 'We reverence all the gods, we reverence the heavens and all the gods that are in heaven. What then, do you attend to the air? Then sacrifice to the air!' 'I do not attend to the air', answered Pionius, 'but to him who made the air, the heavens, and all that is in them.' The proconsul said: 'Tell me, who did make them?' Pionius answered: 'I cannot tell you.' The proconsul said: 'Surely it was the god, that is Zeus, who is in heaven; for he is the king of all the gods.'[1]

The owl of Minerva flies only at dusk: basic mental notions will typically find explicit expression only when challenged or under pressure from outside. The early Acts of the Christian Martyrs present several fascinating illustrations of this: in their dialogues with Christian defendants presenting fundamentally different views on God and theology, Roman officials could be called on to verbalize and rationalize customs and values so basic, so much taken for granted, that they were hardly ever stated without such provocative prompting. The governor who heard the case of Pionius in Smyrna in the days of the Decian persecution, AD 250, furnishes an example. What he and other governors trying Christian defendants demanded of them was not any specific belief, cosmology, reasoning, or philosophy, but simply an action: sacrifice. Dragged, however, into a dogmatic discussion in the context of the traditional pagan rite, sacrifice of wine and incense to the gods, the governor comes out with his own ad hoc cosmology: Zeus had made the world, for he was king of the gods.

Where did he get this answer? No school of philosophy had

[1] *Mart. Pion.* 19.9–13, Musurillo (1972, 160ff.), id. tr. (adapted); Robert *et al.* (1994); Lane Fox (1986, 460ff.).

presented such a cosmology, and none of the stories of mythology told this tale. Apparently the governor himself made up this answer on the spot. What is revealing in the story is that he did *not* employ any of the readily available answers from philosophy or mythology to legitimize the rite demanded of Pionius. That rite, sacrifice, in this case a bloodless one, did not need to be pinned onto a dogmatic or philosophical system to be defended. With impressive tradition behind it, it had always, or so it must have seemed, been the natural way to honour the vastly superior powers of the gods: sacrifice was the core element in divine worship.

The account of Pionius before the governor was penned by a Christian writer, and the governor's dialogue was put in his mouth for the benefit of a Christian audience. It is not to be taken literally as a faithful transcript of the exchange. But its imagery of pagan arguments should not be summarily dismissed for that reason. The didactic message of the text is obvious: each member of the Christian audience savouring Pionius' cruel martyrdom had to be prepared for the same situation. The text was meant to encourage them to display the same nerve, the same unflinching resolve as that of Pionius, a presbyter whose constancy was not even shaken by the fact that his own bishop had lapsed and performed the sacrifice. Recent examinations have upheld the text of Pionius' martyrdom as contemporary and faithful in its details, whenever these can be subjected to control. But whether factual, elaborated, or simply invented, the dialogue is not a mere mythical construct, nor is the pagan adversary portrayed as a madman or a raving disciple of Satan: Christians knew their opponents, knew what to expect from a governor attempting to make them forsake their principles; they had to know in order to prepare for their moment of glory. The governor's insistence on demanding the rite itself without any dogmatic underpinning was indeed telling and typical. It faithfully reflected the edict of Decius where the emperor demanded of his non-Jewish subjects that they should sacrifice, plain and simple, without requesting from them any specific beliefs or theology or recognition of any named gods.

The story of Pionius and Quintilian the governor is one of many that could be quoted to illustrate the fallacies of interpreting traditional religious practice in the light of philosophical or mythological texts or arguments. It illustrates the extent to which this traditional worship lived its own life, independently of philosophical speculation or elaborate mythology. If we were to look for a parallel in our own mental makeup, it would be our ingrained distinction between religion and politics. This dichotomy was unknown to, or at least irrelevant to, traditional Graeco-Roman worship and other honours to benefactors. For divine cult was an honour, differing in degree but not in kind from 'secular' honours;[2] and this by itself implies that there is something wrong with our usual and ingrained oppositions, of religion versus politics, of man versus god, when applied to pagan practice.

Even when avoiding philosophy and mythology it is all too easy to go searching for the mental hinterland behind the pomp and circumstance of cultic practice. When trying to reconstruct a detailed theology from religious rites, we must be on guard: we are then pursuing our own game, not that of the ancients; and we then easily fall into the trap of 'philosophizing' or 'christianizing' Graeco-Roman religion. For Christianity of course combined philosophy, in the shape of detailed systems of dogma, with rituals of divine worship; these rituals acted out the word of God and the sacrifice of His son as contained in Holy Scripture. The rituals in themselves, without this dogmatic underpinning, were nothing. The core and basis of traditional Graeco-Roman religion were precisely the contrary: the rituals, not any verbalized and authoritative texts or dogmas or philosophical reasoning. Only with extreme caution should philosophical treatises, such as Cicero's *De Natura Deorum* or *De Divinatione* be employed in the study of Roman religion; and as for its interpretation, they are best left out of account altogether. It will perhaps be noticed that these and similar treatises, usually seen as core sources for Roman religion, are almost completely ignored in this book. Instead, as I attempt here, interpretation should be based on study of ritual, not merely as a reflection of an underlying theology, but in its own

[2] Nock (1934, 481 f.): emperor worship was 'of the nature of homage and not of worship in the full sense'; contra Price (1984a, *passim*, esp. 15 ff.) (fundamental for religion vs. politics); yet, unlike most modern scholars, Nock recognized that the distinction is a modern one (1972, 241; written in 1930).

right, as what traditional Roman religion was in fact all about: rituals constructing, and not merely reflecting, the theology, the world, and its social order.

RELIGION

By demarcating 'emperor worship' and studying it as a subject in isolation from ancient religion and politics—since it is not clear to which of these categories it belongs—this book may unfortunately further cement our own distinctions, and submerge those of the ancients. Unlike its usage in modern scholarship, 'the imperial cult' had no category of its own in the ancient world. Both our concepts of religion and politics, and thus the dichotomy between them, are in fact modern inventions. Neither Greek nor Latin had any pre-Christian term for 'religion' or 'politics' in our sense of the word. *Religio* meant reverence, conscientiousness, and diligence towards superiors, commonly but not exclusively the gods: 'To be *religiosus* is not merely to hold the sanctity of the gods in great respect, but also to be dutifully obliging (*officiosus*) towards men', as a Roman grammarian stated. In another, narrower sense, the word could be used collectively of the rites and ceremonies of divine worship, and of everything connected with such worship (synonymous with *res divinae* as opposed to *res humanae*).[3] Pre-Christian *religio* was not concerned with inward, personal virtues, such as belief, but with outward behaviour and attitude; in other words, with observance rather than faith, and with action rather than feeling. This does not, of course, amount to saying that pagan worshippers did not experience personal emotions in connection with their worship, merely that this aspect was only marginally relevant, if at all, to the concept and meaning of *religio*. The meaning of this word in the modern sense as a religious system encompassing both action—rituals—and philosophy—theology, dogmas, cosmology, mythology—belongs to late antiquity and was developed specifically in connection with *religio Christiana*, Christianity.

The concept of 'religion' is actually very problematical to

[3] Fest. p. 348L: '*religiosus est non modo deorum sanctitatem magni aestimans, sed etiam officiosus adversus homines*'; narrower: e.g. Cic. *Nat. Deor.* 2. 3. 8: '*religione id est cultu deorum*'; 2. 28. 72.

employ; even today, historians of religion do not generally agree on a definition.[4] Most such definitions are either too broad and all-inclusive, which renders them less useful for practical purposes, or else christianizing, as in stressing individual faith, sincerity, or perceived experience, and hence too narrow. The most useful definition, in my view, interprets the concept of 'religion' as defined by action of dialogue—sacrifice, prayer, or other forms of establishing and constructing dialogue—between humans and what they perceive as 'another world', opposed to and different from the everyday sphere in which men function. Typically, this 'other world' is a realm of gods or God (but not necessarily so: academic Buddhism, which most scholars are loath to exclude from the concept, does not operate with gods). Such a view of 'religion' recommends itself, I believe, to the study of pagan practice: it stresses action as the constituting factor, and avoids christianizing concepts such as 'belief' or 'emotion' as determinants.[5]

The problem with this as with any other definition of 'religion' (except such as simply reject pagan practice as devoid of religious aspects) lies not in the factor of dialogue, clearly definable, but in the notion of the 'two worlds'. On the face of it no problem is apparent: the 'other world' is simply the realm of the gods, with which dialogue is established by ritual action (primarily sacrifices). Yet the fact that such ritual was also employed in connection with humans puts fundamentally in question our whole construction of dichotomies: this world versus that of the gods, man versus god, religion versus politics. The phenomenon of ruler cults has received so much attention because it does not fit into these basic dichotomies, but transgresses them. Was the emperor, when worshipped in divine rites, seen as a man or as a god? Was he a political or a religious figure?

Our distinction between the 'two worlds', between religion and politics, is the fundamental one. The distinction or strong dichotomy between the two spheres goes back to the Age of Enlightenment, and was not directly theologically inspired. Yet the roots of the distinction are clearly founded in Christian theology, and it is a relevant question whether it could at all have

[4] For discussion of definitions see refs. in Liebeschuetz (1979, 72 n. 6); Pfenner and Yonan (1972); Whaling (1983).

[5] For a fine discussion of such christianizing notions see Price (1984*a*, 1 ff.).

been thought of without these antecedents. They are originally represented in the saying of Jesus to 'give unto Caesar what is Caesar's, and unto God what is God's';[6] and later continued in a Christian tradition with St Augustine as the best-known exponent. In his *De Civitate Dei* he unequivocally set up this demarcation line between the realm of God (*civitas Dei*) and this world. Later still, medieval theologians spent much ink and effort defining and arguing about the distinction between temporal and spiritual power and their respective preserves. The two forms of authority were expressed in the institutions of kingship and church, as ultimately personified in the figures of the holy Roman emperor and the pope. These Christian theological categories do not correspond to our categories of religion versus politics. But they certainly represent a precursor and probably a necessary prerequisite for these modern concepts.

So even our view of religion as a dimension, or aspect of the human spirit, separable from other spheres of human experience and common to all mankind, is ultimately christianizing and directly relevant only to a Christian cultural sphere, or such as are influenced by it. Other cultures, including pagan Greece and Rome, lack the religious dimension: it is absent in the sense that 'the divine' or the 'other world' forms a whole with other aspects of human experience, including politics, and can be separated and dissected on its own only at the peril of understanding. The very concept of 'religion' is inherently christianizing—which is not an argument against its use, as long as we are aware of it. But it is all too easy to fall into the trap of treating our own categories as absolute and god-given.[7]

[6] Matthew 22. 19ff.; cf. John 8. 23.

[7] The 'otherness' of Graeco-Roman religion is now commonly recognized in classical scholarship, thus for Roman *religio* Scheid (1985, 7ff.); the realization that the problem of 'religion' is of a general nature, and not only confined to pagan Graeco-Roman cults, seems rarer: Liebeschuetz (1979, 72) raises the problem of defining 'religion', but does not fundamentally tackle it; also Beard (1994, 729ff.), who, however, tends to see the problems of definition as characteristic of Roman state religion in particular; I would rather see them as generally typical of studies of religions outside a Christian cultural sphere. Price (1984a, *passim*, esp. 15ff.) is fundamental for the 'otherness' of pagan religiosity, exhibiting strong and sophisticated awareness of methodological and anthropological discussions on the subject, though curiously avoiding direct discussion of the concept of 'religion'.

To avoid, as far as possible, these pitfalls of method, terminology, and language I shall therefore attempt to base my investigation primarily on the ancient standards and distinctions. The definition of emperor worship or 'the imperial cult' (a more flawed term, because more specific, giving the impression of a neat and independent category) will follow the ancient term of *divini* or *summi* or *caelestes honores*, the highest form of honours, with which gods were cultivated (but probably never gods *only*): sacrificial rites, whether blood sacrifice or bloodless (wine and incense) to the emperor, dead or alive. To identify such cults, the presence of temples and altars is taken as direct evidence (the arguments for doing so will emerge from my treatment). Cults of imperial virtues or circumstances, such as *Salus* ('Welfare'), *Virtus* ('Prowess') or *Providentia* ('Foresight'), with or without the qualification 'of the emperor'—*Augusti*—or, more commonly, as an adjective, *Augusta*, 'august' or 'imperial', will largely be ignored, since these concepts existed as goddesses in their own right.[8]

Two concepts, however, could not stand alone, but always 'belonged' to someone: *Genius* and *numen* (the term '*numen*', divine power, can also simply be synonymous with *deus*). These two terms have played an enormous role in scholarship on the subject, and they will also be included here. Worship of the *Genius* of a man denoted cult on a 'human' level, since all living men (and gods, for that matter) possessed a *Genius*, and its cultivation did therefore not impute divinity, or rather divine status, to its 'owner', as did the 'heavenly honours' (*caelestes honores*). Inclusion of the *Genius* in this treatment does receive some contemporary support; at least to one Christian apologist, writing probably in the early third century, worship of the *Genius* was placed in the same despicable category as direct worship:[9]

Pitiable indeed the man whose hope is stayed upon a mortal man, with whose death all that he builds on comes to an end! True indeed that Egyptians choose a man for their worship; that they propitiate him and him alone; that they consult him on all matters and kill victims to him. But though to others he is a god, to himself at least he is a man,

[8] See, however, further p. 103–6 below.

[9] Min. Fel. 29. 3 ff., tr. Rendall, Loeb edn. (adapted).

whether he like it or no; for he does not impose upon his own consciousness, even if he deludes others. Princes and kings may rightly be hailed as great and elect among men, but homage to them as gods is base and lying flattery; honour [*honor*] is the truer tribute to distinction, affection the more acceptable reward to worth. Yet that is the way men invoke their deity [*Sic eorum numen vocant*], make supplications to their images, pray to their Genius, that is their daemon [*daemonem*]; and think it safer to swear falsely by the Genius of Jupiter than by that of their king.

The passage neatly applies the monotheistic distinction between worship and honours, which has continued to problematize the interpretation of ruler cult ever since. Implicitly the apologist criticizes contemporary practice in Italy, though it is a typical feature of the genre that the specific example singled out for attack is not Roman religion, but the beastly practice of the Egyptians, contempt of which was generally shared by Christians and Roman pagans alike (I shall return to these aspects at the end of this book). Modern scholars have generally continued in this didactic and polemical track by denying or down-playing emperor worship as a *Roman* phenomenon, and instead consistently seeing it as a feature characteristic of the Greek parts of the empire, or of barbarians newly brought under the sway of Rome. In fact, Roman pagan writers for didactic or moralizing reasons employed the same distinction between Roman and Greek or barbarian. Thus Tacitus' term *Graeca adulatio*, 'Greek flattery', has often recurred in modern scholarship on the subject. However, though little acknowledged by scholars, the Roman historian with these words does not criticize the phenomenon as such, but only the granting of divine honours to the ridiculously unworthy (*in casu* Pompey's friend Theophanes of Mytilene).[10]

PUBLIC RITES, PRIVATE RITES

To make sense of a large and seemingly confusing body of material, I shall attempt to divide it into categories that were meaningful by contemporary standards. Thus status consciousness and its implication for the cult forms chosen by wor-

[10] Tac. *Ann.* 6. 18; for a different view of Theophanes' worth see Robert (1969).

shippers in honouring the emperor will play a large part; I shall attempt to distinguish between the status of worshippers in such cults, whether freeborn of high rank and (claimed) social independence, or freedmen and slaves. The obvious advantage of this criterion is that it is objective, and in most cases simple to apply; as to its meaningfulness in contemporary terms, that can hardly be controversial. In close connection with this I shall strictly distinguish between public cults, which were always carried out and controlled by freeborn of high rank, and private worship, where the status of worshippers was more variable. Our own notions of public and private are notoriously ill-suited and difficult to apply to the Graeco-Roman world; and in the field of Roman religion, the terms are too often employed in senses so vague as to be practically meaningless. I shall therefore here follow the Roman legal definitions.[11] The explicit definitions are preserved only by Festus in his second-century epitome of the gigantic dictionary *De Verborum Significatu* of the Augustan scholar Verrius Flaccus. Sacral law was an important branch of Roman jurisprudence, which for obvious reasons had little appeal to Christian posterity, and whose texts have therefore not been preserved. Festus' shorthand definitions in the field raise problems of their own, but are in the main clear enough; thus the basic definition of public versus private *sacra* (Fest. p. 284L):

Publica sacra quae publico sumptu pro populo fiunt, quaeque pro montibus, pagis, curis sacellis: at privata, quae pro singulis hominibus, familiis, gentibus fiunt.

Public rites are those which are performed at public expense on behalf of the [whole] people, and also those which are performed for the hills [*montes*], villages [*pagi*], 'clans' [*curiae*] and chapels [*sacella*], in contrast to private rites which are performed on behalf of individual persons, households, or family lineages.

Publica sacra fall, then, in two distinct groups, of which the first and main one is fairly straightforward. It covers cults performed on behalf of the whole individual city—or 'city state'—and all its citizens (*populus*), by city magistrates, at public expense. These cults, which I will here term public cults, or

[11] Wissowa (1912, 398ff.); Geiger (1914).

outside Rome municipal or civic cults, were then the exclusive privilege of the magistrates (including priests) of the individual 'city state'. The magistrates invariably belonged to the local élites—in Rome the Senate, outside Rome the corresponding city council (*ordo decurionum*)—of their townships. In the case of Rome, such cults may be termed 'state cults' or collectively the 'state cult' (a term often employed in a very imprecise manner).

The second group of the *publica sacra* comprised a small group of archaic Roman state cults which, unlike the main group, were not performed on behalf of the whole people, but only on behalf of parts of the city territory and the citizens who dwelled there. This variation is explicable in historical terms as local cults incorporated into the Roman state cult as a result of synoecism, or cults so early that Rome and its citizens had long ago outgrown the geographical areas they traditionally covered. Thus the rites *pro montibus*, the festival called *Septimontium*, took place on the original seven hills of Rome—not to be confused with the more widespread later seven hills of the city—which covered only a small part of Rome's centre. So did the *Paganalia*, the festival for the villages—*pagi*—of archaic Rome; and the obscure rites for the *curiae*, subdivisions or 'clans' within the old Roman tribes; and the ceremonies of the *sacella*, a rite more commonly known as the rite of the *Argei*.[12] The *Argei* were straw dolls kept in twenty-seven or thirty chapels

[12] Usually *sacellum* in the passage has been taken as synonymous with *compitum* (Geiger (1914, 1662 with lit.)), but this must be wrong; the word *sacellum*, 'small shrine', is generic, and otherwise not specifically used of *compita*: contra Wissowa (1904, 237 with n. 4 and cf. ibid. 219f.); but the instances quoted by him seem rather to be, again, the Argeian shrines, or simply 'shrines' in general; or, whatever the precise term referred to, used in poetry where the word is then employed for metrical reasons. However, Varro, *Ling. Lat.* 5. 48 unequivocally terms an Argeian chapel a *sacellum* (though elsewhere, 5. 45 and 47, calling them *sacraria*, for which *sacellum* indeed seems the obvious synonym). Note further that both *sacrarium* and *sacellum* are vague terms, certainly interchangeable in Varro, whereas *compitum* is an equally short term and quite specific to one type of sanctuary only; it therefore seems inexplicable why the specific and suitable term should have been exchanged for the vaguer one, if the *compita* had indeed been meant in Festus and his source Verrius Flaccus; in prose metrical reasons are out of the question. Lastly, the cults at the *compita* were clearly privately funded (see p. 128–30 below), unlike the rites of the Argeian *sacraria* (see n. 13 below).

scattered over Rome's archaic centre, and annually collected to be thrown into the Tiber from the Sublician Bridge. The survival into historic times of these localized state cults is fascinating evidence of the strong Roman conservatism in religion, but they did not really play any important role in historical times, and represent only a rare and curious variation on the main group of state rites. In any case, such cults were also funded with public money, and performed or presided over by state magistrates.[13]

What is important is not to mix up these localized state cults with other cults in subdivisions of Rome, such as the compital cults. Each of the city quarters, *vici*, of Rome had from archaic times a cult centre, *compitum*, where the inhabitants of the individual *vicus* worshipped its tutelary gods, the *Lares compitales*. The priests in these local cults were, however, mainly freedmen or slaves, and the worship was not publicly funded, but financed by the priests themselves, that is, with private money; state priests or state finances had no role to play in these cults. They were then clearly private, probably within a subcategory encompassing the cults of private, but non-familial groupings, *collegia*.[14] Such private worship is not mentioned by Festus at all, but that is not a great problem, for his shorthand characterization of *sacra privata* is clearly not complete. The only instances he gives are those of individuals and families, and private cults certainly covered much more than such household rites. The category thus also included cults of private clubs, *collegia*, which were ubiquitous during the empire.

[13] Festus' shorthand wording is ambiguous as to the financing, but public funding must be decisive to the inclusion of these cults within the *publica sacra*, and at least for the *sacra pro curis* there is clear evidence of public funding (Dion. Hal. *Ant.* 2. 31. 1; Varro, *Ling. Lat.* 6. 46; generally Hülsen, 1901, 1815ff.); the rites were presided over by the obscure officials, the *curiones*, under a general *curio maximus*. Equally obscure, minor public officials, local *magistri* and *flamines*, presided over the *Septimontium*. For this and the *Sacra pro Argeis*, see Wissowa (1904, 230ff. and 211ff., as well as id. (1912), *passim*). Note that the praetors, *pontifices*, Vestal Virgins, and the *flaminica Dialis* took part in the *sacra pro Argeis*.

[14] Thus apparently Ascon. p. 7C on the compital cults and their games in the late republic: '*Solebant autem magistri collegiorum ludos facere, sicut magistri vicorum faciebant, Compitalicios praetextati, qui ludi sublatis collegiis discussi sunt*'; Lintott (1968, 77ff.); Fraschetti (1990).

The distinction between public and private cults seems clear enough, and was in fact based on objective determinants, even if they may be imperfectly known to us in the case of this or that individual cult.[15] All this may so far seem mere legalistic pedantry, but will, I trust, be shown to make sense when applied in practice. It was decisive in one particular respect. Religion and politics formed a whole in the public sphere of Rome, or indeed of any other city state in antiquity. State religion, the city cult of Rome, was therefore an integral part of the Roman 'constitution' and indeed continually defined it. On a local level the same goes for municipal or civic cults, the public cults in the self-governing city states under Rome's control which were scattered all over the empire: they too defined the 'constitution' of each little city state.

The state cult in Rome functioned on behalf of the whole Roman people, which in the early empire basically meant all the free inhabitants of Italy (i.e. the peninsula as defined by the eleven Augustan regions: without Sicily and Sardinia, but including Histria, now part of Croatia). Roman state gods were simply and exclusively those which received worship in such state cult. Municipal or private cults, on the other hand, had no bearing whatsoever on the Roman 'constitution'. Municipal worship only covered the inhabitants and area of the individual township; and private cults merely affected the private persons

[15] Note the subcategory of *popularia sacra* given by Festus elsewhere (p. 298L): '*Popularia sacra sunt, ut ait* [M. Antistius] *Labeo, quae omnes cives faciunt, nec certis familiis adtributa sunt* [i.e. 'and not confined only to some households']*: Fornacalia, Parilia, Laralia, porca praecidanea*' (Harmon (1978, 1594); further comments by Scheid (1990, 255 and 259); Wissowa (1912, *passim* for the items mentioned)). This appears to comprise rites and festivals which were celebrated *both* in state cult and simultaneously in all Roman private households, an interpretation supported by Varro (*Schol. Pers.* 1. 72 = Varro, *ARD* ed. Cardauns, p. 56): '*Palilia* [= Parilia] *tam privata quam publica sunt*'. The term *Laralia* has usually been taken as = *Compitalia*, a festival celebrated both in the households and at the *compita* in the *vici* (Wissowa, 1912, 399 n. 2; Geiger, 1914, col. 1662). But *Laralia* is otherwise never used as a synonym for this festival, and there is no evidence that the *Compitalia* were ever celebrated in the state cult. The term *Laralia* should rather be understood as covering both the ubiquitous private cult of the *Lares* of each house and the corresponding public worship of the state *Lares*. This would certainly fit the implications of the category as both public and private more neatly.

involved. That means, for instance, that the Roman emperor could in principle be worshipped as a god in all the municipal cults of Italy and in private cults everywhere in Italy, including in Rome itself, without such worship in the least affecting his formal place in the 'constitution' of Rome. Only the public, constitutional sphere of Rome itself mattered in this connection. In the same way a god could be worshipped anywhere in Rome and Italy and still be completely outside the Roman state system, such as the god Silvanus who was extremely popular in private cults everywhere in Italy, but never became a state god.[16] The distinction between public and private cult does not, it should be noted, correspond to our ideas of public versus private. Private cults regularly took place in public, even at public temples, and could be under tight control and scrutiny from the public authorities.

In geographical terms, my investigation will cover Roman Italy, the Roman heartland in the early empire. The state cult in Rome, an integral part of the 'constitution' of the Roman state, will receive the most thorough treatment; the state cult presents complicated problems peculiar to this 'constitutional' sphere, and my investigation will, I hope, add some new dimensions to the history of the development of the principate. For the same reason my main emphasis will be on the early empire, the formative phase of the principate. Conditions in the Greek world, or indeed the world outside Italy, will be almost totally ignored in this book. This is not owing to any disdain for *Graeca adulatio*, but only reflects the fact that the author feels uncomfortable with the Greek versus Roman dichotomy, which has traditionally played such a prominent role in work on ancient ruler cult. By dealing with Italy in isolation, artificial as this may seem, I hope to avoid presupposing either differences or similarities between the Roman heartland and the world outside it, thus also avoiding any temptation to fill in missing bits from other areas of the Roman empire. Informed readers may make their own comparisons and form their own judgement on this, though I trust that Italy will emerge as less deviant from the rest of the empire than most handbooks suggest today.

[16] Silvanus: Dorcey (1992).

FIG. 1.1. A standard state sacrifice in front of the temple of Jupiter Optimus Maximus on the Capitol

Notes: The temple, in the background left, has three entrance doors, for Juno Regina, Jupiter, and Minerva respectively. The officiating priest, the emperor Marcus Aurelius, is pouring a libation in the introductory sacrifice of wine and incense—presented in the little box held by the attendant behind the tripod altar. Right of the altar is shown a flute player. Jupiter's victim, a steer, benevolently watches the proceedings in the background; he is to be slaughtered by the attendant (*victimarius*) with the axe. The other *victimarius* whose main function was to cut open the victim's neck artery with a knife (not visible) carries the tray of salt and spelt (*molae salsae*) on his head. Between the emperor-

SACRIFICE

When the proconsul Quintilian ordered Pionius to throw incense on the altar fire, he went straight to the core of all pagan dealings with the gods—rites of sacrifice. With their stubborn resistance to performing the rite, Christians recognized this as fully as their persecutors: to refuse sacrifice was to refuse the gods.

Sacrifice in the ancient world constituted a system of exchange between worshippers and gods. In return for gifts of food, drink, and pleasant smells, the gods were expected to assist the worshippers with their requests. The standard procedure of the Roman sacrifice could be varied, embellished, or simplified in individual rites, but was generally followed in both public and private sacrifices. There were two types of sacrifice, blood (*immolatio*) and bloodless. The bloodless variant encompassed gifts of wine, incense, sometimes cakes or loaves of bread. In principle any food item could be used, as was presumably often the case in household worship, which for obvious reasons often had to function along less strict lines than the more well-endowed public sacrifices. Bloody and bloodless sacrifices differed in degree, but not in kind; the main difference in their use was simply that blood sacrifice was more costly and prestigious. All sacrifice took place by an altar where the offerings were burnt. The altar was typically situated in front of a temple, rarely inside it; however, sacrifices only presupposed the existence of an altar (which could also be portable and taken to the location for the occasion), not a temple. The most sumptuous victims were oxen, and during the empire they constituted the standard type of victim in most state sacrifices. The bloodless rites formed part also of a bloody sacrifice, which always included at least a preliminary libation of wine in invoking the deity before the slaughter of the victim. A very common bloodless rite was the *supplicatio*, a thanksgiving or collective

priest and the victim stands Jupiter's state priest, the *flamen Dialis*, wearing the characteristic headgear (*apogalerus*) of a *flamen*. Behind the emperor the participation of the Senate is marked by its personification, the bearded and long-haired *genius senatus*. Relief panel from *c*.AD 170, now in the Palazzo dei Conservatori, Rome.

prayer to the gods, either to avert danger or to express gratitude for successes; the rite included sacrifice of wine and incense. The gifts to the gods were always burnt on or by their altar, something which clearly set aside the nourishment given to them from that of men.

The procedure in the typical animal sacrifice was as follows.[17] First silence was proclaimed and the ceremony opened with the words *hoc age*—'Concentrate on this'. The officiating priest then invited the god by a formulaic prayer accompanied by a preliminary sacrifice of wine and incense thrown into the altar fire, either on the main altar or on a portable one next to it (presumably to avoid kindling the greater fire on the main altar before it was necessary, thus saving fuel). Next the sacrificial victim(s) were led forth, sprinkled with wine and salted grains of spelt (*mola salsa*), the main prayer read out, and the victim slaughtered: its head was held down close to the ground, then it was stunned by a mallet blow on the forehead, and its neck artery was quickly cut open. The animal, or animals, was then opened and its internal organs (*exta*)—heart, lungs, liver—examined for signs of abnormalities; if such were found and the victim was then not perfect, the sacrifice had to be repeated with a new animal. If nothing was wrong with them, the *exta*, together with samples of the meat, were removed, strewn with *mola salsa*, and placed on the altar where they were burnt to ashes. Sometimes the pieces would first be boiled in a cauldron on the spot. The rest of the animal's meat was cooked elsewhere on the site and then consumed by the human participants in the sacrifice; or else they would each receive parts of the meat to take home for later consumption. Sometimes cakes, *liba*, and pre-cut carvings of meat would be given to the god as additional preliminary offerings, though it is not clear at what stage in the ritual they would be burnt.

The sacrificial rites were meant to be appreciated and learnt from watching them in progress. They were, in fact, so common and ubiquitous in the Graeco-Roman world that there was hardly ever any point in describing them more closely. Very few such detailed descriptions have therefore been pre-

[17] Wissowa (1912, 409ff.); Latte (1960, 375ff.); further refs. in Scheid (1990, 326 n. 27). More generally for blood sacrifice in the ancient world see refs. in Elsner (1991, 50 n. 2).

served, and most of what we know about Roman sacrifice must be picked out as fragments from texts dealing with other matters, or from among the meagre bits of Roman sacral law preserved by grammarians such as Festus. Amazingly, only one full description of a Roman sacrifice has come down to us from any literary source. In the late first century BC the Greek historian Dionysius from Halicarnassus came to Rome and witnessed her holy rituals. He wrote in Greek, for a Greek audience, and his motivation for describing the Roman rites was to demonstrate that Roman sacrifices basically followed the same procedures as the Greek ones known to his readers, and that Rome had therefore been founded by Greeks. The historian has just described the magnificent procession in the festival of Liber, Libera, and Ceres, whose temple in Rome went back almost half a millennium before Dionysius' time:[18]

> After the procession was ended the consuls and the priests whose function it was presently sacrificed oxen; and the manner of performing the sacrifices was the same as with us. For after washing their hands they purified the victims with clear water and sprinkled corn on their heads, after which they prayed and then gave orders to their assistants to sacrifice them. Some of these assistants, while the victim was still standing, struck it on the temple with a mallet, and others received it upon the sacrificial knives as it fell. After this they flayed it and cut it up, taking off a piece from each of the inner organs and also from every limb as a first-offering, which they sprinkled with grits of spelt and carried in baskets to the officiating priests. These placed them on the altars, and making a fire under them, poured wine over them while they were burning. It is easy to see from Homer's poems that every one of these ceremonies was performed according to the customs established by the Greeks with respect to sacrifices . . .
>
> These rites I am acquainted with from having seen the Romans perform them at their sacrifices even in my time; and contented with this single proof, I have become convinced that the founders of Rome were not barbarians, but Greeks who had come together out of many places.

Dionysius drew the wrong conclusion from a correct observation. Greek culture had for centuries spread far beyond the areas settled by Greek-speakers, and central Italy and Etruria had been strongly influenced by Greek ways and religion ever

[18] Dion. Hal. *Ant.* 7. 72. 15–18, tr. Cary, Loeb edn. (adapted).

since the later eighth century BC. It may be that the specific cult described was particularly Greek in character or origins[19] (which would of course not make it less Roman). But such an observation is little more than an inference from Dionysius' text, and it ignores the central, and correct, statement Dionysius is making. Traditional Greek and Roman worship could vary in points of detail—as such details also varied in different areas or sanctuaries within the Greek world—but the two systems were basically identical, functioning on the same premises and by the same fundamental rituals. Sacrifice was a major feature in the perceived common culture that united Greece and Rome; both parties could immediately recognize what such rituals were about when they encountered them abroad.

THE ARVAL BROTHERS AND THE STATE CULT

Till the last generation scholarship has focused all too much on the oldest layers of Roman religion, about which we know little, and practically nothing from contemporary sources. In contrast, Roman religion from about 200 BC onwards has till recent years received less attention, despite (or perhaps because of) the fact that from this period onwards we do have sources giving us more than the curious fragments deprived of context which form the evidence for archaic Roman rites.

What is, however, almost always lacking in our sources are descriptions of the actual rituals, as opposed to short references in passing or philosophical interpretations of such rites and systems. But there is a striking exception to this observation. Our main source for Roman state cult during the empire is not any literary text, but the amazing corpus of inscriptions known as the *Arval Acta*. The Arval Brothers were a state college of priests, twelve in number, dedicated to the worship of the old and obscure goddess Dea Dia in her sacred grove by the Via Campana, five miles from Rome. The college went back to a very early age but came into prominence under Augustus who had the college restored or revived as part of his restoration programme for the old cults of Rome. From Augustus onwards

[19] Thus Latte (1960, 161 f.).

the ruling emperor was always a member of the college, which otherwise was filled with senators of high rank.

Thus far, however, there is nothing very remarkable about the Brothers; they were a state college among several others, and, though prestigious, not among the most prominent or important of these priestly groupings, unlike, say, the college of the Augurs or the Pontifices.[20] But, uniquely among such colleges, the Brothers from the reign of Augustus till well into the third century adopted the curious habit of every year having their Acta, that is records of the rites they had performed during the past year, engraved on marble stelae posted in their grove. Through more than four centuries past, fragments of these inscriptions have turned up on the site.[21]

These fragments, altogether taking up well over two hundred pages in their respective publications, are without comparison our most important source for the Roman state cult during the early empire. Though the Arval Brothers were not one of the four major colleges, nor were their rites central to the workings of the state cult, their *Acta* enable us to follow the ceremonies, their occasions, their form, and their calendar, of what was for all we know a typical college of state priests. As in a splintered mirror the texts enable us to trace developments in the life of the college, and, used with caution, in the state cult at large.

The *Acta* are obviously not unproblematic sources. Since we have nothing comparable from any other state colleges, it is difficult to know whether and to what extent developments in the Arval worship reflect such trends in the state cult at large. Furthermore, the fullness of the recording varied considerably over time. Sometimes the same rites could for some years be described quite fully, while in other years merely being

[20] The four highest state priesthoods, the *summa* or *amplissima sacerdotia* were the *pontifices*, the *augures*, the *XVviri sacris faciundis* and the *VIIviri epulonum*; the Arvals appear to have been the most prestigious college below these: Augustus *RG* 7. 2 lists his membership of the Arval college immediately below the four major colleges, as number five of the seven state priesthoods he held. The Arval college is rarely mentioned in literary sources, see Scheid (1990).

[21] Arvals: Scheid (1990); texts in Henzen (1874); *CIL* VI. 2023–119, 32338–98, 37164f. and later finds in Scheid (1990, 789f.), now all superseded by Scheid (1998) with French translations.

recorded as having been performed, and these differences are often difficult to explain. More generally, the number of Arval celebrations per year decreased considerably after the Julio-Claudian era, and for most of the second century the Brothers only functioned, it seems, in connection with the New Year vows and the traditional sacrifices of Dea Dia's cult. And lastly, the record is very incomplete: little survives from the reign of Augustus (but including the calendar, *fasti*, of the college), more from that of Tiberius, much from the first years of Caligula (with the entries for AD 38 preserved in their entirety), some fragments from Claudius' reign, a very good record for that of Nero and his shortlived successors in AD 69; then some fragments from Vespasian, everything from AD 81 and much from later in Domitian's reign; intermittent fragments from the period Trajan to Marcus, much from Commodus' reign, almost nothing from that of Severus, and very much, though still with gaps, from his successors till the 240s; then, abruptly, the records cease. Apparently the Arvals gave up recording their rites in inscriptions around this time, though the college continued to function till at least into the early fourth century. Another problem, to some extent general in the study of ancient epigraphy, is caused by the fragmentary state of most of the inscriptions. They are generally completed with modern restorations, of varying likelihood or certainty, whose basis can be difficult to assess for the non-specialist and which can therefore be dangerous, because non-Arval scholars may then tend simply to accept them on a par with the text actually preserved.

The *Arval Acta* are, as mentioned, by far our best source for the Roman state cult under the emperors. Still, they have till recent years been curiously ignored, with the exception of the ancient Arval hymn, engraved in the record for the year 218, and other items reflecting, or taken to reflect, the archaic origins of their cult. In older studies the record of the Arval rites have received attention mainly for what they could say about the archaic religion, the contemporary and complete ceremonial ignored as late and decadent, corrupted by Greek ideas and emperors. But recent years have seen interest in the *Acta* in their entirety deservedly revived, mainly owing to the publications of John Scheid, in particular his monumental *Romulus et ses frères* (1990). The inscriptions still have much to give.

The Arval college was dedicated to the worship of Dea Dia, celebrating her yearly festival in her grove every May or June. However, in the Julio-Claudian period, at least, this was only a small part of the Brothers' activities. During the rest of the year they met at various temples in Rome to sacrifice to the Roman state gods for the welfare of the emperor and his family. A wide variety of gods are encountered in this worship, almost always cultivated to lend their support to the imperial house. Typical occasions were imperial anniversaries, such as the emperor's birthday and accession anniversary; or birthdays of his family, or those of dead and deified members of the imperial family; or extraordinary sacrifices in celebration of military victories or the detection of conspiracies; or the yearly vows every 3 January to Jupiter, Juno, and Minerva and other gods on the Capitol. These vows promised the gods to give them victims the next year, if the emperor and his family were still alive and well on the next 3 January. At the same time the promised victims from the vows the year before were paid, if the stated condition had been met. In most cases the information given is brief, confined to listing place, god, and occasion; at other times the information is fuller, sometimes giving the sacrificial procedure in telegrammatic form, such as at the fulfilling of the New Year vows on 3 January AD 87:[22]

. . . eodem die ibidem in area C. Salvius [Li]beralis, q[ui v]ice magistri fungebatur, ture et vino in igne in foculo fecit immolavitq(ue) vino, mola cultroque Iovi O(ptimo) M(aximo) b(ovem) m(arem), Iunoni Reginae b(ovem) f(eminam), Minervae b(ovem) f(eminam), Saluti Publicae p(opuli) R(omani) Q(uiritium) b(ovem) f(eminam); exta aulicocta reddidit.

On the same day in the same place [the Capitol] in the court [of Jupiter's temple] Gaius Salvius Liberalis, functioning on behalf of the chairman [of the college], offered incense and wine on the fire of the brazier [i. e. portable altar] and sacrificed with wine, grains of spelt and sacrificial knife to Jupiter Best and Greatest a steer, to Queen Juno a cow, to Minerva a cow, to the public Welfare of the Roman people a cow; after the inner organs had been boiled in a cauldron he returned them [to each god] [i.e. they were burnt on the altar].

The New Year vows were given and, if they had been effective,

[22] Scheid (1998, 146 l. 18ff. = *CIL* VI. 2165 l. 18ff.)

fulfilled every year by all the priestly colleges, as well as by the consuls. The same presumably goes for the other occasions the Arval Brothers celebrated, apart from the rites to Dea Dia which were exclusive to this college. The Arvals offer striking and detailed evidence of the extent to which the emperor and his house quickly came to dominate the state cult in Rome, without, however, receiving direct worship in this sphere, and without supplanting the more traditional cults and celebrations.

The *Acta* also, with their dry style, give evidence of the strict regulations governing the Roman state cult. Thus the order of the gods in listings such as the one quoted was always the same, reflecting the relative rank of the gods worshipped. Likewise, specific victims were appropriate to each god in different rites, and this too never varied. The general rule in the Roman state cult—valid also for the civic cults all over Italy—was that male gods received male victims, goddesses female victims. The male gods were further split up in those of the underworld: Dis Pater, Pluto, the *Di Manes* (spirits) of the dead, who received castrated victims, and the celestials, who received fertile victims. There was traditionally one major exception: Jupiter, though a celestial, received castrated male victims. Whatever the reason for this, it is lost in the mists of prehistory. During the Empire, dead and deified emperors, the celestial *Divi*, also received castrates, seemingly because their rites were modelled on those of Capitoline Jupiter, the most prestigious cult in the Roman pantheon. The Arvals overwhelmingly sacrificed the costliest types of animals, namely bovines; the terminology of the three types of bovine victims were *taurus*—bull, *bos mas*—steer, *bos femina* or *vacca* (synonyms)—cow or heifer.[23]

[23] The type of *taurus* is well known from depictions of the *suovetaurilia* (Ryberg, 1955, *passim*); the *vacca* and *bos femina* are clearly synonyms in the *Arval Acta* (and termed *iuvenca*—heifer—in Juv. 6. 46); the *bos mas* is commonly taken to be a steer, i.e. castrated (thus Wissowa, 1912, 413); this is doubted by Krause (1931, col. 258ff.) who instead takes *bos mas* to be a younger animal than *taurus*, but uncastrated (*taurus* Krause takes, bizarrely, to be sometimes castrated, sometimes not). His arguments are, however, unconvincing, and the interpretation of the *bos mas* as a steer is effectively vindicated by the lustration rites of the Arvals, where the more common bovine victims were replaced by the corresponding types of ovile ones; thus (AD 224, Scheid (1998, 314f. l. 8–13 = *CIL* VI. 2107 l. 8–13)) an *aries* (ram, corresponding to *taurus*) for Mars Ultor and a *vervex* (wether, i.e. castrated ram, corresponding

THE MEANING OF SACRIFICE

Sacrificial procedure has much to say about archaic, primitive conceptions of divinity. The correspondence between the sex and nature of the sacrificial victim and that of the receiving deity thus reflects an old notion that the gods needed such gifts to strengthen or maintain their force and power. But it is vital to realize that such notions and ideas are in principle irrelevant to the performing of the rituals in the period where they were recorded. In historical times the rituals were carried out simply because of the impressive tradition behind them. They constituted the 'natural', eternal, and traditional way of communicating with divine powers whose assistance the worshippers required. The theology from which sacrifice had originated did not matter beyond, at the most, simple acceptance of the gods' power and the notion that they appreciated such honours, for whatever reason. That is, it was not important to the observance of the rituals whether the divine recipients simply enjoyed the ceremonial as an 'empty' honour, or whether they physically delighted in the meals offered them. In fact, not even the vaguest notion of the efficacy of such rites was necessarily required to take them seriously: strong traditionalist values supplanted any need for personal faith, or at least rendered it irrelevant to the performance of the ceremonies.

The impressive tradition legitimizing and underpinning the rites of sacrifice was the strongest guarantee of efficacy and, more decisively, the only argument needed to perform them. These traditionalist values were indeed generally shared by all pre-modern religious systems. In antiquity even new religions, such as Christianity or Mithraism, claimed and believed themselves to be age-old, or to be the 'true' representatives of a tradition from time immemorial; and age was commonly used as an argument in itself. No one saw virtue in religious novelty or originality. Amazingly, even professed disbelief in the efficacy

to *bos mas*) for Jupiter; cf. *verveces* for the *Divi*: again, the bovine victim of (male) *Divi* was the *bos mas*; cf. Fest. (p. 372L): '*Solitaurilia hostiarum trium diversi generis immolationem significant, tauri, arietis, verris, quod omnes eae solidi integrique sint corporis; contra †aci . . . † verbices maialesque . . . Atque harum hostiarum omnium inviolati sunt tauri, quae pars scilicet caeditur in castratione*'. For types of bovines, note also Varro, *Rust*. 2. 5. 6.

of communicating with the gods, such as found among the Epicureans or Sceptics, did not usually lead to rejection of the sacrificial systems. Believers in such philosophical ideas were thus commonly found among the senatorial priests in the Roman state cult during the late republic and the empire.[24] It is not adequate simply to ascribe this to love of honours or outright cynicism, a view which prejudices ritual and traditionalist values in favour of philosophical theology. Such arguments, rooted in the modern idea of progress, seriously underrate the positive force of traditionalism, taking it in our terms as a rather tired, predominantly negative feature. It is thus interesting to note, and not to be lightly dismissed, that when the traditional rites in such cases conflicted with philosophical ideas, the old ways usually won the day. Such instances are symptomatic of the extent to which philosophy and religious ritual could and did function independently of each other.

It is difficult for us to grasp a religious system with almost exclusive emphasis on ritual action to the almost complete detriment of theology or speculation. But it is revealing that such pagan theological speculation was confined to philosophy, and that the traditional cultic systems carried on for centuries irrespective of these philosophical discussions. The lack of a systematic or detailed theological system in ancient sacrifice is equally noteworthy. For instance, where was the god in the rite? Different versions were conflated in the normal ritual. In one version, the god dwelt in his temple, from which his cult statue could watch the sacrifice. Then again, the smoke from the offerings went to heaven; so on that argument, the deity dwelt in the sky, or air, where he would partake of his offering. And lastly, he could be presumed to be immediately present at the sacrifice and devour his meal on the altar (in which view he would presumably be in, or identified with, the altar fire). Of course such theological inconsistencies could be explained and rationalized in a secondary, philosophically motivated, analysis. But they were not, or at least they were only debated outside the ritual context. The religious rites were never changed or modified to impart theological consistency or logic to the ceremonies. They were what constituted, and not merely

[24] Liebeschuetz (1979, 31 ff.).

reflected, traditional Graeco-Roman religion. In Christianity, the idea is the exact opposite: there ritual is and was the secondary feature, a reflection of the real basis, namely the word of God and the dogmas built on it.

MEN AND GODS

The Roman sacrificial rites established and defined clear boundaries between the sacred and the profane sphere, as well as between gods, the honorands, and men, the worshippers. The first demarcation, between sacred and profane, was defined in terms both of place, time, and even sound. Sacrifice usually took place on sacred land, dedicated to the god and separate from the profane land beyond the sanctuary; if no such sanctuary was available in the circumstances of the sacrifice, the site had to be carefully chosen and marked out or set aside for the god. In terms of time and sound, spoken formulas opened, finished, and thus framed the rite; and musical accompaniment established a sound wall to shield the rite from profane noise from outside the ritual framework.

The second demarcation, men versus gods, is equally clear, but its interpretation is not. The god was the only participant in the rite who was not visually present in it; the specific deity honoured was named and invoked in the opening prayer; and the food of the deity was separated from that of the worshippers, cooked separately, then burnt on the altar, whereas the human portions of the victims were shared out among the worshippers.

One may stress these demarcations between sacred and profane, between men and gods, and thus neatly isolate Graeco-Roman religion from secular society as an independent category. Such an approach, convenient because it will make the ancient world fit our own categories, may not be entirely wrong, but is far too narrow. One should rather stress the fact that the sacrificial system formed an integral part of a larger social context, which should be examined as a whole to become intelligible in contemporary terms. Temples, priests, and sacrifices were the ingredients of the highest or divine or heavenly honours (*summi, divini, caelestes honores*), and such were the most prestigious honours known to men. But they differed in degree, not in kind, from lower, terrestrial, or—as we would say—secular honours. They were ultimately an aspect of the honours-for-benefactions structure found in all relationships between parties of vastly unequal power and social standing in Roman society, such as in the interplays between subjects and ruler, cities and benefactors, dependants and patrons, slaves and masters.

Sacrifice clearly expressed a dividing line between the gods worshipped and their human worshippers. But it is a simple fact that these heavenly honours could in antiquity also be accorded to mortal men, and this fact raises a fundamental question: what distinction did the man–god divide in these rituals actually signify or reflect? In monotheistic religions the one and true God is vastly superior to men, and vastly different from them. The difference is one of nature or, for lack of a better word, zoology: God is the sole example of another 'species', radically different. That is how we instinctively tend to interpret the man–god divide of Graeco-Roman divine cults. Yet the phenomenon of ruler cult in antiquity—and elsewhere outside monotheistic cultures, for that matter—shows that this interpretation is at best inadequate. One may still attempt to save the model by isolating ruler cult from ancient religion, and declaring it either exceptional, perverse, or political, three options frequently employed in scholarship on the subject.

There is, however, another option: the man–god divide in the pagan context could also be taken to reflect a distinction in *status* between the respective beings, rather than a distinction between their respective natures, or 'species'. That is the model which I will test in this book: divinity as a relative rather than as an absolute category.

2

Before the Caesars

It is a commonplace of handbooks on Roman history and religion that ruler worship fundamentally conflicted with republican tradition.[1] That supposition is in fact very problematic. Ruler cult was obviously absent from the public sphere down to the eve of the republic, that is, to the dictatorship of Julius Caesar; in other words, it played no part in constitutional practice as continually defined by offices, elections, and state sacrifices. That is no more than a truism: ruler cult presupposes the existence of a 'ruler', king, emperor or otherwise, and the Roman republic in the very nature of this term had no ruler. This is not to say that the phenomenon was at any time unknown to Romans in the republican era; it merely reflects that the Roman republic, which finally collapsed with Caesar, was never ruled by a human individual with power perceived as absolute and permanent. The Roman state gods, however, did receive divine worship; our problem with emperor worship only arises with our insistence on seeing such worship as inherently different from that accorded the 'old' or unquestioned gods. Or, in other words, if we insist on seeing religion and politics as two separate and mutually exclusive spheres. The very existence of emperor worship in antiquity should rather cause us to question the relevance of this distinction when dealing with pagan antiquity. We instinctively see Jupiter as a religious figure, a Roman emperor as a political one. This

[1] Taylor (1931, 54): 'the inclusion of a mortal among the gods would not bring to the men of the day the same shock that it would have caused in a time when the native religion was strong'. The claim of religious crisis in the late republic, and the (partial) resurrection of traditional religion under Augustus was formulated by Warde Fowler (1911, 428f.) with much influence on later scholarship, thus Latte (1960, 264ff.: 'Der Verfall der römischen Religion'), Hopkins (1978, 213): 'The emperor's divinity . . . contrasts with earlier republican sentiments'; against the notion of crisis: North (1976) and (1986) (review article).

distinction between religion and politics is christianizing, as is basically the very concept of 'religion' itself. This has long since been recognized in the discipline of history of religion, but rarely in classical scholarship, which still tends to operate strictly along the lines of 'political' or 'religious' history.

Paganism was polytheistic. The gods were not just numerous, but innumerable. This constituted no problem: men worshipped only the gods perceived to be of assistance to themselves. There was obviously not, nor could there be, any claim that the gods were entitled to worship *qua* gods, as with the one God of the Christians or Jews, but by virtue of their powers that might assist or endanger the worshipper(s). With emperor worship, the question that has consistently puzzled modern scholars is whether the emperor was really perceived to be a god, or whether the rites should be interpreted 'politically', as rendered him *as to* a god. This discussion has been able to go on for so long because the sources do not furnish us with a clear answer: the question was simply irrelevant in contemporary, pagan terms. It seems superfluous to us in connection with worship of the 'real' gods, for example Jupiter, but it should not. As stressed by Simon Price, classical antiquity had no generally accepted definition of what a god actually was in absolute terms, or what it took to become one.[2] Price has taken this ambiguity or uncertainty as enabling worship of the emperor in the first place. I cannot completely agree; it seems significant that the question 'what is a god?' (i.e. in absolute terms) was discussed only in philosophical writings, which in fact form the basis of Price's enquiry. And to this genre, in my view, it belonged: there is no evidence that it was ever of relevance to actual cultic practice. State sacrifices to Jupiter were not performed simply because he was a god (though he unquestioningly was): most gods were never worshipped by the Roman state. Such worship took place because Jupiter was the foremost, most powerful god *of Rome*. His immense power over the well-being of Rome gave him divine status in the Roman 'constitution'. His divine status was thus relative to the body honouring him, and it was 'constructed' by the honours accorded him by this body. Jupiter's nature, the aspect of absolute divinity, hardly mattered in this connection; it was

[2] Price (1984*b*).

irrelevant to the *relative* status system constructed in cultic rites.

This claim is supported by contemporary conceptualization of divine worship. As mentioned, our ingrained distinction between religion and politics is not relevant in the pagan Graeco-Roman context, and, correspondingly, pagan antiquity did not distinguish between 'worship' and 'honours'; divine worship was an honour which differed from 'secular' honours, such as, for example, the erection of a statue, only in degree, not in kind. When Augustus died and the Senate accorded him full-blown divine status in the Roman state system, official language did not state that he had become a god in any absolute sense, but that 'heavenly honours were decreed to Divus Augustus by the Senate'.[3] Divine worship was the highest possible honour known in antiquity, expressing a maximum status gap between the recipient and the worshippers, but it made no gods in the absolute—and irrelevant—sense. It merely granted divine status to the honorand in relation to the worshippers. If relative divinity was the important aspect of such relationships between parties of vastly unequal social status, we should then speak of *divine status* rather than of *divinity*, which smacks of the absolute. But these observations are equally relevant to worship of the 'real' gods. Worship of Jupiter likewise expressed his superhuman status in relation to the worshippers, or the body they represented. It did not stress his absolute divinity, his divine nature. Hence missionary measures were practically unknown in the traditional pagan context; if at all, they are encountered only in the context of mystery cults.

Such a system of relative divinity, to which the philosophical, absolute aspect of divine nature is not relevant, may be difficult for us to grasp. Brought up with a monotheistic image of God, we tend to focus instead on the philosophical aspect of absolute divinity. The Christian God is divine and all-powerful in an absolute sense, as the creator and ruler of the whole universe, not only in relation to those asking for His assistance in worship: He is the God even of those who do not recognize Him or His existence.

[3] See my Chapter 12: 'Heavenly Honours Decreed by the Senate': From Emperor to *Divus*.

If my arguments here are accepted, emperor worship presents problems which are apparent rather than real. It differed little from worship of 'real' gods, cultivated likewise for the sake of their enormous power over the worshippers, not because divine nature gave them any claim a priori to such honours.

It is a common claim that divine honours to a human being conflicted with the traditional Roman mentality, and that the phenomenon was fundamentally an import from the Greek world.[4] This view is unfounded if, as I claim here, divine honours were not concerned with the nature of the being worshipped, man or god, but merely expressed his superhuman status and power in relation to the worshippers. In that case there is no fundamental difference between worship of an emperor and of Jupiter, and in this sense the Roman republic was never a republic in our sense of the word: the 'king' of republican Rome was Jupiter. The extent to which men and gods were perceived to form part, not of each their own worlds, but of one and the same world, is worth stressing.

This is not to say that the distinction between men and gods was blurred, a claim commonly found in handbooks as a condition enabling emperor worship to exist. The argument is in fact based entirely on the existence of divine worship of men in antiquity, and is therefore circular as an explanation of divine worship of emperors or other mortals. What is more, the claim is clearly wrong outside the philosophical discussions of absolute divinity examined by Price; these debates should not be allowed to represent Graeco-Roman religion to the detriment of its constituting factor, actual ritual practice. In terms of actual worship (or, in other words, divine cult) the borderline between men and gods was within each ritual set up as clear and unequivocal. For instance, the god worshipped was always invoked by name in prayer before the sacrifice, and in bloody sacrifices the parts of the sacrificial victim given to the god were always kept separate from the meat to be eaten by the worshippers.[5] There was no blurring of distinctions in this con-

[4] The view that emperor worship was primarily a phenomenon of the Greek parts of the empire is still upheld in surveys, e.g. Garnsey and Saller (1987, 164f.); Galsterer (1990, 16).

[5] The strictness of these regulations is not always recognized; thus Elsner

text. Nor was this the case on the immediate linguistic level: the Latin words *di*, gods, and *homines*, men, were plainly antonyms, as were the corresponding terms in Greek. It is quite another matter that the two categories were not mutually exclusive, and that an emperor or another man could in any particular rite or context be worshipped as a god. This follows naturally, if we accept divinity as primarily a relative rather than an absolute concept. Likewise, philosophers could, from the third century BC onwards, argue that the gods had once been mortals who had been honoured with deification after death, a common idea in antiquity, and today known as euhemerism; but such notions did not affect the divinity of the gods in question, or their worship.[6]

A crude parallel may further understanding. For instance, antonyms such as 'large' versus 'small' are relative terms which can be taken, in strict principle, to correspond to 'divine' versus 'human' in Roman pagan terms; the difference is of course that small–large is determined by relative size, whereas the polytheistic human–divine was determined by relative power (as perceived by different participants in the social structure in any given context or situation). To an ant a mouse is large, but to a cow it is small. This does not mean that either the ant or the cow is wrong, or that their distinctions are blurred, confused, or ambiguous. It simply means that there are no absolute criteria to determine what is large and what is small. Unlike monotheistic cultures, pagan antiquity had no absolute criteria by which to determine divinity, nor had it any clergy or holy texts to expound or set dogmas, and thus the only real dogma was tradition itself. Like size, divine status in the pagan world was relative to the beholder. Any individual or any group could in principle confer divinity—divine appellations, names, or worship—on anything or anybody, without such divine status obliging anybody else but the worshippers (and, in a moral sense, the honorand), and then only as long as they themselves chose to continue the dialogue with their gods.

(1991, 54) is wrong in claiming that it was ambiguous who was the recipient of sacrifice at the Ara Pacis Augustae. As evidenced by the *Arval Acta* where the college sacrificed cows at the altar (Scheid (1998, 31 l. 68), the recipient was simply the goddess Pax Augusta; the fact that her epithet Augusta would connote a connection with Augustus is a very different matter.

[6] Euhemerism: Liebeschuetz (1979, 33); Price (1984*a*, 38f.).

Beyond the force of tradition, power was in fact the only common determinant for according divine worship to anyone, celestials or terrestrials. The question whether the one or the other figure was a god or not was not important; in a world with an infinite number of gods, divinity was not in itself an interesting characteristic to worshippers who could only ever get to cultivate a modest number among them. It was any god's power and its relevance to worshippers which determined which deities would be cultivated, not their presumed divinity —or humanity. One might, however, think that immortality was generally taken to be a *sine qua non* for divine status. That was not so. It is not very decisive that we can point to some 'real' gods who were, at least sometimes, perceived as mortal, such as the *Genius* of a man,[7] or to many eastern cults where the god each year died and revived. It is more important that death is not merely a biological fact, but also very much a social construct. In very few cultures, if any, is death generally taken as the ultimate end, rather as a transition where the soul, or life force, actually lives on without the body. The death of an emperor, or indeed of anybody, could be redefined to be anything but death. Shedding the physical body was no more a bar to divinity than possessing one was a prerequisite for it. Hence euhemerism constituted no threat to paganism, and indeed was not in the least 'invented' in opposition to it. It was only later Christian use of the idea which turned it into an argumentative weapon against the old gods.

REPUBLICAN ROME

No terrestrial possessed divine status in the Roman state during the republic. In the nature of things, divine honours were not accorded by the state to a man before the dictatorship of Julius Caesar; the prerequisite for such a cult, power perceived to be permanent and absolute, was possessed by no one before Caesar. This does not mean that the idea behind such worship was absent from the minds of 'primeval' Romans, unadulterated by Greek influence (Roman culture without strong Greek influence never existed). But it means that the phenom-

[7] Hor. *Epist.* 2. 2. 187f.: '*Genius . . . deus . . . mortalis*'.

enon during the republic was confined to the private sphere, where individuals could indeed occupy quasi-monarchical positions, such as that of the master of the house, the *pater-familias*, in relation to his household. This observation entails that our sources must in the nature of things very much let us down in tracing the custom during the republic.

First, literary sources rarely deal with the private sphere, with life in the *domus*; it was largely without public interest, and even when we get bits of information they are therefore usually of a scandalous nature, and hence untypical. The one exception is the genre of comedy, which in itself presents difficult problems of interpretation. Still, as we shall see, comedy is an important source, and in the republic almost our only one. There is a further problem with literary sources. Many scholars have seen the 'phenomenon' of ruler worship as a Greek import. Greek influence is strong in early Roman comedy; but more generally, few literary sources go back earlier than the beginning of the second century BC, when Hellenistic influence in Rome became far stronger and more direct than before. So it is very difficult to argue against the idea of a Greek import on the basis of these sources. More generally, scholars attempting to reconstruct 'original' Roman culture, especially in regard to 'primeval', pre-Greek Roman religion, have had little to build on, and thence little opposition, because of this lack of earlier sources. I have little faith that a pre-Greek Roman religion ever existed;[8] in any case it must remain a mere speculative construct.

Secondly, inscriptions: though in the nature of things, they belong to a public sphere—they 'publish' facts or images to an uninitiated audience—they do on occasion, during the empire, give us glimpses into the cultic life of Roman households. But the overall number of republican inscriptions from Roman Italy is small, and practically non-existent from the private sphere.

Thirdly, archaeological sources are likewise of little help, for several reasons. They are too damaged to show traces of private cult generally (if we had a republican Pompeii, conditions

[8] Thus Hanson (1959, 50) and Muth (1961), denying the existence at any stage of a 'pure' Roman religion; cf. Muth (1978, 300); North (1989) gives a good survey of Roman religion until *c*.200 BC.

would of course be different). Yet the typical elements in house cults, as known primarily from Pompeii, seem, from the scanty references in the literary sources of the republican era, to have remained fairly constant over the centuries. It therefore seems legitimate to use the Pompeian evidence as valid also for house cult in the late republic. Beyond the institutionalized house cults, however, there are further problems with the archaeological sources. Any group of people we may imagine to have rendered worship to a man during the republic must have been of low status and limited economic power. If, as I argue here, such cult presupposed an enormous status gap betweeen the person honoured and the worshippers, this goes without saying; only later, with the emergence of the position of emperor, can we expect to encounter persons of such exalted status that this status gap could involve persons of note, such as the local aristocrats of Italian townships, or even Roman senators, as worshippers. In the republic, only relatively poor and humble people could have had patrons or benefactors so elevated in relation to themselves. The worshippers would therefore rarely have had the resources to erect buildings, stone inscriptions, and other monuments which would stand a chance of being archaeologically traceable today. To this we may add that such worship, if it existed, would have been ephemeral, confined at the most to the lifetime of the individual honoured, which would hardly encourage the erection of monuments to survive the millennia. So the absence of archaeological evidence implies neither that such worship existed nor that it did not.

Before the republic, however, Rome had kings; and we may expect to encounter public worship of the kings in this archaic period. Too little is known, of course, and most is mythical.[9] Yet if any information can be regarded as reliable in this context, it is what we are told of the dress of the kings. It was perpetuated in the attire of the general celebrating a triumph. He was dressed in a purple cloak, later replaced by the embroidered *toga picta*, carried a sceptre surmounted by the figure of an eagle, and wore a golden wreath on his head; furthermore, his face was painted red, as was that of the image of Capitoline Jupiter. The king, and later the triumphator, wore the dress

[9] Momigliano (1989, 87ff.) with refs. for Roman kingship.

of Jupiter, and appeared as an earthly Jupiter, a concept we shall encounter again later. Modern scholars have argued whether the triumphator's dress was that of Jupiter, or of the Etruscan kings, who would then have taken it over from Jupiter; in other words, whether the triumphator appeared as a man or as a god. The distinction is perhaps not very relevant; again, it reflects primarily the importance of the question of man or god to modern scholars. The fruitless nature of the discussion has been convincingly pointed out by Versnel: the triumphator was both king and Jupiter, or rather acted the Roman king who appeared as Jupiter.[10] Whether human or divine was hardly the issue: the dress of the triumphator was simply the emblem of supreme power or status. In relation to this, the philosophical question of the exact nature of the splendid figure in his chariot mattered little, as it mattered little in connection with worship of Jupiter, or other gods. Their power was the main issue, and what made them worth dealing or communicating with in the first place. This power did not spring, nor was it even supposed to spring, from their divinity, as that of God in Christian theology; rather the divine status conferred on them by their worshippers sprang from the enormous power they wielded.

We know nothing as to whether Roman kings were ever the objects of divine worship; any alleged information on the question would in any case be late and unreliable. If anything, however, the factual information on the dress of the Etruscan kings of Rome is reliable; it is important because it indicates, for a very early date in Roman history, that the representational language of supreme power was not concerned with the dogmatical question of man or god. Superhuman power was always reciprocated with superhuman honours, constructing and expressing the status springing from such power. Of course, Rome in the late regal period was also under strong Greek influence (primarily via the Etruscan area). But tracing the phenomenon of ruler cult to this early era renders nonsensical the discussion of Greek influence behind the import of 'ruler cult' into a supposedly 'pure' and uncontaminated Roman culture and religion.

[10] Weinstock (1971, 67f.) with lit. and summary of the discussion; Versnel (1970, 66ff.).

MASTERS AND SLAVES, PATRONS AND CLIENTS

In the republic, no man occupied such a position of supreme power in the state that public divine honours were relevant (with the regal relic of the triumph as the archaic, arcane, and very temporary exception). The private sphere, however, had its 'kings': supreme power wielded over other men was obviously to be found on this level, which is, however, badly illuminated in our sources. The household is a case in point: in theory, at least, the *paterfamilias* was a petty king, with unlimited powers over everybody and everything under his authority. In practice, as Richard Saller has now pointed out, this position of unlimited power was relevant only to the slaves and freedmen of the *paterfamilias*, and not to his wife and children.[11] In relation to his slaves and freedmen, however, his monarchic position was permanent, institutionalized, and hereditary. It was expressed in house cult, the worship which took place in the individual household for its welfare. The main source for such cult is Pompeii, where it is ubiquitous.[12] Republican sources, however, such as Plautus, confirm that this worship, and its common elements, *Genius* and *Lares*, go far back in time.

The *Genius* of the *paterfamilias* was the object of worship in the household. Whether and to what extent the worshippers included the wife and children of the master is not entirely clear. Inscriptional evidence from the empire suggests that the worship was overwhelmingly performed by the slaves, freedmen, and other *clientes* of their master, but the absence there of his wife and children might have something to do with epigraphical habit.[13] In the early empire, as we shall see, worship of the emperor's *Genius* had a servile connotation or stigma.

[11] Saller (1994, 102ff.).

[12] For private cult, De Marchi (1896) is still the only monograph, and still useful; Pompeii: Boyce (1937) and Fröhlich (1991) present the archaeological evidence; for a shorter overview see Orr (1978).

[13] See App. 1, including only inscriptions to the *Genius* of living persons; funerary inscriptions to the *Genius* of the dead are not uncommon, but different in character: they are usually set up by close blood relatives of the deceased, and no status gap between dedicators and deceased is discernible in

The meaning of the word *Genius* cannot be fitted into a narrow definition: 'life force' seems to me the best translation (the meaning of the term implies, but is not confined to, procreative powers). Every man possessed, as long as he lived, a *Genius*, and the god was closely attached to his person, though it was not entirely clear whether the *Genius* was perceived as dwelling within his body or outside it, as more of a guardian spirit (as so often, the system functioned perfectly well without philosophical or dogmatical speculation or precision). The close attachment is clear from the fact that whereas other human virtues or characteristics, such as *Providentia*, *Salus*, or *Virtus*, existed as gods in their own right, a *Genius* did not exist without being attached to someone or something, such as the *Genius* of a place (*Genius loci*), or of a corporation (*Genius collegii*). Parallel to the male *Genius*, the 'life force' of women was called the *Juno*.[14]

In household cult, however, only the *Genius* of the *paterfamilias* was the object of worship; the continued existence of the household (*domus*) and its dependants (*familia*) as a social unit obviously depended on this *Genius* alone, the 'life force' of the *paterfamilias*, including its aspect of procreation. The *Genius* of the master was worshipped at the house sanctuary (today generally termed *lararium*), normally a modest niche in the wall. In Pompeii it was usually embellished with murals depicting the main gods of the cult, the *Lares* and, usually, but not always, the *Genius*: the *Lares* were apparently the main and more important gods. The *Lares* were two in number; in Plautus' comedies, however, we usually encounter only one *Lar* of the *domus*, with one exception.[15] At some stage, presumably around Plautus' time *c.*200 BC, the god apparently became doubled, though the reason for this development remains uncertain; most likely, it reflects influence from the two *Lares*—homonymous, but different in character—worshipped at the crossroads, the *compita*; we shall later encounter their cult. In historic times, it was uncertain to Roman observers what the *Lares* actually were, and whence they originated; they were usually interpreted as collective personifications of dead

this connection. Fröhlich (1991, 28f.) points out that the great majority of *lararia* in Pompeii are found in kitchens or service areas.

[14] Orr (1978) with refs.

[15] Plaut. *Rud.* 1207: '*laribus familiaribus*'; cf. Marx (1959, 208f.).

ancestors of the *paterfamilias*. Much debated in scholarly literature, this view is probably not correct, and most students now interpret them as originally agrarian in character.[16] They were depicted as dancing youths in short tunics, pouring wine from drinking vessels; this iconography, influenced by that of the Greek *Cabiri*, and obviously of relatively late origin, also remains unexplained. Whatever their precise origins, however, they were in historical times gods or spirits of the house. Like comparable creatures in other agrarian societies, such as the Danish *nisser* or Swedish *tomtar*, they do not fit into any narrow, specialized definitions.

The *Lares* are found depicted in practically all the certain *lararia* of Pompeii, the *Genius* in most of them; other, subsidiary house gods were Vesta, depicted in a few instances in Pompeian house sanctuaries, and the *Penates*, whose character is very unclear: originally distinct, though it is difficult to see how they differed in character from the *Lar* or *Lares*, they seem in most of the literary sources to be simply a term for the house gods generally; they are apparently never depicted in Pompeii, and seem to have disappeared as separate house gods by the first century AD. All these house gods had their public equivalents, with state temples in Rome, reflecting a view of the Roman state as a *domus* writ large (the state *Penates* continued to have separate existence after these gods had apparently vanished from house cult). In the public sphere, Vesta was in historical times the most prominent of these gods. The one clear difference is revealing: during the republic, the *Genius* worshipped in state cult was of course not that of a man (if the cult existed under the kings, that may have been the case then, but on this we have no evidence whatsoever), but of the *populus Romanus*.[17] Apart from the house gods mentioned above, there is considerable variation in which other gods are encountered in the Pompeian *lararia*: the *paterfamilias* could have any gods he fancied worshipped in the cult of his *domus*.[18]

Dedicatory inscriptions to the *Genius* of a living *privatus* can hardly ever be dated with precision; they are not numerous—this no doubt merely reflects the private nature and origins of

[16] Harmon (1978) with refs.

[17] Liv. 21. 62. 9 (218 BC) is the earliest reference to the *Genius p. R.*

[18] Boyce (1937) and Fröhlich (1991, *passim*).

such household worship—and none of them is certainly pre-Augustan. I have in Appendix 1 collected the known instances, and they are, without exception, dedicated by the slaves or freedmen of the individual honoured, or in a few cases by his *clientes* (so termed in the inscriptions). Considering the background, the house cult, of such *Genius* worship, it seems legitimate to take this pattern as valid also for the republican period.

What is the meaning of this pattern, and what underlying structures determined it? The concepts of Roman patronage and clientelism have in scholarship tended to be over-employed far beyond their terminology in contemporary Latin. To avoid this, I shall stay as close as possible to the ancient usage.[19] The slaves of the master were under his absolute authority, his *potestas*. The freedmen, on the other hand, were not under the *potestas* of their former master, but still bound to him by bonds of good faith and loyalty, *fides*, and he was their *patronus*. In a strict legal sense they did not belong to his household, but in a more general sense the bond of *fides* and the ex-master's status as their *patronus* implied that they were still very much part of it; for instance, they were often buried in the sepulchre of their former master.[20] Likewise, the term *familia* in the narrow sense was used only of the slaves of the household, but in the wider sense also covered the free dependants of the master, such as his freedmen. Even allowing for the obvious danger of circularity, their continued role in the household worship of his *Genius* provides further support for this connection. Though free after their manumission, ex-slaves were not, at least in legal formality, fully independent. In any case the participation of both slaves and freedmen in the house cult of the *Genius* of their master or *patronus* makes it legitimate to call such worship 'servile'.

The few instances of *clientes* as worshippers in such *Genius* cults may seem more problematic for this characterization. But *clientes* in an overall sense belonged to the same category as freedmen in relation to their superior, even if their respective rights and obligations could differ in details.[21] The opposite number—ex-master or patron—of both freedmen, *liberti*, and

[19] For the terms see Saller (1982, 7ff.).

[20] Brunt (1988, 524 n. 1); Saller (1994, 97ff.).

[21] Differences: Brunt (1988, *passim*, esp. 407ff.).

clientes was termed *patronus*, which clearly suggests that the two groups held comparable positions in relation to him. This linguistic argument could of course be taken to refer only to a remote past, and was not necessarily relevant in the late republic and during the empire. But *liberti* and *clientes* were commonly categorized together in these periods, and *liberti* could even be taken as a subcategory of the broader term *clientes*.[22]

So much seems beyond doubt; what can, however, easily cloud the issue is the fact that the term *patronus* was clearly vaguer and more frequently employed than that of *clientes*, as well as being used in different contexts than was the latter term; for instance, *patroni* of townships are very commonly met with in inscriptions, but that did not imply that the local aristocrats, the *decuriones*, would term themselves *clientes*, individually or even collectively, of him or of anybody else, something which is in fact hardly ever encountered in the inscriptional evidence.[23] So to term someone *patronus* of a town was not necessarily humiliating for local persons of rank, but terming oneself his *cliens* clearly was. The social stigma attached to the term *cliens* is brought out by Cicero:[24]

> But they who consider themselves wealthy, honoured, the favourites of fortune, do not wish even to be put under obligations by a kind service [*beneficio*]. Why, they actually think that they have conferred a favour by accepting one, however great; and they even suspect that a claim is thereby set up against them or that something is expected in return. Nay more, they find it as bitter as death to be under patronage or to be called *clientes*.

[22] Together: Cic. *Inv. Rhet.* 1. 109: '*servis libertis clientibus*'; Cic. *Caec.* 57: '*aut cliens aut libertus*'; *Dig.* 47. 2. 90: '*libertus vel cliens*'; Fronto *Ad Verum* 2. 7. 2 (Loeb edn., vol. ii, p. 151 f.): '*ut neque illum pigeret nec me puderet ea illum oboedire mihi, quae clientes, quae liberti fideles ac laboriosi obsequuntur*'; cf. Juv. 5. 16 and 28; Sen. *De Ira* 3. 35. 1; subcategory: Liv. 43. 16. 4: '*cliens libertinus*'; Suet. *Caes.* 2: '*libertinus cliens*'; cf. *CIL* VI. 14672; cf. Brunt (1988, 408); non-freedmen *clientes* were also frequently buried in the tombs of their *patronus*: Saller (1994, 97 ff.).

[23] A single, though late example (3rd cent.) is *CIL* XIII. 3162 (Thorigny: *amicus et cliens* of govenor).

[24] Cic. *Off.* 2. 20. 69 (tr. W. Miller, Loeb edn., adapted): '*At qui se locupletes, honoratos, beatos putant, ii ne obligari quidem beneficio volunt; quin etiam beneficium se dedisse arbitrantur, cum ipsi quamvis magnum aliquod acceperint, atque etiam a se aut postulari aut exspectari aliquid suspicantur, patrocinio vero se usos aut clientes appellari mortis instar putant*'.

FIG. 2.1. Lararium from Pompeii, House of the Vettii
Notes: The fresco shows the togate *Genius* of the master of the household between the two dancing *Lares*. The snake approaching an altar in the bottom of the painting probably represents an older form of depicting the *Genius*.

The high-ranking Roman senators Cicero had in mind may be an extreme example, but we shall later encounter further evidence that the term *cliens* and the behavioural pattern associated with it was avoided also by local aristocrats. So when I here term worship of a living man's *Genius* 'servile' or, synonymously, 'cliental', it depends on these categories: by terming themselves *clientes*, such people defined themselves as being on the same level in relation to their *patronus* as were his freedmen.

The close attachment between a man and his *Genius* is illustrated by the iconography of the *Genius*. In the Pompeian *lararia*, the *Genius* is depicted as a togate youth, with the rim of his toga drawn over his head in sacrificial posture, engaged in pouring a libation with his right hand (Fig. 2.2). His left hand usually holds a cornucopia, which in some instances is replaced by an incense box (*acerra*). Without the cornucopia, an unequivocally divine attribute of fertility, it is in fact impossible to see whether the figure in itself represents a man or his *Genius* (in practice, there is rarely doubt in such depictions of *Genii*, but that is due to the context, with the *Genius* placed between the two *Lares*). The similarity between the man and his *Genius* should, however, not be overstressed. Scholars have often seen the facial features of *Genii* as portraying the man himself, but that is false; the *Genius* is always, irrespective of the physical appearance of his 'owner', depicted as a generic youth which reflects the fertility aspect of this 'life force'.[25]

Since the *Genius* was so closely attached to his 'owner', it may come as no surprise that the distinction between the man and his *Genius* is at times dissolved in the evidence, resulting in direct cult of the individual concerned. In fact, when the worshippers were slaves or freedmen, the distinction between *Genius* cult and direct, god-like worship seems to have mattered little. In either case, the cult expressed a position of abject social inferiority for the worshippers in relation to the person honoured. We shall later see that persons of servile status can be found in worship of the emperor's *Genius*, as well as in direct god-like cult of the monarch, whereas the cult form chosen by freeborn worshippers was far less equivocal: outside Rome, which is a special case, they always opted for direct cult, as to a 'real' god.

It is in my view a mistake, though a common one, to see the form of *Genius* worship as a more 'moderate' option, chosen to

[25] Boyce (1937) and Fröhlich (1991) for the iconography; portraits presumed e.g. by Mau (1900, 266) who saw the facial features of young Nero in the *lararium* painting from the House of the Vettii, and by J. Scheid in *The Oxford Classical Dictionary*, 3rd edn. (1996), s.v. '*genius*': 'a man's double', close to 'self' (unconvincing). The eternal generic youth in the facial features of the Pompeian *Genii* is clearly evident in the *lararium* paintings of Pompeii; also in the case of the *Genius Augusti*, never a portrait of 'his' emperor: Kunckel (1974, esp. Taf. 8–11) (her A1—from Rome, Augustan?, presumably from a *compitum*—seems certain, but her A2–3 and A5–6 may be city *Genii*, for which see Gradel (1992)); Ryberg (1955, fig. 33); Spinazzola (1953, 190ff.).

Fig. 2.2. Another lararium painting from Pompeii, now in the Museo Nazionale, Naples

Notes: Flanked by the *Lares* as usual, the *Genius* is shown in the centre pouring a libation to himself. The sacrifice is attended by a flute player and a small boy carrying the tray with *molae salsae* (cf. Fig. 1.1). Another attendant, a *victimarius*, leads forth a pig to be sacrificed to the *Lares*. In the bottom two snakes (for symmetry or perhaps representing the *Genius* and *Juno* of the master and mistress respectively) partake of eggs placed on an altar.

avoid divine cult, often imputed by modern scholars to have been blasphemous. In fact opposition for this reason to divine honours conferred on men is very rarely encountered in a pagan context, and it is christianizing to impute major importance to it. Rather, the *Genius* worship should be seen and interpreted in its proper institutionalized context within the *domus*. The cult formulated the identity of the slaves, freedmen, and other possible *clientes* participating in it as a social unit, a *familia*, or *collegium*. This unit was held together and defined only as consisting of people who were all under the authority, *patria potestas*, of a single man, the *paterfamilias*, or bound to him by *fides*. Only his continued existence and ability to produce an heir, the future *paterfamilias*, ensured the continued existence of the unit. Hence it makes good sense that the cult, rather than focusing on an individual, was centred on his *Genius*, the very quality of the master which could ensure this continued existence. The cult did not express gratitude to an individual for personal benefactions he had bestowed, but merely focused on the existence, vital to the worshippers, of a *paterfamilias*, present and future.

'MY EARTHLY JUPITER!'

It is different when we come to less permanent and institutionalized honours offered by social underlings to their benefactors; more personal in nature, such honours in some cases took the form of divine worship. Belonging to the private sphere, the instances are in the nature of things rarely encountered in the sources; significantly, when they are it is exactly in the genre focusing on this sphere, namely comedy. In Plautus' comedies, belonging to the period around 200 BC, the theme of divine worship, or assimilation to deities, accorded to human beings is in fact quite common. A few examples should suffice.[26]

In the play *Persa* (99f.) we encounter the parasite Saturio, on the lookout for a free meal, exclaiming to his patron Toxilus (a slave!): 'Ah my earthly Jupiter [*Iuppiter terrestris*]! Your table-

[26] Hanson (1959, 52; 69); generally fundamental for religion in Plautus. His suggestion that the Plautine passages referring to divine cult of men should be of relevance to studies of the imperial cult has not been taken up by scholars; a partial exception is Weinstock (1971, 167ff.).

mate has to accost you!' A more extreme case is found in Plautus' *Pseudolus*. The title figure is a clever slave whose half-witted young master, the lovesick Calidorus, is driven to despair by the prospect that his sweetheart Phoinicium, a slave girl, will be sold by her owner, the low-life pimp Ballio. When Ballio tells Calidorus that he will postpone the sale, the young man's emotions burst out (323 ff.):

CALIDORUS. Oh wonderful, you dear, delightful man!
BALLIO. That's nothing. Want me to make you even happier than happy?
CALIDORUS. How then?
BALLIO. Because I haven't actually got Phoinicium for sale now.
CALIDORUS. Haven't you?
BALLIO. No, by God I haven't.
CALIDORUS. Go, Pseudolus! Fetch victims, bovines, and them that slay them, that I can sacrifice to this supreme Jupiter! For he is now to me a much mightier Jupiter than Jupiter!
BALLIO [*modestly*]. No major victims please—I will be placated with lamb's inner organs.

Still in Plautus, we also encounter the grotesque case of the slave Libanus demanding divine worship from his master's young son Argyrippus (*Asinaria*, 712 ff.). The slave has cunningly acquired the money needed by Argyrippus to buy his sweetheart Philaenium, but before handing it over teases the youth with a drawn-out Saturnalian charade of inverting the normal social order. Libanus orders his young master to go down on all fours, so he can ride him like a horse; he demands kisses and embraces from Philaenium, and finally reaches the height of megalomania with his last condition for handover: 'Only if you also erect a statue and an altar to me and sacrifice an ox right here to me as a god—for I am now your Salvation [*Salus*]'. Nothing here is serious, but the fun depends entirely on the inversion of the normal social roles (including a master's sexual access to his slaves); thus Argyrippus offers to carry the money, arguing: 'O Libanus, my *patronus*, give it to me—it is more proper that the *libertus* rather than his *patronus* should carry a burden in public'. In another instance (*Captivi*, 860 ff.) a parasite bringing the good news to an old citizen that his son is alive and well orders the old man to bring sacrificial implements and sacrifice a fat lamb to him: 'For I am now to you the mightiest Jupiter, and likewise Salvation, Fortune, Light, Joy, and Happiness [*Salus, Fortuna, Lux, Laetitia, Gaudium*]'.[27]

It is interesting to note that none of these instances contain any indication that the person worshipped is a god, or divine in any absolute sense of the word. He merely occupies a (claimed) position *in relation to* the worshipper, corresponding to that of Jupiter, Salus, and so on. The patron demands or is offered divine honours, but his exact nature is quite irrelevant to the relative status hierarchy, involving patron and worshipper only, constructed and expressed by these supreme honours. This suggests a problem which has commonly been taken as fundamental in scholarship on imperial cult. We hardly ever receive an answer to the question whether the emperor in such a context was perceived as a god (in the absolute sense), or merely received honours *as to a god*—that is whether such treatment implied identification or merely a parallel. The question is so difficult to answer because it is the wrong one to ask; it implicitly misunderstands the nature and purpose of traditional pagan worship. As in the passages from Plautus, the absolute nature of the honorand was simply not relevant in such worship. Nor did this dogmatic question matter in worship of the 'real' Jupiter; such cult likewise constructed and expressed a status relationship between him and those cultivating him. It entailed no claim that Jupiter was the king of gods in the absolute sense, the main god for all men anywhere, but only for those performing the worship (or, as in state cult, for the *populus Romanus*, on whose behalf this cult took place).

Plautus is, however, a problematical source: Roman comedy is so influenced by Greek models that it may not be very relevant for Roman conditions; and much of Plautus' humour may in fact depend on what his audience recognized as Greek or

[27] *Persa* 99f.: '*O mi Iuppiter | terrestris, te coepulonus compellat tuos*'; Woytek (1982, 196f.) takes *terrestris* with *coepulonus* rather than with *Iuppiter*; I find this unconvincing, as does Jocelyn in *CR* 33 (1983, 198 n. 15); *Pseud.* 326ff.: 'CAL. *Pseudole, ei accerse hostias, | victumas, lanios, ut ego huic sacruficem summo Iovi; | nam hic mihi nunc est multo potior Iuppiter quam Iuppiter*'; *Asin.* 712ff.: '*si quidem mihi statuam et aram statuis | atque ut deo mi hic immolas bovem: nam ego tibi Salus sum*'; *Capt.* 860ff.: '. . . *sed iube | vasa tibi pura apparari ad rem divinam cito, | atque agnum afferri proprium pinguem . . . nam ego nunc tibi sum summus Iuppiter | idem ego sum Salus, Fortuna, Lux, Laetitia, Gaudium*'. Further examples in Plautus: Hanson (1959, 69).

Roman phenomena.[28] The argument could perhaps equally well be turned around: the fact that the Greek genre could work so unproblematically in a Roman context to some extent belies our strongly ingrained dichotomy between Greek and Roman. In fact the instances of personal worship in Plautus find no parallel in Greek comedy, nor in Terence whose plays follow Greek prototypes more closely. It is therefore commonly recognized that the instances from Plautus quoted here were in fact added by him, and not taken over from any Greek prototypes.[29]

Comedy is very difficult to employ as a historical source; we can to a large extent understand the humour in Plautus from our knowledge of social conditions in the 'real' world outside the theatre, but it is quite another matter to reconstruct this world from comedies. We will need extraneous sources to appreciate fully these instances of personal worship in Plautus. The most we can say is that caricature must still be immediately recognizable to fulfil a comical purpose. What is more, the instances of personal worship were apparently not funny simply because the behaviour of the characters was *in itself* so grotesque in these cases. It is striking that the normal or expected example of personal worship, that of someone vastly inferior to someone vastly superior in social terms, is not encountered in Plautus. All his examples represent inversions of this pattern which we would take to be the more common social circumstance in which such supreme honours would arise. Instead we meet slaves demanding divine worship from their masters, or a parasite from a social superior, or worship being offered to a repellent pimp (responding with mock modesty).

The other type of situation where we should expect such behaviour from potential worshippers would be in cases of supreme benefactions, impossible to repay by more modest

[28] For Greek vs. Roman in Plautus see Harvey (1985–6); Shipp (1955); Lowe (1989); and the essays in Lefèvre *et al.* (1991).

[29] Thus Fraenkel (1922, 115f.) = id. (1960, 109f.) on *Pseud.* 326ff. and *Asin.* 712ff.; cf. id. (1922, 96f.; 225) = id. (1960, 90f.; 216); id. (1922, 70) = id. (1960, 66) on *Capt.* 863ff. Contra Taeger (1957, 407): 'Auffällig ist, dass Plautus diese Motive übernommen hat, obwohl sie wenigstens in ihren letzten Hintergrunden für seine Hörer so gut wie unverständlich sein mussten, so sehr diese bisweilen über die derbe Situationskomik gefreut haben werden'.

means, and therefore answered with supreme honours given to the benefactor. Typically this should be the case of one person saving the life of another, or benefactions on a similar scale. Instead the notion of divine cult is triggered off in Plautus by a pimp agreeing to postpone—not even to cancel—the sale of the highly-strung worshipper's sweetheart, or in the expectation of a free meal, or as reward for simply bringing good news—without even having engendered it. Such instances are funny because of their grotesque extravagance, but this extravagance may well depend on the inversion of a more normal pattern. Contrary to what we might expect, this normal pattern is not encountered at all. Divine worship of men was then not sufficiently funny in itself—perhaps because it was not in itself that grotesque, but part of conceivable, everyday social behaviour.

The instances of 'human' worship encountered in Plautus are commonly taken to be original to Plautus, and not reflections of any Greek prototypes. But even if one were to argue that the phenomenon encountered in Plautus still depended on Greek influence, specifically in Plautus or more generally in Roman culture, such a view may well be correct, but it explains nothing. As mentioned already, Roman religion or culture, taken in the sense of being free of strong Greek influence, never existed. If of any point at all, the question should rather be when and why this way of honouring benefactors or other social superiors entered Roman culture. Even this question is ethnocentric, and should rather be turned round: when and why did such honours become monopolized by 'real' gods? Or rather, whence came the sharp, exclusive dividing line between human and divine, between religion and politics, presupposing such monopolization? The question then reverts to our own concept of religion as an aspect of the human spirit which can be isolated, and interpreted in isolation, from other aspects of human mentality. This is in fact not difficult to answer: 'religion' as a mental concept in Western culture has Christian roots, as I have claimed above. In this light, divine worship of humans, as of gods, an aspect of the 'relative' as opposed to the 'absolute' status system, is indeed the 'natural' state; only the later invention of 'religion', and the concept of the realm of God as sharply distinct and separate from this world, has problematized the phenomenon. Indeed this concept probably presupposes a monotheistic system, with one God of absolute status and omnipotent power, the God of all men, not only of his worshippers.

APPOINTING THE GODS

The complex problems of Plautus' passages cannot be solved here; arguments based on internal criteria in Plautus can hardly lead to very strong conclusions as to this worship. Instead I shall attempt to present some arguments external to Plautus' comedies, arguments which suggest that the instances quoted here are not so alien or grotesque as we might think. In fact, the Plautus passages do receive some support from other sources as indicative of social behaviour in contemporary Rome. We may note the theme of the 'earthly Jupiter' in some of Plautus' passages; as the supreme honour payable to a benefactor the theme should not surprise us, though it may seem ridiculously extravagant (and is so in connection with the unworthy recipients in Plautus). We have already encountered the same idea in connection with the Etruscan kings of Rome, who seem to have appeared in their emblematic dress exactly as such earthly Jupiters. Another parallel to the Plautine imagery, closer in time and circumstance, is encountered in a phenomenon as genuinely 'Roman' as any. The origins of the *corona civica*, the military distinction of an oak wreath, are lost in prehistory, but the employment of it can be followed back to the third century BC. It was bestowed for the saving of the life of a fellow citizen on the battlefield; in historical times the distinction was bestowed by the commanding general, but tradition had it that it was originally awarded by the soldier saved to his saviour.[30] To save the life of another man was naturally the greatest possible benefaction, and had to be reciprocated by the greatest possible honour. The winter oak, from whose leaves the wreath was made, was Jupiter's tree and symbol; though it has to my knowledge not been noted, the award seems obviously explicable as the appointment by the soldier saved of his rescuer as an earthly Jupiter for himself.[31]

[30] Gell. 5. 6. 11; *corona civica*: Maxfield (1981, 70ff.) with the other sources.

[31] Plin. *Nat. Hist.* 16. 5. 11: '*Civica* [corona] *iligna primo fuit, postea magis*

In the course of history, the *corona civica* came to take on an institutionalized life of its own, and the original significance of the custom seems to have been lost or forgotten by the late republic, though its connotations of Jupiter, who also wore it, remained obvious. When Augustus in 27 BC received the privilege of having the wreath placed above the door to his house, the Jovean wreath became an imperial emblem, employed as such by later emperors too. Its use in this context served a double purpose, one explicit, the other by association: it was explicitly decreed to the emperor, because he had saved his fellow citizens from civil war. Beyond this, however, it furthermore fitted perfectly the obvious parallel between the heavenly and the earthly monarch, which was so often employed in literature and art, and, no doubt, always present in the popular mind, if not in official ideology (it was of course incompatible with the formal notion of Augustus as first among equals).[32]

This later development is, however, not relevant here; if the original meaning of the wreath was the one I have claimed here, it was long forgotten in the Augustan age. Our sources only mention that the bestowal of the wreath obliged the soldier saved to honour his rescuer as a father.[33] This is indeed close enough to the original meaning, and may contain an echo of it; rather than merely a biological term, *pater* of course, as in *paterfamilias* and indeed *Juppiter*, connoted a position of absolute authority over those employing the term *pater* of someone in order to express his relationship to them. In connection with the *paterfamilias* we have already encountered the more institutionalized form of worship conferred on his *Genius* by his *familia*; this form of worship focused, as mentioned, on the continued existence of the household as a social unit. The appointment of a *Juppiter terrestris* seems more in keeping with

placuit ex aesculo Iovi sacra, variatumque et cum quercu est ac data ubique quae fuerat custodito tantum honore glandis'. This may reflect an older distinction between a terrestrial Jupiter, whose emblem was made from the less noble holm-oak, whereas Juppiter Optimus Maximus was characterized by the grander winter oak; later, however, the parallel was further stressed by the use of leaves from the tree of the 'real' Jupiter. But Pliny's version may be a later rationalization of variations in the exact type of leaves employed, which may reflect no more than that any oak tree at hand near the battlefield could suffice.

32 See p. 110 n. 4 and 269 n. 14 for instances of the parallel.

33 Father: Polyb. 6. 39. 7; Cic. *Planc.* 72; Weinstock (1971, 163 ff.).

the singular and personal benefaction involved; it was furthermore a greater honour than *Genius* worship, corresponding to the magnitude of the benefaction. In both instances, however, the message of such worship was roughly the same: the worshipper subjected himself to the unlimited (in principle) authority of the honorand, to his *potestas*. He thus expressed his own enrolment into the *familia* of the person worshipped. Whether this person was termed *patronus* or even *deus* or *Juppiter* was then a difference in degree rather than in kind.

Tenuous and misty as are both the emblematic dress of the Roman king and the origins of the oak *corona civica*, they suggest that the instances of personal worship in Plautus are not merely comical inventions (the comical aspect rather lies in the rather modest benefactions triggering these extravagant honours, and the unworthiness of their recipients, in the passages quoted). They also imply that the phenomenon of personal worship was not merely a Greek import to Italy in the middle or late republic, but that it goes back so far in a Roman context that any talk of Greek influence in this connection becomes meaningless. If such honours seem absent before the late republic, this merely reflects the nature of our sources, which are predominantly late and largely ignore the private sphere. We do, however, get a few glimpses of such honours. In 86 BC people in Rome erected statues of a praetor, Marius Gratidianus, in street shrines (*compita*), and sacrificed wine and incense to the images in gratitude for beneficial currency reforms attributed to him (wrongly, as it happened).[34] The worship at the *compita* took place in public, even if it was private in legal terms. But after Gaius Marius' great victories over the Teutonians and Cimbrians in the late second century BC people included him in the honours habitually afforded to their house gods at meals, and poured libations to him.[35] Both these instances—and others could be quoted[36]—are only encountered because the public sphere, the Roman body politic, came to interfere with the private level. Without such interference or overlap, we cannot expect any information. It seems

[34] Cic. *Off.* 3. 80; Sen. *De Ira* 3. 18. 1.

[35] Val. Max. 8. 15. 7; Plut. *Mar.* 27. 9.

[36] Weinstock (1971, 293ff.) (with some instances more convincing than others).

that emperor worship conflicted with republican tradition only in the banal sense that the Roman republic in the nature of things did not have an emperor; the novelty lies in the gradual emergence of monarchy, and not in the history of Roman religion and mentality.

Honours bestowed on a man (or god) by other men defined relative status, and the power structure between the two parties involved. The highest honours—divine worship—expressed the maximum status gap and the absolute power wielded by the person worshipped over his worshipper. For the latter, the object of his homage was a god in the decisive sense that his power over the worshipper was as absolute as that of a god—'for he is now to me a much mightier Jupiter than Jupiter!' in the words of a Plautine worshipper (*Pseud.* 326 ff.). Again we should bear in mind that pagan Roman thought did not include any clear distinction between 'honours' and 'worship'. Divine worship differed in degree, not in kind, from 'political' or 'secular' honours. Massive differences in social status—as that between gods and humans—found expression in weighty honours. Such massive status gaps were either permanent in the existing social order, as between the Roman state gods and the Roman people (*populus Romanus*), or between the *paterfamilias* and his subjects, his *familia*; or they could be 'constructed' by benefactions of such magnitude that *summi honores* constituted the only means of repaying them. Cicero may furnish an example of this. When he returned to Rome from exile, he delivered the following homily to P. Cornelius Lentulus Spinther, who had made possible his homecoming (*P. Red. Quir.* 11): 'parent, god, and Salvation of my life, fortune, reputation, and name' (*parens, deus, Salus nostrae vitae, fortunae, memoriae, nominis*). Cicero did not, however, worship Lentulus in cult; for this, his own social position was too high, and the 'status gap' between the two fellow senators was of too transitory a nature. The 'gap' was closed by the honour of this, to our ears extravagant, laudation in a public speech by which Lentulus' supreme benefaction was repaid. The main principle involved, that of gift exchange, expressed in the formula *do ut des* ('I give so that you will give'), is well known; mutual obligations permeated Roman culture. This strong, morally mandatory obligation to repay benefactions with honours and vice versa may be difficult to understand in our culture with its ideas of personal liberty.

The structure functioned along the same lines whether directed towards gods or men. To dismiss divine worship of human beings, including the Roman emperor, as a 'political' rather than 'religious' phenomenon is to miss the point. Absolute and permanent power probably found expression throughout Roman history in divine honours bestowed on men as well as on gods. Only in the private sphere, however, was this power to be found in the hands of men under the republic. The public sphere, the Roman state, had no monarch or *paterfamilias* or anyone filling a similar position till the republic finally collapsed under Caesar's dictatorship. The reactions of the Senate, and the way in which the Roman 'constitution' was made to respond to this new situation will form the subject of my next chapter; the dictator's case raises questions fundamental to any interpretations of emperor worship.

3
Caesar's Divine Honours

I have argued in my preceding chapter that, in terms of mental history, ruler cult was the traditional republican response to monarchy, whether the monarch was Jupiter or Caesar. The case of Julius Caesar illustrates and exemplifies many of the problems of ruler cult, as well as adding some of its own. The secondary literature on Caesar and his divine honours is enormous (though the rate of increase has, mercifully, shrunk considerably over the last decades) and often bogged down in detail or discussion several times removed from the sources; its sheer bulk and detail has unfortunately tended to overshadow the ancient evidence and makes it legitimate largely to ignore modern scholarship here in favour of the primary sources.[1]

There were three main phases in the Senate's honours to the dictator. The first was after the battle of Thapsus in 46, when the senators decreed him a chariot and statue to be placed on the Capitol; the statue was to have an inscription stating that he was a demigod—*hēmítheos* in Cassius Dio's Greek.[2] In the second phase, after the battle of Munda in 45, his statue was to be placed in the temple of Quirinus with an inscription declaring him an unconquered god.[3] Thirdly, the culmination came in the last months of Caesar's life, when he was decreed state divinity, with a cult name (*Divus Iulius*), a state priest (*flamen*),

[1] I shall largely quote two works here: Weinstock (1971) because his book presents all the ancient evidence, direct and parallel, and seems to me still by far the best major work on the subject, clearly written and argued (though at times somewhat bizarre in its conclusions), and consistently taking its starting-point in the ancient evidence rather than in the jungle of views of other scholars; and Fishwick (1987, 56–72) because he supplies a fine and fairly recent overview from which later literature can be gleaned. A useful outline of scholarship as well as an extensive bibliography can be found in Gesche (1976, esp. 154ff.).

[2] Dio 43. 14. 6; Weinstock (1971, 40ff.); Fishwick (1987, 57ff.).

[3] Dio 43. 45. 3; Weinstock (1971 *passim*, esp. 133ff. and 175ff.; Fishwick (1987, 57ff.).

a state temple, and a sacred couch—*pulvinar*—for his image. These honours represent all the paraphernalia of the main gods of the Roman state. A persistent branch of scholarship has denied that Caesar was ever deified by the Senate in his lifetime. This view is untenable unless we simply rewrite the sources, something which has in fact been done too much. Immersed in nitty-gritty details and extreme speculation, the literature on the sources to Caesar's dictatorship can by now scare away most of us. Yet, surprisingly perhaps, the state of the sources is actually relatively good, and presents fewer problems than might be thought from a look at the secondary literature. As for the crowning honours from the last months of Caesar's life, they are confirmed by Suetonius, by Dio, by Appian, and, most importantly, by Cicero in his second *Philippic*.[4]

Much of the discussion on points of detail is caused by this relatively large amount of written source material (one source only would of course not contain contradictions, and its information would therefore more easily be established as historical 'facts'). The discussion of minor points is therefore understandable, but the fact that several scholars have rejected outright that Caesar was appointed state god, with all the *summi honores* mentioned as features in the public worship of the supreme gods of the Roman state, is surprising, for on these points the sources are basically in agreement (only Plutarch, rarely rated highly as a historical source, seems to date the divine honours after Caesar's death).[5] One detail over which

[4] Cic. *Phil.* 2. 43. 110; Dio 44. 4ff.; App. *BC* 2. 106; Suet. *Caes.* 76. 1; 84. 2; Weinstock (1971, 270ff.); Fishwick (1987, 60ff.).

[5] Plut. *Caes.* 67. 4: '*ἡ δὲ σύγκλητος ἀμνηστίας τινὰς καί συμβάσεις πράττουσα πᾶσι Καίσαρα μὲν ὡς θεὸν τιμᾶν ἐψηφίσατο*' refers the honours to a senate meeting of 17 March, i.e. immediately after the murder when the Senate tried to steer a middle course between Caesarians and tyrant-slayers, upholding Caesar's acts, but at the same time granting an amnesty to his murderers; a deification at this time and in this context seems incongruous, and the meeting is not mentioned by either Dio or Appian, so the passage is usually rejected, thus by Gesche in Wlosok (ed.) (1978, 370), Alföldi (1975, 175), Fishwick (1986, 65f.); upheld by Charlesworth (1935, 25); perhaps Plutarch's statement refers only to the funerary arrangements, as stated by Weinstock (1971, 354f.). Alternatively, he means that the Senate voted to uphold Caesar's recently decreed divine honours even after he was dead (in principle only, then, for nothing was done to implement the measures), or he simply

much discussion has accrued, and to which I shall return, is the new name or title, *Divus Iulius*, accorded Caesar, but mentioned only by Cicero. In general, his testimony is the decisive one, for though it is brief and undetailed, it basically corroborates the later writers, and makes it impossible to reject them on the grounds that they are late (though that in itself would not be a strong argument anyhow). With scathing sarcasm Cicero in his second *Philippic* (110), purporting to have been delivered on 19 September 44, scolds Mark Antony for neglecting Caesar's memory, calling his bluff in his attempt to appear as Caesar's avenger and political heir:[6]

> And are *you* zealous in respecting Caesar's memory? do *you* love him now he is dead? What greater honour had he obtained than to have a couch [*pulvinar*], a cult image [*simulacrum*], a temple pediment to his house [*fastigium*], a flamen? As Jupiter, as Mars, as Quirinus has a flamen, so the flamen to Divus Julius is Mark Antony. Why then delay? Why not be inaugurated? Select your day; look out for your inaugurator; we are colleagues; no one will say no. O detestable man, whether as priest of Caesar or of a dead man!

So all the sources are basically in accordance with each other on the main points, though it seems clear that the measures were in fact never implemented before Caesar's death; as stated by Cicero, his flamen, Mark Antony, had not yet been inaugurated by the Ides of March. In the complicated political situation caused by the murder of the dictator, the crowning honours were simply ignored. Only at the formation of the second triumvirate at the end of 43 BC did the triumvirs have the honours implemented, as well as adding new ones, such as taking 'an oath and making all the rest [of the senators] swear that they would consider all his acts binding'; also they began the erection of a temple to Divus Julius in the Forum, on the spot

misunderstood his source in the light of consecration procedures of *Divi* in his own day. Apart from this item, Plutarch ignores Caesar's divine honours.

[6] (tr. Ker, Loeb edn., adapted) *Et tu in Caesaris memoria diligens, tu illum amas mortuum? Quem is honorem maiorem consecutus erat, quam ut haberet pulvinar, simulacrum, fastigium, flaminem? Est ergo flamen, ut Iovi, ut Marti, ut Quirino, sic Divo Iulio M. Antonius. Quid igitur cessas? cur non inauguraris? Sume diem, vide, qui te inauguret; conlegae sumus; nemo negabit. O detestabilem hominem, sive quod Caesaris sacerdos es sive quod mortui!*

where he had been cremated, instead of the temple to Caesar and his *Clementia* voted before his death.[7] Antony, however, to some extent still tried to steer a middle course and hesitated to be inaugurated, since Caesar's honour would now primarily reflect on young Octavian, his adopted son and Antony's rival; in fact, the inauguration only took place in 40 BC.[8] The later implementation of Caesar's deification by the triumvirs has given rise to some controversy as to when the measures were actually voted. But the controversy seems superfluous: Cicero's passage, supported by the later sources, leaves no doubt that the honours of state divinity were in fact passed in Caesar's lifetime. The protracted discussions on the issue do not, I believe, primarily reflect any uncertainty or ambiguity in our sources, but rather the fact that the measures have seemed so strange and alien to scholars that outright rejection or forced interpretation of the evidence have seemed the only alternatives to concluding that Caesar (and the Senate) had gone insane in accepting such proposals. The incredulity displayed by modern scholars reflects modern concerns, interpreting the state divinity in christianizing terms of man versus god. The ancient sources, however, should show us that our own terms are the wrong ones to apply here.[9]

[7] Dio 47. 18. 3 ff.; cf. 44. 6. 4; App. *BC* 2. 106; Weinstock (1971, 386) presupposes a new senatorial decree in this connection; that is possible, but Dio in fact does not mention any such thing, and presumably it would have sufficed simply to implement the dormant honorary decrees from Caesar's last months; only the new measures, such as the oath and the new temple probably presuppose the passing of new decrees. The implementation at this date led to the later, Augustan version, as I see it, that Octavian deified his father, as stated by App. *BC* 2. 148 (and implied in Dio 51. 20. 6, see p. 74 n. 2 below); in Augustus' reign, the lifetime deification, blatantly incompatible with the Augustan constitutional settlement, was an inconvenient version.

[8] Plut. *Ant.* 33. 1; Weinstock (1971, 399).

[9] Most handbooks and shorter accounts still leave open the question whether the honours were in fact posthumous or from Caesar's lifetime, e.g. Price (1987, 71 f.), eventually settling on 42 BC; since Cicero's account seems difficult to circumvent, ambiguity has been kept alive by Gesche (1968) who suggested that the measures dated from Caesar's lifetime, but were only meant to come into effect at his death, that is, she projects backwards the system from the imperial age when emperors could only become *Divi* after death; the suggestion attempts to steer a middle course between the ancient evidence and modern incredulity, but nothing of the kind is mentioned in any of the ancient sources. Her theory is rightly rejected by most scholars, e.g. Alföldi (1970,

In connection with Caesar's honours in general, the classic questions have been two: what was Caesar's programme and did he want to become king?[10] Too much attention has been focused on the personal aspect inherent in these questions. What is most striking, however, is the fact that scholars have reached such diametrically opposite conclusions. Once again, this may be not because the answers are wrong, but because the questions are. Almost all scholars, Meyer, Gesche, Weinstock, Dobesch, to name but a few, have taken it more or less for granted that behind all Caesar's honours lurked a programme of his. Fewer have asked whether such a programme ever existed, or should have existed.[11] The question is pertinent, however. One of the reasons for the differing reconstructions of Caesar's programme seems to me to be that the honours and privileges accorded to Caesar do not really add up to any consistent whole. So, depending on which of these honours, or refusals of honours, are emphasized, almost any result can emerge.

Taking our sources and their lists of honours at face value, Caesar's supposed programme is in fact far from obvious; as suggested directly by Cassius Dio, his role appears to have been primarily a passive one, responding only to honorary measures proposed to him by the Roman Senate.[12] In this flow of measures there is little reason to claim any consistent programme. Still, it might be argued, Caesar could have controlled this flow in the direction he preferred simply by picking out the honours consistent with his own ideas and rejecting those which were not. Often, however, he was not in Rome and was apparently not even asked. This appears for instance to have been the case with the sculptures decreed to him on the Capitol, where he later had the title of demigod ('*hēmítheos*') chiselled out from

175) and Fishwick (1987, 64f.). I believe, however, that she is right in interpreting the oath of Octavian, quoted by Cicero (*Ad Att.* 16. 15. 3, November 44: '. . . *iurat "ita sibi parentis honores consequi liceat"*'), as demanding that Caesar's honours be implemented, rather than that Octavian should himself attain to the same honours.

[10] Hellenistic-type kingship: Meyer (1963, *passim*); fundamentally the same view in e.g. Taylor (1931), Dobesch (1966), and Weinstock (1971); Roman-style kingship: Alföldi (1953); no kingship: e.g. Fishwick (1987, 70f.).

[11] Meyer (1963); Gesche (1968) and (1976); Weinstock (1971); Dobesch (1966); contra Balsdon (1967); Fishwick (1987, 71).

[12] Dio e.g. 44. 6. 1; 3; North (1975, 172f.).

his statue base. And if the crowning divine honours had really been of his own devising, it seems inexplicable that he did not have their measures carried out before departing for the East, as he was about to do on the Ides of March.

The argument that Caesar could simply have implemented his claimed programme by picking and choosing among the honours voted him misunderstands the whole system of granting and accepting honours in Roman society. Honours were a way to define the status or social position of the person or god honoured, but it was also a way to tie him down. The bestowal of honours to someone socially superior, whether man or god, obliged him to return them with benefactions. Or, we might say, to rule well. It could indeed be honourable to reject excessive honours, and, for example, the elder Scipio had excelled in this *gloria recusandi*. On the other hand, refusing honours also entailed rejecting the moral obligations that went with them, even to the point of recognizing no bonds whatsoever. So it would be socially irresponsible to reject all such proposals. The emperor Tiberius, and his rather hesitant and inconsistent policy when Roman provinces presented him with divine honours is a case in point. He accepted a provincial temple to himself in Asia in 24, but a year later rejected one in Farther Spain (Tac. *Ann*. 4. 37f.). Tiberius has been lauded by modern scholars for these refusals of worship. More surprisingly, perhaps, his rejection caused adverse comments at the time, if we believe Tacitus: 'for disdaining one's reputation will lead to disdaining all moral quality' (*nam contemptu famae contemni virtutes*). Claudius' letter to the Alexandrians is another example; it illustrates the correct balance in the emperor's accepting some honours and rejecting others, neatly mirroring his mixture of benevolence and dismissal in dealing with the requests of the Alexandrians.[13] The balance was a delicate one, and Caesar's fate shows that he did not manage to keep it. But there is no need to see in his acceptance or refusal of honours any evidence of a consistent programme or policy. Caesar wanted to be the first man in Rome; how this position should be expressed and formalized in the state system may well have

[13] Smallwood (1967, no. 370); tr. and comm. in Levick (1985, 125ff.), lit. in Sherk (1988, 83ff.).

been left to others, primarily the Senate. Indeed, this appears to have been the case.

Another perennial discussion is that of Caesar's craving for kingship; once again, the results reached by scholars have been diametrically opposed. And once again, the question has often been put the wrong way. For instance, when the Senate decreed that Caesar's statue should be placed on the Capitol next to those of Rome's kings, did this imply monarchy?[14] The statue of L. Brutus who had expelled the kings from Rome stood in the same group; so did this honour instead present Caesar as an anti-king, a liberator? Discussion has been rife. But the question is flawed. As there was no standard and authoritative definition of what a god was, so it was with a king. Many of Caesar's honours had clear connotations of kingship, both that of ancient Rome and the different version of the Eastern, Hellenistic world, but there was no standard recipe for what a king really was. All we can say is that Caesar never took or accepted the two most unequivocal emblems of kingship, the title of Rex or the diadem. Furthermore, discussions of whether this statue of Caesar's made him a king, or a Brutus, or a new founder of Rome misses the essential ideological point in such iconographical representations. It was a strength, not a weakness, that their message was equivocal, and could create different connotations, and hence cater for several, even conflicting, views on Caesar. The search for an exact ideological meaning in representations of Hellenistic monarchs or Roman emperors as Zeus or Jupiter represents a parallel misunderstanding.

With Caesar the republic collapsed. His honours are to be seen as the Senate's attempt to formulate the new and unique position of Caesar, hence their lack of consistency. In dealing here only with Caesar's divine honours, as opposed to his secular ones, I am consciously anachronistic. Both types of honours are regularly mixed up completely in the ancient sources, without any attempt at making distinctions.[15] That is not surprising,

[14] Dio 43. 45. 3; Weinstock (1971, 145ff.).

[15] The only feeble and imprecise indication of such a distinction is in Suetonius' (*Caes.* 76. 1) group of honours '*ampliora . . . humano fastigio*'; but the group includes, revealingly, such an item as '*sedem auream in curia et pro tribunali*', as well as the divine honours of *templa, aras, simulacra iuxta deos,*

for our ingrained distinction between religion and politics is largely irrelevant when dealing with pagan antiquity. Caesar's divine honours are an obvious example that religion and politics were not only two sides of the same coin, but simply part and parcel of the same phenomenon.[16]

DIVUS CAESAR?

The first divine honours accorded Caesar by the Senate were decreed after the battle of Thapsus, fought on 6 April 46. There were several honours, but Dio unfortunately records only the ones actually accepted by Caesar, so perhaps only the more moderate ones (though by what standards we cannot really say).[17] In Dio's version the Senate voted him a chariot to be placed on the Capitol, facing Jupiter, and a statue of Caesar placed on top of the inhabited world, accompanied by an inscription stating that he was a demigod. The appearance of the sculptures has once again given rise to much debate, but it seems reasonably clear that two separate sculptures are described, and that the one of Caesar—without chariot—represented him as world ruler, *pantokrator*, probably placing his raised foot on a globe. Whatever the precise scheme employed, the motif was clearly borrowed from such representations of Hellenistic kings, even if perhaps no king in particular. The chariot, probably with another statue of Caesar in it, was to be placed facing Jupiter; whether by this is meant the Capitoline temple or simply a statue of Jupiter which stood on the Capitol, is not entirely clear.

I am, however, not concerned here with these ghostly sculptures, but with the inscription decreed to accompany the statue with the globe. It was to state that Caesar was a demigod—*hēmítheos* is the word used by Dio. Much discussion has been spent on this word, namely what the Latin inscription actually said, or was to have said. The word *hēmítheos* in Latin seems to

pulvinar, flaminem, etc. The distinction is clearly not founded on any dichotomy between religion and politics, but on moral (and anachronistic) criteria determined by the behaviour of good vs. bad emperors from Augustus till Suetonius' own day.

16 Thus Beard (1994, 729ff., esp. 734).

17 Dio 43. 14. 6; 21. 2.

be ruled out by the fact that it is first encountered in the fourth century AD, and the Latin translation *semideus* is first found in Ovid, and may indeed have been coined by him. Both words would in any case have been extremely weird and inexplicable in this context. Other suggestions include the word *Genius*, but this is invariably translated by Dio, and other Greek authors, as *túchē*. Weinstock simply gave up on the problem, but later Fishwick has returned to it and persistently argued that the only solution should be a *name* of a specific 'demigod', in which case the only option would be Romulus. Fishwick has drawn attention to other instances where Caesar was clearly associated with the founder of Rome who would also be an obvious associative parallel to the dictator. Thus Fishwick points to another honour to Caesar, when the Senate decreed that Caesar's statue should be erected in the temple of Quirinus with an inscription stating that he was an unconquered god. Once again, the source is Dio, but in this case it is easy to restore the Latin equivalent to his Greek, namely *deus invictus*. It was commonly accepted that Quirinus was the name accorded to Romulus when he had been deified after his death.[18]

However, Fishwick's interesting theory runs into unsurmountable problems. The statue in the Quirinus temple was voted a year later than the statue on the Capitol, namely after the battle of Munda in 45. The coupling of Caesar with the founder of Rome was obviously suggested to the responsive Senate by the fact that news of the victory reached Rome on 20 April, the day before the anniversary of the founding of Rome; so another of the Senate's honours on this occasion was that the Parilia of the following day should be dedicated to the celebration of Caesar's victory, as if he had thereby founded Rome anew. All honours coupling or associating Caesar with Romulus/Quirinus belong after this time, and there is no trace in our sources that the notion was used before this occasion. This fact was also felt by Fishwick to constitute a problem, so much so that he claimed that Dio was mistaken and had reversed the two inscriptions; surely this is going too far to save a theory. It is true that the wording *Deo invicto* would have been very appropriate indeed to the statue on the Capitol with

[18] Weinstock (1971, 53); Fishwick (1975), reiterated in Fishwick (1987, 57).

its globe under foot, but this very appropriateness makes it more difficult to see how or why Dio or his source should have made this mistake and switched the inscriptions. Even more damaging is a simpler argument: if the Capitoline inscription described Caesar as Romulus, why should Dio or his source not simply have quoted this, instead of making a hazy translation? So Fishwick's theory must fall victim to Occam's razor.

It may appear that Weinstock was right in dismissing the whole project as hopelessly speculative. However, I believe it is not; but the answer should be sought not in the sources for Caesar's last years and his countless honours, but in something more down-to-earth, namely Dio's vocabulary. One of the numerous suggestions for the elusive word has been *Divus*, which was, however, promptly dismissed by scholarship.[19]

By Dio's time the word *Divus* was used of a dead emperor, posthumously deified by the Senate. The precedent was set by Caesar's case: whatever titles he received while he was still alive, he was deified under the name Divus Julius in 42 BC. The next deification was that of Augustus, declared a god of the Roman state by the Senate immediately after his death in 14. In Dio's day the list of *Divi* had grown monotonously long and the process of state deification had become totally routine, to the extent that a contemporary writer, Herodian (4. 2. 1), could describe to his Greek audience—cynically or naively, but correctly—that the Romans had the custom of deifying any dead emperor who left behind a son to succeed him. Originally *Divus* had simply been synonymous with the word's by-form *Deus*, but by Dio's time the word was so closely attached to dead emperors that Dio regularly translated the word into the Greek *hērōs*, a dead man worshipped. Only in some cases, when citing the full *name* of a *Divus*, does Dio use the original and official translation into Greek, namely *theiós*, for example when citing the name *theiós Augoustos*, Divus Augustus.[20]

So the term *Divus* to Dio and his Greek audience in the early third century implied simply a dead man deified, a *hērōs*. Sometimes, however, Dio ran into difficulties with his vocabulary. If the Capitoline inscription, or Dio's Latin source quoting it,

[19] Weinstock (1957, 232) (no arguments); abandoned in id. (1971, 53).

[20] For Dio's vocabulary I have consulted the *Ibycus*.

read *Divo Caesari*, Dio's usual translation would not do, since Caesar was clearly not dead at the time. Hence he used *hēmítheos*. This could be dismissed as mere speculation, if it was not for the fact that Dio's vocabulary elsewhere confirms the idea. His account of Augustus' funeral furnishes us with some neat examples. Describing the funeral procession he says (56. 34. 2):

Behind these [images] came the images of his ancestors and of his deceased relatives (except that of Caesar, because he had been numbered among the *hērōes* [*hóti es toùs hērōas esegégrapto*]) and those of other Romans who had been prominent in any way, beginning with Romulus himself.

Likewise a little later, in Dio's version of Tiberius' funeral oration to the people in honour of Augustus (56. 41. 9):

It was for all this, therefore, that you, with good reason, made him your leader and a father of the people . . . and that you finally made him a *hērōs* and declared him to be immortal.

These are examples of Dio's normal usage. Earlier in the same funeral oration, however, Dio makes Tiberius mention Caesar (56. 36. 2):

For this, indeed, is one of the greatest achievements of Augustus, that at the time when he had just emerged from boyhood and was barely coming to man's estate, he devoted himself to his education just so long as public affairs were well managed by that *hēmítheos* Caesar . . .

In this context a setting is presented from a time when Divus Julius, Caesar, was *alive*, and Dio therefore uses '*hēmítheos*' to stress this—so here he felt '*hērōs*' to be inappropriate. This is the only other instance where Dio uses the word '*hēmítheos*', which goes to show that the use must be quite deliberate, and presumably harks back to the earlier instance. It is in any case clearly used here as a synonym for '*hērōs*', and the word was in fact generally employed in this way. However, whereas the term *hērōs* presupposed death, that was not necessarily the case with *hēmítheos* which was suitably more vague (thus *hērōs* can be seen as a subcategory of this more general term).[21] So Caesar

[21] Synonyms: already Hesiod, *Op.* 160 speaks of 'the divine breed of human *hērōes* who are called *hēmítheoi*'. Cf. Dion. Hal. *Ant.* 7. 72. 13: *hēmítheoi* are gods 'whose souls after they had left their mortal bodies are said to have

is the only person of whom Dio uses the word, since Caesar was the only man to be termed *Divus* when alive. Likewise when Dio ran into the wording of the Capitoline inscription from 46 BC. Here '*hērōs*', the dead man, was totally inappropriate; hence the term '*hēmítheos*'.[22] So we may plausibly reconstruct Caesar's inscription as something like *Senatus populusque Romanus Divo Caesari.*

If this is correct, Dio's translation into Greek was of course anachronistic, but he often is. Originally the word *Divus* was simply a by-form of the word *Deus*, and the two words were completely synonymous, as they continued to be in poetry. At some point, however, Roman grammarians tried to work out a difference in etymology and meaning between them. The explanation was, as far as we can judge, wrong in terms of etymology, but that is not important. It was established or at least supported by Caesar's contemporary, the learned and highly influential scholar Varro; and, probably due to Varro's authority, it was believed, as Caesar's and later Augustus' title of *Divus* goes to show. Varro's treatment of the words seems to have been presented in the lost part of his treatise on the Latin language, *De Lingua Latina*. But Servius, fourth-century commentator on Virgil, refers to Varro's discussion:[23] 'Deus or dea is the general term for all [gods]. . . . Varro to Cicero in the third book [of *De lingua Latina*]: "That is the reply they would give as to why they say *dii*, when the ancients said *divi*

ascended to Heaven and to have obtained the same honours as the gods, such as Heracles, Asclepius, the Dioscuri, Helen, Pan, and countless others'—i.e. full-blown gods (unlike *hērōes*) except for the fact that they were once mortal; further instances in Liddell and Scott's dictionary s.v. ἡμίθεος.

[22] Cf. Serv. *Ad Buc.* 9. 46: . . . *quam quidam ad inlustrandam gloriam Caesaris iuvenis pertinere existimabant, ipse animam patris sui esse voluit eique in Capitolio statuam, super caput auream stellam habentem, posuit: inscriptum in basi fuit 'Caesari emitheo'.* Often quoted, the passage is in fact irrelevant, for Servius' wording may well ultimately be based on Dio. All that can be said is that by Servius' time the word '*(h)emitheus*' had entered Latin as a synonym for '*heros*', cf. Serv. *Ad Aen.* 8. 314.

[23] Serv. *Ad Aen.* 12. 139 (= Varro, *Ling. Lat.* fr. 2, ed. Goetz-Schoell): '*Deus autem vel dea generale nomen est omnibus: nam quod graece δέος, latine timor vocatur, inde deus dictus est, quod omnis religio sit timoris. Varro ad Ciceronem tertio: "ita respondeant cur dicant deos, cum [de] omnibus antiqui dixerint divos"*'.

about them all."' Elsewhere Servius further employs what was probably the same passage in Varro's work:[24]

The poet [Virgil] usually employs 'of the *divi*' [*divum*] and 'of the *dii*' [*deorum*] indifferently, although there should be a distinction in that we call the immortals '*dii*', whereas '*divi*' are created from men, inasmuch as they have ended their days; from which we likewise call [dead] emperors '*divi*'. But Varro and Ateius hold the opposite opinion, claiming that '*divi*' are eternal, whereas '*dii*' are such as are held in honour because they have been deified, such as is the case with the '*dii manes*'.

Varro's main arguments seem clear from these passages: *divi* are in his view a subcategory of the general term *dii*, the 'élite division', so to speak, of the gods, for *divi* are eternal gods—and originally all deities were eternal ones—whereas men who have become gods are called by the more general term, such as the deified spirits of the dead, the *dii manes*. We do not know whether the Ateius likewise mentioned by Servius was a contemporary of Varro's or belonged to the next generation.[25]

The date of Varro's work on the Latin language, where his discussion was apparently found, is interesting. It was finished in the early months of 44 BC, that is, exactly the time when the Senate conferred the novel title *Divus* Julius on Caesar. Parts of Varro's work were, however, published a few years earlier, and we have no way of knowing if the discussion was to be found in the earlier version or not. In any case, Varro's definition belongs to exactly the period when senators debated Caesar's titulature, either in 44 or in 46 when the monument on the Capitol was set up. Though certainty is beyond our reach, it seems likely that Varro dealt with the problem in response to the debate on what novel titles the dictator should receive, or even as a result of being consulted by senators on the issue.

[24] Serv. *Ad Aen*. 5. 45 (= Varro *fr*. 424, *Grammaticae Romanae fragmenta*, ed. Funaioli): '*"divum" et "deorum" indifferenter plerumque ponit poeta, quamquam sit discretio, ut deos perpetuos dicamus, divos ex hominibus factos, quasi qui diem obierint; unde divos etiam imperatores vocamus. Sed Varro et Ateius contra sentiunt, dicentes divos perpetuos deos qui propter sui consecrationem timentur, ut sunt dii manes*'. Cf. Price (1984*b*, 83 n. 38–9); Weinstock (1971, 391 f.).

[25] He is either the contemporary Ateius Praetextatus (Varro *fr*. 12, ed. Funaioli *op. cit*.), or the Augustan Ateius Capito (*fr*. 15, ed. Funaioli).

In any case, the discussion was not merely one of academic pedantry: it was political dynamite during these very years.

Thus, according to the influential scholar, *Divi* were gods who had always been so, whereas creatures who had at some point been consecrated as gods were termed *Dii*. The word *Divus* then implied the noblest condition, that of the eternal gods, and was therefore the more dignified term. This explains why it was chosen in relation to Caesar, in 46 and then again later; and this was again why Augustus became *Divus* Augustus when the Senate deified him after his death. So these men had actually always been gods, even if this characteristic was only recognized belatedly. However, we should not press such a dogmatic expression too far; what mattered was probably just that the title *Divus* represented an honorific maximum—and, decisively, circumvented any uncomfortable connotations of death.

Ironically, this Varronian use of the word '*Divus*' ensured that Varro's definition was eventually turned upside down. Centuries later, Servius was struck by the apparent eccentricity of the older grammarian's definition of '*Divus*', because he failed to realize this chronological development. Also in Servius' day the term '*Deus*' was the more general one, of which '*Divus*' was a subcategory. But whereas Varro's *Divi* had formed the immortal élite division of the *Dii*, posthumous deification of emperors with the title of *Divus* entailed that *Divi* instead came to be regarded as the lowest category, dead emperors deified, unlike the immortal and eternal gods who were always termed *Dii*. The subjects of the Empire evidently cared little about their emperors once they had died; their interest was mainly focused on the living emperor. Thus the word *Divus*, chosen for Caesar and for Augustus at his death as the most splendid expression of unequivocal divinity, eventually failed to impress as intended and became devalued. The lack of interest in dead emperors is in fact evident even in relation to the one case where we might have expected otherwise, that of Divus Augustus. Shortly after the emperor's death and deification the governor of Bithynia, Granius Marcellus, had Augustus' head taken off one of his statues to have it replaced by that of Tiberius. Furthermore, Dio explicitly states that some of the towns in Italy which erected temples to Divus Augustus did so only after pressure from Tiberius;[26] such intervention in the civic cults of Italy is, significantly, never evidenced in connection with municipal temples to a living emperor. It was not necessary.

My claim here that Caesar's inscription on the Capitol actually called him a *Divus* is important, if correct. This would then be the first time the term was applied to a ruler in Rome, and thus significant to the history of imperial deification in Rome. On the view presented here, Caesar was termed *Divus* by the Senate already in 46. He was certainly not accorded this as a title, as apparently happened later, but only named so in a public inscription, as for instance Claudius was later termed *divinus princeps* in the *Arval Acta*; but the use in official vocabulary certainly represents a significant step towards granting him the official state title.

Dio tells us a little more about the sculptures and inscription on the Capitol, namely that Caesar at first ignored these monuments, but at some point later had the term '*hēmítheos*' removed from the inscription.[27] Caesar's next batch of honours were presented to him by the Senate a year later, after the battle of Munda fought on 17 March 45 BC. Once again Dio (43. 45. 3) is the main source and once again he did not mention all the honours, but only those that seemed noteworthy to him.

News of the victory arrived at Rome on 20 April, and the Senate followed the hint and decreed that the Parilia, anniversary of the founding of Rome, of the following day should in the future be dedicated to celebrations of the victory. In a procession, apparently decreed for the occasion, from the Capitol to the Circus, Caesar's image was to be carried in the company of the gods. A letter of Cicero (*Ad Att.* 13. 28. 3) sug-

[26] Marcellus: Tac. *Ann.* 1. 74. 3; Dio 56. 46. 3; see p. 336–9 below.

[27] Dio 43. 21. 2; Fishwick (1975, 624ff.) argues that Dio's wording '*τὸ τοῦ ἡμιθέου ὄνομα*' (emphasis added) suggests a proper name rather than a title; I fail to see why the article cannot simply be anaphoric, since Dio had mentioned the inscription shortly before—contra id., 626 n. 15. It is an open question whether Dio is really such a conscious stylist that his grammar can bear examination so detailed as Fishwick's is here; in any case, Fishwick's claim that Dio knew that the inscription contained a proper name seems contradicted far more convincingly by Dio's wording in 43. 14. 6: '*ὅτι ἡμιθεός ἐστιν*'; on Fishwick's interpretation we should certainly have expected '*ὅτι τίς ἡμιθεός ἐστιν*' *vel sim.* here.

gests that it was carried next to that of Quirinus. These honours would have carried divine associations, but they did not deify Caesar; thus the image in the procession corresponds, for example, to the later inclusion of Augustus' name among those of the gods in the hymn of the Salii. In both instances, the main point was not to declare or present the ruler as a god in any absolute sense; the measures could be interpreted both as divine honours or as singular honours to a man. The main point was to express a superhuman status of absolute power, divinity in a relative sense.

The Romulean association was exploited even further, when it was decreed that Caesar's image should be placed in the temple of Quirinus. There has been some discussion whether Caesar actually became a *sunnaos theos* with Quirinus in the temple, or whether his statue was merely placed there without any rededication of the sanctuary. The more moderate option seems by far the likelier one, but this question does not matter much here. Caesar's statue was to have an inscription naming him an *anikētos theós*, that is, *deus invictus*, thus further elaborating on the theme that Caesar had refounded Rome by his victory at Munda.

DIVUS JULIUS

The Senate's steadily escalating series of honours to Caesar reached its climax in the last months of his life. The exact chronology of these decrees is not absolutely clear, but need not concern us here. Dio gives a very long list of the honours; among the motions proposed was even that Caesar should be allowed to sleep with as many women as he pleased (apparently this one was not passed). More importantly, perhaps, Dio's rather monotonous summary of the measures makes little sense from a literary point of view, and gives the clear impression of ultimately paraphrasing the primary documents themselves, both the decrees actually passed, and the *Acta Senatus*. There is little point in going through all the items in his list, so I shall merely pick out the culminating ones, which deified Caesar outright. As mentioned, the passing of these honours, and Caesar's acceptance of them, are basically confirmed by

Suetonius, Appian, and, most importantly, by Cicero whose shorthand listing is in fact very close to Dio's account, and goes far to confirm it, as well as supporting the view that Dio (or his source) had good and primary sources at his disposal.[28]

There is, however, one conflict between the accounts of Dio and Cicero, which has caused much debate. Several scholars have seen a problem in the fact that Cicero gives Caesar's cult name as Divus Julius, whereas Dio (44. 6. 4) informs us that the senators 'addressed him outright as Jupiter Julius [*Día Ioúlion*] and ordered a temple to be consecrated to him and to his *Clementia* [*Epieikía*], electing Antony as their priest like some *flamen Dialis*'. On the face of it, there should be no difficulty: Cicero is the contemporary, well-informed source, so the cult name must have been Divus Julius.[29] Dio's version does, however, make good sense in the contemporary context, where Caesar was often likened to Jupiter, as has been convincingly argued by Weinstock.[30] Caesar's remark when refusing the royal diadem and dedicating it in the temple of Jupiter, namely that the only king in Rome was Jupiter, would seem to render the title of Jupiter Julius an obvious choice. Even more convincing is the fact that no plausible reason can be given as to why and how Dio should have made this mistake—he was certainly aware that Caesar was later named Divus Julius. So Weinstock actually followed Dio, ignored Cicero, and opted for Julian Jupiter. The apparent discrepancy of the cult name has

[28] As noted by North (1975, 175), though generally sceptical as to Dio's reliability; Dio is clearly the main source for Weinstock (1971): for criticism see North (1975). Source refs.: p. 55 n. 4 above.

[29] Thus North (1975, 175); his reiteration of the common suggestion that Dio's '*Día Ioúlion*' arose from 'confusion, corruption or misunderstanding from Cicero's "divus"' entails several problems. If Cicero's passage was used by Dio, it was clearly not his only or main source, and the similarity between the texts may rather depend on Dio's ultimate dependence on a source summarized by Cicero: if so this ultimate source can hardly have been anything but the senatorial decree itself, which would have been very well known to Cicero and his audience. Dio was perfectly familiar with the word '*divus*' and the terminology, and 'corruption' would in any case be easier to explain in Cicero's case, i.e. *Iovi Iulio* corrected to *Divo Iulio* in early MS tradition, from the later and well-known *Divus* Julius. But 'corruption' is a dangerous argument: it does not seem methodically sound to rewrite our sources when they make sense, simply because we disagree with them.

[30] Weinstock (1971, 287ff.).

even been used by some scholars to reject the whole thing as fictive, on the more or less clearly expressed notion that Caesar was too sensible to accept such a silly plan.

A closer look at Dio's text does, however, provide an obvious answer. The list of honours is presented in several stages, perhaps each representing a particular decree. After the first two listings Dio breaks his enumeration with the comment that Caesar was pleased with the honours mentioned, and hence presumably accepted them as they stood. No such comment is given in connection with the last and crowning honours of temple, priest, and cult name. Dio clearly summarizes all the measures contained in the decrees (or at least he thought he did). So eventually the senators addressed Caesar as Jupiter Julius; it is actually not specifically stated that this was to be his cult name. But it seems likely that this was indeed the name offered to him. It is, however, nowhere stated that he accepted this. Dio says after the listings that Caesar 'accepted all but a very few of their decrees'. Plausibly the cult name offered to him was one of the items he rejected, so the more vague and modest version of Divus Julius—'Julian god'—was either substituted by Caesar himself or offered him instead by the Senate. As I have argued above, the Senate had probably employed the word *Divus* before in connection with Caesar, namely in the inscription on his Capitoline statue in 46. Nowhere does Dio actually state or imply that the name Jupiter Julius was accepted by the dictator; only—at the most—that it was offered him;[31] so there is really no conflict whatsoever with Cicero's testimony. Instead we may have gained an insight into the dealings between Caesar and the Senate; both the cult names mentioned in our sources would then be authentic. If correct, this interpretation goes some way towards confirming that Dio, or rather his source, had had access to the text of the decrees themselves.

It is all too easy to misunderstand Caesar's divine honours by a monotheistic view which places undue emphasis on the distinction between man and god. The distinction is a dogmatic one, central to the theological systems of Christianity and

[31] A parallel case would be Dio's statement that the Senate decreed a temple to Caligula in 40, which was apparently rejected by the emperor. See Chapter 6.

Judaism. On the contrary, traditional Graeco-Roman religion was characterized by the lack of any but the most rudimentary dogmatic system, and could indeed function and work with what would in terms of strict logic seem to be blatant inner contradictions. The honours, such as temple, priest, the title of Divus Julius, the inscription to Caesar as '*Deus invictus*' after Munda, should be seen as an expression of relative divinity, that is, divine *status* in relation to all other men. The words obviously did not exclude that Caesar really was a god in an absolute sense, but this question, one of dogma, was simply irrelevant. It was in fact generally irrelevant in pagan worship, whether of Caesar or of Jupiter. What mattered was power, again *relative* divinity, and Caesar's power was at this stage unquestioned, as was Jupiter's. Absolute power entailed divinity and vice versa. Caesar's heavenly honours expressed his new status far above the position of any other man, past or present, in the Roman republic.

4
Beyond Rome: 'By Municipal Deification'

The literary sources have little to say of the civic worship accorded to Augustus and his successors in the towns of Italy.[1] As usual, these sources concentrate almost exclusively on conditions in Rome, and even there overwhelmingly on the narrow sphere of the relationship between *princeps* and senate. Our source material for civic emperor worship outside Rome is, however, comparatively rich, though it has not been given its due in scholarship. It consists mainly of inscriptions mentioning temples or priests dedicated to the emperor. Furthermore, the ruins of several imperial temples are still standing, though in most cases we depend on the epigraphic evidence for their identification as such. Despite this comparatively rich material, scholars have traditionally focused on one late literary source, which, in an aside of four words, has always been taken to deny outright the existence of emperor worship in Italy, namely Dio Cassius (51. 20. 6–8). The year is 29 BC, and the historian describes Octavian's administrative measures whilst in the East after the conquest of Egypt:[2]

Caesar [Octavian], meanwhile, besides attending to the general business, gave permission for the dedication of sacred precincts in Ephesus and in Nicaea to Roma and to Caesar, his father, whom he

[1] The term *municipali consecratione* is employed of civic cults in general by Tertullian, *Ap*. 24. 8, neatly bringing out the irrelevance to the 'constitution' of the Roman state of such cults. Vitr. 5. 1. 7 mentions a *pronaos aedis Augusti* in connection with his basilica at Fanum; this *aedes* is rejected, unconvincingly, as a temple by Ohr (1975, 113ff.), followed by Hänlein-Schäfer (1985, 2 n. 8).

[2] (tr. Cary, Loeb edn., adapted) '*Καῖϲαρ δὲ ἐν τούτωι τά τε ἄλλα ἐχρημάτιζε, καὶ τεμένη τῆι τε Ῥώμηι καὶ τῶι πατρὶ τῶι Καίϲαρι, ἥρωα αὐτὸν Ἰούλιον ὀνομάϲαϲ, ἔν τε Ἐφέϲωι καὶ ἐν Νικαίαι γενέσθαι ἐφῆκεν· αὗται γὰρ τότε αἱ πόλειϲ ἔν τε τῆι Ἀϲίαι καὶ ἐν τῆι Βιθυνίαι προετετίμηντο. καὶ τούτουϲ μὲν τοῖϲ Ῥωμαίοιϲ τοῖϲ παρ' αὐτοῖϲ ἐποικοῦϲι τιμᾶν προϲέταξε· τοῖϲ δὲ δὴ ξένοιϲ, Ἕλληνάϲ ϲφαϲ ἐπικαλέϲαϲ,*

had named the hero Julius [i.e. Divus Julius]. These cities had at that time attained chief place in Asia and Bithynia respectively. He commanded that the Romans resident in these cities should pay honour to these two divinities; but he permitted the aliens, whom he styled Hellenes, to consecrate precincts to himself, the Asians to have theirs in Pergamum, the Bithynians theirs in Nicomedia. This practice, beginning under him, has been continued under other emperors, not only in the case of the Hellenic nations but also in that of all the others, in so far as they are subject to the Romans. For in the capital itself and in the rest of Italy no emperor, however worthy of renown he has been, has dared to do this; still, even there various divine honours are bestowed after their death upon such emperors as have ruled uprightly, and, in fact, shrines are built to them.

Dio's passage has been taken by all scholars to say, plainly and simply, that there was no worship of the living emperor in Rome and the rest of Italy under Augustus, or indeed later. Most scholars have accepted the statement, and overlooked the epigraphic evidence, which seems to conflict with Dio's claim; a small minority have instead accepted these contemporary sources, and rejected Dio as being in error.[3]

First, however, we should pay attention to what Dio is actually saying, for that is in fact not so immediately obvious as it has commonly been taken to be. As for the distinction between Romans and non-Romans in the cults mentioned by Dio, there is no evidence that it was upheld for very long and the cults of Roma and Divus Julius seem to have quickly disappeared, leaving little trace in other sources.[4] That, however, is not of much relevance here. It should be noted that the usual interpretation of the passage is simply wrong. Dio's outlook,

ἑαυτῶι τινα, τοῖϲ μὲν Ἀϲιανοῖϲ ἐν Περγάμωι τοῖϲ δὲ Βιθυνοῖϲ ἐν Νικομηδείαι, τεμενίϲαι ἐπέτρεψε. καὶ τοῦτ' ἐκεῖθεν ἀρξάμενον καὶ ἐπ' ἄλλων αὐτοκρατόρων οὐ μόνον ἐν τοῖϲ Ἑλληνικοῖϲ ἔθνεϲιν, ἀλλὰ καί ἐν τοῖϲ ἄλλοιϲ ὅϲα τῶν Ῥωμαίων ἀκούει, ἐγένετο. ἐν γάρ τοι τῶι ἄϲτει αὐτῶι τῆι τε ἄλληι Ἰταλίαι οὐκ ἔϲτιν ὅϲτιϲ τῶν καὶ ἐφ' ὁποϲονοῦν λόγου τινὸϲ ἀξίων ἐτόλμηϲε τοῦτο ποιῆϲαι· μεταλλάξαϲι μέντοι κἀνταῦθα τοῖϲ ὀρθῶϲ αὐταρχήϲαϲιν ἄλλαι τε ἰϲόθεοι τιμαὶ δίδονται καὶ δὴ καὶ ἡρῶια ποιεῖται.' For the version here implied that the title Divus Julius was given (rather than confirmed or implemented) to Caesar by Octavian (i.e. in 42 BC) see also App. *BC* 2. 148 and p. 57 n. 7 above.

[3] Rejected by Mommsen (1887–8, ii (3)) (1887, 757 Anm. 1); Habicht (1973, 49f.); Hänlein-Schäfer (1985, 17ff.).

[4] Price (1984*a*, 76f.; 254); Fishwick (1987, i. 130).

typical of Roman historians, is narrowly confined to the *Staatsdenken* of the capital and its senatorial class (though, as I shall argue later, it may be relevant to the interpretation of the passage that Dio is writing for a Greek, i.e. provincial, audience). Thus the whole aspect or sphere of private cults is simply ignored by him, and there is in fact, as I shall argue later, ample evidence of private divine cults—temples, altars, sacrifices—dedicated to the living emperor, both in Rome itself and in the rest of Italy. The traditional interpretation of the passage is therefore wrong in any case. But private cults concerned only the individuals involved in them and were therefore without interest to Dio—or to his readers—as long as they did not conflict or interfere with the interests of the state. There is nothing strange in this: 'political' history is of course by definition 'public' history. Dio's omission was therefore natural and is in fact generally paralleled in Roman historical writing, for instance by Suetonius' parallel statement as to Augustus' policy in this field:[5] 'Although well aware that it was usual to vote temples even to proconsuls, yet in no province would he accept one save jointly in his own name and that of Rome [i.e. *Dea Roma*]. In the city itself he refused this honour most emphatically . . .'. It is more curious, perhaps, that the 'narrow-mindedness' of the ancient writers in this matter has continued in modern scholarship, for even there almost all attention has been focused only on the public imperial cults to the point of ignoring the testimonies of emperor worship on the private level.

With regard, however, to the state cult in Rome there can be little doubt that Dio and Suetonius are basically right. Divine state worship of the living ruler spelt out a monarchical 'constitution', and since the principate as established by Augustus was not—formally—a monarchy, the phenomenon was constitutionally impossible, so other ways were instead followed in the attempt to formulate the emperor's position in the Roman state system.

The formulations of Dio and Suetonius are quite close to one

[5] Suet. *Aug.* 52 (tr. Rolfe, Loeb edn., adapted): '*Templa, quamvis sciret etiam proconsulibus decerni solere, in nulla tamen provincia nisi communi suo Romaeque nomine recepit. Nam in urbe quidem pertinacissime abstinuit hoc honore* . . .'.

another, so there may be a connection between the two sources. Suetonius, however, deals with only two levels: that of provincial cults, under close imperial control or supervision, and that of the state cult in Rome. The problem arises from Dio's additional remark 'and in the rest of Italy'. Like Suetonius, Dio deals with the level of provincial cults in his passage, but since Italy was not a province, his words can refer only to the municipal level, or so one would think at first sight, and so his passage has hitherto been interpreted. In that case, he is simply wrong, as we shall see. That would not matter much to our investigation of the evidence, but it is surprising none the less: Dio was a consular senator, and owner of a villa near Capua.[6]

He may, however, merely be making a didactic point to his Greek—provincial—audience. His passage deals with provincial cults, common to and functioning on behalf of a whole province, in this case Asia. In my view he may merely claim that no emperor had dared to establish a parallel cult of himself, which functioned on behalf of all Italy, that is, in analogy with a provincial cult, and unlike municipal cults, which functioned on behalf of the individual town or city only. Now, the state cults in Rome (or, in some instances, elsewhere in Italy) were conducted on behalf of the *populus Romanus*, all Roman citizens, and in Augustus' day that would basically mean the free population of Italy. In the Greek provinces, such as Asia and Bithynia (whence Dio himself came, namely from Nicaea), provincial cults were likewise concentrated in the provincial capitals. However, many provincial cults were located in other cities within the province: this Dio himself mentions here when he relates that Ephesus and Nicaea 'had at that time attained chief place' in their respective provinces, yet then goes on to show the cults to Roma and Octavian being placed in cities other than these provincial capitals. And this, I suspect, is probably the reason behind Dio's words 'and in the rest of Italy': neither in Rome nor anywhere else in Italy had any emperor dared to establish a cult to himself which functioned on behalf of all Italy, that is, which would be an equivalent of a provincial cult. The comparison between provincial and Italian conditions is not far-fetched: several Roman state cults were

[6] For Dio see Millar (1964).

indeed also situated or established in Italy outside Rome.[7] If this interpretation holds, Dio is actually not speaking of municipal cults in the passage, and it can be left out of account in this connection.

Alternatively, Dio is simply wrong. Inscriptions from all over Italy testify to the existence of temples, priests, and sacrifices to the living emperor, and the evidence is in fact most abundant from Augustus' reign. Depending, however, on Dio's four words on Italy, scholars have from the 19th century onwards ignored these sources, or twisted their interpretation. Pompeii and its imperial temple have played a major role as keystone. There have been persistent attempts to reconcile Dio's statement with the apparently conflicting evidence from Pompeii and elsewhere by claiming that worship of the living emperor in Italy was dedicated, not to himself in god-like fashion, but rather to his *Genius*. Since all men possessed a *Genius*, this worship did not impute divinity to its 'owner': so Dio was right after all. In this way it became, with dubious support from Dio's remark, possible to maintain worship of the living emperor as a phenomenon characteristic only of sycophantic Greeks, and fundamentally alien to the sane and earthbound peasant mentality of the Romans (for some reason, the undoubted cult in Rome of the *Divi*, dead emperors, has never provoked the same opposition and consternation from scholarship).

The most enduring version of the *Genius* theory was formulated between the wars by Lily Ross Taylor. The idea itself was

[7] Thus the Arval grove of Dea Dia five miles outside Rome; the Latin Festival at the Alban Mount and similar state rites (shared with other Latin communities: Wissowa (1912, 124f., cf. 519ff.)); the shrine, established in AD 16, of the *Gens Iulia* at Bovillae, where the *sodales Augustales* met and worshipped this goddess and Divus Augustus (Tac. *Ann.* 2. 41; Wissowa (1912, 346)); probably the similar shrine at Antium for the *Gens Claudia* and *Gens Domitia* (Tac. *Ann.* 15. 23; Wissowa, 1912). A probable further instance is the temple to Divus Augustus at Nola in Campania, erected where Augustus had died, and dedicated by Tiberius in 26 (Tac. *Ann.* 4. 57; Dio 56. 46. 3; if so, this may well have been the main specific instance Dio had in mind). In the light of such instances I do not understand Fishwick's (1995, 20) claim that 'at no time did such a possibility exist' (i.e. of establishing a state cult of the emperor in Italy outside Rome), commenting on my earlier presentation of the idea in Gradel (1992).

much older, but as presented in her elegant and influential work from 1931, *The Divinity of the Roman Emperor*, it has stood unchallenged till recent years. Her theory was, as were earlier versions of it, based on the monuments of Pompeii:[8]

Was Dio simply mistaken in his statement that Italy knew no such worship? . . . For an answer to the question we may turn to the monuments of Pompeii which here, as so often, have preserved for us the solution to a puzzling problem. There is on the east side of the Forum of Pompeii a small temple with a deep forecourt. . . . In the court directly in front of the temple stands a quadrangular marble altar adorned with the civic crown and the laurel branches, emblems that show its relation to the cult of the emperor. On its front is a sacrificial scene in which the victim is clearly a bull. . . . The victim is the regular offering to the Genius.

The altar and the temple to which it belongs were then evidently the centres of the cult of the Genius of the emperor. At them the *sacerdos Augusti*, known in the records of Pompeii, officiated. The word *genius* was, to be sure, suppressed in the title of temple and priest, but that was not without parallel. At Trimalchio's dinner, when the guests poured the customary libation to the Genius of the living emperor, what they said was simply *Augusto patri patriae feliciter*. . . . Thus Dio's statement that Augustus and the later emperors were not worshipped in Italy until after they had died is shown to be in a sense true, for the cult was offered not to the emperor in person but to his shadowy attendant spirit. Thus too we see that the Genius of the emperor, which had been worshipped for some years in the *vici* of the cities, was made an object of official cult that concerned not merely the lower stratum of the population but all the citizens . . .

Taylor's arguments, some employed before her, some her own, are in fact an elaborately circular construct. It is true that a bull was the proper sacrificial victim to the *Genius* of the emperor; thus in the state cult of Rome, where the living emperor's *Genius* was worshipped from the mid-first century, as evidenced in the *Acts of the Arval Brothers*. In Roman sacrifice, the sex and nature of the victim usually corresponded to those of the gods who received them. Thus gods received male vic-

[8] Taylor (1931, 216ff.); her version first presented in Taylor (1920). For the temple, previously dated the last generation of Pompeii's existence, but now commonly accepted as Augustan in date, see Gradel (1992, 48) with refs.; for the altar, likewise of controversial date, see Ryberg (1955, 81ff.); Kockel (1986, with lit.).

tims, and goddesses female ones; celestial gods received fertile victims, such as bulls, whereas the gods of the infertile underworld received castrated animals, such as steers. Jupiter was the odd exception to these rules, since his victims were castrated animals such as steers.[9] According to these rules, we would expect the proper bovine victim, that is, the costliest and most honorific type of animal, to have been a bull to the living emperor, and there is in fact good evidence that this was so, even apart from the depiction of the Pompeii altar (e.g. my Fig. 9.1).[10]

The key weakness in Taylor's argument is that the word *Genius* should have been suppressed whenever it is not mentioned in the sources. This claim of suppression cannot be disproved or even argued against, for it basically takes the discussion beyond the realm of scholarly argument: no evidence whatsoever can conflict with it. As for the parallel example of 'suppression', the libation to the emperor at Trimalchio's dinner, the claim of suppression in fact rests on the same notions as Taylor's other arguments, namely that Dio was right and there was no worship of the living emperor in Italy. I shall later examine the case and argue that the libation was indeed to the emperor himself, as to a god, not to his *Genius*.[11]

The small temple of the imperial cult was then not dedicated to a *Genius*, for there is no trace of such a deity in the shrine or on the altar's iconography, to which I shall later return. The altar seems, by common stylistic criteria, Augustan.[12] Protracted controversy over the dating of the temple to which it belongs has, however, clouded the issue. The building was earlier dated to the last period of Pompeii's existence, but on no decisive arguments. More recently scholars have redated the shrine to the Augustan age, and there now appears to be a consensus on this among the experts on Pompeian architecture and building techniques (I am not one).[13] This dating should be

[9] Wissowa (1912, 412ff.).

[10] Gradel (1992, 45ff.) for refs. and detailed refutation.

[11] See p. 207–12 below.

[12] For the altar see Dobbins (1992), giving a convincing technical analysis (254ff.) and an unconvincing iconographical analysis (260ff.).

[13] Thus Dobbins (1996, 99 with n. 6 (refs.)); Richardson (1988, 192ff.); Zanker (1995, 94f.).

accepted in the absence of arguments to the contrary. It fits the altar, as well as the fact that we know Pompeii to have had a public priest dedicated to Augustus from at least before 2 BC.

THE EMPEROR'S TEMPLES

Since the publication in 1985 of Heidi Hänlein-Schäfer's fine monograph on temples to Augustus from all over the empire, increasing doubt has spread as to Taylor's *Genius* theory, though it is still found, in one form or another, in most recent handbooks (often conflated with the idea that *numen* was another word for *Genius*).[14] Hänlein-Schäfer sensibly preferred to accept the sources on the more immediate level, and since the *Genius* was not generally encountered in the evidence from Roman Italy, she rejected Taylor's interpretation, and Dio's remark with it, as wrong. Practically all scholars, including Hänlein-Schäfer, have, however, accepted the instance of the imperial temple in Pompeii as certainly dedicated to Augustus' *Genius*. This was because of a fragmentary architrave inscription (*CIL* X. 816) from Pompeii—though its provenance is otherwise unknown—which has for more than a century been thought to belong to it (hence the labelling of the temple by scholars in the 19th century as *tempio del genio di Augusto*):[15]

M[a]MIA P(ublii) F(ilia) SACERDOS PUBLIC(a) GENI[o Aug(usti) s]OLO ET PEC[unia sua . . .

Mamia, public priestess, daughter of Publius, to the *Gen[ius* of Augustus] on her own land and with her own money . . .

Strangely, Taylor is to my knowledge the only scholar who has

[14] Opposition to Taylor's theory by Habicht (1973, 49ff.); Hänlein-Schäfer (1985, 17ff.); S. Price in review of her book, *JRS* 76 (1986, 300); they all, however, accept the temple of Pompeii as dedicated to the emperor's *Genius*. This is doubted by Fishwick (1987, i. 1. 91 n. 55), ignoring Mamia's inscription, for which see below.

[15] The theory that the temple and its cult in Pompeii were dedicated to Augustus' *Genius* rather than to himself (a possibility simply rejected a priori in older lit.) was first advanced by Fiorelli (1875, 261 f.) (*non vidi*) on the basis of the inscription as restored by himself, and on the argument that the bull was known to be the sacrificial victim to the living emperor's *Genius* in the *Arval Acta*; see also Nissen (1877, 270ff.); Overbeck and Mau (1884, 117ff.); Hänlein-Schäfer (1985, 133ff.); Gradel (1992, 48).

rejected it as evidence;[16] hence she used other arguments to arrive at the same result. Her attitude was most sensible, however, for the decisive part of it is a restoration: so the whole *Genius* theory ultimately rests on a lacuna. The tendency to attribute all sorts of dubious Pompeian evidence to the emperor and his cult is far from a recent development. I have argued at length elsewhere that the inscription cannot have belonged to the imperial temple—its measurements simply do not fit it—and that the decisive lacuna should rather be restored '*GENI[o coloniae* or *Pompeiorum s]OLO* . . .', that is, 'to the *Genius* of the colony (of Pompeii)' or 'of Pompeii'; cults of city *Genii* are known from numerous other instances, especially in Campania, where it appears to have been common. Furthermore, I have suggested a location for the temple to which the inscription belonged. Suffice it to say here that the inscription must be left out of account in connection with the imperial cult, and with it goes the *Genius* theory, for there is no other example of a municipal temple (nor of any other temple, for that matter) dedicated to an emperor's *Genius*.[17]

In fact, the pattern of temples and priests dedicated to Augustus and later emperors in their lifetime is surprisingly uniform. As Hänlein-Schäfer has convincingly demonstrated, the temples to Augustus were modelled on traditional temples to the 'old' gods; no independent, idiomatic architectural language was employed or developed to set Augustus apart from these traditional gods,[18] and in fact, without inscriptional evidence, or iconographic representations of the imperial emblems, such as we find on the altar from Pompeii, it would not be possible to identify these temples as dedicated to Augustus rather than to one of the traditional divinities. That is significant, and it corresponds, as we shall see, exactly to the titles of imperial flaminates, likewise modelled closely on the titulature of such priesthoods dedicated to other gods. There is little point in paraphrasing Hänlein-Schäfer's book at length here, so I shall limit myself to a short overview.

A temple (*tò Kaisar[eion]*) is attested in an inscription

[16] Taylor (1920, 129 n. 49); but accepted, hesitantly, in id. (1931, 278).
[17] Gradel (1992).
[18] Hänlein-Schäfer (1985, 23 ff.; 49 ff.).

dealing with the games in honour of Roma and Augustus, which were established at Neapolis about 2 BC; the same inscription mentions a sacrifice to Augustus.[19] Neapolis was Greek-speaking, and the evidence has predictably been rejected as unrepresentative on that score.[20] An epistyle inscription from Terracina testifies to a temple to Roma and Augustus.[21] Another dedicatory inscription, from Beneventum, comes from a *Caesareum* erected to Augustus and the *colonia Beneventana* by the wealthy knight P. Vedius Pollio, personal friend of Augustus and best known for feeding slaves to his murenas; he died in 15 BC, which then gives the *terminus ante quem.*[22] From Superaequum another Augustan inscription mentions an *[. . . aedes?] Romae et Augusti.*[23] Pisae had an *Augusteum* in AD 2, in which the town's *decuriones* met.[24] (Hänlein-Schäfer has generally included temples called *Augusteum* or *Caesareum* in her list, even when they are undated, in which cases it is not certain whether they were dedicated to Augustus or only to later emperors.) In Pola on the Istria (now Croatia) there still stands—though bombed in the Second World War and re-erected later—a well-preserved temple dedicated to Roma and Augustus in the emperor's lifetime.[25] Several inscriptions from Ostia testify to a temple to Roma and Augustus in the city, and its remains (including fragments of the statue of Roma) have been excavated in its forum. The temple is traditionally dated to after Augustus' death, and Hänlein-Schäfer, oddly and without arguments, accepted this dating. It is, however, based on nothing more than the idea that there was no worship of the living emperor in Italy (a stylistic dating of the architectural fragments points to late Augustan or early Tiberian, but is of course too imprecise to settle the issue). Discarding that notion,

19 Olympia V, *Die Inschriften* (1896, no. 56); Hänlein-Schäfer (1985, 128 ff.).

20 Taylor (1931, 215).

21 *CIL* X. 6305: '*Romae et Augusto Caesari Divi f. A. Aemilius A. f. ex pecunia sua f(aciendum) c(uravit)*'; Hänlein-Schäfer (1985, 135 ff.).

22 *CIL* IX. 1556: '*P. Veidius P. f. Pollio Caesareum Imp(eratori) Caesari Augusto et coloniae Beneventanae*'; Hänlein-Schäfer (1985, 141 ff.), cf. Dio 54. 23.

23 *AE* 1898. 79; Hänlein-Schäfer (1985, 144 ff.).

24 *CIL* XI. 1420–1; Hänlein-Schäfer (1985, 148).

25 Its epistyle inscription is *CIL* V. 18: '*Romae et Augusto Caesari Divi f. patri patriae*'; Hänlein-Schäfer (1985, 149 ff.).

we can note only that Augustus is not named *Divus* in the temple's title, and hence date it as probably Augustan.[26]

These are merely examples from Hänlein-Schäfer's valuable work. Two temples may be added to her listings, both from Volsinii in Tuscany: a *Caesareum*, very likely Augustan; and another undated *Caesareum*, dedicated by an imperial freedman and *procurator*.[27] With the last example we may be in the private sphere, but the other instances mentioned here, as well as the others which can be found in Hänlein-Schäfer's book, appear to be municipal temples, judging from either their size and situation (Pompeii, Pula, Ostia), the status of their dedicator(s) (Beneventum, Terracina), other information in the inscriptions (Pisae), or the sheer size and monumentality of the inscriptions themselves. Though temple buildings may also be encountered in private cults,[28] Hänlein-Schäfer's investigation, in dealing with temples only, is mostly limited to the municipal sphere, and her book must be the obvious starting-point for discussions of emperor worship at this level. The *Genius* theory of Italy had stood unmolested till the appearance of her book, and in fact is still the commonly advanced version. This is a sombre illustration of the dangers of specialization on the part of historians, archaeologists, and epigraphists, and of the too common tendency of archaeologists not to venture large-scale interpretations of their material, but to wait for, or merely trust, historians to do this work.

Much is left out of her account by its exclusive (though perfectly legitimate) concentration on temples; cults did of course not depend on the existence of a temple, but only of an altar. We may therefore add still further examples to the list of imperial cults in Augustan Italy: a sacred grove dedicated to the emperor at Perusia; or a monumental altar, probably also

[26] Hänlein-Schäfer (1985, 130ff.); the temple's title (*aedes Romae et Augusti*) is given in *CIL* XIV. 73.

[27] *CIL* XI. 948 (presumably Augustan: the dedicators lack *cognomina*); 7220.

[28] One particularly prominent category are the *Augustea* erected by or for the *ordo* or *collegium* of the *Augustales* or *seviri Augustales*, buildings which also functioned as their assembly halls. These shrines and their cults are left out of account here, because in legal terms they were private (i.e. belonging to the *sacra privata*), but see further p. 229f.

municipal, from Aquileia, dedicated to Augustus in AD 14 (but apparently before his death).[29] Recently published documents from a money-lending business at Puteoli have revealed an astounding imperial presence in the forum of the city; the business transactions regularly took place by one of the two altars to Augustus erected in the forum, each named after a noble family of the city, people who had then paid for the erection (*ara Augusti Hordionia* and *ara Augusti Suettiana*). These altars stood in connection with two statue galleries, *chalcidica*—presumably with portraits of the imperial family—likewise named after and hence, it seems, erected by Hordionii and Suettii. Furthermore, a *chalcidicum Caesonianum* and a *chalcidicum Octavianum* were also to be found in the forum, and the fact that no altars are mentioned in connection with these galleries may be no more than a coincidence. It looks as if the noble families of Puteoli virtually competed with each other in erecting monuments to the emperor.[30]

It is not my aim to be comprehensive here, nor will I deal with geographical distributions within the Italian peninsula. I shall limit myself to a general characteristic of these cults, and ignore local differences. As will, I trust, become evident, the cult forms chosen, and the ways in which the emperor was worshipped in this context, appear in fact to have been so uniform from one end of Italy to the other that such cursory treatment is warranted.

With the addition of the one Volsinian example to Hänlein-Schäfer's list, we now know of sixteen public imperial temples from Italy outside Rome; of these, seven are Augustan, and only one or, at the most, two are certainly posthumous (p. 90f. below), whereas the rest are undated (and some of them, called *Augusteum* or *Caesareum*, may in fact have nothing to do with Augustus, but that is not of great import here). Considering that Augustus received state deification and public cult in the capital itself only after he had died, this pattern may surprise, and it must depend far more on local conditions than on emulation of those in the capital.

[29] Grove: *CIL* XI. 1922–3; Aquileia: *CIL* V. 852.

[30] The *tabulae ceratae* from Murecine: Camodeca (1992, 274, s.v. Puteoli).

PRIESTS

On the last local coinage issued anywhere in Italy, the town of Paestum in Lucania proudly advertised its flaminate dedicated to the emperor Tiberius.[31] This same ruler is frequently recorded as having refused offers of divine worship presented to him. Such refusals were important in the interplay between emperor and Senate in Rome, but they had little relevance to what took place at the municipal or civic level. We do not know if the grandees of Paestum were aware of Tiberius' attitudes, but they clearly did not consider this relevant for themselves. In this they were no doubt right: the relationship between emperor and Senate in the capital was only of marginal relevance to them, and Tiberius' hesitations and refusals were presumably never meant to curtail his worship at this level.

The largest group of sources testifying to imperial cults at the civic level consists of inscriptions, mainly honorary, some funerary, to local aristocrats, specifying among their offices any imperial priesthoods they may have held. Though this group of sources is quite large, it presents problems which preclude full use of it without extensive registration and autopsy of the inscriptions. First, they are usually impossible or difficult to date on the basis of the text alone as published in the *Corpus of Latin Inscriptions* (*CIL*) or elsewhere, making autopsy and attempt at dating by the letter forms necessary. Secondly, they give evidence for the existence and titulature of such priesthoods in different localities, but only exceptionally supply us with any further information.

Practically everywhere in Italy where we possess a reasonable inscriptional record, civic priests of imperial cults are encountered, always with the titles *flamen* or *sacerdos*; already in Augustus' day they can be found all over Italy. *Sacerdos* was the more general term, meaning 'priest', and *flamen* was a more narrow term signifying a special priest dedicated, in principle,

[31] Burnett *et al.* (1992, nos. 610–12); the common dating to the reign of Tiberius may not be absolutely certain—some of the readings of the rare coins are doubtful, and that of 610: *Fla(men) Aug(usti) Ti(berii) Caesar(is)* could perhaps be taken as a flaminate to both Augustus and Tiberius, before the death of the former; no. 612 displays the cap (*apex*) of the *flamen* on its reverse.

to the worship of one god only.[32] Thus *flamines* were a subcategory of *sacerdotes*. As we would expect from this, the two terms could be used synonymously (all *flamines* were *sacerdotes*, though not vice versa). In Pompeii one man, M. Holconius Rufus, is named in the inscriptions as priest of Augustus, first in two contemporary ones: *Augusti sacerdos*, *flamen Caesaris Augusti*, then in two later ones (one of which can be absolutely dated to 2 BC): *Augusti Caesaris sacerdos* and *flamen Augusti*.[33] So obviously both titles could be used for the same office; I shall here employ the term *flamen* as covering both titles.

In Pompeii another holder of the priesthood in Augustus' lifetime, M. Holconius Celer, is, logically, labelled *sacerdos Divi Augusti* after the emperor's death, when the emperor received the title of *Divus* from the Roman Senate.[34] The title *flamen/sacerdos Augusti* or *flamen/sacerdos Augustalis* is, however, encountered in Italy long after the death of the first emperor. Since all emperors carried the name or title Augustus, these instances must signify priests dedicated to the living emperor, whoever he was.[35] In no instances is the *Genius Augusti* mentioned; the titles always designate the holder of the office as priest of the emperor himself, just as when dedicated to the worship of other gods. And exactly the same titles are encountered from the rest of the Western half of the empire, where scholars have always taken them to indicate direct, divine worship (for Dio's supposed claim only sets Italy apart).[36] The hundreds of imperial *flamines* encountered in the Italian inscriptions give us the titles only, and we are ill-informed as to the content and details of the offices. On the

[32] Thus Cic. *Leg.* 2. 8. 20: '*Divisque aliis* [*alii*] *sacerdotes, omnibus pontifices, singulis flamines sunto*'.

[33] *CIL* X. 837; 947; later: 830 (2 BC); 838. The distinction between the terms has been much discussed, see Fishwick (1987, i. 1. 165ff. (n. 109 for the municipal level)), attempting to distinguish; I strongly (and heretically) suspect that the Pompeian synonymity is valid also for the term as employed at the provincial level, and that the terminology is therefore far less stringent than supposed by modern scholars.

[34] *CIL* X. 840, 943–4 (*Augusti sacerdos*); 945–6 (*sacerdos Divi Aug.*).

[35] Geiger (1913, 14ff.); Toutain (1905, i. 45ff.); Étienne (1958, 287ff.).

[36] This is implicitly admitted by Taylor (1931, 218): 'The altars and temples and priests in other cities of Italy, perhaps in municipalities of the west generally, were, like those of Pompeii, places for the cult of the *Genius*'.

provincial level, a fragment of the charter of Gallia Narbonensis, now securely dated to the reign of Vespasian, gives us part of the *lex* for the *flamen Augustalis* of Narbonensis, specifying his duties and privileges.[37] The provincial flaminate at Narbo was held for one year at a time, and one of the duties of the *flamen* was to have portraits of the emperor erected in the provincial sanctuary, paid for from the public funds; furthermore he had the right to erect statues of himself after his tenure. When the *flamen* performed the cult, he had the right to lictors. As a provincial flaminate, the Narbo office is not directly comparable to the municipal parallels; but, by and large, the same model was probably employed. For instance, on the altar from the imperial temple in Pompeii, the priest—who must be the town's *flamen Augusti*—is accompanied by lictors; and the municipal flaminates likewise appear to have been annual.[38]

I have in Appendix 3 collected all the imperial *flamines* of Italy outside Rome known from published inscriptions. Of these roughly 56 *flamines* are mentioned as dedicated to the worship of the living emperor, roughly 100 to that of the *Divi*, emperors posthumously deified by the Senate in Rome. These numbers should, however, be interpreted with caution, for a person who had occupied a flaminate would hold the title for the rest of his life, that is potentially long after he actually functioned in the office. Thus many of the *flamines* of the *Divi* may actually have held the office while 'their' emperor was alive, and therefore really have been priests of the living emperor. After the death of the relevant emperor, his name was then updated with the title of *Divus* in the titulature of the *flamen*, something we can say with certainty happened in the inscriptions of M. Holconius Celer from Pompeii: first termed *Augusti sacerdos*, his title was updated to *sacerdos Divi Augusti* after the death of the emperor: '[former] priest of the [now] deified Augustus'. The only alternative, that Celer was actually *flamen* in AD 14, the year of Augustus' death, and that the title was therefore 'upgraded' when he was in office, seems out of the question from the fact that we know of a Pompeian *flamen*

[37] McCrum and Woodhead (1961, 52 no. 128 = *CIL* XII. 6038); Fishwick (1987, i, ii. 240ff. with pl. XLIII).

[38] Geiger (1913, 46); Étienne (1958, 236f.); Ladage (1971, 80ff.); Mouritsen and Gradel (1991, 149).

Caesaris Augusti from the town's last years.[39] The Augustan form of the title clearly indicates that the priesthood had functioned uninterruptedly from Augustus' day onwards. On the other hand, there is no evidence that Pompeii ever had a flaminate to any *Divus*. The focus was, in this instance at least, on the living emperor.

It is an interesting question how such a cult would in practice have been transferred from one emperor at his death to his successor. But it cannot at present be answered. Rededicating a cult to the new emperor was a delicate business and it stood in glaring contrast to official policy in the state cult of the capital, where an emperor could receive divine worship only after he had died. It is therefore not surprising that the sources do not tell us anything about this process: discretion must have been vital to the exercise, and it would certainly have been crude to publicize it in inscriptions or otherwise. The title of the flaminate in Pompeii may contain a hint: the cult went with the name of Caesar Augustus, titles held by all ruling emperors, but not by dead ones. Perhaps this made it possible to avoid an embarrassingly formal and public ceremony of rededicating the temple, so that it was merely required, with as little fuss as possible, to remove the cult image of the old emperor from the temple *cella* and install that of his successor there. But we do not know.

It is difficult to judge from the overall figures of imperial priests whether Pompeii's concentration on the living ruler was general to such city cults in Italy, but it seems to have been the case. Most of the relevant inscriptions naming these priests would have to be studied by autopsy, since only palaeographic criteria could give a dating, however rough, of them. However, those inscriptions of *flamines* to *Divi* which can in fact be dated from information in their text only very rarely postdate the lifetime of the emperor mentioned in them by so many years that we can say with near certainty that the ex-*flamen* could not have held the office during the lifetime of the *Divus*. In almost all these datable instances the priest must have functioned either in the lifetime of 'his' emperor, as in Celer's case, or shortly after his death. If the emperor was not deified by the Roman

[39] *CIL* IV. 1180; Sabbatini Tumolesi (1980, 42f.).

Senate after his death, we may reasonably surmise that the original title of *flamen Augusti* or the like was still employed for the ex-priests who had functioned during his reign (as is usually the case with, for instance, the title *legatus Augusti*, if the relevant Augustus suffered damnation of his memory). If we could surmise the usual age at which a man would attain to the flaminate, we could perhaps do something with the rough 56 : 100 ratio, but we do not know. It seems that flaminates could be occupied at least at the age of 25, the usual minimum age limit for holding municipal office.[40] But knowing the minimum age does not really assist us here.

A city like Ostia certainly had specific flaminates established to some *Divi*, as well as a flaminate to Roma and Augustus (i.e. the living emperor);[41] but the size and wealth of Ostia, as well as its proximity to Rome, where the cult of the *Divi* was most relevant, means that it cannot count as typical. Since the worship was paid for from the public money of the individual township, a large number of flaminates would impose a strain on its finances. What the datable inscriptions *can* tell us is that such flaminates dedicated to *Divi* were short-lived and did not generally last for more than a generation after the death of the emperor honoured. This observation is still valid, even if and when such flaminates were in fact established to a particular *Divus*, that is, after the death of the particular emperor (or, rarely, empress). It does, however, seem simpler and easier to explain the pattern generally in the terms of Pompeii instead: the overwhelming number of Flamines to a *Divus* encountered in the inscriptions had actually been priests of the living emperor, and then updated their titulature after his death and deification. We know too little to test the 56:100 ratio convincingly against this claim; but the ratio certainly does not conflict

[40] Ladage (1971, 71f.), based on municipal flaminates generally, from the West of the empire, argues for manhood only (i.e. assumption of the *toga virilis*) as criterion of age; the youngest imperial flamines I have found in the Italian inscriptions (funerary) died at the ages of 12 (*AE* 1988. 211: Ostia), 18 (*AE* 1987. 204: Portus), 25 (*CIL* XIV. 292), and 26 (*CIL* V. 6517); since 25 was the usual minimum age for holding the municipal *aedilitas*, this may be generally valid for the flaminate too, Ostia excepted; but see Mouritsen and Gradel (1991, 148) for a possible child *flamen* with an exceptional title.

[41] Meiggs (1973, *passim*, esp. 378 ff.).

with it. Rather, it roughly corresponds to what we might expect on the basis of it (noting also that the number of inscriptions, as is generally the case, is largest in the second and early third centuries, when most emperors did in fact become *Divi* at their death).

The partial exception to this pattern is, not surprisingly, Divus Augustus, to whom I have found some flaminates so long after his death that they must certainly count as posthumous (there are five instances). As for the next emperor to become *Divus*, namely Claudius, I have encountered three Trajanic instances; they are just in the balance where they *might* have been held in his lifetime, but probably were not. There are, however, no later instances where flaminates to a *Divus* postdates his death by more than a generation (though again we should bear in mind that most of the inscriptions cannot be dated). This image corresponds to, and receives some support from, the temples to Augustus assembled by Hänlein-Schäfer and treated above: outside Rome, she found only two temples certainly dedicated to Divus Augustus. One of these, at Nola where Augustus died, was dedicated by Tiberius, and thus cannot count as evidence of great enthusiasm for the new god of the Roman pantheon; it may even have been a state temple rather than a municipal one.[42] As for the other instance, it seems doubtful to me whether this temple, from Luceria (reg. II), really had anything to do with Divus Augustus: its dedicatory inscription runs *Apollini Divo Augusto*, the interpretation of which is not easy: 'To Apollo [and?] Divus Augustus' or 'To Apollo the august god' (both the words *divus* and *augustus* of course existed before they were used in connection with the first emperor).[43] In either case, this temple cannot weaken the

[42] Nola: Dio 56. 46. 3; Tac. *Ann.* 4. 57; Hänlein-Schäfer (1985, 129f.); see further p. 77 n. 7 above and p. 337 below.

[43] *CIL* IX. 783; Hänlein-Schäfer (1985, 142f.), interpreted by Ribezzo (1937, 20), followed by Hänlein-Schäfer, as a syncretistic combination of the two characters, since there is no '*et*' or other conjunction between the two names. The argument is unconvincing, for that is in fact generally the case in dedications to more than one god. Alternatively, Divus Augustus was *sunnaos theos* with Apollo, though the association between Apollo and Augustus in his lifetime was hardly relevant after his death, and is in fact unparalleled (despite the *Divus* title, Ribezzo (1937, 18) interpreted the temple as dedicated to Augustus in his lifetime, theoretically possible, but unlikely). A third option,

conclusion: the municipal cults in Italy mostly, if not exclusively, concentrated on the living emperor rather than on the *Divi*, the dead ones.

RITUAL

About the ritual content of these cults we know very little. The decisive point, however, is that they are closely modelled, in their aspects of temple architecture and priestly titles, on the traditional worship of the 'old' gods, and that there is no reason not to take this close and deliberate parallel to imply that the imperial cults to the living emperor in the Italian towns included sacrifices to the emperor, not to his *Genius* or merely on his behalf. The depiction on the altar from Pompeii (Fig. 4.1) can now be taken to represent the sacrifice of a bull to the living emperor, presumably Augustus.[44] The depiction may have more to reveal than has usually been deduced from it. Thus the presence of *vela*, sun shades on the temple in the relief, seems to indicate that the sacrifice takes place in the summer. The character of the sacrifice in the relief may also be specified further. It takes place on a—temporary, no doubt—movable tripod altar, though the altar itself is a square marble altar. This seems to imply that the ceremony depicted is not merely a standard one of a sacrifice being repeated year by year.

The obvious interpretation would be that the ceremony

which seems preferable to me, is that the temple was dedicated only to Apollo, and that the words *divo* (= *deo*) *Augusto* are simply epithets.

[44] The dating of the altar is controversial (Ryberg (1955, 81 ff.); V. Kockel in *AA* (1986), 457), tied as the argument is to the dating of the temple, since it is shown on the altar front; the temple now standing has usually been dated to the last generation of Pompeii's existence, and since Maiuri's limited excavation of the site appeared to show that no earlier temple had stood there (Maiuri, 1942, 43 ff.), this would give a similar dating for the altar; in recent years some scholars have, however, argued for an Augustan date of the temple (Richardson (1988, 191 ff.); V. Kockel in *AA* (1986, 457 n. 52); A. M. Small in *EMC/CV* 34 n. s. 9 (1990, 314 f.)) and hence also of the altar, which seems stylistically Augustan. The traditional dating of the temple is based on its construction in *opus testaceum*; the chronology of Roman building techniques is based on monuments in Rome, which I do not believe can be rigidly applied also in Pompeii, so I accept the Augustan dating. The fact that Pompeii had *flamines* of the emperor from at least 2 BC has really no bearing on the date of the temple: cult only presupposed an altar, not a temple.

A

B

FIG. 4.1.A–B. The altar in the imperial temple in the Forum of Pompeii

Notes: A: The front of the altar depicts a sacrifice to the emperor, probably Augustus, performed by Pompeii's *flamen* or *sacerdos Augusti*; in the background are the walls of the raised temple *cella*. B: Back of the altar, showing imperial emblems, the oak wreath and laurels decreed to Augustus by the Roman Senate in 27 BC; the short sides of the altar show standard utensils of sacrifice, such as wine jar and incense box.

shown is the dedication of the temple, taking place before the present altar was made or finished. And most likely, this dedication ceremony, the *dies natalis* of the cult, was placed on an imperial anniversary. Under Augustus, the two most important and celebrated of these dates were 1 August, anniversary of the conquest of Alexandria in 30 BC, and generally regarded as the beginning of his rule (though the term *dies imperii* is not used in Augustan sources—young Caesar had had *imperium* from 43 BC—the use of this anniversary corresponds to the later term); and his birthday on 23 September. The presence of the *vela* points to the former date.

Though the depiction on the Pompeian altar, taken in conjunction with the evidence of *flamines* to Augustus from at least 2 BC onwards, seems clear and unambiguous, it has in fact been taken by Taylor to support the *Genius* theory. We know of no certain cult images from these cults, though the great scarcity of life-size depictions of the *Genius Augusti* in the round[45] further undermines the idea that he should have been the central figure in this context. But we have at least a depiction of such a cult image. Though almost completely overlooked, we do in fact possess another altar, presumably municipal, showing a sacrifice (a libation) to the emperor. It is a round marble altar from Abellinum (in Campania, now Avellino), decorated with reliefs all round (Fig. 4.2).[46] The altar has been almost completely overlooked in scholarship, and I shall not lose myself in its interpretation here, especially since I have not studied it by autopsy; suffice it to say here that the scenery includes a *togatus* pouring a libation to another figure placed on a base, and so without doubt meant to represent a statue. The depiction of a military trophy and a Victoria in the scenery can leave little doubt that the figure is an emperor; he is dressed in a toga, and the statue does not represent a *Genius*.

[45] Life-size statues: Kunckel (1974, A1–3) seem likely or possible. Her identification of these statues is in fact uncertain; for instance, her A5, with *torques*, must surely represent a city *Genius* rather than the *Genius Augusti*, and this may in fact be the case for all her statues of the emperor's *Genius*. Thus A1–3 may all come from Puteoli, where we know that the *Genius coloniae* was a popular figure, see Gradel (1992, 49f., n. 48 and 55 n. 73).

[46] Pescatori (1975, 39f.) (unconvincing interpretation) with Tav. 35–7; no measurements given.

FIG. 4.2.A–H. Marble altar from Abellinum, now in the Museo Irpino, Avellino

Notes: A togate priest, presumably a local priest of Abellinum, is pouring a libation in front of a togate figure—clearly a statue, since it is depicted standing on a base; right of the priest stands another statue, this time heroically semi-nude. The sacrifice may be intended for both statues, though it is not clear whether they are meant to represent two different characters (Drusus Minor and Germanicus?), or two versions of the same person (Augustus?). The complex iconography of the altar awaits further study.

E

F

G

H

So much for the iconographic depictions of these civic cults. As for the textual sources, there is one precious piece of evidence, namely a sacrificial calendar from Cumae (*Feriale Cumanum*);[47] and an inscription from Forum Clodii, describing the cult at the *ara numini Augusto* there. This is, however, a special case, for it is the only known instance of a municipal cult in Italy dedicated to the emperor's *numen*; I shall deal with it in Chapter 10.

The *Feriale Cumanum* gives us an invaluable view into the festivals of the civic cult of Augustus at Cumae; it can be dated from internal criteria to within the last decade of Augustus' reign. Apart from this inscription there is indeed no evidence that Cumae had an imperial cult, but since all the entries in the calendar are concerned with imperial anniversaries, there can hardly be any doubt that the inscription belonged to such a cult. It is furthermore inconceivable that the inscription should have belonged to a private cult, for they are usually much more modest in character, and there is no known instance from Italy that private cult associations had their calendar engraved for public view.[48]

The entries of the calendar correspond closely in character to public *Fasti*, more general calendars, discovered at other sites in Italy (though these, unlike the *Feriale Cumanum*, of course contained many other items than imperial festivals, such as a marking for every day of the year, and festivals of other gods). On most of the anniversaries of the *Feriale*—birthdays of members of Augustus' family and highlights of the emperor's earlier career—the rites, always *supplicationes*, are directed to traditional Roman state gods, such as a *supplicatio* to Vesta on the birthdays of Tiberius Caesar and other male members of the imperial house. But there are two exceptions. The entry for 16 January has: '*Eo d[ie Caesar Augustu]s app[e]llatus est. Supplicatio Augusto*'—'On this day Caesar was named Augustus: thanksgiving to Augustus'. And on Augustus' birthday, 23 Sepember: '. . . *N]atalis Caesaris. Immolatio Caesari hostia, supp⟨l⟩icatio [Vestae?]*'—'Caesar's birthday: sacrifice of a victim to Caesar, thanksgiving to [*Vesta*?].' The name of Vesta is supplied on the basis of *supplicationes* to her on the

[47] Degrassi (1963, 278 ff.). [48] See p. 216–24 below.

birthdays of other members of the imperial family in the calendar; though Degrassi does not express any doubt on the issue, it is of course possible, since this birthday was a special case, that the restoration is wrong, but that matters little here. The entry of Augustus' birthday is the only one in the preserved parts of the calendar where a blood sacrifice is mentioned. This clearly points to this day as the main feast day of the cult. However, neither the beginning nor the end of the calendar has been preserved. It seems most probable that the cultic year began on 1 August, the anniversary of the taking of Alexandria; this day and Augustus' birthday were generally by far the most celebrated of his anniversaries during his reign. So 1 August may also have contained rites beyond the usual *supplicationes*.

The sacrifice to Augustus on his birthday (no doubt of a bull, the appropriate victim to the emperor, as also on the Pompeii altar) should, one would think, have settled once and for all the question of the nature of emperor worship in Italy. Not so. But Taylor deserves credit for not simply ignoring this evidence: she claimed that the word '*Genius*' here, as elsewhere, was 'suppressed'.[49]

CONCLUSION

I have stressed here the uniformity of municipal cults to the living emperor, as well as the much lesser role accorded the *Divi* at this level. This uniformity, however, craves an explanation. The simplest explanation would be that the municipal cults were controlled and regulated from Rome, implying that there was a centrally ordained standard model applied everywhere. That is not much believed today, and for good reason. Only very rarely do we find that the emperor was personally involved in the establishment or running of cults at the civic level, and in those cases his role seems to have been a passive one; in some instances at least he would be informed of the establishment of these cults, or his permission asked.

For instance, when Pisae established a cult to the recently deceased L. Caesar in AD 2, the town sent ambassadors to Rome to inform the emperor; two years later, when Lucius' brother

[49] Taylor (1920, 129 ff.).

C. Caesar also died and the Pisans established a cult for him too, no delegation could be sent, since Pisae in that particular year did not have any magistrates because of dissension of some kind among the candidates; instead the *decuriones* requested the *flamen Augustalis* of the town to inform the emperor by letter, which was accordingly done.[50] A century later, the younger Pliny wished to build a temple for a collection of imperial portraits he had inherited, and give this temple to the town of Tifernum. He requested permission, first from Nerva, then from Trajan to add their portraits to the group. Without the portrait of the living emperor, Pliny evidently saw no point in going ahead with the scheme, and in fact nothing was done about it before the imperial permission had been granted; that is worthy of note in connection with the major role accorded to the living emperor rather than to the *Divi* in such cults, according to my arguments here.[51] Many years before this, Pliny's father had in fact begun building a similar temple, or so it seems; when his father died, it was completed and dedicated by Pliny for his home town Comum.[52] Also at Comum, Pliny had been *flamen Divi Titi*, though we cannot tell whether he received the office before or after the death of Titus.[53]

Most revealing is perhaps a story quoted by Quintilian in a chapter on jokes and laughter. When a palm tree grew out of the municipal altar to Augustus in Tarraco, the town sent a delegation to Augustus to inform him of the miracle. His answer, quoted by Quintilian as a joke, was: 'That goes to show how often you light it' (i.e. for sacrifice).[54] Witty as the remark was, the delegation from Tarraco can hardly have found it very amusing. As this story can be quoted to show, there is little doubt that Augustus appreciated such honours.[55] The *domi*

[50] *CIL* XI. 1420–1 (=*ILS* 139–40 = Ehrenberg and Jones (1955, 68–9); lit. in Sherk (1988, 34)).

[51] Plin. *Ep.* 10. 8; 3. 4; 4. 1.

[52] Alföldy (1983); the temple was dedicated *aeternitati Romae et Augustorum*, which seems to match perfectly the ideological implications of the later temple, with its collection of past and present *Augusti*.

[53] *CIL* V. 5667; Scott (1936, 61 f.).

[54] Quint. 6. 3. 77: '*Et Augustus, nuntiantibus Tarraconensibus palmam in ara eius enatam, "apparet" inquit "quam saepe accendatis"*'. Fishwick (1987, i. 1. 171 ff.).

[55] Cf. his remark in a letter to Tiberius on his liberality at the gaming table (Suet. *Aug.* 71. 3): '*benignitas mea me ad caelestem gloriam efferet*'; perhaps

nobiles of towns travelling to Rome to inform the emperor of such honours may also have appreciated the direct link they and their town could thus establish with the emperor. This has often been claimed as a reason for these honours; though no doubt true, the argument is, however, too often used as a convenient and reductionist way to dismiss the meaning and significance of such honours. Whereas the passing of such measures in a local town could certainly fulfil this function, it cannot explain the continued existence of cults for generations: the emperor would be informed only at the inception of these honours.

These instances (and numerous others could be quoted)[56] reveal that the initiative behind the establishment of municipal cults and other honours to the emperor came from below; the emperor was never asked to specify which form of worship or other honours he would prefer, nor in any other way given a say in the matter beyond refusal or acceptance.

With local initiative as the exclusive driving force, how are we then to explain this uniformity? Why is worship of the emperor's *Genius* totally absent from municipal cults, and why were these cults always modelled on those to the traditional gods?

Worship of a living man's *Genius* and *Lares* was a phenomenon of the house cult where the *familia*—slaves, freedmen, and other *clientes*—of the *paterfamilias* in this way ritually expressed their subordination to his authority (p. 38 ff. above). As I have already mentioned, dedications from Roman Italy to a living man's *Genius* are invariably set up by his slaves or freedmen or *clientes* (so denominated). The same goes for dedications to the living emperor's *Genius*: the dedicators are always slaves or freedmen or *clientes* of the emperor.[57] At the

humorous, as claimed, too dismissively, by Griffin (1984, 211 f.), but none the less revealing for that (see p. 281 below).

[56] e.g. Tiberius' reply to Gytheion: *SEG* XI. 922–3 = Ehrenberg and Jones (1955 no. 102); tr. and lit. in Sherk (1988, 57 ff.); or Claudius' letter to the Alexandrians: Smallwood (1967 no. 370), tr. and lit. in Sherk (1988, 83 ff.); generally Charlesworth (1939).

[57] The only freeborn dedicators in these inscriptions are found in a group of second-century altars dedicated by the *equites singulares*, members of the mounted imperial bodyguard, obviously of low rank and standing in a cliental relationship with respect to the emperor; see App. 2 and p. 231 below.

cultic level, there is only one exception to this pattern, though a striking one: from the mid-first century (but not under Augustus) the living emperor's *Genius* received state worship from senators in the priestly colleges of the Roman state. I shall soon return to this sphere; in this connection we can leave out the capital, and in Augustus' day the pattern was in any case unambiguous, with or without the state cult in Rome.

The pattern is confirmed by Suetonius in a passage dealing with the client kings (an appropriate term, as we shall see) of Rome in Augustus' day:[58]

His friends and allies among the kings each in his own realm founded a city called Caesarea, and all joined in a plan to contribute the funds for finishing the temple of Jupiter Olympius, which was begun at Athens in ancient days, and to dedicate it to his Genius; and they would often leave their kingdoms and, clad in the toga and without the emblems of royalty, not only at Rome, but even when he was travelling through the provinces, show him the attentions usual from dependants [*more clientium*].

The temple-and-*Genius* project never materialized, but that matters little here. Roman nobles, with their claimed abhorrence of kingly titles, had for centuries had a strong fascination with kings and kingship, and a particular fondness for seeing genuine kings grovelling at their feet; we may note the proud display of subject kings paraded by Augustus in the *Res gestae*.[59] The full donning of cliental uniform and behaviour by kings dealing with Rome was a *topos* first presented by Polybius in his description of the Bithynian king Prusias' dealings with Rome when pleading his cause before the Senate in the second century BC.[60] Kings could, and apparently did, exploit this Roman weakness by performing these, to Roman eyes, delight-

[58] Suet. *Aug.* 60: '*Reges amici atque socii et singuli in suo quisque regno Caesareas urbes condiderunt et cuncti simul aedem Iovis Olympii Athenis antiquitus incohatam perficere communi sumptu destinaverunt Genioque eius dedicare; ac saepe regnis relictis non Romae modo sed et provincias peragranti cotidiana officia togati ac sine regio insigni more clientium praestiterunt*' (tr. Rolfe, Loeb edn., adapted).

[59] *RG* 31. 1 ff.

[60] Polyb. 30. 18; cf. Liv. 45. 44. 4ff.; for 'client kings', see Braund (1984), who argues against this term, but strangely ignores these instances of 'cliental' behaviour.

fully humiliating rituals of *clientela*. To client kings this was then, paradoxically, a price to pay for kingdom, and it was presumably bearable because this behaviour took place outside, and independently from, their 'own' social hierarchy of their kingdoms. The fact that this *topos* of cliental behaviour is most clearly encountered in connection with these rather untypical *clientes* may cause us to wonder how common such cliental rituals actually were, but that is of slight importance: what matters is that the *topos* and its behavioural elements were known to and immediately recognizable to a Roman audience. And, as one element in such behaviour, Suetonius places the planned temple to Augustus' *Genius*: this too was *more clientium*, 'cliental custom', albeit on an absurdly massive scale.

Cult not only formulated the position of the being worshipped, but also relatively of the worshippers themselves. The top and politically decisive layer of each local city council (*decuriones*) consisted of a local aristocracy, the social élite of the community. These local grandees, the *domi nobiles*, as Cicero termed them, were the driving force behind establishing and running the imperial cults in the towns of Italy. Each of them had slaves, freedmen, and other *clientes* who cultivated his *Genius*, and thereby expressed their social subjection and dependence on him within his extended household. But the *domi nobiles* had themselves never been in such a position of extreme social inferiority in relation to another man as to have exhibited this behaviour, and any definition of themselves as *clientes* of another human would have been abhorrent to them. As Cicero put it (*Off.* 2. 20. 69): 'But they who consider themselves wealthy, honoured, the favourites of fortune . . . find it as bitter as death to be under patronage or to be called *clientes*'. There was, however, nothing socially humiliating in subservience to beings of divine status, the gods—that was the lot of all men—and public worship of the gods on behalf of the city was traditionally their domain. If we see divinity, and divine honours, in pagan terms as primarily concerned with status rather than nature, ruler cult will begin to make sense. In terms of the traditional, republican social hierarchy there could be little doubt: Augustus had burst out of the top of the social structure, into the level of the gods; his power was divine, that is, absolute in his sphere of control. Divine cult would be, and was, the traditional response to this new situation; and the higher the emperor was placed on the social ladder, the higher also was the possible place of his worshippers. Status consciousness thus entailed for these men an intrinsic tendency to construct the emperor not as a human *dominus* or *patronus*, but as a god—and to be serious about it. They therefore uniformly chose to place him on the superhuman level, deliberately and emphatically so.

With this in mind, there is no reason to operate with terms such as flattery, or to presume lack of interest or seriousness among these worshippers, and the obvious popularity and flowering of these cults in Augustan Italy will begin to become understandable. And there was, then, nothing untraditional or even unrepublican about these cults. The option uniformly adopted was the traditional way of accommodating supreme power and, hence, status into the public sphere of self-governing townships; and it was the obvious way to neutralize the potentially disrupting novelty of the emperor and his position. Modern scholars have consistently emphasized the novelty of the phenomenon, but they may have done so on the wrong premises, by focusing overwhelmingly on the absolute distinction between man and god (or rather God), which is as central to Judaeo-Christian theology and mentality as it seems irrelevant in the pagan religious context. The novelty was the principate itself, not, in terms of mental history, the response to it. By placing and constructing the emperor on the divine level in the 'constitutions' of these townships, the world of these *domi nobiles*, and their place in it, remained unchallenged: their pantheon had merely received another member.

I have argued here that this response to the imperial power was really the 'natural' reaction and the one to be expected. If so, the problem of interpretation is then shifted from these cults to the sphere where emperor worship was not to be found, and, as we shall see, forever remained absent, namely that of the state cult in Rome. Augustus' formal position was ambiguous in the Roman state system (though his subjects in Italy, as we have seen, clearly perceived it as that of a monarch); yet, as the principate slowly but steadily developed into a monarchy, we would expect this position to be eventually defined and expressed also in the state system in the same terms as we have encountered in the towns of Italy, by divine state worship. My next chapters will attempt to explain why this 'natural' development never took place. First, however, I will make a detour to take a closer look at Pompeii, where handbooks have tended to claim an astonishing imperial presence.

A NOTE: THE FORUM OF POMPEII

Pompeii has indeed played a large role in studies on emperor worship, perhaps too large. Conversely, emperor worship certainly appears to have played too large a role in Pompeian studies. The Campanian town is the obvious place to look for illuminating a wide range of questions on Roman Italy. Then again, in many instances this expectation has meant that the Pompeian evidence has perhaps been over-exploited. Unique circumstances have left us Pompeii in a generally splendid state of preservation. But these conditions do not apply everywhere in the town. Its public forum was already in antiquity thoroughly plundered to the extent that it is the most badly preserved part of the town. Its state of preservation is in fact not remarkable even compared to many other sites which were never affected by the eruption of Vesuvius or similar disasters.

Recent handbooks on Pompeii have tended consistently to claim a stunning presence of the emperor and his cult in Pompeii.[61] Thus three buildings in the forum are commonly accepted as shrines of the imperial cult, a large imperial altar has been postulated to have stood in the centre of the square, and the temple of *Fortuna Augusta* to the north of the forum is frequently taken as yet another imperial temple, dedicated to Augustus' Fortune.[62] This case may merit a few comments, because it is commonly taken as a straightforward aspect of 'the imperial cult', which is not strictly legitimate.

There is, I believe, much more of a difference between august Fortune, *Fortuna augusta*, and the Fortune of Augustus, *Fortuna Augusti*, than is generally supposed (though rarely

[61] Thus in Zanker's work on Pompeii, e.g. (1995, 88ff.): the word '*Kaiserkult*' appears three times on his map of the forum on p. 93, as well as '*Augustusaltar*?'

[62] For the temple see Richardson (1988, 202ff.); Zanker (1995, 90ff.) with further lit.

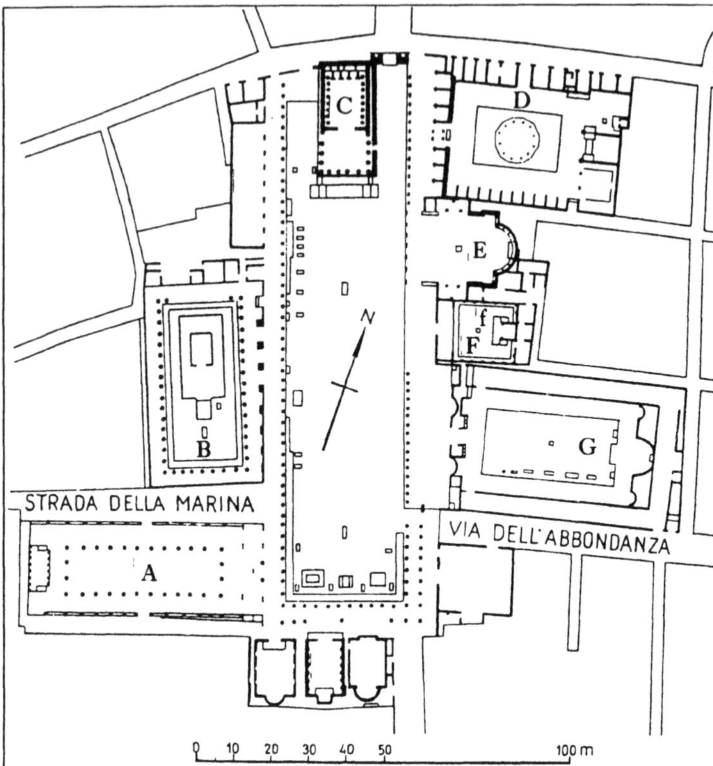

A: Basilica; B: Temple of Apollo; C: Temple of Jupiter; D: Macellum; E: 'Shrine of the public Lares'; F: Imperial temple (f: altar); G: Building of Eumachia.

FIG. 4.3. The Forum of Pompeii (after Mau)

argued).[63] The adjective '*augustus*' would certainly connote the emperor, but on the formal level it was simply an epithet to a divine name, one which had indeed been employed as such before Augustus' day (see p. 113 below). The use of the epithet in the imperial age enabled all gods to be associated with the emperor and vice versa, but the very vagueness of this connec-

[63] The standard treatment of *augustus/Augusti* is now the interesting discussion and presentation by Fishwick (1990, i. 3. 446 ff.), taking the two appellations as practically synonymous, as is usual.

tion was an advantage: a goddess such as *Fortuna Augusta* could cater for several perceptions of herself, the emperor, and her relationship to him, exactly because the connection was vague and implicit—unlike the unequivocal use of the emperor's name in the genitive with names of gods, a usage which explicitly appropriated such deities as his personal tutelary gods. One advantage in lack of explicitness can be presented here. Any existing temple of any god could be subtly transformed by terming its deity '*augusta*' or '*augustus*'. But the associations this would conjure up in the mind of an observer were perfectly compatible with the traditional deity: there was no discrepancy on the formal level. In contrast, an old temple to Fortuna would simply have to be re-dedicated to *Fortuna Augusti*, because this was indeed a new goddess, a Fortuna unknown before Augustus. The much more subtle and ambiguous employment of '*augustus*' as an adjective entailed no such problems. The deity could be transformed in people's perceptions and yet formally remain the same. The use of the title as an adjective offered wonderful scope for innovation without breaking with tradition, and it enabled the novelty of the emperor to be painlessly latched on to the worship of the old and traditional gods.[64] In the case of Pompeii, the temple of *Fortuna Augusta* was in fact built under Augustus, and the connotation to the emperor was indeed obvious. His statue was furthermore placed in the sanctuary (though not as a cult image), further underlining the point.[65] But *Fortuna augusta* (or *Augusta*—the ancients would, conveniently, not have had to choose) could also at the same time be a tutelary goddess of

[64] Thus e.g. *CIL* XIV. 2156, a dedication to the age-old Diana *Nemorensis*, now termed Diana *augusta*; note also e.g. *CIL* XI. 3076 (=ILS 116): '*Genio* | *aug(usto) h(uius) l(oci)*', interpreted by Fishwick (1995, 26 n. 35) as the *Genius Augusti* 'appropriated as a *genius loci*'; the interpretation, which seems strained to me, follows from Fishwick's claim of virtual synonymity between the adjective *augustus* and the genitive of the imperial title *Augusti*. I find it more obvious to take the inscription as just one among several other pieces of evidence that the adjective (which, we should remember, existed before 27 BC, see p. 113) and its employment were more subtle and ambiguous than Fishwick supposes. In the present instance it appears to be simply an honorary epithet, shared with the emperor and exploiting the prestigious aura of his title in a completely generic way, without any specific connection whatsoever between him and the *Genius loci*.

[65] *CIL* X. 823; cf. Richardson (1988, 204); Zanker (1995, 92).

Pompeii, or indeed of anyone so wishing, in a way which would not have been possible for *Fortuna Augusti*.

At least the temple of *Fortuna augusta* is known and identified beyond doubt. We should now move to the forum of the town, where the same claim does not always apply. The large 'altar' in the square may be taken as symptomatic: all that is preserved is a lump of concrete in the pavement. This may well have formed the core of an altar, but it could equally well have been a statue base. Accepting it as an altar, let alone fantasizing about to whom it was dedicated, seems futile.[66]

Apart from the possible altar in the forum, Pompeii is commonly claimed also to have housed in its main forum no fewer than three imperial temples. The one housing the well-preserved marble altar with its unequivocal imperial emblems seems irrefutable. Immediately north of this temple is an unidentified building, termed the 'Shrine of the public *Lares*', or now often 'The imperial cult building'. This latter terminology is unfortunate, for it cannot but spread confusion in relation to the certain imperial temple right next to it. The unidentified building clearly housed many statues, for niches for them are still visible in its walls. However, not a single fragment of the building's statues has ever been found, nor any of their inscriptions. The claim that the building had a connection with 'the imperial cult' is without any foundation whatsoever, no matter how broadly we take this commonly abused term.[67] One is left to wonder how it can be that, in the case of Pompeii, normally banal criteria, such as evidence of some kind or other, can be so easily and completely suspended. Perhaps it reflects an implicit refusal to recognize that there are in fact questions which Pompeii cannot answer, and evidence it cannot supply.[68]

[66] Altar for Augustus: thus Zanker (1995, 115) (though with question mark).

[67] Zanker has repeatedly suggested the new identification, thus (1995, 94) (though sensibly sticking to the traditional appellation of the building); Dobbins (1996, 99 ff.) takes the idea as fact, renaming the structure as 'The Imperial Cult Building'. Even if imperial statues were erected in this, or any other, building, this would of course not transform it into a temple of imperial cult, unless these statues were cult images, as opposed to merely ornamental images; cf. Suet. *Tib*. 26. 1.

[68] Cf. the remarks of Mouritsen (1988, 27) on excessively optimistic use of Pompeian evidence.

North of this building is a complex which can indeed be identified, the market or *macellum* of the town. To this complex is connected a shrine or statue gallery, commonly taken to be an imperial sanctuary. At least there is in this case some evidence to go by. The connection with the emperor has been taken as established with the find in the 1820s of the arm, holding a globe, from a statue. The arm has never been published or depicted anywhere, and seems to have been lost.[69] This alone makes it almost worthless as evidence. The most that can be said is that statues of emperors could commonly show them globe in hand, thus typically when the monarch was shown in the guise of Jupiter. But 'real' gods, such as Jupiter or Fortuna, are also found with the globe, so we cannot know whether the statue from which the fragment stemmed represented an emperor. If the arm should ever turn up again, there may be some basis for discussion; as it is, this vanished fragment can be used or abused to anyone's liking. Then again two complete marble statues, of a youth and a woman, have been found on the site. Imperial iconography is by now well known, and, notwithstanding some claims to the contrary, neither of the statues represents members of the imperial family. They must be, as Paul Zanker among others has pointed out, local notables.[70] Furthermore, there is no altar in front of or in connection with the building. This suggests that the building was not a shrine at all—cult presupposed an altar—but a statue gallery.[71] At best, the imperial shrine in Pompeii's *macellum* is highly doubtful.

The sweeping claims of imperial presence in Pompeii's main forum are not necessarily wrong, but they are unfounded. Pompeii's forum is simply too badly preserved to support—or reject—them. The illuminating work of Paul Zanker has portrayed in vivid fashion how the new Augustan imagery was enthusiastically received, copied, and re-employed all over Italy during the reign of the first emperor.[72] This conclusion does not depend on Pompeii's forum, but hypothesis has

[69] *Macellum*: Richardson (1988, 198 ff.); Shrine: Small, 'The Shrine . . .' (1996); arm: ibid. 118 f.

[70] Thus Zanker (1995, 94) with lit.; contra Small, 'The Shrine . . .' (1996).

[71] Thus also Richardson (1988, 201).

[72] Zanker (1987)/(1988).

nevertheless been piled on conjecture to make the central public square in our model town of Roman Italy support it. Furthermore, a fashionable term such as 'the imperial cult' ought to be reserved for actual cults, if it is to have any meaning at all. To use the term indiscriminately will only blur the multifaceted and subtle ways in which imperial imagery and ideology were adopted and adapted to suit local contexts and conditions in and outside Rome: if everything is 'imperial cult', then nothing is.

It is sad to pursue an argument which is so negative, but it may sometimes be necessary: it is now, it seems, becoming accepted as fact that the emperor and his family completely dominated the public centre of Pompeii, and that half the forum was filled up with imperial cult buildings. Yet, on the present state of the evidence, the only shrine of the imperial cult in Pompeii is the one with the well-preserved marble altar in its courtyard.

5
The Augustan Settlement

At the end of his life, Caesar the dictator was appointed a god of the Roman state by the Senate. Whether or not he had in fact aimed for the title of king, this certainly entailed a formal monarchical position in the state (which should, one would think, have made any such title superfluous). In the short run, the scheme resulted in Caesar's murder; in the long run, the effect was to demonstrate to his son and eventual successor how *not* to go about reforming the Roman constitution.

The Augustan settlement that eventually evolved during the principates of Augustus and his immediate successors never returned to the explicit, or even crass, Caesarian formalization of absolute power. Even when the principate in practice evolved into an office with unlimited powers, rather than a position resting on a conglomerate of different prerogatives and general *auctoritas*, this was never completely formalized in the constitutional façade of Rome. No living emperor ever became a state god after Caesar; though the sources have sometimes been taken to imply cases such as Caligula and Domitian as exceptions, this was, as we shall see, not the case. The *topos* of the good emperor, an image shaped by senatorial hopes and demands, was modelled on the constitutional conservatives (or, less benevolently, the hypocrites): the *principes* who, no matter how absolute their power was in practical terms, kept up the game and avoided explicitly formulating this power, but kept alive the image of themselves as fellow senators. Ghostly as this image may seem to us, its long life and the monotonous sequence of emperors who were murdered for disrespect towards it, should caution us against an all too easy mistake, that of searching only for the 'reality' or *Realpolitik*, and downplaying the formal aspects, the 'empty' façade, as of importance in history. Strange as it may seem to us, trained to be on the lookout for empty rhetoric and newspeak in politics, the imagery of the emperor as first among equals was felt to be of importance by the political establishment of Rome, so much so that it determined the shape of imperial monarchy till late antiquity.[1]

The man responsible for defining this imagery, though not for upholding it for so long, was Augustus. The general development of the Augustan principate cannot be dealt with here; nor can the whole ideological and literary background to emperor worship in this period.[2] The imagery of Augustus as a god on earth, or a god-like individual, is frequent in contemporary poetry and private iconography.[3] Such imagery could express or satisfy views on Augustus which were not accommodated in the formal constitutional façade of Rome. But poetry or panegyric were irrelevant to this formal makeup; any poet was, for instance, free to declare Augustus a god, or—suitably ambiguous—to liken him to Jupiter, which was a common *topos* in Augustus' lifetime.[4] Similarly, when Tacitus informs us that 'worshippers of Augustus' were to be found 'in all Roman households' shortly after the emperor's death, this must reflect conditions in his later years as well.[5] The passage has usually been ignored by scholars who have repeated, almost to the point of a mantra, that there was no imperial cult, no divine worship of Augustus, in Rome in his lifetime. For this, other evidence is often quoted, such as Suetonius, *Aug.* 52:[6] 'Although well aware that it was usual to vote temples even to proconsuls, yet in no province would he accept one save jointly in his own name and that of Rome; and in the city itself he

[1] For the *civilis princeps* see the fine study of Wallace-Hadrill (1982).

[2] A small sample only of the vast lit. on the subject: Syme (1939) is the classic study; for later views see the articles in Millar and Segal (1984) and Raaflaub and Toher (1990); for archaeological aspects see *Kaiser Augustus und die verlorene Republik* (1988) and Zanker (1987, 1988); for religious aspects see Liebeschuetz (1979, 55ff.); Kienast (1982, 185ff.); more specifically the Arval college: Scheid (1990).

[3] Poetry: e.g. Taylor (1931, *passim*, esp. 1442ff.); Taeger (1960, *passim*); Griffin (1984). Iconography: Zanker (1987, 1988).

[4] Jupiter: Fears (1981, 3 ff.); in art: Zanker (1988, 230ff.), also in statues, id. 317f.; Fuchs *et al.* (1989, 61ff., 137ff. (Augustan?)); I suspect that several of the portrait heads of Augustus with the *corona civica* may in fact represent him in the guise of Jupiter, a question I cannot pursue here.

[5] Tac. *Ann.* 1. 73 (AD 15): '*cultores Augusti qui per omnis domos in modum collegiorum habebantur*'; for the passage see Chapter 8.

[6] See p. 75 f above for interpretation.

refused this honour most emphatically . . .'. The statement can be paralleled, for example, by Cassius Dio in a passage (51. 20. 6 ff.) which raises problems of its own, since Dio adds a remark on Italy beyond Rome (see p. 73 ff above). What has not usually been realized is the legal point and limitation of these and similar statements. In fact they do not claim that there was no divine worship of the emperor in Rome, only that he never received a state temple. Suetonius and Dio, as I have stated, completely ignore the private aspect, and there is in fact unequivocal epigraphic evidence that later emperors at least were worshipped in private cults. There can be little doubt that this was the case under Augustus too, and that Tacitus' offhand remark on such cults was correct. The problem is one created primarily by modern scholarship. Suetonius, Dio, and other historians were simply not concerned with the private level. Nor is there any obvious reason why they should have been: Dio wrote political history, which by definition was—and is—concerned with public policy, and the biographer Suetonius dealt with the public behaviour and private lives of his subjects only. In fact Suetonius' description deals only with the level of provincial cults and the state cult; even municipal worship is ignored (as also, it seems, by Dio).

It was only almost four centuries after Augustus' time that a writer found the phenomenon of emperor worship of such interest that he purported to give a general characterization of it (Aur. Victor, *Caes.* 1. 6):[7]

> [Augustus] was named Father of the Fatherland because of his mildness and granted tribunician power for life, and hence temples, priests and corporations [*collegia*] were consecrated to him, as to a god, in Rome and throughout the largest cities of all the provinces, both while he was alive and posthumously.

When these words were written in the late fourth century, the world was a very different one from that of Suetonius. Christianity had become a state religion of the empire, and pagan cults were soon to be banned altogether. This context must have determined the interest Aurelius Victor, an intelligent pagan, took in the phenomenon of divine worship of the

[7] '*Pater patriae ob clementiam, ac tribunicia potestate perpetuo habitus, hincque, uti deo, Romae provinciisque omnibus per urbes celeberrimas vivo mortuoque templa, sacerdotes et collegia sacravere.*'

ruler. It is a sobering thought that none of his predecessors, at least those that have come down to us, found the idea noteworthy enough to deal with it on a general level. What may surprise us is that Victor's brief characterization was essentially correct. Cult of Augustus could be found anywhere in the empire, also in Rome where private associations were dedicated to his worship, as we shall see later. Aurelius Victor had been or was about to become *praefectus urbi*, 'mayor' of Rome, when he wrote his short biographies of the Roman emperors.[8] He must have known Rome well, and his information on corporations worshipping Augustus was most likely based on his having seen monuments of such groupings in the cityscape of Rome. So must earlier writers. But such memorials were simply too matter of course and too uncontroversial to be noted by Suetonius and Cassius Dio. It took Christianity to problematize ruler worship enough to draw attention to the humble private, constitutionally irrelevant form of it.

On the state cult level, however, Augustus consistently avoided direct deification, though the option was always there, his to take, as Suetonius says, had he accepted it.[9] He consistently refused it, remembering the unfortunate precedent of his father Julius Caesar. On all other levels, however, namely those of provincial, municipal, and private cults, all of which were constitutionally irrelevant, there is no evidence that he was averse to the idea. In municipal cults we know of no prohibitions, and since such cults, depending entirely on local initiative, became very widespread indeed, active encouragement was superfluous; passivity was more than sufficient. The same appears to have been the case with private worship. On the provincial level, Augustus' regulation was limited to insisting that Roma be worshipped with him in the same temple.

Even on the formal level of the state cult in Rome, Augustus encouraged or accepted measures that went to the very limit, though never beyond it: thus his title, or name, of Augustus, granted him by the Senate in 27 BC. An archaic word, it

[8] *CIL* VI. 1186 (=*ILS* 2945); the *Caesares* go up to AD 363, but the date of its composition is not known.

[9] Cf. Agrippa's attempt to turn his newly built Pantheon into a temple to Augustus: Dio 53. 27. 3; though we have no further specific evidence, there were no doubt other attempts, cf. p. 142 ff. below.

smacked of Roman origins; the educated observer would remember the line of Ennius, in which Rome was founded 'by august augury' (*augusto augurio*); and the word was used of votive offerings, temples, and sites dedicated to the gods. This at least is the explanation Suetonius gives us, perhaps paraphrasing part of the senatorial motion in which Munatius Plancus proposed the title.[10] What is striking is that Suetonius' interpretation appears so academic and avoids the obvious synonyms or parallels to the word: this would indeed seem to reflect the motion in the Senate, carefully avoiding the cruder interpretation, which I suspect would have been the more immediate one to the man in the street. Ovid sees it as synonymous with '*sanctus*' or even '*divinus*' and his version is probably closer to the more banal and immediate connotations of the word.[11] For young Caesar was neither a votive offering nor an augury; and in the only instance before 27 BC where the word is found used as an adjective to a name or being, it is in fact tied to the names of gods: a dedication from 59 BC, from Gallia Cisalpina, is to the '*[A]ug(ustis) Laribus*', here clearly the *Lares compitales*, to which I shall return shortly;[12] small gods perhaps, but still gods who received divine worship all over Roman Italy. That this is the only known parallel example of the use of the word before 27 BC seems surprising, especially

[10] Suet. *Aug.* 7. 2: '. . . *Augusti cognomen assumpsit . . . Munati Planci sententia, cum quibusdam censentibus Romulum appellari oportere quasi et ipsum conditorem urbis, praevaluisset, ut Augustus potius vocaretur, non tantum novo sed etiam ampliore cognomine, quod loca quoque religiosa et in quibus augurato quid consecratur augusta dicantur, ab auctu vel ab avium gestu gustuve, sicut etiam Ennius docet scribens: "Augusto augurio postquam incluta condita Roma est"*'. Whereas the first part of the passage may paraphrase the motion, for further and general explanation of the word Suetonius or his source appears to have looked it up in Verrius Flaccus' *De verborum significatu*: cf. Festus p. 2 L: '*Augustus locus sanctus ab avium gestu* . . .'. Cf. Syme (1979, i. 417, 431) (a rare word coming into vogue).

[11] The aspect of divinity is stressed by Ovid, *Fast.* 1. 607ff., though presumably with some poetic hyperbole in ranking the name with Jupiter; after interpreting other grand *cognomina*, such as *Magnus* and *Maximus*, he proceeds: '*sed tamen humanis celebrantur honoribus omnes: | hic socium summo cum Iove nomen habet. | sancta vocant augusta patres, augusta vocantur | templa sacerdotum rite dicata manu; | huius et augurium dependet origine verbi, | et quodcumque sua Iuppiter auget ope.*' For the passage see Herbert-Brown (1994, 122f.).

[12] *ILLRP* 200 (=*CIL* V. 4087) (*agri Mantuani*).

since the abbreviation may seem to presuppose that the word was well known in the context where we find it employed. Perhaps the word was used mainly in ritual, formulaic language, of which we have only a few republican examples; it certainly had strong religious connotations, as is evident from Suetonius' passage. However, whereas the word *sanctus* could also be employed of humans of pure *mores*, what little evidence we possess suggests that this was not the case with *augustus* before 27 BC. Hence it was perhaps closer in meaning to *divinus*, though suitably more vague and less explicit. In any case, it denoted a superhuman status, also, no doubt, to people who did not know their Ennius by heart. A writer slightly later than Suetonius, Florus, was, in ideological terms, closer to the significance and meaning of the title (perhaps based on Livy, Florus' main source):[13]

> It was also discussed in the senate whether he should not be called Romulus, because he had established the empire; but the name of Augustus was deemed more holy and venerable [*sanctius et reverentius*], in order that, while he still dwelt upon earth, he might be given a name and title which raised him to the rank of a deity [*consecraretur*].

So *augustus* can be seen as basically a somewhat obscure synonym for the more straightforward *divinus*. Yet Suetonius—and presumably the senatorial motion, whose wording he may well depend on—did have a point in stressing only the more remote and harmless connotations of the word. Whatever it meant or connoted, it was a title only; it conferred no formal powers, and it was therefore constitutionally irrelevant. It was only after Augustus, when the novelty of his settlement had worn off and become an institution, that the title came to mean 'emperor' and sum up an office and all its prerogatives. Yet, ambiguous and vague as was *Augustus* compared to the blunt *Divus Iulius* conferred on Julius Caesar, the title is good evidence that it was not any citizen's divinity or humanity *per se* which caused resistance among senators, but only its constitutional implications. In Caesar's case they had been unambiguous: the name of *Divus*, with state priest and temple; in

[13] Flor. *Epit.* 2. 34. 66 (tr. Forster, Loeb edn.): '*Tractatum etiam in senatu, an, quia condidisset imperium, Romulus vocaretur; sed sanctius et reverentius visum est nomen Augusti, ut scilicet iam tum, dum colit terras, ipso nomine et titulo consecraretur.*'

Augustus' case, his new title had no constitutional or practical consequences. It was simply an honorary name, certainly differing in degree, but not in kind from other such names formally conferred on prominent senators under the republic.

Though it is clear that Augustus did not become a god of the Roman state until he had died, it has generally been believed that his position was expressed in state cult by public worship of his *genius*. Scholars have usually linked this development with Augustus' election as *pontifex maximus* in 12 BC. Tradition prescribed that the holder of this office should live in the *villa publica* in the forum, but since Augustus did not wish to leave the Palatine, he handed over the *villa publica* to the Vestal Virgins and instead made part of his own house on the Palatine public. Here he set up a shrine to Vesta, a replica, apparently, of Vesta's old sanctuary in the forum (which, confusingly, continued to exist). Up to this point, there can be little general disagreement, though the exact details and their interpretation have caused much debate.[14] But Wissowa, followed by L. R. Taylor and later scholars, furthermore believed that Augustus in making part of his house public thereby also turned his household cult, the worship of his *Lares* and his *Genius*, into a public cult. Wissowa and his successors then proceeded to link the worship of Augustus' *Genius* in the city districts, the *vici* or *compita*, which took place from at least 7 BC, to this development. Since the theory has found general acceptance in scholarship, it merits further investigation.[15]

This acceptance is unwarranted, since it seems clear from the written sources that Augustus' house cult did *not* form part of the new state cult on the Palatine. The passage of Ovid usually quoted as evidence in fact mentions only Vesta in the new cult on the Palatine; when Ovid goes on to state that 'one house holds three eternal gods', namely Augustus, Apollo of the Palatine whose temple had been built by Augustus next to his house, and Vesta, this is merely poetic hyperbole, typical of Ovid, treating the whole Palatine complex as Augustus' *domus*.[16]

[14] For the latest treatment, see Herbert-Brown (1994, 63 ff.).

[15] Wissowa (1912, 77); Taylor (1931, 183 ff.); generally accepted by later scholars, e.g. Liebeschuetz (1979, 70); restated, not very clearly, by Fraschetti (1990, 358 ff.); cf. Fishwick, *Historia* (1990, 478 n. 22).

[16] Ov. *Fast.* 4. 949 ff.: '. . . *cognati Vesta recepta est | limine: sic iusti*

Elsewhere Ovid employs the same imagery, in a prayer to 'Vesta dedicated among the Caesarian Penates, and with Caesarian Vesta you too, domestic Phoebus [Apollo]'.[17] Again, this is poetic language, and should not be taken literally; but even if we were to do so, the implications should indeed not be that Augustus' house cult became public, but that the grandiose temple of Apollo and the new cult of Vesta were part of Augustus' domestic cults: that is private, not public. In factual terms this is simply nonsense. But as a poetic statement of Augustan ideology, it works very well: the Palatine temple of Apollo—plainly public—was indeed situated next to Augustus' house; he had built the shrine, and Apollo was his personal tutelary god. Ovid's characterization is ideology dressed in poetic imagery, not statements of legal facts. This ought to have been recognized from reading Ovid himself; but at least there is another, more down-to-earth source to confirm it. The Calendar from Praeneste mentions Vesta, and only Vesta, in the new cult on the Palatine: no *Genius* or *Lares* or *Penates*.[18] So the thesis that this cult included Augustus' house cult and turned it public should be rejected. We are then left with the worship accorded to Augustus' *Genius* at the *compita*.

THE COMPITAL CULTS AND THEIR IMPACT

Around the year 7 BC Augustus reorganized the administrative system of the city of Rome. The capital was subdivided into 14 *regiones* and 265 *vici*, or city quarters.[19] From time immemorial (or, in Roman terms, from the days of King Servius Tullius)

constituere patres. | *Phoebus habet partem, Vestae pars altera cessit;* | *quod superest illis, tertius ipse* [Augustus] *tenet.* | . . . | *stet domus: aeternos tres habet una deos.*'

[17] Ov. *Met.* 15. 864f.: '*Vestaque Caesareos inter sacrata penates* | *et cum Caesarea tu, Phoebe domestice, Vesta* . . .'.

[18] Degrassi (1963, 133) (*Fasti Praenestini*, 28 Apr.): '*Feriae ex s(enatus) c(onsulto), quod eo di[e signu]m et [ara?]* | *Vestae in domu Imp. Caesaris Augu[sti po]ntif. max.* | *dedicatast Quirinio et Valgio co(n)s(ulibus)*'. Whether the cult included a temple to Vesta has caused much debate, which is, however, irrelevant in this connection; see Kolbe (1966–7); Herbert-Brown (1994, 63ff.).

[19] Dio 55. 8. 6f.; Suet. *Aug.* 30. 1; Plin. *Nat. Hist.* 3. 5. 66; Niebling (1956);

Rome had been subdivided into *vici*, and each *vicus* had had a cult of its own, the worship of the *Lares* of the crossroads (*Lares compitales*). The cults were run by *magistri* of the *vicus*, and the festival of the *Compitalia* (which was likewise celebrated in the households) and games (*ludi compitalicii*) were also celebrated at the shrines (*compita*). We know little of the republican institutions, but in the late republic the cults in the *vici* became centres of political and popular unrest, and were several times suppressed by the Senate, the last time under Caesar.[20] Outside Rome, however, the bans did not affect the cults which had been established on the Roman model in several townships all over Italy, and where they continued when the cults had been suppressed in the capital.[21]

The previous history of these cults in Rome demanded tight governmental control, when they were finally re-established around 7 BC; this revival took place as part of the general Augustan scheme of restoring age-old cults and traditions which had fallen into disuse in the political and, as it was felt, moral collapse of the late republic. Typical of such Augustan restorations, the new cults from 7 BC onwards had, below the formal level, little resemblance to their republican precursors. The two *Lares compitales* of the republic were henceforth unanimously termed *Lares augusti*, and with them entered the worship of a new and third god, the *Genius Augusti*.[22] We are relatively well informed as to these cults, since several inscribed and relief-decorated altars from the Augustan cults have been

Nicolet (1988, 209 ff.); Fraschetti (1990, 204 ff., esp. 255 ff.). The year 7 BC is given by Dio and confirmed by the majority of inscriptions of the new cults, whose calendar began in that year (*CIL* VI. 36809; H. v. Hesberg in *Kaiser Augustus und die verlorene Republik* (1988, 368 ff.), both Augustan; but *CIL* VI. 30975 (Palmer, 1990, 17 ff.) gives 8 BC); two later inscriptions (*CIL* VI. 449 and 452, dated 83 and 109) each give another first year. Either the process was more gradual than Dio suggests, and took place over a number of years, or else the chronology of the two later inscriptions (whose first year is not the same) may be explained as calculating errors, as suggested by Niebling (1956, 304 ff.). However, whether the first year of the cult was the same in all *vici* in Rome or not, does not matter much here.

20 Treggiari (1969, 168 ff.).

21 e.g. *ILLRP* 200 (=*CIL* V. 4087); *CIL* I². 777 (Pompeii); XIV. 4710 (Ostia).

22 Ov. *Fast.* 5. 145 ff.: '*mille lares geniumque ducis, qui tradidit illos* | *urbs habet et vici numina trina colunt* . . .'

preserved.[23] The cults were each run by four *magistri vici* chosen annually from (perhaps by) the inhabitants of the *vicus*. The *magistri* were overwhelmingly, though not exclusively, freedmen (perhaps freeborn wealthy enough to perform the tasks had better options elsewhere), assisted by four *ministri* who were slaves. This was apparently traditional enough; also in the republic the compital cults, and the yearly festival *Compitalia* celebrated at the sanctuaries (though also in each private household), seem to have been especially connected with people of servile status or origins.[24]

Such traditional patterns may have made the function unattractive to prospective freeborn candidates, which perhaps explains the almost total dominance of freedmen among the *magistri*, though these supposedly in some way represented all the inhabitants of their respective *vicus*. What we do know, however, is that the *magistri vici* were allowed to wear the magistrates' purple-bordered toga (the *toga praetexta*) and be accompanied by a lictor when they performed the cult. We cannot say to what extent these privileges were new; also during the republic the *magistri* had worn the *toga praetexta*, at least when giving games (*ludi compitalicii*), and the same may have been the case with the lictor, though here we have no information.[25] But the Augustan reform certainly gave new functions to the *magistri vici*. Apart from their role in the cults at the *compita*, they now had administrative tasks, such as organizing fire-fighting and perhaps conducting censuses for the grain dole.[26]

[23] For reasons of brevity I will deal here with only a few aspects of the iconography of these altars; the monuments are assembled by Hano (1986), but a full-scale monograph is lacking; Ryberg (1955, 55ff.); Zanker (1969, 1970–1, and 1988, 129ff.); Hölscher (1984, 27ff.); Hölscher in *Kaiser Augustus und die verlorene Republik* (1988, 390ff. with lit.); for architectural aspects see Holland (1937); H. v. Hesberg in *Kaiser Augustus* (1988, 398ff.). The inscriptions of the cults are found in *CIL* VI. 33–5; 441–54; 760–5; 30954; 30956–62; 36809; 36813(?); 36851(?); most of these plus related inscriptions in *ILS* 3609ff.; also Degrassi (1947, 279ff.); Panciera (1987); Dondin-Payre (1987) (*compitum Acilium*).

[24] Only three Augustan freeborn *magistri vici* known from Rome: Degrassi (1947, 285 l. 5–6 (two)) and *CIL* VI. 445 (=*ILS* 3613) (father unknown: *Sp(urii) f(ilius)*); later: 36 out of 275 *magistri* in *CIL* VI. 975 (=*ILS* 6073) (AD 136). Republic: Treggiari (1969, 168ff.).

[25] *Toga praetexta*: Ascon. p. 7C.

[26] Nicolet (1988, 209ff.).

Augustus himself was strongly involved in the reform and revival which suggests that this local level of administration was of great significance to the working of the city administration. The emperor even, at least in some cases, presented the shrines with their new cult images.[27] His involvement and the place of the *magistri* in local administration as, in practice, small pegs in the state machinery should not, however, overshadow the fact that the cults were financed by the *magistri* themselves. On the Augustan compital altars, often of very fine sculptural quality, the *magistri*, and sometimes also the *ministri*, always appear in the inscriptions as dedicators, and there is no sign of public financing. There is indeed explicit, albeit later, evidence that the cults and their monuments were paid for by the *magistri*.[28] Such financial demands do perhaps suggest why Augustus, by direct interference and the conferral of status symbols unique for freedmen, went to such lengths to make the positions attractive. There is also evidence of direct financial support for the *magistri* from emperors: in 37 they were beneficiaries of Tiberius' will, perhaps reflecting that such further support was by then needed to keep the system running.[29]

Yet, at least in the slightly longer run, these props were perhaps not enough. We later encounter inscriptional evidence of restoration programmes, again controlled by the public authorities, of the *compita* from the late first and the early second century, and later from the early third century.[30] But there is for instance no evidence whatsoever of restorations after the great fire in Rome under Nero, though this disaster must have destroyed a good number of compital shrines. Likewise, though the administrative functions of the *magistri* seem to have continued without interruption—the Augustan dating system was employed at least till the third century—it appears that only repeated state intervention ensured the

[27] Degrassi (1947, 285): '*Imp. Caesar August[us, pontif. maxim.,] cos. XI, tribun. potes[t. X] VII, lares augustos mag(istris) vici dedit*'; Ov. *Fast.* 5. 145 f. (n. 22 above).

[28] *CIL* VI. 449(?)–52; 30960 (= *ILS* 3617–21); 30958 (dates, in same order: AD 83; 98/9; 100; 109; 223; 116); Panciera (1987, 61 ff.).

[29] Suet. *Tib.* 76: '*plebeique Romanae viritim atque etiam separatim vicorum magistris*'.

[30] See n. 28 above.

A

B

C

FIG. 5.1. Two Augustan compital altars
Notes: A: Front of an altar from the first year of the reorganized cult (7 BC or thereabouts), showing the togate *Genius Augusti* (left) and the two *Lares Augusti*. B: Short side of the same altar, showing two of the *magistri vici* engaged in pouring libations, accompanied by a flute player; the other short side is identical, so that all four *magistri* are shown. C: Front of another altar, dedicated by the *magistri* of the ninth year of their cult (AD 2–3 or thereabouts), showing a scene of sacrifice: the four *magistri vici* pour the libations of the introductory sacrifice, while the victims, a pig for the *Lares* and a bull for the *Genius*, are led forth by two *victimarii*; the *magistri* are accompanied by a lictor and by the flute player usually present at sacrifices.

restoration of dilapidated shrines, albeit still with the private money of the *magistri*.

The new Augustan compital cults had an enthusiastic reception all over Italy. Local versions of these cults had not been affected by the suppresion in Rome in the late republic. But they were overwhelmingly reformed to reflect the new, Augustan version of the capital. These local *compita* are quite common in the streets of Pompeii (though, it should be noted, not situated at crossroads, but merely on the pavement at the side of main streets). They typically consist of a humble, undecorated altar erected against a house wall, on which were painted images of the cult and its gods, the *Genius Augusti* and the *Lares Augusti*, and sometimes other deities as well.[31] Monuments of this type will not usually be traceable below the unique level of preservation in Pompeii.

The imagery of the ubiquitous *lararia* in Pompeian houses furthermore shows an amazing degree of influence from the iconography of the Augustan compital cults. In the domestic shrines the *Lares*, here clearly those of the individual house, were typically depicted with flanking laurels, reflecting the laurel trees planted outside Augustus' house by decree of the Senate in 27 BC.[32] As with the new uniform title of the *Lares Augusti*, the laurels in the compital iconography suggested the connection to the emperor and the new identity of the gods, now Augustus' own house *Lares* rather than the old gods of the crossroads (at least by association if not explicitly: the title means 'the august *Lares*', not 'the *Lares* of Augustus'). In the house shrines the laurels seem to have been taken over rather mechanically and often without clear knowledge of the original significance of the trees. In some Pompeian *lararia* we thus find *each* of the two house *Lares* flanked by two laurels, so that the paintings depict four laurels.[33] This is rather senseless if taken as a deliberate allusion to the two laurels of Augustus, and it is therefore clear that the trees were merely incorporated as generic status symbols. This doubling of the laurels is interesting, because it suggests the ways followed by the imagery from outdoor *compita* to household *lararia*. On the compital stone altars from Rome, the *Lares augusti* are typically shown on the

[31] Spinazzola (1953, 190 ff.); with some of these shrines it is uncertain whether they are compital ones, or dedicated to the *Lares viales* (if these were distinct from the compital *Lares*). But four instances where the four *magistri vici* are either depicted or mentioned in a painted inscription are certain as compital cults; in two of these the *Genius Augusti* is depicted with the *Lares*.

[32] Boyce (1937) and Fröhlich (1991, *passim*): most of the paintings well enough preserved for judgement show the laurels; note Boyce (1937, no. 410, pl. 20) where the *Lares* are not even depicted, but merely represented by the laurels. Note that my dependence on Boyce (1937) here does not reflect any dissatisfaction with the impressive work of Fröhlich (1991) which has largely superseded him, but merely that this book has been only sporadically accessible to me whilst writing this.

[33] Thus Boyce (1937, no. 468, pl. 22. 1, and no. 99, pl. 17. 1).

short sides of the altar, one on each side, and each flanked by the two laurels. This makes perfect sense as alluding to the two laurels of Augustus, because only one of the *Lar*-cum-laurels depictions could be seen at a time. The copying of this imagery onto a two-dimensional surface, as in some Pompeian *lararium* paintings, resulted in two *Lares* with four trees visible at the same time, and thus no consciousness of the specific message of the two laurels. Presumably this non-specific use of the imperial symbols was typical for the way imperial imagery entered the iconography of domestic cults.[34]

The *Genius* of the *paterfamilias* was likewise in the late Pompeian *lararia* commonly depicted wearing the *toga praetexta* worn by the *Genius Augusti* in the compital paintings of Pompeii. As shown by the instance of the laurels, it is too simplistic to take such iconographic loans literally in terms of the content of the house cults, as some scholars have done, but they are none the less interesting for that.[35] They subtly assimilated the house cults found in practically all Roman homes to that of Augustus, carrying imperial imagery, however generically employed, into the most private sphere. There is parallel evidence on the linguistic level: at least in one instance the house *Lares* were termed 'the august *Lares*', *lares augusti* (an honorary title employed also before Augustus' time for the compital *Lares*, as we have seen).[36] The strong assimilation in represen-

[34] A parallel instance is the depiction of an oak wreath (*corona civica*) above the front door of a Pompeian house (reg. II. 2. 4: Eschebach (1978, fig. 203)), as above Augustus' house on the Palatine; this should of course not be taken as evidence that the owner was an emperor, or had won the distinction in the army.

[35] Taken by e.g. Alföldi (1973, 55 f.) and Hänlein-Schäfer (1996) as evidence that the *Lares* and *Genius* of the Pompeian *lararia* were no longer those of the house and of the *paterfamilias*, but of the emperor; there is no direct evidence for such a striking development (for the emperor's presence in private households, see Chapter 8). The interpretation presupposes a somewhat simplistic view of iconographic language, and note clear evidence that the *Lares* and *Genius* in Pompeian *lararia* were still, as they remained, those of the house and of the *paterfamilias*: *CIL* X. 860–1 (=*ILS* 3640–1); XI. 356; 6806 (see my App. 1); further Censorinus, *De Die Nat.* 3. 3 with Wissowa (1912, 177 n. 2). In contrast, no dedications to the *Genius Augusti* are known from houses in Pompeii or elsewhere; and the *toga praetexta* was a generic status symbol which was of course used not only by the emperor and his *Genius*, note e.g. Plin. *Ep.* 8. 8. 5 for an image of the river god Clitumnus dressed in the *praetexta*.

[36] Boyce (1937, no. 47).

tational language between the compital cults and the house cults must depend on the fact that the two cult types catered for the same social groups, namely predominantly slaves and freedmen (plus a few freeborn *clientes*). The enthusiastic response from these groups to the new compital cult is striking, even when its imagery and terminology were simply employed for their generic prestige or 'snob value'. But there was probably nothing new in this strong linkage between *compita* and *lararia*: centuries before Augustus' time the originally single *Lar* of the house, as commonly found in Plautus, had become doubled, presumably under influence from the two *lares compitales* of the street shrines.

Returning to the Augustan restoration in Rome, there was probably, on the formal level, less novelty in the new form of the cult than scholars have supposed. *Compitum* means crossroads, and the cult with its main festival, the *Compitalia*, was in the republic dedicated to the *Lares compitales*, liminal gods guarding the point where two roads crossed each other. The cult was also celebrated in the countryside where it may have had its origins; presumably it was there originally dedicated to the *Lares* as guardian gods of the limits of the estate. The fact that the *Compitalia* were, in historical times, a festival of the household seems a remnant of these origins, as does the fact that the cult and the festival were especially popular with the slaves and freedmen of the household. As the house cult of the *Genius* and *Lares* of the *paterfamilias* expressed the identity of the *familia* as a social unit—defined as all those under the authority of the same man—so the compital cult presumably did the same in geographical terms, as expressing the identity of the *familia* as a unit defined by its connection with a particular plot of land (and the plot was of course defined by its four corners, or crossroads). Agrarian in origins, the cult would seem to have lost its original sense when transplanted to a city with myriads of crossroads, and people from entirely different *familiae* cohabiting the same land and in the same apartment blocks. It did, however, as did the household cults in general, preserve its character of a cult form for slaves and freedmen.

Given this character and probable origins of the cults, and although the meagre sources do not mention any such thing, it seems reasonable to surmise that the *Genius* of the *paterfamilias* might also have played a role in the agrarian cult and been rendered worship there with the *Lares compitales*. When the cult became urbanized, this element vanished, since there was no single *paterfamilias* for any *vicus*. Still, remnants may be traceable. In all the *vici* of Rome the populace in 86 BC erected statues of a benefactor, the praetor Marius Gratidianus, and offered sacrifice to them; a *vicus* is known to have erected a statue to the dictator Sulla in Rome; and later, in 29 BC, a *vicus* in a Campanian town did likewise for Octavian and Agrippa. These instances may be rejected as too vague, since they do not involve the *Genii* of the men honoured. But from the Italian settlement on Delos in the late second and early first century BC are preserved several frescoes relating to the cult and the celebration of the *Compitalia*; and a *Genius*, of the togate type, with cornucopia, is depicted in one of these frescoes (Fig. 5.2).[37]

One may be enough. If the *Genius* of the *paterfamilias* was worshipped in the rural cult, this god in any case played a minor role; the *Lares* were the main gods, and the fact that worship of the *Genius* is nowhere mentioned in connection with the *Compitalia* may reflect no more than this subordination. Likewise, in the house cult, the *Lares* usually received a blood sacrifice, a pig, on festive days, whereas the *Genius* received only bloodless offerings, wine and incense; and a large number of the *lararium* paintings of Pompeii depict only the *Lares*, not the *Genius*.[38] The same pattern recurs in the altars from the Augustan compital cults in Rome, where the dedicatory inscription in all cases but one runs *Laribus augustis*, with no mention of the *Genius*.[39] Similarly, those of the altars which

[37] Marius Gratidianus: Cic. *Off*. 3. 80; Sen. *De Ira* 3. 18. 1; Sulla: *CIL* VI. 1297; Octavian and Agrippa: *CIL* X. 4830–1. For the Delian material generally see Bruneau (1970); the fresco with the *Genius* was already destroyed in 1926 (Bulard 1926, 79 n. 2), but is depicted and described in Bulard (1908, fig. 24 and p. 75 ff.); Bruneau (1970, 605 f.).

[38] Bloodless to *Genius*: Tibullus 1. 7. 49; Orr (1978, 1571); pig to *Lares* and *lararium* paintings: Fröhlich (1991, *passim*); Hänlein-Schäfer (1996) (62 of 159 paintings depict only the *Lares*).

[39] The exception is *CIL* VI. 445, wrongly restored '*Laribus augustis, g[enis Caesaru]m*' on the analogy with this wording in late first-century and second-century compital inscriptions; Hano (1986, with refs.); however, MS tradition (*CIL* loc. cit.) appears to give the last letter as an I, thus: '*Laribus augustis, g[enio August]i*'.

FIG. 5.2. Fresco relating to the pre-Augustan compital cult of the Italic colony on Delos

Notes: In the centre is shown a male god holding a cornucopia and, as it seems, pouring a libation, apparently a *Genius*; the wreath above his head is labelled 'of Zeus Eleutherios'—'Zeus the Liberator', an appropriate deity for the ex-slaves prominent in the compital cult—but the iconography of the *Genius*(?) below does not look like any Zeus. The figure is flanked by two identical females, also with cornucopiae, hence goddesses and both perhaps representing Fortune (*Túchē*). To the left is a centaur galloping (the interpretation is uncertain), while to the right a naked athlete is placing a wreath on his own head, presumably referring to the althletic games held in connection with the compital festival. The interpretation of the unique depiction is uncertain, but the central figure may well represent the *Genius* of a former master of the ex-slaves running the compital festival, here honouringly termed Zeus the Liberator as an allusion to their manumission. Magasin à la baignoire, late second-early first century BC

Source: From Bulard (1908), fig. 24.

carry figurative relief sculpture always depict the *Lares*, but only in a few instances the *Genius Augusti* (of the traditional togate type). In fact, were it not for the literary evidence, we would have no way of knowing that the *Genius Augusti* was always included in the cult together with the *Lares*.[40]

[40] The *Genius* is mentioned in only one inscription on the altars from Rome

The other apparent innovation in the Augustan reform seems easier to judge. The *Lares compitales* (who had long ago lost any obvious connections with crossroads) were henceforth uniformly termed *Lares augusti*. As stated above, the word *augustus* is always an adjective in this connection, and not a genitive of the emperor's name. Still, by association, and because of their new partnership with the *Genius Augusti*, they must henceforth have been seen as Augustus' own *Lares*, and the cults thus became affiliations or copies of Augustus' own house cult. Yet there was, formally speaking, nothing new in their title, as evidenced by the dedication to the *[a]ug(ustis) laribus* from 59 BC.[41] The fact that the title now became uniform, and is found without exception on all the Augustan altars, shows that it must have been decided upon from above, perhaps in a senatorial decree ordering the restoration of the cults,[42] or else by Augustus himself or by magistrates acting with his connivance. The effect of the popular unrest formerly centring on the sanctuaries was to attach the new cults closely to the person of the emperor. Henceforth their main feast day on which *magistri* and *ministri* changed was 1 August, anniversary of the fall of Alexandria in 30 BC. In the ideological,

(see n. 39); on the same altar he is also depicted together with the *Lares*, as well as on another altar, without inscription, in the Villa Medici, see de Azevedo (1951, 70ff. with fig. 51). On the altar from *Vicus Aesculeti* the *Genius* is neither depicted nor mentioned in the inscription, though he was certainly included in the cult, as is clear from the sacrificial depiction of the altar, which includes a bull to the *Genius* as well as a pig to the *Lares*: Hano (1986, pl. V. 10).

41 The inscription (n. 12 above) and its implications seem to have been overlooked: e.g. Fraschetti (1990, 261) sees the title of the *Lares* in the new Augustan compital cults as a '*nuovo appellativo*'.

42 The existence of such a decree is not evidenced in the sources, but since the cults in the late republic were suppressed by senatorial decree (Treggiari, 1969, 168ff.) it seems difficult to imagine that their resurrection took place without the involvement of the Senate; under Trajan (AD 116) a restoration of the compital shrines apparently involved a decree of the senate (*CIL* VI. 30958): '*[. . . e]x s(enatus) c(onsulto) qui aediculas la[rum augustoru]m sua impensa restitueru[nt mag(istri) vic(orum)] urbis reg[ionum XIIII]*'; see now P. L. Tucci in Bianchi and Tucci (1996, 47ff. with figs. 10ff.). Note also involvement of the Senate in connection with the *lex Iulia* apparently enabling the re-formation of the *collegia* after the bans in the late republic (*CIL* VI. 2193=4416=*ILS* 4966): '*Dis manibus. Collegio symphoniacorum, qui sacris publicis praestu* [sic] *sunt, quibus senatus c(oire) c(onvocari) c(ogi) permisit e lege Iulia ex auctoritate Aug(usti) ludorum causa*'.

though of course not factual, sense the *magistri* and *ministri* performing the new cults expressed their enrolment in the emperor's household or *familia*, for the worship of a man's *Genius* and *Lares* was traditionally performed by his slaves and freedmen, and was perceived as cliental behaviour, as argued above (p. 38 ff; 99 f).

Another aspect which seems to have been imposed from above is the sacrifice to the *Genius Augusti* of a bull, which is depicted on the altars showing the sacrificial rites of the cult; the *Lares* received a pig, as in house cults, but in this sphere the cult of the *Genius* was, as mentioned, usually bloodless. Since the *Lares* appear pre-eminent in the altar inscriptions and relief decoration, it is surprising to note that the *Genius* received the more costly victim in sacrifice. However, the iconographic representations differ from altar to altar, as do their dedicatory inscriptions; these matters were clearly left to the initiative of the *magistri*, who then displayed a somewhat surprising conservatism in stressing the gods who had traditionally been pre-eminent in the cult.[43] The new title of these gods, the introduction of the *Genius Augusti*, and his bull sacrifice, must then, on the other hand, have been ordained from above, since, as far as we can judge, these features seem universal. The implication of the costly sacrifice is that the *Genius* was the main divinity of the cult, and this feature is an interesting reflection of policy to which I shall shortly return.

THE STATE CULT

Scholars have unanimously followed Wissowa and Taylor and taken the compital cults as evidence that Augustus' *Genius* was henceforth worshipped in state cult. As I have argued, the idea that this development stemmed from Augustus' arrangements at his appointment as *pontifex maximus* in 12 BC does not find support in the sources. As for the compital cults, where the worship of Augustus' *Genius* is beyond doubt from at least 7 BC, there is a basic problem of definition. Though it has not been noted by scholars, the compital cults cannot be termed state cults. They were not part of the *sacra publica*, but were instead

[43] Zanker (1970–1); Hölscher (1984, 28).

categorized as cults of private groupings (*collegia*), and hence belonged to the *sacra privata*. The state cult in Roman terms (as in ours, if the term is to have any meaning at all) was defined as rites performed by state officials on behalf of the whole *populus Romanus*, and for its welfare, paid for by public funds; or the rare, archaic subcategory of cults, also publicly funded and run by state officials, which were performed for subdivisions of the ancient Roman city territory.[44]

It is a very different matter with the compital cults. They functioned on behalf of the individual *vicus*, and the rites were performed and paid for by the officials, *magistri*, usually freedmen, and *ministri*, slaves, of the *vicus*. It is true that the *magistri vici* also had administrative functions besides attending to the cult, such as organizing fire-fighting, and they were allowed to wear the magistrates' purple-bordered toga (*toga praetexta*) and to be accompanied by a lictor when they performed their worship. Such prestigious emblems were presumably meant to encourage candidates for the office, which could be quite expensive to perform, and they were certainly aped from the public sphere of state magistrates and state priests. But they did not transform the *magistri vici* into state magistrates (quite apart from the absurdity of the idea that such magistracies and a state cult would in that case be in the hands of freedmen). The cults at the *compita* do not conform to our ideas of private worship, and they were obviously under tight control from the state machinery. But that is not relevant. The cults, games, and festivals in the *vici* were clearly privately funded—by the *magistri vici*, perhaps also to some extent by other inhabitants in the individual *vicus*, but in any case not from the public coffers; and the *magistri vici* were not state priests. Nor were the *ministri* assisting them public slaves, as were those who assisted at state sacrifices. In no way were the compital cults then connected with the state cult or the Roman constitution, or public funds. Even though the cult took place in Rome, the *compita* and their worship were as irrelevant to the Roman state cult and the Roman constitution as were any other cults on the private, or municipal, or provincial level.[45]

[44] See p. 9 ff above.

[45] Thus in at least one later instance, the worship of the *Genius* in a compital cult had in fact been exchanged for or supplemented with worship of the

The connection scholars have persistently detected between developments in the state cult and the compital worship is a ghost. For instance, Augustus at an unknown date restored the shrine of the *state Lares* on the Velia,[46] and some scholars have claimed that the form of the compital cults reflects a reorganization of this state cult in connection with this restoration.[47] What little evidence we possess runs in the opposite direction, and revealingly so: an inscribed base of a dedication to these *Lares* of the Roman state, dedicated by Augustus, is from 4 BC, so clearly after the compital reform;[48] but its wording is 'To the public *Lares*', *Laribus publicis*, not 'To the august *Lares*', *Laribus augustis*, as is uniformly the case in the compital cults. So the worship of the state *Lares* was *not* reorganized along the lines of the compital settlement, or vice versa, nor is there any indication that Augustus' *Genius* was included in this cult. If anything, the inscription is evidence of the tight shutters between the servile, popular level of the compital cults, and the constitutional level of the state cult.

In fact, though accepted in scholarship, there is no evidence whatsoever that Augustus' *Genius* was ever worshipped in state cult, or ever became a state god. The first time we can find the phenomenon is in the *Arval Acta* of AD 55, and the Augustan evidence points in the opposite direction. A man's birthday was the main feast day of his *Genius*, and under later emperors we encounter sacrifices to the ruling emperor's *Genius* on that day. Augustus' birthday was, however, not celebrated in this way.

emperor himself (*CIL* VI, 451, cf. 449 and 452): '*Laribus augustis et genis Caesarum, Imp. Caesari Divi Nervae filio Nervae Traiano . . .*' (AD 100). The form *genis Caesarum* seems easiest to explain as the inclusion in the cult of the *Genii* and *Iunones* (the female equivalent) of all members of the *domus Augusta* (apparently = Caesares, for Trajan was at this point the only 'Caesar').

[46] *Res Gestae*, 19: '*aedem Larum in summa sacra via . . . feci*'; Ov. *Fast.* 6. 791 f.; *Fasti Ant. mai.*: Degrassi (1963, 474).

[47] Hölscher (1984, 27), repeated and elaborated in *Kaiser Augustus und die verlorene Republik* (1988, 397 ff.).

[48] The inscription, *CIL* VI. 456 (Palmer, 1990, 17), was found north of the arch of Titus, corresponding to the *summa sacra via* where the *Aedes Larum* is located in the sources (Platner and Ashby, 1929, 314 ff.); Taylor (1931, 190 n. 17 with lit.) suggested that another inscription (*CIL* VI. 30954) had a connection with this sanctuary. But there is no reason whatsoever to suppose so: the wording *Laribus aug. sacrum* is common in the compital inscriptions.

The *Fasti* of the Arval Brothers were engraved at some point between 36 and 21 BC, and subsequently kept up to date with further entries. Thus later in Augustus' reign, after 12 BC, the calendar received an entry mentioning sacrifices on Augustus' birthday, 23 September, 'To Mars [and] Neptune in the Campus [Martius], to Apollo at the theatre of Marcellus'—a neat triad of Augustan tutelary divinities who had assisted him in his victories by land and sea through his early career.[49] This celebration in the state cult, with its somewhat undiplomatic emphasis on civil war victories, would seem to date to immediately after Actium; the fact that the Arvals took up these rites only after 12 is fascinating evidence of the way Augustus' person gradually entered state cult and eventually came to dominate it during his long reign. Later, under Tiberius, the Arval Brothers on Augustus' birthday sacrificed to Jupiter Optimus Maximus, as they did also on the birthday of the living emperor under Tiberius and later.[50] Since Augustus was deified by the Senate immediately after his death and became a state god, we would perhaps have expected a sacrifice to him, as became the case on his birthday later, after the dedication of his

[49] Degrassi (1963, 35, 512): '*B np. M[er]k(atus). F(eriae) ex s(enatus) c(onsulto), q(uod) e(o) d(ie) Imp(erator) Caesar Aug(ustus) pont(ifex) ma[x(imus)] natus est: Marti, Neptuno in Campo, Apo[l]lini ad theatrum Marcelli*'. Taken by Degrassi to give the *dies natales* of the three temples of these gods, but this seems clearly wrong: the Arval celebrations at the sanctuaries simply mark the birthday of Augustus, and have nothing to do with the dedication dates of the temples. The addition to the *Fasti* at 12 BC or later, underlined here, is all contemporary and in the same hand (thus also Degrassi), and there is no reason to take it as two separate pieces of information. Note the sole fragment of the *Fasti Palatii Urbinatis* (Degrassi, 1963, 63; taken as evidence at 512): '*Apollini, Laton(ae) ad theatr(um) Marc(elli), Feli[c]itati in Cam(po) Mart(io), Iovi Stator(i), Iun(oni) Reg(inae) ad cir(cum) Flam(inium)*'; this, apparently unconnected with imperial celebrations, seems rather to indicate the founding dates of the sanctuaries mentioned. But it is worthless as dating evidence (though frequently quoted as such), since the date is lost in the inscription, and Degrassi only assigns it to 23 Sept. on the basis of the Arval text. The *Fasti Antiates Maiores* (Degrassi, 1963, 18) have rites to Jupiter *Stator* for 5 Sept., which then seems a better candidate for the day of the *Fasti Palatii Urbinatis*, thus also Wissowa (1923, 387). Apparently due to Degrassi's authority his forced interpretation has won general acceptance, thus by Ziolkowski (1994, 262) and F. Zevi in Steinby (ed.) (1996, iii. 227) s.v. 'Mars in Circo'.

[50] Henzen (1874, 56).

temple in 37.[51] The posthumous sacrifice to Jupiter makes sense best as reflecting state cult practice in Augustus' later lifetime, the emphasis on civil war exploits having been abandoned. In any case, there is no trace of his *Genius*.

In fact, the state worship of the ruling emperor's *Genius* is a later development. In Augustus' day, it appears to have been a cult form for persons of slave and freedman status only, as I have already argued in dealing with the municipal cults to Augustus in Italy. State worship of the living emperor's *Genius* implied, then, that he was *paterfamilias* of the Roman state household, and that the senators performing such cults, indeed the whole *populus Romanus*, were his *clientes*. No matter how the institution functioned in practice, the *paterfamilias* was, in law, tradition, and formal ideology, monarch of his household, with unlimited formal powers; he was not first among equals.[52] The time at which the living emperor's *Genius* began to receive state worship may thus be taken as the point where the Roman state formally acknowledged itself to be a monarchy; I shall soon return to this development. Under Augustus (and Tiberius), however, there was no clear-cut constitutional definition of the position of the *princeps*.

A FAILED SCHEME?

Though Augustus' *Genius* was never a state god, there are, however, some indications that such a scheme may have been approached or contemplated. A late Augustan statue base from Sorrento depicts on its reliefs a series of Augustan gods and sanctuaries of the Palatine, all favourite characters in Augustan ideology, such as Vesta and Apollo.[53] One of the sides of the base (Fig. 5.3) shows in the background Augustus' house on

[51] Temple: Fishwick (1992). Augustus' birthday from 37 onwards: Henzen (1874, 56f.); Scheid (1998, 31 l. 92–4).

[52] See now Saller (1994, 114ff.), who convincingly questions the traditional image of *patria potestas*: in practice, at least, the celebrated *ius vitae necisque* amounted to nothing. But Saller's view should only marginally affect my argument here, which is based on the public image—or mythology—of the term, and its connotations, rather than its use in practice; cf. Gaius, *Inst.* 1. 55, too down-played in Saller's picture.

[53] For the base see Rizzo (1933); Ryberg (1955, 49ff.); Kolbe (1966–7), 94ff.); Guarducci (1971, 89ff.); Hölscher (1984, 30ff.).

Fig. 5.3 The Sorrento base

Notes: Only the right half of this battered and weathered side has been preserved, showing from right to left Mars, Amor, and a *Genius* in front of Augustus' house on the Palatine.

the hill, unequivocally identified by the *corona civica* placed over the door. In front of the building stands Mars, cuirassed and helmeted, in the type which has been identified as Mars Ultor (hence the date must be after 2 BC when the temple of Mars Ultor was dedicated). To his left stands the putto Amor. The left half of the relief has not been preserved, but parallel iconography and the figure of Amor strongly suggest that Venus was placed there. Between Mars and, probably, Venus is preserved half a figure, seated towards the right, with a garment loosely draped over his thighs, and holding a cornucopia in his left hand; his face is unfortunately missing. The cornucopia, however, makes it almost certain that the figure is a *Genius*, the only male divinity who is regularly depicted with this attribute. Enough of the figure's body and drapery is preserved to show that he is not of the togate type of *Genius* commonly depicted in Pompeian *lararia*, but of the heroically semi-nude and youthful type of the *Genius populi Romani*. The iconography of this god was already fully developed in the late republic, as can be seen from numismatic evidence.[54] The *Genius populi Romani* can in the instances known to us be found grouped with Dea Roma or, later, with the bearded *Genius senatus*, but not, however, with Mars (or Venus).[55]

Most scholars have identified the relief figure with the *Genius Augusti*. The divinities shown on the other sides of the base—Vesta, Magna Mater, Apollo, Latona, Diana—all had their temples founded or restored by Augustus. Furthermore, all these gods had sanctuaries on the Palatine, and the images of Vesta and Apollo with his relatives seem to depict the cult images of the gods in their Palatine shrines.[56] The cuirassed figure of Mars on the relief reflects the god as Mars Ultor whose imposing temple, central to Augustan ideology, was dedicated in the Forum of Augustus in 2 BC; Venus probably

[54] Kunckel (1974) for the iconography of *Genii*.

[55] With Roma: denarius *c*.90 BC: BMC Grueber I, 233, no. 1705, pl. 32. 9 = Kunckel (1974), M III 1 (Taf. 4. 1 and p. 122 with lit.); likewise grouped with her on the Boscoreale cup of Augustus: Kunckel (1974, Taf. 13)—see now Kuttner (1995). With the *Genius senatus*: Arch of Titus (Hannestad, 1986, 124ff. (fig. 80); Cancelleria panels (Hannestad, 1986, 124ff. and 132ff. with lit.).

[56] Hölscher in *Kaiser Augustus und die verlorene Republik* (1988, 376ff. with refs.).

stood next to him in the shrine.[57] Unlike the gods on the other sides of the base Mars and Venus had no temples on the Palatine; neither did the *Genius populi Romani*, but, more decisively, there is no evidence that his shrine, situated in the Roman Forum, was ever restored by Augustus.[58] The depiction of Augustus' house behind Mars and the *Genius* on the base further supports the common interpretation of the figure as the *Genius Augusti*, certainly a local inhabitant. So does, perhaps, the fact that the *Genius* is seated. Personifications of places or rivers are likewise commonly shown seated or lying to show their connection or identification with one particular site or topographical feature, that is as an indication of stationary residence; and, again, Augustus (with his *Genius*) resided on the Palatine. Altogether, the *Genius* Augusti seems a likelier candidate than that of the Roman people.[59]

Augustan depictions of the *Genius Augusti* otherwise show him as the common togate type encountered also in the Pompeian *lararium* paintings of the *Genius* of the *pater-familias*.[60] Under Nero, however, coin emissions from 64–6

[57] V. Kockel in Steinby (1995, ii. 289 ff.) s.v. 'Forum Augustum'.

[58] Temple of *Genius p. R.*: Dio 47. 2. 3 (43 BC); 50. 8. 2 (32 BC); D. Palombi in Steinby (1995, ii. 365 ff.) s.v. '*Genius Publicus/populi Romani*'.

[59] Hölscher (1984, 31 n. 115) and in *Kaiser Augustus und die verlorene Republik* (1988, 377) suggests an identification with Romulus instead, owing to the somewhat similar stance displayed by a minute tympanum figure he interprets as Romulus in the so-called Hartwig fragment, depicting the front of the temple of Quirinus (contra Paris, 1994, 39 ff. and 52 f., with best depictions, suggesting instead Aeneas) with a representation of Romulus' *augurium* at the founding of Rome. But whoever the badly preserved, seated figure in the tympanum is, he can hardly be Romulus who is shown elsewhere in the scene. It is not possible to see whether an apparent cornucopia (which must in fact form the whole basis for the comparison) is held by this figure or by the female figure to his right. Hölscher's mysterious argument that the garment of the figure on the Sorrento base is too short for the *Genius* of the emperor seems to suggest that he is familiar only with the togate type of the *Genius Augusti*.

[60] *Genius Augusti*: Helbig, 4th edn., I Nr. 83 (E. Simon) = Hölscher (1984, 27) with Abb. 37–9 = my Fig. 5.1.A above (compital altar, 7 BC); de Azevedo (1951, 70 ff. with fig. 51 (Augustan?)); Ryberg (1955, 62 f.); cf. Spinazzola (1953, 190 ff.); Kunckel (1974, 78 (A1–3) with Taf. 8–10): statues—but most of her identifications are very uncertain: her A1–3 (all from Puteoli?) may equally well be city *Genii*, for which see Gradel (1992) (much evidence from Puteoli), and her A5–6, with torques, seem certainly to be city *Genii*. *Lararium* paintings: Fröhlich (1991, *passim*).

depict the semi-nude *Genius*, with cornucopia, pouring a libation over an altar (Fig. 5.4); the figure is completely of the type of the *Genius populi Romani*, even in his hairstyle, which is curly below his diadem, and smooth above it. He is, however, labelled '*Genio Augusti*'.[61] The question is whether this iconography may go back to Augustus. In any case we may ask why the two types of *Genii*, that of the Roman people and that of the emperor, became so totally mixed up as to be indistinguishable without an inscriptional label. Even if the traditional togate type had been felt to be inappropriate as resembling the *Genius* of any other man, a new imagery could have been created, as was so often the case in Hellenistic and Roman divine iconography. Furthermore, there seems to be no obvious theological similarity in the nature of the two types of *Genii* which could warrant this total overlap.

The explanation probably lies elsewhere. When the compital cults were revived (or reinvented) around 7 BC they were in reality a new cult, and the *Lares augusti* were no longer, at least primarily, the old gods of the crossroads. The iconography of the old *Lares compitales* and the *Lares augusti* was, however, exactly the same, and this formal continuity may have made it easier to accept the new cult form. If Augustus or his supporters desired a more formal and explicit definition of the emperor's place in the constitution, the imagery of the *paterfamilias* would have been the obvious one to use. Although an explicit formulation of Augustus' position as that of a *paterfamilias* for the Roman state household was not compatible with the notion of him as first among equals, it held other advantages. It was traditional Roman imagery that did not smack of Hellenistic kingship (which was the form of kingship known to contemporaries, and in whose light also the archaic Roman monarchy was perceived); in fact it circumvented any regal connotations. In the republic, when the state had had no *paterfamilias*, this had been expressed by the figure of the *Genius populi Romani*.

Augustus, or a later emperor, as head of the Roman state could therefore be supposed to take over and exploit this figure.

[61] BMC i. 248, nos. 251–3, pl. 45. 1; 272 no. 366–72, pl. 47. 3–4; Kunckel (1974), Taf. 4. 3–4; see further p. 188 below.

FIG. 5.4. *As* of Nero, AD 64–66; reverse: the *Genius Augusti* (i.e. of Nero) sacrificing to himself

And this was probably the background of the iconographic overlap between the two *Genii*, if the *Genius* on the Sorrento base is indeed that of Augustus. It would make sense as a preparatory step, by Augustus or by his supporters, towards his *Genius* taking over the place of the republican *Genius* of the Roman people. Again, as with the compital *Lares*, continuity in the iconography would have made innovation easier to accept. In fact, this was what at least happened later, as evidenced by the Neronian coin type. If we accept the figure on the base from Sorrento as the *Genius Augusti*, it must have been 'in the air' already under Augustus, though the depiction of course cannot be taken as evidence of any cult (it may reflect a statue group on the Palatine, in front of Augustus' house, or it may simply be a reference to the gods as connected with the emperor). There is one further indication of such a scheme. In the new compital cults, the *Genius Augusti* received bulls as victims. This is strange, perhaps, since worship of the *Genius* of the *paterfamilias* was usually bloodless in the household sphere, from where the notions and iconography of the compital *Genius Augusti* were obviously taken. The sacrificial animal of the *Genius populi Romani* was, however, a bull[62] (as it was later also to the emperor's *Genius*, when this god became the object of state cult). The sumptuous bull sacrifice to the *Genius Augusti* in the compital cults clearly seems to have been ordained from above, as I have argued. Again, in its own right this does not make much sense; as a preparatory step, however, to introducing Augustus' *Genius* in the state cult, it does.

[62] Animal sacrifice to the *Genius populi Romani* is mentioned by Liv. 21. 62. 9 in 218 BC: '*Genio maiores hostiae caesae quinque*'; bulls as victims: *Arval Acta*: Scheid (1998, 101 l. 61; 102 l. 87) (AD 69).

Yet, from the evidence we possess, this plunge was never actually taken under Augustus. If the imagery of *paterfamilias* and *Genius* possessed some advantages, it could also offend. Since such worship, as known from the household sphere, was characteristic of slaves, freedmen, and (other) *clientes*, it could be humiliating for the high-ranking senators performing the rites of the state cult; and in fact, as we shall see, even when the living emperor's *Genius* did enter the state cult long after Augustus' death, it remained a controversial figure into at least the later second century. Instead a more vague and less specific version of the same imagery was adopted or accepted by Augustus. In 2 BC, the Senate formally conferred on him the title of 'Father of the fatherland', *Pater patriae*, to which Augustus himself apparently attached immense weight. Less specific than terms such as *paterfamilias* or, for example, *pater rei publicae*, the title must have connoted the same idea and exploited the household imagery. But its appropriate vagueness made it also possible to stress instead the connotation not of power, but of fatherly love without its *potestas*, as it became almost a *topos* in literature. This was assisted by the fact that the title, like that of Augustus, was only an honorary one which entailed no formal powers or prerogatives whatsoever, and carried no practical consequences either, such as state worship of the emperor's *Genius*. Still, the connotations of the title were not merely benevolent and philanthropic, as is borne out by the fact that Augustus' successor Tiberius consistently refused to take it. The fact that it later became part of the stock of imperial titulature should not lead us to view this steadfast opposition as mere personal idiosyncrasy.

In the state cult, Augustus' unique position was then formulated only by sacrifices to the traditional gods on Augustus' behalf, typically for the welfare of the emperor (*pro salute Augusti*), and by worship of 'Augustan' gods, such as *Pax augusta*. Again, on the formal level there was probably no innovation in this use of the adjective '*augustus*'. It was a very different matter from personal gods whose name was followed by that of Augustus in the genitive, such as *Fortuna Augusti* (like the *Genius Augusti*, that type of deity is, significantly, not found in the state cult under Augustus). Yet after 27 BC, the use of the adjective '*augustus*' as an epithet to the names of gods obviously suggested a connection, suitably vague, between the divinities in question and the emperor (though it actually began the other way round: young Caesar received the title, because it was traditionally used, however rarely, with the names of gods only). But the main point remains: there was no state worship of Augustus, or his *Genius*, in his lifetime.[63]

[63] For the supposed *ara numinis Augusti*, which has often been taken as evidence to the contrary, see Chapter 10.

6

The Augustan Heritage and Mad Emperors

The long reign of the conservative Tiberius has its main relevance in this context for adding a further twenty-three years to the final Augustan scheme of the principate, thereby establishing it as an institutional precedent beyond the lifetime and person of Augustus. Under another emperor, with ideas of his own, the principate might very well have continued to develop; but Tiberius' faithful, even rigid, adherence to the Augustan scheme ensured that it did indeed turn into a system in its own right, with a precedent and life of its own beyond and apart from Augustus the individual.

Tiberius had succeeded to Augustus' position (*statio*) by formal powers accumulated before Augustus' death, by his adoption as Augustus' son, and by the terms of Augustus' will which instituted him as the main heir, and gave him the title *Augustus*. At the accession of Caligula, the situation was formally much less clear-cut. Tiberius had instated him as heir together with a mere boy, Tiberius' grandson by blood Tiberius Gemellus. The Senate therefore declared the will invalid. Since Caligula could then not simply claim the principate by the *auctoritas* inherited from his adoptive grandfather, the Senate had to invest him with the imperial power, presumably defining it in a decree. This for the first time clearly and unequivocally defined the principate as an office. Furthermore, the formal definition of the supreme office entailed in this procedure ran counter to the notion of the emperor as *princeps* in the word's original sense of first among equals.[1]

Time was then, so to speak, ripe for a development in the definition of the emperor and his status in the formal aspects of

[1] For Tiberius' and Caligula's accessions, see Levick (1976, 68ff. and 220); Barrett (1989, 50ff.); Brunt (1977) on the *Lex de imperio Vespasiani*.

the state and its 'constitution'. The separate powers granted to Caligula did not answer such a need of overall definition. Nor did his title Augustus. Indeed it had never been anything more than a title only, which in itself did not entail any formal powers or prerogatives. Likewise, its connotations of superhuman status had never been clearly expressed or formulated in the constitution of the Roman state, where sacrifices, prayers, festivals, and powers had never been granted to Augustus or Tiberius as to individuals above the human world. Once the definition of the principate as an office with absolute powers was formally made, the conflict inherent in the Augustan settlement from the moment it began to develop into a fixed system therefore flared up. Caligula's (and the Senate's) attempt to solve this conflict has stamped him as a madman ever since. His case can, like that of Caesar, illuminate several features of the place of divine honours in the relationship between emperor and Senate, and furthermore function as a test case for later 'mad' emperors who are likewise credited with demanding divine worship of themselves. Because of this, I shall deal with it in detail.

Perhaps the earliest development was the Senate's decree ordering sacrifices to be made to Caligula's *Genius*. The emperor vetoed the proposal, 'and even caused this action of his to be inscribed on a tablet'.[2] The measure, mentioned by Dio under the year 37, belongs to Caligula's early rule, when he went to great lengths to appear modest and accommodating to the Senate. The publication of his veto marks the gesture as a popular one, and it is not difficult to say why. The *Genius* of the *paterfamilias* was worshipped in house cult by his slaves and freedmen, and the cult form therefore defined the worshippers as of servile or cliental status. I have shown above that worship of the emperor's *Genius* was carefully avoided in the municipal cults of Italy and beyond. Instead, outright divine cult was the scheme unanimously adopted at the municipal level. This in turn involved less or no social humiliation; it was furthermore the traditional way to accommodate superior powers in city cults.

On the other hand, the decree of the Senate makes sense as an attempt to define the imperial office by developing the

[2] Dio 59. 4. 4; the Greek translation of *Genius* is here, as usual, *túchē*.

logical consequence of Augustus' title *pater patriae* (which had also, and revealingly, been purely honorary). The notion of the *paterfamilias* was known to everybody, and was, as is indeed shown by the *pater patriae* title, an obvious choice for defining the emperor's position. The power of a *paterfamilias* was in principle and in law unbounded, though (it was hoped) blunted by affection. To formulate the emperor as head of the household, *familia*, of the Roman state and people would certainly solve the problem of definition, and much of the senators' unease when dealing with the emperor and not quite knowing which foot to stand on (a common theme in Tacitus' account of Tiberius and the Senate). By now it perhaps did not matter much that such a scheme would deal a final blow to the notion of the emperor as a fellow senator—whatever a *paterfamilias* was, it was not first among equals. More importantly, such a formalized position of senators as *clientes* was deeply humiliating. Left to themselves, local aristocracies in the townships of Italy adopted, as we have seen, a different and more comfortable scheme. Why did the Roman Senate not follow the same course towards a divine monarchy?

Left to itself and its own free will, it probably would have done so. But the Romulean, Caesarian, and Augustan precedent, upheld by Tiberius, had probably now become codified beyond change: the ruler of Rome received state deification only in connection with his death. Caesar's horrid murder immediately after receiving these culminating honours taught a clear lesson of the close connection between death and divinity in the Roman state. The notion is unequivocally encountered a generation later. When the consul designate with more loyalty than tact proposed the erection of a state temple to *Divus Nero* in 65, Nero himself immediately vetoed the measure to avert the omen.[3] So, contrary to the municipal level, this course was closed to senators.

[3] Tac. *Ann.* 15. 74. 3: '*Reperio in commentariis senatus Cerialem Anicium consulem designatum pro sententia dixisse, ut templum Divo Neroni quam maturrime publica pecunia poneretur. Quod quidem ille decernebat tamquam mortale fastigium egresso et venerationem iuste hominum merito, [sed ipse prohibuit, ne interpretatione* (suppl. Halm, exempli causa)*] quorundam ad om[en mal]um sui exitus verteretur: nam deum honor principi non ante habetur, quam agere inter homines desierit.*' Another possibility is the reading *omen futurum* of the contro-

The offer of state divinity had in fact been presented to the living emperor several times before, thus to both of Caligula's predecessors. Agrippa had intended to build in the Campus Martius an *Augusteum* to the first emperor, with his cult image inside it. Augustus had forbidden the scheme, and the temple, later known as the Pantheon, was dedicated to other purposes, with Augustus' statue instead placed in its pronaos.[4] And Tiberius received the same offer, recorded (albeit indirectly) by Suetonius:[5]

He forbade the decreeing of temples, flamens and priests to himself, and even the setting up of statues and images without his permission; and he only permitted it on the condition that they were not to be set up among the cult statues of the gods, but among the adornments of temples.

Suetonius as usual ignores the private sphere and the world outside Rome, and the ban on setting up images without permission would be absurd if taken to be general to the empire (where public cults to the emperor were ubiquitous anyway). Tiberius' injunction on placements of his images in state temples closely mirrors the story of Augustus' statue in Agrippa's temple; and the words on temples, flamens, and priests were, as we shall see, a formula for such a packet of divine honours as the Senate had passed for Augustus at his death in 14.[6] Dio gives what seems to be a garbled version of the same story under the year 14; in that case the deification of Augustus was the immediate inspiration for a proposal in the Senate that the same packet should be voted to Tiberius.[7]

versial Leyden MS L: note now the close parallel *spem futuram* in the *SC de Cn. Pisone patre* 129 (Eck *et al.* 1996); the sense is in any case not in doubt. Tacitus clearly found the proposition strange and felt a need to explain its point to his readers: in his day the principle of posthumous deification had become completely codified.

4 Dio 53. 27. 3; for the temple see Ziolkowski (1994); but there is no reason to take the temple as ever having been a private one, as he suggests.

5 Suet. *Tib.* 26. 1: '*Templa, flamines, sacerdotes decerni sibi prohibuit, etiam statuas atque imagines nisi permittente se poni; permisitque ea sola condicione, ne inter simulacra deorum sed inter ornamenta aedium ponerentur*'.

6 See p. 278 below.

7 Dio 57. 9. 1: '*Ταῦτά τε οὖν δημοτικῶϲ διῴκει, καὶ ὅτι οὔτε τεμένιϲμα αὐτῷ οὐχ ὅπωϲ αὐθαίρετον ἀλλ' οὐδ' ἄλλωϲ τότε γε ἐτεμενίϲθη, οὔτε εἰκόνα ἐξῆν αὐτοῦ οὐδενὶ ϲτῆϲαι· ἄντικρυϲ γὰρ παραχρῆμα ἀπηγόρευϲε μήτε πόλει μήτ' ἰδιώτῃ τοῦτο*

Shortly after becoming emperor, Claudius too is recorded as having forbidden anyone to offer him sacrifice, though in this case the generic wording does not enable us to say whether he reacted to an offer of state divinity, or professed his disdain for private worship accorded him in Rome.[8] This does not matter much: there were no doubt other, unrecorded, offers in the Senate of state divinity to the living emperor (we can hardly expect proposals not passed to be systematically recorded in our sources). As we shall shortly see, Caligula too was apparently offered a state temple by the Senate, and it does indeed seem that the motion was a standard one proposed for all the Julio-Claudian emperors. It was constantly rejected from Augustus onwards, probably more because of the ominous link between death and state divinity than because of any modesty on the part of emperors, though such proposals also furnished an opportunity too good to miss for display of *moderatio* (a quality otherwise not very characteristic of Nero or Caligula). The fact that the motion was, in spite of its sinister connotations (obviously more worrying for emperors than for senators), suggested again and again, even as late as 65, goes to show how obvious was the idea of state divinity as a way to define the imperial position. For most senators, the passing of such a motion would have been the most comfortable way to close the issue. Only because this option was steadfastly barred by emperors did the ruler's *Genius* present himself.

Caligula's honeymoon with the Senate quickly soured, and he gradually came to do his utmost to humiliate this body by

ποιεῖν. προcέθηκε μὲν γὰρ τῇ ἀπορρήcει ὅτι "ἂν μὴ ἐγὼ ἐπιτρέψω," προcεπεῖπε δὲ ὅτι "οὐκ ἐπιτρέψω"'. Probably the same story, muddled and confused. Dio perhaps found in his source a presentation similar to that of Suetonius, who does not state explicitly that the bans dealt with the state cult in Rome (presupposed, in line with his general preoccupation with the capital only); and Dio then interpreted the ban as a general measure, which seems, however, absurd (certainly unenforceable). But the possibility remains that Dio's story may be a different one, the similarity then due to Tiberius' standard formulations on the topic. The silence of Tacitus on the issue is not a strong argument for anything, though it is of course possible that Dio misplaced the episode from AD 31 (cf. 58. 8. 4), after the fall of Sejanus (where Tacitus' account is lost), because it fitted thematically with his account of Tiberius' modesty in the early part of his reign.

[8] Dio 60. 5. 4; see further p. 232 below.

constantly emphasizing his limitless powers. The Senate duly co-operated, and though personal fear may be enough to explain its attitude, what I have suggested above indicates that the development was not necessarily unwelcome to nobles who had traditionally bowed their heads to gods only. Many scholars have taken our literary sources to show that Caligula was indeed deified in the Roman state. On the other hand, epigraphical and archaeological sources show no trace of this, either in Caligula's titulature, as encountered in the inscriptions, or in the iconography of his coinage.[9] The list of unprecedented titles claimed by Suetonius to have been assumed by Caligula must therefore have been for informal use only.[10] Likewise, the *Arval Acta* show no sign of anything of the kind under Caligula; indeed they present an image of traditionalism which appears to conflict with the figure of an imperial eccentric encountered in the ancient writers. The conflict, on the face of it a problem of either-or, has in my view never received any satisfactory solution, though more or less subtle or evading interpretations of modern scholars abound. They will for the sake of brevity be largely ignored here in favour of the ancient sources.[11]

[9] This has often been pointed out, e.g. by Taeger (1960, ii. 289f.); Fears (1981, 72) appears rather desperate in ascribing this to the brevity of the reign. For the coinage see Hannestad (1986, 96ff.).

[10] Suet. *Cal.* 22. 1.

[11] Barrett (1989) is a recent biography of Caligula, useful and comprehensive in assembling the material. However, like his predecessors, B. does not fundamentally deal with the decisive question of the 'otherness' of Roman mentality (for which the case of Caligula would be an obvious starting-point), but steers a middle course between accepting and rejecting the monstrous accounts of the problematic literary sources; and he somewhat avoids taking a stand on their general reliability. These weaknesses are nowhere more apparent than in B.'s rather hesitant treatment of Caligula's divine honours (140–53); his conclusion, that Caligula's temple in Rome was probably dedicated not to Caligula directly, but to his *Genius*, is an unhappy compromise, which lacks any foundation whatsoever in the ancient evidence. It is based on the common premise, going back to Taylor and her case of 'suppression', that *Genius* cult was a priori a more moderate form of worship. The case of Caligula ought rather, however, to serve as a basis for reflections on our own views on religious (and other) matters as opposed to those in Caligula's day. This criticism is generally valid also for earlier work on Caligula, e.g. Balsdon (1934), who avoids the problem by the view common in his day on Roman state religion, e.g. on the Roman state gods (169): 'That any thinking man believed in the physical or metaphysical reality of these gods is unlikely'—in other words, it was all a sham anyway, so we need not take Caligula's flirt with divinity too seriously.

The problematic nature of the literary sources is obvious. Suetonius is sensationalist and in his portrayal of Caligula as an emblematic *monstrum*, everything an emperor should not be, suspends his critical faculties.[12] Dio displays no critical ability whatsoever in his account, and in the main copies his predecessors; his account of Caligula's last year is lost and preserved only in summaries or epitomes, though generous ones. Both Dio and Suetonius have the habit of generalizing from single incidents. In Seneca's philosophical writings scattered references employ Caligula as an *exemplum* of vice; they obviously supply no coherent picture, and the only point that clearly emerges is Seneca's hatred of the emperor. The Jewish writers Philo and Josephus are our main sources for Caligula's conflict with the Jews, but of little value for other aspects. They, not surprisingly, make much of Caligula's claim to divinity. What is striking, however, is that this aspect in itself does not play a very prominent role in the pagan accounts; their main theme is in fact Caligula's *crudelitas* or *saevitia*, followed by his *superbia*, of which his desire for divine honours is one example, but not even the main one. Clearly, as was evident also in Caesar's case, this aspect was less shocking to the pagan writers than to Jewish contemporaries or Christian posterity. The stereotyping of Caligula the *monstrum* does not depend on his craving for divine honours.

DRESSING UP

First, there is Caligula's penchant for dressing up as and impersonating different gods. Philo, Suetonius, and Dio all basically agree on this habit of his, even insisting that such masquerades took place in public. This is decisive—Caligula may have derived personal enjoyment from fancy dressing, but that is not very interesting in itself. His use, however, of emblematic dress in his public representation, and what this may tell us of his conception of himself and his office, is what matters here.[13]

[12] Wallace-Hadrill (1983, 61, 171, 174).

[13] Suet. *Cal.* 52; Dio (Xiph.) 59. 26. 6ff.; Philo, *Leg.* 75–114; Balsdon (1934, 162) and Barrett (1989, 146) are too reductionist in stressing the costumes merely as evidence for Caligula's transvestism or whims, though

Characteristically, the Jewish writer Philo took his behaviour as implying a literal claim to divinity. His account, the only contemporary source, portrays Caligula as beginning with gods who were part men, such as Hercules and the Dioscuri, then progressing to full-blown gods, such as Mercury, Apollo, and Mars. Philo is mainly concerned with presenting an edifying tale of blasphemy and punishment, and should be used with caution. It has, however, been noted as striking that Jupiter is not included in Philo's catalogue, though both Suetonius and Dio make much of Caligula's impersonations of the king of gods.[14] However, Philo's main point is not to present the specifics of Caligula's dress habits, but to point out the inappropriateness of the individual identifications, contrasting imperial vice with divine virtues. In such a tell-tale sermon, Jupiter did not fit the general theme, for the similarity between the king of men and the king of gods was clear to all, a theme which had repeatedly been employed in art and literature since Augustus at the least. For instance, sculptural representations of the emperor in the guise of Jupiter had been employed for both of Caligula's predecessors, and it would have been strange indeed if this most obvious of parallels had been ignored in Caligula's masquerades. Characterized more by power than by virtue, Jupiter did not fit Philo's scheme. The fact that Philo is a contemporary source means little: he is also a very bad source for developments which did not specifically involve the Jews (as is Josephus).

The pagan writers, Suetonius and Cassius Dio, presented Caligula's behaviour as a sign of madness rather than blasphemy.[15] This should not bother us unduly; the accusation of

Barrett is right in claiming that 'these accounts . . . say almost nothing about any claim to divinity'. For the emperor's dress styles in the early empire and their functions, see Wallace-Hadrill (1982).

[14] Barrett (1989, 149); Simpson (1981, 492); Fears (1981, 71ff.) argues that Caligula tried to present himself as Jupiter's divinely appointed viceregent, a programme maliciously distorted by Suetonius or his source; the view is too reductionist, and while it may be partly true, such a programme should not be seen as so dogmatically rigid as to exclude Caligula himself from appearing as Jupiter also. In any case, such a programme is hardly relevant here.

[15] Some of the stories may originate in jokes of Caligula's; one of Suetonius' stories (*Cal.* 33), of Caligula standing beside a statue of Jupiter and asking the

lunacy was, then as now, a convenient way to avoid taking persons seriously. If we continue the line of argument sketched above, and see Caligula's dress habits as a way to bring formality into line with the reality of the imperial office, they do indeed make sense. The usual official dress of the emperor was simply the same as that of his fellow senators, and consciously so, for this presented him as a fellow senator, first among equals. On the contrary, the exalted status of the Roman state gods, Jupiter in particular, spelt another message of absolute power and monarchical position. Dress always signified status in Roman society, the uniform of Jupiter as well as that of the senators. We may remember that the dress of the Roman king, as it survived in the triumphal procession, was that of the heavenly king, Jupiter. The triumphator in his brief moment of absolute glory was allowed to possess and display this kingly and divine status. Tellingly, Caligula often donned this garb.[16] The importance of status in this connection is correspondingly borne out by one of the honours decreed by the Senate to Caligula in 40. Till then, the emperor had literally been placed on the same level as the others in the Senate; henceforth 'the emperor should sit on a high platform even in the very senate-house'.[17]

Caligula's emblematic uniforms of divinity should be seen in the same light, as an expression of status. The issue has been confused by the ancient writers who refused to take such a programme seriously, and by the christianizing views of modern scholars who have taken it to imply divinity. As I have argued, the question of absolute divinity, that is, of divine nature, was not very relevant in pagan antiquity. What was expressed in imperial cults was rather relative divinity, that is, divine *status*, and the absolute power it entailed in relation to the worshippers. This is not to say that Caligula's uniforms should be taken metaphorically; his behaviour certainly did not exclude his being divine in an absolute sense, but this question was simply irrelevant. When dressed up as Jupiter, Caligula, as the king and triumphator of old, appeared to his spectators as a divine

actor Apelles which of the two was greater, is recorded *inter varios iocos*. For Caligula's jokes see Barrett (1989, 146 and *passim*).

[16] Also before celebrating his triumph after his German campaign: Suet. *Cal.* 52; Dio 59. 7. 1; (Xiph.) 59. 27. 1.

[17] Dio (Xiph.) 59. 26. 3.

monarch whose power knew no bounds. The same would go for the emblems of other gods, but we lack information of the specific contexts in which Caligula dressed up as different gods (appropriately, it seems from Philo that he appeared as Bacchus and Apollo in the theatre).[18] Caligula appearing in public as Jupiter would spell out the message to anybody, particularly the senators. To others, the message was perhaps rather superfluous; doubt had never existed as to the status of the emperor in relation to the Roman *plebs*.

A story recounted by Dio appears to support my idea that the target of Caligula's divine appearances, as much of any emperor's behaviour in Rome, was indeed the Senate. When uttering oracles from a high platform in the guise of Jupiter, Caligula spotted a Gaul moved to laughter by the sight, and asked him: 'What do I seem to you to be?' The man answered: 'A big idiot'. 'Yet', Dio continues, 'the man met with no harm, for he was only a shoemaker.'[19] Shoemaker or not, if Caligula's point had really been to stress that he was a god, he would no doubt have been less good-humoured.

The emperor could, however, dress up as anything he liked without that affecting his formal role in the Roman constitution. Perhaps exactly this point made emblematic dress a suitable way to define a position without courting death, as state deification would have done. Many scholars have, however, claimed that Caligula did receive such formal divinity and the literary sources, hostile and confused though they are, may appear to support such a view. Towards the end of his reign, a temple was apparently built to Caligula in Rome.

GAIUS THE GOD?

The evidence for this is found in Suetonius and Dio (epitomized);[20] archaeological evidence, to which I shall return later, suggests that much of their information is confused and

[18] Philo, *Leg.* 95–7; for imperial hymns sung in the theatre cf. e.g. Phaed. 5. 7. 27; Dio (Xiph.) 59. 26. 6 plausibly links Caligula's appearance as Neptune with the building of his notorious bridge across the bay of Baiae.

[19] Dio (Xiph.) 59. 26. 9; Barrett (1989, 146 n. 32).

[20] Suet. *Cal.* 22. 2–4: '*Templum etiam numini suo proprium et sacerdotes et excogitatissimus hostias instituit. In templo simulacrum stabat aureum iconicum*

unreliable. Suetonius describes the temple and its cult in this manner:

> . . . he built out a part of the Palace [*or* 'the Palatine'] as far as the Forum, and making the temple of Castor and Pollux its vestibule, he often took his place between the divine brethren, and exhibited himself there to be worshipped by those who presented themselves; and some hailed him as Jupiter Latiaris. He also set up a special temple to his own godhead, with priests and with victims of the choicest kind. In this temple was a life-sized statue of the emperor in gold, which was dressed each day in clothing such as he wore himself. The richest citizens used all their influence to secure the priesthoods of his cult and bid high for the honour. The victims were flamingoes, peacocks, woodcock, guineahens and pheasants, offered day by day each after its own kind.

The epitome of Dio, on the other hand, is totally muddled, apparently because Dio was himself confused by his sources, and close analysis of the text seems pointless; it mentions a temple which had been voted by the Senate; this, or another, temple was then built on the Palatine (or 'in the palace') at Caligula's own expense. Grammatically, at least, only one temple is mentioned, though most scholars have seen two in the text, and connected the temple decreed by the Senate with yet another building of which Dio had some vague notion: 'It seems that he had constructed some sort of quarters [*katálusin*] on the Capitoline, in order, as he said, that he might dwell with Jupiter'. It is certainly not clear from the text whether this building was actually the same as the temple decreed by the Senate, and Dio himself appears not to have known this. Suetonius, however, merely describes it as a house (*domus*), and Dio's phrase *katálusis* seems to support this—it is never used of temples. The epitome then reports how Caligula cut in two the temple of Castor and Pollux to make 'through it an approach to the Palatine (or 'the Palace') between the two statues, in order, as he was wont to say, that he might have the Dioscuri for gatekeepers'. Dio's epitome proceeds to characterize his cult, in which he styled himself Jupiter or Jovean (59. 28. 5: '*diálión*';

amiciebaturque cotidie veste, quali ipse uteretur. magisteria sacerdotii ditissimus quisque et ambitione et licitatione maxima vicibus comparabant'; 57. 4; Suet. *Claud.* 9. 2; Dio (Xiph.) 59. 28. 2–8.

the text is apparently corrupt at this point), clearly the same as that described by Suetonius.

Different interpretations of the texts have been offered by scholars.[21] To me, the likeliest course of events seems to be that Caligula extended the palace with some buildings, *including* the one dedicated to his own worship, namely the temple described by Suetonius. This building was situated behind the temple of the Dioscuri which was even incorporated into it as its vestibule (as we shall see, this is probably nonsense, but revealingly so). There is some slight uncertainty as to whether the temple was situated on the Palatine or in the palace (both Suetonius' and Dio's wording can mean both), but a location behind the temple of Castor and Pollux, at the foot of the Palatine, suggests the palace rather than the hill; so does Suetonius' account: an extension of the palace, rather than the Palatine, seems the more obvious meaning.[22]

There is one further complication: the temple of Divus Augustus, dedicated by Caligula, was likewise described, in some cases, as *in Palatio*, though it was situated at the foot of the hill. Hence, to account for this, it has been suggested that the Palatine *region* (also *Palatium*), as opposed to the hill itself, extended into this part of the forum. However, as has recently been pointed out by Fishwick, this explanation of the term is a modern construct, which receives no support from other sources; instead he argues, convincingly I believe, that the

[21] For Dio (Xiph.) 59. 28. 2ff., see Simpson, 1981, 504ff., rightly rejecting the common view that the Capitoline *katálusis* was the temple decreed by the Senate; for Suetonius' account (*Cal.* 22), see Wardle (1994, 205ff.); Hurley (1993, 88). For Caligula's building programme, possibly in accordance with older plans of Octavian, see Wiseman (1987, 406ff.); Fishwick (1992, 251ff.).

[22] The wording of Suetonius *Cal.* 22. 3f. is ambiguous on whether he considered the extension of the palace and the temple (*etiam*) to be separate buildings, or the temple to be a part of the extension; but the fact that the two building projects are mentioned together, and that Suetonius gives no hint as to the situation of the temple perhaps rather supports my view. Even more so does the fact that Suetonius in the sentence describing the extension claims that this took place '. . . *datoque negotio, ut simulacra numinum religione et arte praeclara, inter quae Olympii Iovis, apportarentur e Graecia, quibus capite dempto suum imponeret*'; the same story occurs in Dio (Xiph.) 59. 28 who adds that the statue of Olympian Zeus was to have been placed in Caligula's Palatine/palace temple, a scheme prevented, however, by divine intervention.

temple of Augustus was incorporated into Caligula's palace extension, hence '*in palatio*'.[23]

The story that Caligula styled the Discouri his gatekeepers also implies a close physical connection between their temple and his own sanctuary. Caligula would then have received worshippers in the *propylon* to his own temple precinct, standing between Castor and Pollux and thereby appearing as Jupiter, father of the divine brethren. The title Jupiter *Latiaris* used by worshippers in Suetonius' version appears rather strange; it is difficult to see why Caligula should have been dressed as this particular, rather obscure Jupiter when appearing between his gatekeepers. Suetonius' statement that 'some' hailed him thus may suggest a daring joke: at least in later sources Jupiter Latiaris is presented as a god enjoying *human* blood in his cult. Dio recounts that Claudius after Caligula's death 'restored to Castor and Pollux their temple'. This too appears to support the idea that their temple had really to some extent been incorporated into the precinct of Caligula as its vestibule.[24]

The second temple, decreed by the Senate, is mentioned only by Dio who clearly lacked specific information about it. Had it existed, we should certainly expect Suetonius to mention it too; hence it never existed. But there must have been a reason for Dio's mistake—the information is factual and cannot be explained by the writer's obvious confusion in the passage. The most likely explanation would be that Dio or his source had read or knew of a senatorial decree which presented Caligula with a state temple in his own honour. What happened then, Dio obviously had no idea. Presumably the offer was, unknown to Dio, rejected by the emperor who *instead* built another temple, with flamingo cult and all, at his own expense and on his own land, indeed in his own palace.

This interpretation, if correct, would imply that the temple and its cult were private, not public. Confirmation comes from what we are told of the cult. Dio's epitome explicitly states that the temple was erected at Caligula's own expense. Further-

23 Hänlein-Schäfer (1985, 124); contra Fishwick (1992, 251 ff.): there is no evidence that the Palatine region did not correspond to the hill. Ibid. for the *templum novum Divi Augusti*.

24 Jupiter Latiaris: see Gradel (2002); temple restored: Dio 60. 6. 8.

more, the priests appointed for the cult paid exorbitant sums for the honour (Dio's epitome says 10 million sesterces each).[25] This has, rightly, puzzled some scholars, for there is no other evidence that state priests paid entrance fees (*summae honorariae*) when becoming members of priestly colleges. At the most, state priests could be called upon to finance games or feasts given by their colleges on special occasions.[26] Caligula may of course not have bothered about normal procedure and simply used the cult to squeeze out funds from wealthy senators. But another explanation presents itself as more likely. Public cults were paid for from the public funds; this was indeed one of the definitions of public versus private cult.[27] Private cults were financed by the participants and priests themselves. Clearly Caligula's cult was wildly extravagant, involving victims whose relevance apparently lay in their costliness alone. Making everything as expensive as possible probably amused him, and Dio's story that he appointed his horse Incitatus priest in the cult also suggests that he squeezed as many malicious laughs (and, to the senators involved, humiliation) out of the cult as possible. Also, and more reliably, the offerings of dainty birds must presumably count as one of Caligula's pranks.[28] The cult and temple apparently took place on Caligula's own land, in his palace: bearing in mind Fishwick's suggestion that the temple of Augustus, unequivocally a public one, was incorporated into the palace, that may not be a strong argument. More decisive are the clear statements that Caligula's temple and his cult were paid for by himself and his fellow priests. Hence I submit that it was a private or domestic cult, unconnected with constitutional aspects; it did nothing to formulate his formal position in the Roman state, but only in relation to the worshippers involved. Though private, its priesthoods were apparently open only to members of the imperial family and wealthy, high-ranking senators. And, though private, this worship could just as well as any

25 Suet. *Claud.* 9. 2 gives the figure of 8 million in Claudius' case.

26 Wissowa (1912, 491); Barrett (1989, 147 with n. 34); contra Gordon (1990, 223) who interprets this as normal practice.

27 Festus p. 284 L; see p. 9 ff above.

28 Artemidorus, *On.* 1. 70 and 4. 56 may be relevant: birds were associated with women and flattery, the peacock in particular with love of honour.

public cult fulfil the function of spelling out to top senators their abject inferiority in relation to the divine monarch. The cult admirably served Suetonius' purpose as one illustration among others of the emperor's *superbia*; and his sensationalist approach gave him no interest in specifically stating that this worship was private, though it is implied in his and Dio's account (Dio was, as it seems, simply confused by the whole thing). Had it in fact been a state cult, Suetonius would no doubt have said so, for added good measure.

So much for the literary sources. Extensive archaeological excavations have been carried out on the site of Caligula's claimed palace extension, partly at the turn of the century, and partly in recent years. The site, south of the temple of Castor and Pollux, is now occupied by massive brick constructions from the period of Domitian and Hadrian. Under these, traces of earlier buildings have been unearthed. Directly behind the temple of the Dioscuri parts of an impressive *atrium* have been identified (outer measurements 26.5 by 22.3 m., and thus the largest example known from the Roman world). To the east of this, the excavations identified the remains of a large *piscina*, basin or pond, in the wall of which was found a fragment of an inscription to Caligula, probably from a statue base, and thus supplying a *terminus post quem* for this basin.[29] The atrium may very well be of Caligulan date, and indeed appears to confirm his palace extension. Its size clearly points to representational functions connected with it, and traces of a room projecting from its south side and placed on its central axis (a *tablinum*?) could very well have housed Caligula's cult image (from which the inscription *may* have come); the view from outside into this room, through the columns of the *impluvium*, would certainly have been impressive. But all this is mere speculation.

What recent excavations have, however, established beyond doubt is that the temple of the Dioscuri cannot have been incorporated into these buildings in any physical sense. First, the *atrium* is in no way aligned with the temple, which would at the very least have been aesthetically unfortunate.[30] More decisive is the fact that recent excavations on the temple have

[29] Barrett (1989, 207ff.); Hurst (1988, 13–17); inscription: Huelsen in *RM* 17 (1902), 81.

[30] Tamm (1964).

established that no alterations were made to it in this period: no walls were built against its back wall, there is no trace of any doorway having been built into this wall, nor of any alterations to the base of the temple's cult images, the core of which is almost completely preserved.[31] So Suetonius' statement that the temple was incorporated into Caligula's buildings, further elaborated by Dio, must be wrong; the whole story was probably developed from one of Caligula's quips, such as the one that the Dioscuri were to be his gatekeepers.[32] More mysterious remains Dio's statement that the temple was restored to Castor and Pollux by Claudius. Perhaps Caligula's statue was placed somewhere in the temple, and removed by his successor,[33] though this cannot really accommodate Dio's wording; nor would such a statue have had anything to do with Caligula's own temple, but the two may have been mixed up in the fertile historical tradition. Once again, this is highly speculative. In any case, the close physical proximity between the temple of Castor and Pollux with Caligula's palace and his own sanctuary seems very likely; apparently this very proximity, and Caligula's joke, gave rise to popular gossip elaborating on this core and totally mixing up the two cults. So the stories of Caligula and the Dioscuri once again suggest that his temple was actually situated in his palace extension, and so was a private, even a domestic, one. Individually, the arguments for this may indeed be tenuous and weak; in combination, however, I believe them to be very strong.

The bickering and competition in the struggle for the priesthoods in Caligula's cult may surprise. As Keith Hopkins has noted: 'Perhaps fear prompted the senators to humble themselves with flattery, but fear does not explain the form which their flattery took. Nor was it fear which induced the "richest citizens to use all their influcnce to compete with each other to

[31] The Italian-Scandinavian excavation project has not yet (1998) published their findings on this phase of the temple's history, but the editor Mrs Pia Guldager Bilde has kindly supplied me with this information.

[32] The joke apparently parodies the story that Augustus declared his newly built temple of Jupiter Tonans on the Capitol to be a janitor's quarters for Jupiter Optimus Maximus, after the king of gods had complained in a dream that the newcomer was stealing his worshippers (Suet. *Aug.* 91. 2).

[33] Suggested by Barrett (1989, 147).

obtain the priesthoods" of the temple to Caligula'.[34] In this particular instance, fear may perhaps be explanation enough. However, as suggested above, the divine status of the emperor may not have been unwelcome to senators. Grovelling at the feet of gods was a natural, even an ancient practice; but to do so in relation to another man, even a fellow senator, was to plumb the depths of humiliation. Or, as Cicero put it:[35] 'But they who consider themselves wealthy, honoured, the favourites of fortune . . . find it as bitter as death to be under patronage or to be called *clientes*'. The higher the emperor was placed on the status ladder of the world, the higher was the relative placement of the senators themselves; if the emperor possessed outright divine status, the role and self-esteem of prominent senators would be as in the good old days, when they, first among men, lorded it over the world.

Dio indeed claims that divine honours were paid to Caligula not only by the common people, but 'from those also who stood in high repute', that is, high-ranking senators. The arch-flatterer L. Vitellius is a case in point; on the model proposed above he and his peers would actually have shared an interest with Caligula in expanding the status gap between the emperor and themselves. Caligula was, still according to Dio, called by divine titles (Jupiter, *deus*, and *divus* are explicitly mentioned) to the extent that such names even found their way into documents—of an official nature, that is, or the comment would be pointless. Probably Dio or his source had found such epithets in senatorial decrees. But that does not mean that they became part of official titulature until formally decreed by the Senate, which clearly did not happen. Such informal titles could be used by individual senators, or by others, or indeed by the whole Senate in decrees without entailing any consequences for the Roman constitution. For instance, the Arval Brothers described Claudius as *divinus princeps* in their *vota*, engraved in their official Acts, and certainly not from fear or imperial pressure.[36]

[34] Hopkins (1978, 213).

[35] Cic. *Off.* 2. 20. 69; see p. 40 above.

[36] Dio (Xiph.) 59. 26. 5: *deus* and *divus* (=*hērōs*, as usually in Dio's Greek); (Xiph.) 28. 8: *Jupiter* and documents; (Xiph.) 27. 2ff.: Vitellius; the story that his life was threatened by Caligula is probably not true (Barrett, 1989, 236; id., 150f. for other instances—but his distinction between worship and servile

It appears, then, that Caligula never received state deification or divine worship in the Roman state. This would certainly explain the apparent conflict between the literary sources on the one hand and the inscriptional and archaeological evidence on the other. On the reconstruction presented above, the Senate probably offered Caligula state divinity, as it later did to Nero; and probably Caligula, like Nero, rejected the offer, for the same reason, namely that precedent linked this with death. Instead Caligula developed the system in the private sphere, where no such sinister precedent existed; both Augustus and Tiberius had apparently been worshipped extensively in Rome in private cults, and while not, so far as we know, actively encouraging the phenomenon, they neither tried to nor perhaps could prevent it.[37] Caligula's cult was then far less sensational than might be expected from its treatment in modern scholarly literature. This would also explain why the contemporary Jewish writers, Josephus and Philo, did not mention any such thing. In any case, the mythologizing character of both their accounts makes them almost worthless as sources on specific developments in Rome; their main interest was obviously to fit Caligula into the *topos* of enemies of God punished for their blasphemy, on the model of Antiochus Epiphanes in 1. and 2. Maccabees. Even beyond this, Philo had additional interest in laying all blame for such blasphemy on Caligula, instead of tactlessly wallowing in an incident which, for better or worse, involved leading senators of the day (including the ruling emperor Claudius who had gone bankrupt to pay for one of the priesthoods).[38]

Discretion may similarly explain Seneca's silence on the cult. Only one passage in his works perhaps contains an implicit reference to it; in *De Tranquillitate Animi*, which unfortunately cannot be dated precisely, he describes the heroic death of the Stoic philosopher Julius Canus under Caligula. When Canus was led out to execution, Seneca lauds his equanimity till the very end, even when 'the tumulus, where a daily sacrifice was

flattery is modernizing and irrelevant); Scheid (1998, 52f. (his dating to 54 is possible, but not certain)). Note also Suetonius' (22. 1) examples of earlier titles assumed by Caligula, clearly of similarly informal nature.

[37] See Chapters 8 and 9 below.

[38] Suet. *Cal.* 22. 3; *Claud.* 9. 2; Dio (Xiph.) 59. 28. 5.

offered to our god Caesar, was already close at hand'.[39] The tumulus must be the mausoleum of Augustus, and though some scholars have taken Seneca's words literally as mentioning sacrifices to Caligula, the location would have linked such worship with death in a way which is very difficult to accept. The reference to daily sacrifices is rather a bitterly ironic euphemism for incessant executions.

Yet the ironic imagery might seem somewhat pointless if it is not implicitly contrasted with a well-known real cult of Caligula: the 'worship' by the tumulus was, however, of a form much more appropriate for this particular god! Seneca was a senator, and the description of Caligula as *Caesar deus noster* presumably depends on this. *Noster* was a term implying affinity, and is, for example, common among slaves referring to their (present) master, or as a term of affection; it is never used of dead emperors, so Seneca can hardly allude to *Divus* Augustus in the tumulus.[40] The allusive way of referring to the actual cult of Caligula seems to presuppose knowledge of it from Seneca's audience, and the allusion, bitter and cryptic as it is, illustrates how uncomfortable would be any direct mention or description of the incident, if my interpretation holds. In any case, the fact that contemporary sources are silent on the issue cannot warrant an outright rejection of the testimony of Suetonius and Dio.

Caligula was without doubt a disaster as emperor; there is, however, no reason to assume that it was particularly or primarily his cult or flirtation with divinity which caused his murder. This should rather be ascribed to his general incompetence and singular ability to insult everybody who mattered.[41] For instance, the heroic tyrant-slayer of the ancient writers,

[39] Sen. *Tranq.* 14. 9: '*Nec iam procul erat tumulus in quo Caesari deo nostro fiebat quotidianum sacrum*'. It is not clear whether the work was written under Claudius or Nero, see Griffin (1976, 396 and *passim*). The passage has been much discussed, but the wording clearly suggests that this was where Canus was to be executed; for lit. see Barrett (1989, 150 n. 52) and Bickerman (1973, 17).

[40] *Caeser deus noster* = *Divus Augustus*: thus Pippidi (n.d., *c*.1939, 79ff.) in a very thorough treatment; further Simpson (1981, 489f. n. 1). The doctor Scribonius Largus terms Claudius *deus noster Caesar* which must also reflect Caligulan usage (79. 21; 5. 5 ed. Teubner, 1983); his name suggests he was freeborn, but no more can be said as to his status.

[41] Cf. Sen. *De Const. Sap.* 18. 1ff.; Seneca's writings, full of venom against

Cassius Chaerea, apparently decided to murder the emperor because Caligula teasingly and repeatedly questioned his masculinity. However, Caligula's overall, almost complete failure as emperor obviously entailed that his behavioural pattern was something for emperors to avoid in general. Perhaps it also extended the link between death and divinity somewhat; henceforth emperors would be more anxious to avoid any too obvious and active flirt with the notion of divinity, whether public or private. Simply because the scheme was his, Caligula's behaviour may well have given worship of the living ruler a worse name than it had before.[42]

LATER 'MAD' EMPERORS

Caligula's cult was, then, a private one, which had no consequences for his place in the formal 'constitution' of the Roman state. The specific statements in ancient sources that Caligula received a temple and divine worship have constituted a thorny problem of interpretation, which may now be resolved. As for any later emperors, who are credited by our sources with a craving for divine honours, there can be no doubt on that point: any worship they received in Rome was of a private nature. In fact, as we shall see later, 'good' emperors were also worshipped on the private level in the capital, as well as in the rest of Italy; and it appears that senators too were regularly found among the worshippers (see p. 228 below). Thus Caligula's case was probably less bizarre than we may at first think. He was, however, unique in actively furthering and controlling such worship by high-ranking senators; in all later instances, emperors reacted with pious prohibitions or, more often, passivity. However, two emperors drove passivity in this field to such lengths that in practice it amounted to encouragement: Domitian and Commodus. Since their cases in the main present only variations on the theme I have analysed in depth in Caligula's case, a few remarks on them will suffice.

Caligula, spell out his cruelty, but ignore his divine honours; cruelty is in fact the main theme also in Dio and Suetonius.

[42] Tiberius was, according to Tacitus, criticized for refusing a temple to himself and his mother offered by the province of Baetica (*Ann.* 4. 38. 4f.): '*nam contemptu famae contemni virtutes*'.

Domitian's craving for divine titulature is invariably stressed in the ancient sources dealing with him, but it has been stressed even more, and too much, by modern scholars:[43] thus the title 'master and god' (*dominus et deus*) by which he was regularly addressed in his later years. As in Caligula's case, it was never a formal title: it was never granted by the Senate, and it is never found in inscriptions. In fact, it is little realized that Domitian probably did not invent this titulature. Suetonius is explicit in stating that the term was first employed in the imperial administration by, not surprisingly, the emperor's *procuratores*, that is, freedmen members of his staff or extended household (*familia*). And the term was always used *of* or *to* Domitian, never by himself in the first person. True, Suetonius claims that he dictated a letter in the name of his procurators with the following preamble: 'Our master and god orders this to be carried out' (*Dominus et deus noster hoc fieri iubet*), and thus, according to the biographer, began this practice of addressing him or referring to him.[44] Yet how would Suetonius know that Domitian actually dictated these words? The fact that Suetonius can come up only with this dubious example, and cannot supply any instances where Domitian used it in the first person, is revealing; had there been such instances, he would undoubtedly have quoted them. Certainly, Domitian did nothing to prevent this titulature, and he was probably very pleased with it; but that is not relevant here.

The younger Pliny mentions sacrifices to Domitian on the Capitol, and I shall later return to his passage (see p. 227 below). All such worship and titulature were, however, as in Caligula's case, of a private and informal nature, no matter how common. As with Caligula, Domitian's coinage and the *Arval Acta* reveal nothing of all this, and that is decisive.

Commodus may seem, and to some extent is, a different case. In the last year of his life, he in fact received the official title of *Romanus Hercules* from the Senate, as well as other extravagant honours. This has been taken by some scholars to imply that he was declared a god by the Senate.[45]

[43] The ancient evidence is conveniently assembled by Scott (1936, 88 ff.).

[44] Suet. *Dom.* 13.

[45] Thus Speidel (1993, 109); ibid. for the titulature and refs.; cf. *CIL* XIV. 3449.

The close link between state divinity and death established by the institution of the *Divi* may then be taken to have been ignored in this instance. In fact, that was not so. The *Romanus Hercules* never received any state worship—no temples, priests, or sacrifices in the state cult[46]—and Hercules had in fact only ascended to the stars and divinity at his death; so despite the unique extravagance of the title, it does not basically conflict with the notion that the emperor could become a state god only after he had left this world. The title was sufficiently ambiguous or equivocal to avoid direct conceptual association with the emperor's death (or so he must have felt). As it turned out, and since Commodus was murdered some months after receiving the title, the idea did not work; after this, names of gods were never again part of a Roman emperor's titulature. Commodus' title may be seen as the last of several attempts to turn the empire into a formally acknowledged divine monarchy, to bring formality in line with reality, without direct conflict with the dangerous notion that formal divine status had become linked with the emperor's death.

[46] Only the HA *Com.* 17. 11 claims that Commodus 'planned' to have a *flamen* in Rome; Dio knows nothing of this.

7
The Emperor's *Genius* in State Cult

The sinister connotations of the emperor's state divinity left only one option for clearer formulation of the imperial office in the Roman state: the *Genius* of the living emperor, a cult which did not imply divinity, but certainly did imply social humiliation for the senators involved. Contrary to accepted belief, I have attempted to show that Augustus' *Genius* was never worshipped in the state cult. Indeed, the first certain instance of the practice is found in the rites of the Arval Brothers for the year 55.[1] This year, when young Nero was firmly in the grip of his tutors Seneca and Burrus, appears rather unlikely as the point of institution of such ceremonies. Now, the *Arval Acta* are very sporadically preserved from the reign of Claudius. Under Nero and his shortlived successors the *Genius* was worshipped primarily on the living emperor's birthday, as we would expect, and his accession day, *dies imperii*. Neither of these anniversaries is preserved in the *Acta* from Claudius' reign. So we are left with Caligula or Claudius as the institutor of this practice. As mentioned above (p. 141), Caligula early in his reign rejected state sacrifices to his *Genius*, and the Arval Brothers celebrated his *dies imperii* in 38 with the traditional sacrifice to Jupiter Optimus Maximus only. Caligula may, however, have changed his mind later.

Indirect evidence for this may be found in oath formulas. At some point a formula by Jupiter Optimus Maximus, the *Divi*, and the *Genius* of the ruling emperor became standard to the extent that it has been termed 'the official state oath'. Indeed, official status for the formula seems to be supported by the inclusion of the *Divi*, prominent in the public sphere in the capital, but far less so on the private level (see p. 339 below).

[1] Scheid (1998, 57 = *CIL* VI. 32352), preserved only in a faulty manuscript tradition; as for the occurrence of the *Genius Augusti*, there can, however, be little doubt.

For a long time the formula could be traced only to the reign of Nero, where it was evidenced in the business archive of Caecilius Jucundus from Pompeii. A later find, in the so-called Murecine or Sulpician tablets, likewise from the Pompeii area, has, however, supplied an example dated to 15 September AD 39, albeit with the slight variation that the formula is not directly by Divus Augustus, but by his 'divinity', *numen* (the difference is trifling, as will be evident from Chapter 10 below). Also, some scholars have interpreted Suetonius' statement that Caligula executed many for never having sworn by the *Genius* as evidence for this oath formula. However, slaves swore by their master's *Genius*, and Suetonius' remark seems to refer to this practice; he does not say that people *refused* to swear by the *Genius* (i.e. in a newly established public oath), merely that some had never done so.[2] Such oaths therefore reflect long-established private and informal usage. High-ranking freeborn Romans would probably, given a free choice, have avoided such formulation of their own position as a servile one, and even preferred the version implying the emperor's divinity, swearing by his name (for which formula, significantly, no resistance is recorded in our sources).[3] Caligula, however, with his nasty penchant for humiliating senators and others of rank and social pride, would have interpreted such avoidance as refusing to recognize himself as *dominus*.[4] Perhaps the reason for these executions was merely a convenient excuse, but in any case the story has no bearing on the *Genius* in state worship or oaths. Nor does the story that Caligula swore by the *Genius* and *Salus* of his horse Incitatus; it probably reflects a humorous inversion of a common oath formula by the emperor's tutelary divinities, but whether of official or merely private usage, we

[2] Murecine: Camodeca (1999, 164ff.); Weinstock (1971, 213f.); Barrett (1989, 153); Suet. *Cal.* 27. 3, executions e.g. '*quod numquam per genium suum deierasssent*'; compare Tacitus' wording in a case, AD 25, involving refusal to swear the official oath of obedience to the acts of Divus Augustus (*Ann.* 4. 42. 3): '[Tiberius] . . . *Apidiumque Merulam, quod in acta Divi Augusti non iuraverat, albo senatorio erasit*'.

[3] Thus, by the *Genius*, under Augustus and Tiberius: Dio 57. 8. 3; 9. 3; 58. 6. 2; contrast the divine formula, oaths by the name, id. 58. 12. 6 (here explicitly, and revealingly, by senators); 59. 11. 3 (Diva Drusilla).

[4] As later, when suspected Christians were required to swear by the emperor's *Genius*, evidenced in the *Martyr Acts*: Musurillo (1972, *passim*).

cannot know.[5] Only the formula first evidenced in 39 stands; and it seems fairly likely that this official state oath formula would reflect the *Genius* of the emperor as a state god.

There is another bit of possible evidence, a fragment of the *Arval Acta*, commonly restored to mention a sacrifice to the emperor's *Genius*. Since the fragment also mentions Diva Drusilla, Caligula's sister, whom he had deified, it should belong to his reign. But the inscription preserves only '*Gen[. . .]*', and the restoration is in fact quite uncertain. Alternatively, as Panciera has claimed, cult of Diva Drusilla may well have continued beyond Caligula's death, if not much beyond—her deification was never actually revoked, merely ignored; so the fragment might date from the early years of Claudius' reign.[6] This is possible, if not very likely. In any case, it does not matter much. Even if Caligula at some stage changed his mind and had his own *Genius* worshipped in the state cult, this did not create any useful precedent. On the contrary: if Caligula was really the emperor behind this development, that would have been an argument against it. It was far more decisive that Claudius—if not exactly one of the 'good' emperors, then certainly a useful one for establishing precedent—apparently allowed the state worship of his *Genius*. Young Nero is still theoretically possible as the innovator, but as we shall see, there are further arguments for linking this development with Claudius. It is not unimportant—the worship for the first time explicitly formulated the emperor's position in the Roman state (as that of its *paterfamilias*), and considering the social humiliation this would have entailed for the high-ranking senators involved in the cult, the need and pressure for this formulation must have been strong indeed.

[5] Weinstock (1971, 213); cf. Pers. 6. 48 (private games to Caligula's *Genius*); *CIL* VI. 811 (AD 38): '*pro salute et pace et genio Caesaris Augusti*'.

[6] *CIL* VI. 32345 = Scheid (1998, 42); Panciera (1968, 324 n. 41 with Tav. IIa); Scheid (1990, 385 n. 1) believes that the fragment may belong to Caligula's *dies imperii* AD 39, and possibly joins other fragments certainly from that year. An alternative restoration of the text could be a sacrifice to the *Genius populi Romani*, only attested with certainty in the *Acta* from AD 69; or a sacrifice '*gen[ti Iuliae vaccam . . .]*': for the *ara gentis Iuliae*, situated on the Capitol, where the preceding sacrifices of the fragment apparently took place, see E. La Rocca in Steinby (1995, ii. 369 f.) s.v. '*Gens Iulia, ara*' (speculative);

THE '*FRIEZE OF THE VICOMAGISTRI*'

The *Genius* of the emperor appears unequivocally in a source from about this time, namely the so-called *Frieze of the Vicomagistri*, which, judging from its size and technical quality, must have belonged to a state monument. Here young attendants carry statuettes of the emperor's *Genius* and *Lares* in procession. Some disjoined pieces of other, and seemingly contemporary, state reliefs contain similar *Lar* carriers, but they are too fragmentary to allow of interpretation or to show whether the *Genius* may also have been included in these instances.[7]

The frieze was found in two parts in the Campo Marzio under the Palazzo Cancelleria in 1937–9 together with the larger and perhaps more well-known Cancelleria relief panels, belonging to a monument in honour of Domitian. The find context was clearly secondary, a sculptor's workshop, where the reliefs had been taken for reuse, apparently some time during the second century.[8]

The relief slab, preserved at both ends, depicts a religious procession with togate figures, musicians, attendants, and sacrificial animals. Its height is 1.05 m., of which about a third is occupied by sculpted cornices, a narrow one at the top and a broader and more elaborate version at the bottom. The length of the frieze as it is now set up in the Vatican Museums is 4.74 m., but as has been established beyond doubt by Maxwell

however, a text of such fragmentary character should perhaps not be restored at all: nothing can really be gained from the endeavour.

[7] For the *Frieze of the Vicomagistri* see Anderson (1984); Helbig 4th edn., I, 203ff. (E. Simon); Amelung and Lippold (1956, iii. 2. 505ff. with Taf. 229–33 (best photos)); Ryberg (1955, 75ff. with fig. 37a–d); Hölscher in *Kaiser Augustus und die verlorene Republik* (1988, 396ff.). Other *Lar* carriers are found on a fragment of the so-called Valle-Medici reliefs and a fragment from the Lateran collections: Ryberg (1955, 66ff. and 80 with figs. 34–6); Valle-Medici reliefs: Kleiner (1992, 141ff. with lit.). The commonly accepted theory that the Valle-Medici reliefs belonged to the *Ara Pietatis Augustae* has been convincingly questioned by Koeppel (1982, 453ff.) where he reveals this altar to be a construct of modern scholarship. Instead we may think of the *Ara Gentis Iuliae* known from the *Arval Acts*, but the game seems meaningless: the reliefs are simply too fragmentary to allow a convincing reconstruction.

[8] Anderson (1984, 33f.); Cancelleria Panels: Hannestad (1986, 132ff.).

Anderson (1984), a piece is actually missing where the two slabs apparently join. The fact that the two halves of a togate figure appear at first sight to join perfectly must be due to the standard *schemata* employed by the sculptors in representing togate figures. The missing part, entirely from the left slab, was apparently damaged and hence sawn off when the frieze was removed to the sculptor's workshop for reuse. Both the original join and the point where the missing piece was sawn off were naturally placed where the slab was thickest, that is, in the vertical centre of a figure, where the risk of the slab breaking was smallest; so the false join, which was unanimously accepted until Anderson's article, was apparently never intended as such. Anderson has argued convincingly on both structural and compositional grounds that the part missing cannot have been very big. The patternwork on the lower cornice supplies a module for reconstructing the original length of the frieze. Anderson argues for inserting three missing segments of patternwork, 30.7 cm., in the reconstruction; this would give enough space to fill out the two half-figures in the foreground and add another background figure, a scheme which is followed throughout in the frieze. So, according to this reconstruction, the total length of the frieze would have been about 5.05 m. (Fig. 7.1.1).

The frieze must have formed part of a rectangular monument of some kind, for both the left and right edges preserve traces of reliefs, which would have continued on slabs joined at right angles to these edges. To the left is preserved the right half of a boy attendant, a *camillus*, looking left and holding a long-handled *patera* in his left hand (Fig. 7.1.6). The lower part of the figure has been extensively cut down, presumably in

FIG. 7.1.1. The 'Frieze of the Vicomagistri', arranged according to Anderson's reconstruction

the workshop where the relief was found, and the figure must have stood behind or on an object now destroyed, for he is too small for his feet to have reached the ground line. The strong difference in scale between the *camillus* and the figures on the frieze shows, however, that the procession did not continue round the corner. Presumably this should then also apply to the scenes on the missing slab joining the right edge of the frieze; this is important, for it establishes that the procession before us is roughly complete and self-contained, and we should therefore stand a fair chance in venturing an interpretation. On the right edge is clearly preserved only a lion's paw. The rest has been chopped down, but just enough is preserved to show that the paw must have formed part of the hind leg of a throne; of the front leg there remains only the left side of the bottom part, looking like a spinning top (Fig. 7.1.7).[9]

The frieze itself shows, from right to left, two almost frontal togate figures, turning their badly weathered heads towards each other; behind them walk three lictors (Fig. 7.1.5). Then follow two tunicate figures, presumably *camilli*, behind whom three horn-blowers mark the transition to the next group, three bovine victims, each pulled by a *victimarius*, sacrificial butcher (Fig. 7.1.4). The victims are, as noted by Ryberg, a bull, a steer, and a young heifer; somewhat alike at first sight, they are in fact subtly characterized in relation to each other. The bull is larger than the steer, who is again larger than the heifer. Likewise, the bull is stoutly muscular and full of vigour, as shown by his

9 The scheme is roughly the same, in mirror reflection, as the throne of Augustus on the *Gemma Augustea*, where the hind leg is of a slightly simpler form, without the lion paw; compare e.g. the depiction of the *Gemma* in Hannestad (1986, 79).

Fig. 7.1.2. The 'Frieze of the Vicomagistri', detail of left part with a group of togate figures; the presumed emperor is the headless figure fourth from left

vehemently lashing his tail and being held in check by the front *victimarius* only with extreme difficulty. The steer also in these respects forms an intermediate image between the bull and the smaller heifer who is tamely led along, her tail hanging down motionlessly. Trivial at first, perhaps, these details are in fact, as we shall see, important in the characterizations of the victims and the gods to whom they are offered.

After the victims follows a group of musicians (Fig. 7.1.3 and 4). This is where a part of the frieze is missing, so we cannot be entirely sure of their number, but Anderson's reconstruction with two foreground flute players, both half-preserved, and two background lyre players, one entirely preserved and one missing, seems by far the likeliest option. Following the musicians and depicted in almost frontal position come four barefooted youths, dressed in long ungirded tunics and with a shawl, the *ricinium*, draped over their heads (Fig. 7.1.3); this

FIG. 7.1.3. The 'Frieze of the Vicomagistri', detail with young Lar-carriers

uniform marks them as attendants, as they are known from depictions of the compital cults, where the four *ministri* of each cult were dressed like this. The four *ministri* (as we might as well call them, for the time being) each hold objects in their hands; on the first, the objects are broken off, the three following hold statuettes of two *Lares* and a togate *Genius* respectively. The procession is finished off by a group of laureate *togati*, four of whom are shown in a particularly prominent position (Fig. 7.1.2). Apart from the figures described here, the background of the relief is crowded with several minor figures, all laureate, carved in low relief. For instance, behind the bull is shown a *victimarius* carrying a tray with some unidentifiable objects, perhaps parts of a pig to be offered as introductory sacrifice (to the *Lares*?), and behind the heifer a similar figure carries over his left shoulder a rather unusually shaped, small cauldron (for boiling the innards—*exta*—of the victims).

Fig. 7.1.4. The 'Frieze of the Vicomagistri', central part with sacrificial victims (heifer, steer, hind part of bull)

Fig. 7.1.5. The 'Frieze of the Vicomagistri', right end part with victim (bull) and two togate figures heading the procession

FIG. 7.1.6. The 'Frieze of the Vicomagistri', left-hand corner with fragment of sacrificial attendant

FIG. 7.1.7. The 'Frieze of the Vicomagistri', right-hand corner with relief fragment (leg and foot of a throne?)

Though the frieze has been published and depicted countless times in scholarly literature, its iconography has never really received thorough treatment. The name '*Altar of the Vicomagistri*' stems from the four prominent togate figures and four *ministri* on its left part, who have unanimously in scholarship been interpreted as respectively the four *magistri vici* and the four *ministri vici* of a compital cult. Further, the relief has usually been interpreted as forming one side of an altar like the *Ara Pacis*. Here, however, agreement ends.

Inez Scott Ryberg, in the most thorough treatment to date, believed the relief to come from an altar to a personified imperial virtue (like the *Ara Pacis*), and interpreted the bull as a victim to the *Genius* of the emperor, since a statuette of this god was carried in the procession. The steer she saw as a victim to Divus Augustus, a natural choice in connection with the *Genius*, and the heifer should then go to an imperial virtue, such as *Pietas* or the like. Hölscher, on the other hand, believed the monument to have belonged to the shrine of the state *Lares* on the Velia, though he simply ignored the three victims, whose nature seems totally inappropriate in such a context. Both interpretations failed to explain why the staff of a compital cult should participate in such a ceremony. Lastly, Anderson saw the monument as indeed belonging to a compital cult, and again ignored the fact that the three victims seem utterly inappropriate in such a context.

A closer look at the imagery can, I believe, bring us much further, when combined with what we know of Roman sacral law and ritual custom. Interpretation is made difficult by the fact that the relief belongs to such an early stage of depicting religious state ceremonies that the iconographic vocabulary has not yet frozen into the stock depiction of the emperor sacrificing, so well known from later representations (as for instance Fig. 1.1). Thus the ceremony shown on the *Ara Pacis*, the first representative of the tradition during the empire, has even today not received a commonly accepted interpretation.[10] What the depiction of the *Frieze of the Vicomagistri* may, however, lack in symbolic or emblematic clarity on the other hand means that it is more specific in its representation of a particular event. This is not to say that it necessarily gives a reliable or 'photographic' depiction of such an event. But the relief contains a great many details unknown in any of the other, quite numerous, representations of Roman sacrifice known to us, and these details must therefore depend on a particular rite represented, rather than on any stock iconography. To take only one of the more obvious examples, the precise combination of sacrificial victims shown on the frieze is unique in the preserved iconography.

First, we may concentrate our attention on the groups of togate figures and *ministri* ending the procession. The identification of these characters as *magistri* and *ministri vici* has completely overlooked the fact that there are *more* than the customary four togate '*magistri*' here. Hence they are not *magistri*

[10] For the latest attempt, interpreting the ceremony as a *supplicatio*, see Billows (1993); personally I find this interpretation most convincing, but only time can tell if it will gain general acceptance.

vici. There are actually nine of these togate figures in this part of the relief, two of whom stand in the background behind the *ministri*. It is true that four of them are depicted in more prominent positions than the others, and as far as we can see only these four wear the high-girded shoes of the patricians (*calcei patricii*). However, this footwear is also found on the two togate figures at the head of the whole procession, and in any case the patrician shoes were of course not worn by the *magistri vici*, who were overwhelmingly of servile origins. Furthermore, the prominent four in the frieze are clearly not shown on an equal footing, as the quadruplets of the compital cults.[11] The *togatus* at the very left of the frieze is shown in three-quarters profile behind the three more prominent ones, and is thus in an intermediate position between foreground and background figure. So we are left with only three *togati* in the foreground. Even these are not shown in equal positions, for the middle one, most of whose head is unfortunately broken off, is clearly enhanced in relation to the others (Fig. 7.1.2, fourth figure from left). Alone in the entire procession, he is shown in a completely frontal position, even his head apparently having been so. Furthermore, the two *togati* on each side of him both turn their heads to watch him; and lastly, he is slightly taller than any other foreground figure in the relief. It is strange indeed that more attention has not been paid to this figure, for all these means of emphasis are well known in Roman historical reliefs to mark the one figure of exceptional importance in such depictions: the emperor. To name but the most obvious parallel, this is exactly the same scheme employed for the depiction of Claudius in a fragment of the so-called Valle-Medici reliefs, even the gestures of arms and hands being similar.[12]

[11] For *calcei senatorii* and *patricii*, see Pollini (1978, 133ff.).

[12] For such means of compositional emphasis, note also e.g.: frontality: the emperor on the Vesta relief in Palermo (Ryberg, 1955, fig. 27), the sacrificing *togatus* on the Belvedere altar (Ryberg, 1955, fig. 28*b*); height: emperor in Louvre *suovetaurilia* (Ryberg, 1955, fig. 54*a*), Augustus on *Ara Pacis* (e.g. Hannestad, 1986, fig. 45). The common identification of the figure on the Valle-Medici fragment as Claudius has been doubted by some scholars, thus Kleiner (1992, 144), but no strong counter-arguments have in my opinion been presented: the figure is immediately recognizable as Claudius to any observer familiar with his physiognomy in sculpture, and this must have been the case also in antiquity. The fact that his head does not correspond to any

Next, the *ministri*. The fact that their togate followers do not belong to the compital sphere, must establish the same for these youths. It is true that they look exactly like compital *ministri*, but this probably reflects nothing more than that *ministri* in general looked like this when performing their duties, and the compital *ministri* are simply the examples of this species that we know best. Indeed, there is other evidence that such attendants or *ministri* were dressed like this in cults other than the compital ones.[13] The fact that there are four of these attendants here, as in a compital cult, then appears to be no more than a coincidence. In state cults such attendants were not technically termed *ministri*, though performing the same functions, but consisted of two groups: one of these was the *publici*, public slaves assisting at the sacrifices. They were, however, not merely boys, as the four in the frieze, who may instead be identified as belonging to the second group, the *pueri ingenui patrimi et matrimi*, senators' young sons, both of whose parents were alive, so that death would not taint the rites of the celestials. Such youths would by their assisting the priestly colleges get acquainted with the rituals in which they themselves would one day function as priests. The number of four such assistants may not be a complete coincidence: the Arval Brothers likewise had four of them, suggesting that this was perhaps a standard number in some colleges.[14]

The four boys occupy very prominent positions on the

known portrait type is irrelevant to this observation, and is in any case not to be expected in a relief portrait, which could not be 'mechanically' copied to the extent of portraits in the round. The fact that Claudius wears the cap of a *flamen*, the *apex*, may mean that the depiction is 'retrospective', i.e. represents events from before Claudius' accession (such as the Domitianic Cancelleria panel of Vespasian's homecoming in AD 70 (Hannestad, 1986, 132ff.)); but he may well have held the flaminate of *Divus* Augustus after becoming emperor and *pontifex maximus*: though such double tenure was technically not allowed, the Senate would no doubt have granted him a dispensation, had he wanted to keep his flaminate. It does not seem possible to judge whether the figure on the *Frieze of the Vicomagistri* wore the *apex*.

[13] Ryberg (1955, 87f.); cf. Suet. *Aug.* 100. 4: '*Reliquias legerunt primores equestris ordinis, tunicati et discincti pedibusque nudis, ac Mausoleo condiderunt*'.

[14] Wissowa (1912, 496f.); Scheid (1990, 539ff., 547ff. and *passim*); Henzen (1874, 42f.) e.g. p. CV = Scheid (1998, 125 l. 8–10) (AD 80): '. . . *ad peragendum sacrificium per fratres Arvales epulantes et frugibus ministrantibus pueris ingenuis patrimis et matrimis senatorum filis referentibus ad aram in pateris*'.

frieze, in particular the three of them carrying the *Genius* and *Lares*; they are placed almost frontally and are relatively tall as well. Ryberg attempted to explain these features by their being princes of the imperial house, and one scholar has even elaborated further on this, attempting to date the frieze by speculating on the identity of these princes.[15] The problem is, of course, that at no time in the early empire are there enough imperial princes available for this group of four. Furthermore, though Ryberg argues that these statuette carriers look like Julio-Claudian princes, none of their faces corresponds to any known types in this rather confused department of Roman imperial iconography; the similarity is generic, reminding the observer of portraits of Caligula or young Nero simply because the relief belongs to roughly this time (Fig. 7.1.3). The argument is thus based entirely on the prominence accorded these statuette carriers in the depiction, and for this there is a simpler explanation. The youths are brought forward in the composition owing to the importance of the images they carry; simply because of their small size, the statuettes could easily be overlooked. This explanation seems confirmed by the fact that the boys each draw further attention to their small images by pointing at them with their free hand. The youth heading the group is less prominent, and though whatever he carried has broken off, it seems certain that it was not another statuette, which would have left a break. Probably the object he carried was less important to the reading of the scene, hence his more reticent position.[16]

So far I have attempted to establish that the relief depiction, contrary to accepted belief, has in fact no connection with the compital cult; hence the frieze, as we would certainly expect from its size and quality, formed part of a state monument, depicting a state cult. The question now is, which cult?

[15] Ryberg (1955, 79f.); Alföldi (1973, 28f.), who devotes a whole chapter to princes as *Lar* carriers; but there is no evidence that members of the imperial family ever performed such functions.

[16] From the remnant preserved by his right hand, Ryberg believed the object to have been a book scroll partially unrolled; a small scroll seems likely indeed, but since no break is visible between his hands, it was probably held, rolled up, in his right hand only, any—other—object in his left hand being completely destroyed.

To answer this, the sacrificial victims are decisive, and their nature and order in fact gives the answer. The creatures have simply been ignored by most interpreters, whose attempts will not be dealt with here. Ryberg, however, took the animals seriously. Owing to the appearance of the statuette of the emperor's *Genius*, she saw the bull as the victim to this god, and considered the steer behind it to be a victim to Divus Augustus (though not really presenting any arguments, she was probably right, as we shall see). Lastly, the heifer would, she believed, go to an imperial virtue, such as *Pietas* or *Pax Augusta*. The interpretation depends on the commonly accepted idea that the frieze belonged to an altar on the lines of the *Ara Pacis*, and the individual animals would certainly fit the gods she proposed. I shall later return to the problem as to which type of monument the relief may have belonged; any answer to this question should, however, depend on the interpretation of the frieze itself, not the other way round.

Ryberg ignored one important aspect, namely the order of each animal in the procession: *first* the bull, *second* the steer, *third* the heifer. This order should reflect the order of the sacrifice and the relative rank of the three gods involved. Rome was a strictly hierarchical society, among gods as well as among men. This is clearly confirmed by the *Arval Acta* where the rank of each god worshipped is strictly codified and followed without variation all through the first century.[17] For instance, in sacrifices to the Capitoline triad, the order of sacrifice was always first Jupiter, then Juno, then Minerva. Numerous examples can be adduced to show the importance of ranking in such listings of gods (and men).[18] So, the god receiving the bull was the highest-ranking in the triad of the frieze. The relative

[17] For the Arval college, see Scheid (1990). Variation is encountered only in connection with minor gods, recently admitted: namely imperial characteristics; thus in 59 Nero's *Salus* is listed after his *Genius* (Scheid (1998, 71 l. 37 = *CIL* VI. 2042. l. 37)), in 55 apparently before the *Genius* (Scheid (1998, 57 = *CIL* VI. 32352)): but note the faulty MS tradition; the *Salus Publica* is always listed before the emperor's *Genius*. However, the emperor's *Salus* and *Genius* always, as would be expected, appear in direct connection with each other in the *Acta*, so the steer of the frieze, placed between the bull and the heifer, in any case seems to exclude the possibility that the heifer is to be offered to the emperor's *Salus*.

[18] e.g. Herod. 5. 5. 7; Tac. *Ann.* 3. 64.

status of the major Roman state gods in the early empire is known very well from the *Arval Acta*. Let me begin with the steer, the *bos mas* in Roman sacral terminology. Usually in Roman sacrifice, the characteristics of the victim, including its sex, corresponded with those of the god to whom it was offered. In fact, not many gods received the infertile steer as victim, only male and infertile gods, such as those of the underworld; also, and oddly (since, at least in historical times, infertility seems inappropriate), Jupiter; and lastly, modelled on Jupiter's case, male *Divi*.[19] Now, Jupiter is out of the question in this case, since he was the most high-ranking of all gods, and his victim should therefore have headed the procession of the animals here. Gods of the underworld, such as Pluto, would be utterly inappropriate in connection with the living emperor's *Genius* whose image is also carried in the procession. So we are left with a *Divus*: till AD 54 Divus Augustus would be the only candidate. Next, we have the heifer, the *vacca* in the Roman terminology. Imperial virtues—*Pax* or *Pietas Augusta* or others—uniformly ranked over the *Divi* (and over the living emperor's *Genius*), so Ryberg's suggestion should be rejected. In fact, the only goddess ranking below a *Divus* was a *Diva*, so the *vacca* must be to a deceased and deified empress.

The Arval Brothers worshipped all the *Divi* together, beginning with Divus Augustus and then adding later *Divi*. Presumably this was typical in the state cult. So the fact that we are here dealing with one *Divus* and one *Diva* allows a dating. Claudius deified Livia as Diva Augusta in AD 42; in AD 54 he was himself deified as Divus Claudius (oddly, he ranked *below* Diva Augusta, which presumably reflects the fact that the ranking of *Divi* must have depended less on sex than on seniority). Since the heifer is not followed by a steer to Divus Claudius, the frieze must antedate his deification.

This suggests a date between 42 and 54; annoyingly, there is, however, an earlier, albeit short-lived *Diva*, namely Caligula's sister Drusilla. I shall postpone her case a little, since it

[19] For types of victims and the identification of the *bos mas* with a steer, see p. 22 above. The intermediate victim of the frieze must beyond doubt be a *bos mas*, since the only male bovine victims known from the *Arval Acta* are the *bos mas* and the *taurus*, clearly the animal heading the procession, as known also from numerous depictions of the *suovetaurilia*.

depends on further interpretation of the frieze. There is still the bull—*taurus*—to be dealt with. The statuette of the emperor's *Genius* makes this god a likely candidate, who would fit the sequence, for this god ranked over the *Divi*. There are, however, other possibilities, such as, for example, Mars or Apollo. Once again, the *Arval Acta* must be called upon to settle the question: the only bull-demanding god worshipped with the *Divi* was in fact the living emperor's *Genius*. A good example, containing our triad, is the Brothers' sacrifices in 58 on 13 October, anniversary of Nero's accession:[20]

. . . *L. Salvius Otho Titianus mag(ister) collegi fratrum Arvalium nomine immolavit in Capitolio ob imperium Neronis Claudi Caesaris Aug(usti) Germanici Iovi b(ovem) marem, Iunoni vaccam, Minervae vacc(am), Felicitati publicae vacc(am), Genio ipsius* [sc. Neronis] *taurum, Divo Aug(usto) b(ovem) marem, Divae Aug(ustae) vaccam, Divo Claudio b(ovem) marem.*

. . . L. Salvius Otho Titianus, chairman of the college, sacrificed in the name of the Arval Brothers on the Capitol for the [anniversary of the] accession of Nero Claudius Caesar Augustus Germanicus: to Jupiter a steer, to Juno a cow, to Minerva a cow, to public Felicity a cow, to his [i.e. Nero's] *Genius* a bull, to Divus Augustus a steer, to Diva Augusta a cow, to Divus Claudius a steer.

We may also reverse the chain of argument: if the bull was to the emperor's *Genius*, the steer and the heifer must have been to a *Divus* and a *Diva* respectively. For *Divi* were the only state gods who ranked under the emperor's *Genius*.

The gods worshipped in the procession have now, I believe, been identified. The next questions must be when and where; what was the occasion for this particular rite, obviously of some importance in imperial ideology, and where did it take place?

As mentioned, the *Arval Acta* from 55 onwards contain several examples of sacrifices to the living emperor's *Genius*. Usually the god was worshipped with the *Divi*, as on our frieze, but also in most instances with the Capitoline triad, as in the specimen of the *Acta* quoted above; in these cases the rites therefore took place on the Capitol. The Arval records contain only one instance where the sacrifices of the college included only the *Divi* and the emperor's *Genius* (and, parallel

[20] Scheid (1998, 65 = *CIL* VI. 2041).

with this, the *Juno* of the empress, first recorded in the latter part of Nero's reign). This rite is found in the *Acta* from the year 66 and took place 'in the new temple of Divus Augustus' (*[in templo Divi Augusti] novo*).[21]

The Arval rites of 66 thus seem to point to this temple for our procession. The sanctuary is known from numerous sources. Though voted by the Senate immediately after Augustus' death and completed under Tiberius, it was only dedicated by Caligula on his own birthday in 37. It was clearly the main state temple to Divus Augustus in Rome, pivotal to the ideology of the Julio-Claudian dynasty; yet its relationship to other temples to Divus Augustus in Rome remains somewhat obscure, for the terminology of the sources is not very consistent.[22]

It seems clear, however, that the 'new temple of Divus Augustus' was rededicated already in 42 to house also his wife Livia, deified by Claudius on 17 January that year under the name of Diva Augusta. The date was the anniversary of her wedding to Augustus, and her statue was placed in the temple, seated next to that of her husband.[23] The deification was of immense ideological value to Claudius and his claim to the throne. Proclaimed by the Praetorians against the wish of the Senate, Claudius had greater problems with claiming legitimacy as emperor than any of his predecessors, and he was furthermore the first of Augustus' successors who did not descend from the first emperor. His link to Augustus, of vital importance to all the Julio-Claudian rulers, went through his grandmother by blood, Augustus' wife Livia. So there is nothing surprising in his stressing this connection by getting the Senate to pay Livia the crowning honour, even though she had in fact been dead for thirteen years.

[21] Scheid (1998, 81 l. 5ff. = *CIL* VI. 2044c. l. 5ff.): fragmentary, but the restoration of the emperor's *Genius* seems assured by the last god in the listing: '*[. . . Iunoni] Messalinae vacc(am)*'.

[22] Dio 59. 7; see now Fishwick (1992).

[23] Dio 60. 5. 2; the date is given in the *Arval Acta*, Scheid (1998, 45f. = *CIL* VI. 2032): '*XVI k(alendas) Febr(uarias): [ob consecr]ationem Divae Aug(ustae) i[n] tem[plo novo] Divo Augusto bovem mar[em, Divae Augusta]e vaccam*'; the year by inscriptional evidence. The two statues are depicted on coins issued under Antoninus Pius: BMC, Ant. P., 352, no. 2064.

In my view, this consecration is probably the ceremony shown on the frieze, and as we shall see there are actually further reasons for connecting the relief with the *templum novum*. However, as I mentioned above, there was an earlier *Diva*, Caligula's sister Drusilla, dead and consecrated in 38 and dropped from the pantheon shortly after the murder of her brother. But whereas we know that Diva Augusta was consecrated in the temple of Augustus and worshipped with him there, that was not the case for Diva Drusilla. On the contrary, Dio, who gives a long list of her divine honours, mentions that she was instated in the temple of Venus Genetrix, to be worshipped there with the ancestress of the Julian house, and that furthermore a temple was to be built to Diva Drusilla in her own right.[24] So whereas she and Augustus could of course be worshipped together in individual ceremonies, they shared no established cult. The procession of the frieze, clearly an occasion of pivotal importance, since it was depicted on this stately monument, would thus not fit Drusilla very well.

I have already claimed that a figure of central compositional importance, unfortunately without his head, is shown in the procession, and that he must be an emperor. This figure, enhanced in the group of *togati* in the left part of the frieze, and hence at the beginning of the 'reading direction', would then be Claudius. He is depicted as taking part in the procession marking the consecration of Livia and the rededication of the temple to both ancestors of the dynasty. One may object that Claudius does not head the procession. This function is performed by two togate figures, rather small so as not to steal the focus of attention, but wearing the patrician boots (*calcei patricii*) also shown on the feet of Claudius and his three prominent peers at the left end. The two togate figures at the head of the procession have been claimed to be the consuls of the year, but the number of three lictors accompanying them does not fit this theory. Indeed we must ask who are all these togate figures, and there is an obvious answer, namely the *sodales Augustales*. This priestly college was established in 14 for the worship of Divus Augustus, and was henceforth closely connected with the imperial family and its *Divi*, to the extent

[24] Dio 59. 11. 1ff.

that Tacitus characterized it as the personal priesthood of the imperial house (*proprium eius domus sacerdotium*). The *sodales* were 21 in number, to which were added members of the ruling family. Claudius was a member, and is then shown on the frieze among a representative sample of his fellow priests; the two small togate leaders of the procession would then be *magistri* of the college for this particular year. Their three lictors may seem a strange number, but this actually lends some support to my identification of the college. The *sodales Augustales* were headed by three annual *magistri*; this is presumably reflected in the three lictors, one to accompany each official. The fact that we only have two *magistri* here is not a great problem: there is good evidence that the college still functioned if one or more of them were absent, which must often have been the case.[25] The lictors here carry both *fasces* and reed-like rods, which set them apart from lictors as we usually see them depicted; they must be of the kind attending priestly colleges, the *lictores curiatii*, of whom we know very little.[26]

The placement of Claudius is interesting, but entirely explicable in consideration of the time of the ceremony, 17 January 42. He is shown among his peers as a fellow senator, no more, and is brought forward in the depiction by compositional means only. In the early part of his reign, particularly before the rebellion of Camillus Scribonianus in Dalmatia later in 42, Claudius went to great lengths to accommodate the leading

[25] *Sodales Augustales*: Tac. *Ann.* 1. 54; 2. 83. 1; 3. 64; Claudius a member: Suet. *Claud.* 6. 2; *CIL* III. 381; three annual *magistri*: Degrassi (1947, 311–15) (fragments of the *Fasti* of the college); absence of *magistri*: the *Tabula Hebana* l. 59ff. (Crawford, 1996, no. 37) speaks of the *sodales Augustales* at the annual memorial service to the dead Germanicus. To ensure that the total number of *magistri* would always be present at the ceremony, those of them unable to attend (61: '*unus pluresve*') should be replaced for the occasion by *magistri* designated for future years. The extraordinary and extremely honorary measures, decreed to ensure that their total number would always be present at this particular ceremony, suggests that they, under normal circumstances, regularly functioned even though one or more *magistri* were absent (as here, if my interpretation holds).

[26] *Lictores curiatii*: Ryberg (1955, 45f. and *passim*); Mommsen (1887–8, i. 374ff.). The iconography of these attendants is confusingly varied as to their number and whether they carry only the rods or the *fasces* as well; Schäfer (1989, 227ff.).

senators and distance himself from the absolutist pretensions of his predecessor. After Caligula's murder, the top men of the Senate had refused to recognize Claudius, and had in fact been forced to do so only because Claudius had the backing of the military units present in Rome. Neither party forgot the events of those days, but Claudius did his utmost to appear modest as well as legitimate, and actually honoured the amnesty he had granted for these senators.[27] The depiction of the frieze would indeed fit this dating admirably.

The monument must, however, have been made and set up in connection with rebuilding of some sort. Once again, a closer look at the slabs furnishes us with some clues. It has usually been seen as forming part of an altar like the *Ara Pacis*, or the altar from which stem the so-called Valle-Medici reliefs. Yet its dimensions do not make such a reconstruction obvious. Whereas the processional reliefs on the north and south sides of the circuit wall of the *Ara Pacis* measure *c.*1.55 m. in height, the height of the figural part of our frieze measures only *c.*65 cm.; and the figural frieze on the *Ara Pacis* itself measures only about half of that figure.[28] There is more. The missing slabs joining the frieze at right angles by its right and left edges are cut through by the join: rather inelegant for a monument meant to be walked around and seen from all sides. On the *Ara Pacis*, this problem was avoided in the obvious way, namely by corner pilasters. The fact that this was not done on our frieze must indicate that the sides joining it were secondary, and that the front of the monument, namely the part preserved, was that of the main or optimum view. Furthermore, we may note the state of preservation. The right part of the frieze was discovered face up, and due to this position its surface is rather worn and weathered. The left part, however, lay with its face down, and its surface is in a remarkably pristine condition. This was also the case for the Domitianic Cancelleria reliefs found next to the frieze, but in this case the brilliant preservation seems to be accounted for, since the slabs were apparently never placed on whatever monument they were meant for, or

[27] Levick (1990, 60; 93f. and *passim*).

[28] Ara Pacis, 1.55 m.: Moretti (1948, Tav. IV, VI, XII); frieze on the altar itself: 39 cm. (id., Tav. VI: the measurement includes the upper and lower cornices; without, the height of the frieze appears to be *c.*32 cm.).

were placed there only briefly.[29] This seems much more difficult to believe in the case of the older frieze, but as with the Cancelleria reliefs the reason must be that the monument had always stood indoors. Lastly, the massive bottom cornice, above which the frieze tapers inwards, would appear very clumsy if placed as the processional reliefs of the *Ara Pacis*. This element actually seems to indicate that this part more or less finished off the bottom of the whole monument, not only the frieze: placed far above the ground, the cornix would appear too heavy. Actually, the 'optimum view' of the figural relief, the point from which it was meant to be seen, appears when it is raised about a metre, no more, above ground level.[30]

All these features of the frieze seem to point to one type of monument only: a statue base in a temple. The frieze would then have constituted the front covering panel on the concrete core of such a base for the cult image, or images, in a temple. Placed there, the panels joining the frieze to the right and left would have been in the shade and accessible only through a narrow passage between the base and the side walls of the temple. The 'optimum view' would, overwhelmingly, have been the frontal one towards the cult images and the base. Furthermore, the bottom cornice would then really have constituted the bottom of the base, or been quite close to it. And the size of the frieze would be perfect for two colossal statues.

There can be little doubt that alterations were in fact made to the statue base in the *templum novum* when Livia was consecrated there. On that occasion, her statue was placed as cult image in the temple, next to that of Augustus.[31] Furthermore, it seems reasonable to infer that the base actually had to be enlarged to accommodate two statues instead of one. Perhaps

[29] Hannestad (1986, 132ff., esp. 133).

[30] This is evident when the monument is studied by autopsy, as I did in 1991; the 'optimum view' is the point at which the relief is displayed to greatest advantage for a viewer standing in front of it, or, in other words, from which the execution of the monument made it meant to be seen. For instance, the figures on the triumphal reliefs in the archway of the Arch of Titus are not completely vertical, but taper outwards from the bottom upwards, because the scenes were to be seen by spectators standing below them; this feature is not present in the frieze.

[31] Dio 60. 5. 2; the two statues are depicted next to each other in the temple on coins of Antoninus Pius, see n. 23 above.

even Augustus' statue was exchanged, being too big to be pushed to one side of the base. A story in Dio about Claudius, recounted under the year 42, lends some support for this:[32]

He was constantly giving gladiatorial contests; for he took great pleasure in them, so that he even aroused criticism on this score. Very few wild beasts perished, but a great many human beings did, some of them fighting with one another and others being devoured by the animals. For the emperor cordially detested the slaves and freedmen who in the reigns of Tiberius and Gaius had conspired against their masters, as well as those who had laid false information against others without cause or had borne false witness against them, and he accordingly got rid of most of them in the manner related, though he punished some in another way, and handed many over to their masters themselves for punishment. So great, indeed, was the number becoming of those who were publicly executed, that the statue of Augustus which stood on the spot was taken elsewhere, so that it should not either seem to be witnessing the bloodshed or else be always covered up. By this action Claudius brought ridicule upon himself, as he was gorging himself upon the very sights that he did not think it fitting for even the inanimate bronze to behold.

The bronze image featured here was a famous one: the seated and radiate statue of Divus Augustus by the theatre of Marcellus, mentioned in several sources and depicted on Tiberius' coinage (Fig. 7.3.A). It was dedicated in 22 by Livia in person, on the anniversary of Augustus' adoption of Tiberius; by placing her own name first in the dedicatory inscription, Livia was believed to have caused great offence to her touchy son Tiberius. The event of the dedication was entered in the *Fasti Praenestini*, and the Arval Brothers sacrificed in front of the statue.[33] Dio's story quoted here, under the year 42, is the latest testimony to its existence; after that, it disappears from the record. We can now perhaps say why: it was wrapped up for transport and removed from its

[32] Dio 60. 13. 1–3; tr. Cary, Loeb edn.

[33] Statue, generally, with sources and refs.: Torelli (1982, 67ff.); coins: BMC I, 130, nos. 74–5 with pls. 23. 17; offence: Tac. *Ann.* 3. 64. 1f.; *Fasti Præn.*: Degrassi (1963, 477), cf. Torelli (1982, 69 with n. 27); Arval sacrifice, in 38 on the anniversary of the original dedication: Scheid (1998, 30 l. 24–6); theatre of Marcellus and Augustan ideology: P. Gros in *L'Urbs* (1987), 319–46.

location to be the new cult image in the *templum novum*. Popular gossip, however, followed by Dio, found another and juicier explanation, clearly nonsensical. The cult statue of Livia, presumably made for the occasion in 42, was closely modelled to match it; it is depicted on an issue from the Roman mint featuring on the obverse the radiate head of Divus Augustus, on the reverse the seated statue of the new *Diva* (Fig. 7.3.B). Though the coin type is undated, there can be little doubt that it belongs to the event celebrated in 42.[34]

The missing frieze slabs joining the left and right edge of our preserved part with its procession would presumably have shown other scenes from the consecration and rededication of the *templum novum*, henceforth sometimes termed *templum Divi Augusti et Divae Augustae*. The part on the right, where the edge of a throne is preserved (Fig. 7.1.7) would then have depicted the new, colossal cult images of the *Divus* and the *Diva*, or one of them, with perhaps a sacrifice taking place before the image(s). On the left edge is preserved part of a *camillus* holding a long-handled *patera*. Some object, almost completely chopped down, was placed in front of the lower half of the figure, for his feet cannot have reached the ground line (Fig. 7.1.6). In any case, the figure testifies that a sacrifice must have been depicted on this side. The boy, with stance, long-handled *patera* and all, has a close parallel in a beautiful sestertius type of Caligula's, celebrating his dedication of the temple of Augustus in 37 and depicting his dedicatory sacrifice in front of the building (Fig. 7.2).[35] This similarity may not be entirely coincidental. The small scale of the *camillus* indicates that the slab contained an important object of superhuman dimensions; the obvious guess would be, as on the sestertius, the temple, with Claudius sacrificing in front of it at its rededication. For such a depiction, the compositional scheme already existed.

[34] BMC I. 195, no. 224 with pl. 37. 7; the statue is apparently shown again on an issue of Galba, id., 317, no. 54 with pl. 55. 16.

[35] BMC, I. 253 no. 41 ff. with pls. 28. 6 and 9.

THE *GENIUS AUGUSTI* IN STATE CULT

On the reconstruction proposed above, it was only at a rather late stage that the ruling emperor's *Genius* joined the state pantheon of Rome. The decisive development in this direction took place under Claudius, who joined this cult to that of his deified ancestress Livia and her husband Augustus. The ideological connotations were obvious, stressing Claudius as the true heir of Augustus. With the worship of his *Genius*, the emperor's position in the state was for the first time clearly expressed in constitutional terms as that of a *paterfamilias* for the whole Roman people. I say for the first time, because the title *pater patriae* had till that time been merely honorary, involving no practical consequences or formalized powers. Even so, it was not entirely innocuous; by implication, if the emperor was a mega-*paterfamilias*, his fellow senators would be his *clientes*, that is occupying a servile position in relation to him. So the title *pater patriae* had indeed seemed to disappear with Augustus; his successor Tiberius, always extremely cautious and deferential in his formal dealings with the Senate, had never accepted it. Caligula, however, took it very early in his reign, but his case could hardly have been a recommendation.

What ensured the title's permanent place in imperial nomenclature was the fact that Claudius followed Caligula's precedent in this regard. Clearly the title must have been important to him: he needed a formal definition of powers and *auctoritas* he could not claim merely on the basis of blood or election by the Senate. Claudius apparently went one step further and linked the title with its logical consequence in practice, namely state worship of his own *Genius*, as the *Genius* of a *paterfamilias* was worshipped by his *familia* in the Roman household. (Even if we accept that Caligula's *Genius* also received state worship during his reign, this development clearly belongs to a significantly later stage than his becoming *pater patriae* in Sept. 37.) The chronological link is important here: Claudius received the title of *pater patriae* on 12 January 42, and Livia's deification took place on 17—hardly by sheer coincidence.[36] At her consecration

[36] *Pater patriae*: Scheid (1998, 45 = *CIL* VI. 2032); Scheid (1990, 434) for the exact date.

in the temple of Divus Augustus, Claudius' *Genius*, as we have seen, was apparently included in the ritual. The cult of the ruling emperor's *Genius* henceforth was probably centred around this temple. There was, however, a clear limit to this god's prominence: he did not receive a cult statue in the temple, nor was it apparently ever consecrated to him. Indeed, the god never seems to have received a temple in Rome (nor in any other public cult). His reticent position in the state pantheon must have been calculated to minimize the provocation involved in this worship.

With our Judaeo-Christian mental baggage we may find it hard to grasp the extent of this provocation. Surely, the measure was moderate in relation to outright state deification of the emperor? The fact remains, however, that the Roman state cult is the only example known to us in the whole empire of the emperor's *Genius* being worshipped by freeborn persons of high rank, whereas divine worship was ubiquitous in city cults from Augustus onwards. And even in Rome, the custom of *Genius* worship did not last very long.

The worship of the *Genius*, as we have already seen, continued under Nero in the form given it by Claudius. Indeed it appears from the *Arval Acta* to have grown much more frequent, being no longer confined to the main imperial feast days, the emperor's *dies natalis* and *dies imperii*. In accordance with this increasing prominence, the god was even depicted in Nero's late coinage, shown sacrificing and surrounded by the legend *Genio Augusti* (Fig. 5.4). This *Genius* was, however, not the togate one familiar from the house cult, from the *Compita*, and from the statuette carried in the 'Vicomagistri Frieze', but the heroically semi-nude iconography of the *Genius populi Romani* (or *Genius Publicus*).[37] Perhaps not very surprising: right from Augustus, the state cult had regularly replaced prayers, sacrifices, and ceremonies for the Roman state and its people by the person of the emperor. In the light of this, the *Genius* of the Roman people must have come to look somewhat anachronistic as a cult object, and its replacement by the emperor's *Genius*, as suggested by the iconography of the Neronian coin type, entirely logical (cf. p. 132–8 above).

[37] BMC I. 248, no. 251–3 with pl. 45. 1; 272, no. 366–72 with pl. 47. 3–4; Kunckel (1974, Taf. 4. 3–4), *passim* for the iconography of *Genii*.

Logical perhaps, but not harmless; the absolutist pretensions inherent in the cult and the new iconography of the god were unmistakable. The frequent worship of the monarch's *Genius* seen in Nero's later years continued, probably routinely, under his short-lived successors Galba, Otho, and Vitellius, again judging from the *Arval Acta* (as usual our only parameter for judging developments in the state cult at large). With Vespasian, however, a reaction appears to set in. We have practically no *Arval Acta* preserved from his reign, but on his coinage, and later that of Titus, is again shown the semi-nude *Genius* sacrificing: exactly the same depiction as under Nero, but now carrying the inscription *Genio p(opuli) R(omani)*.[38] The type appears already in Vespasian's first year, and it is difficult to see it as anything but a deliberate refutation of Nero's similar, yet differently labelled coin type. Likewise, the *Arval Acta* are completely preserved from the last year of Titus, and the emperor's *Genius* is totally absent. So are in fact the *Divi* after Nero, and there is certainly the possibility that other reasons, such as economy, lie behind the more modest rites of the Arval Brothers in this period, as compared with the sumptuous Julio-Claudian entries.[39] In any case, the Flavians would obviously have had less interest in the *Divi* of the earlier dynasty, with whom Vespasian, as the first of Nero's successors, could not claim even the most tenuous family link. The argument is not, however, valid for the living emperor's *Genius*, and taken in conjunction with the imagery of the coins, there should be little doubt that this god really did disappear from the state pantheon, presumably expunged when the Senate in 70 ordered a commision to 'clear out in the public calendars

[38] BMC II. 85, no. 417f. with pl. 14. 14f. (denarius, Illyrian issue, 69–70); RIC II. 94, no. 677 (as, Titus, 76); BMC II. 266, no. 210 with pl. 50. 10 (as, Titus, 80–1); Kunckel (1974, Taf. 1. 6–7). The *Genius populi Romani* also appears on anonymous civil war emissions from Spain and Gaul in 68, as an emblem of the Roman people in rebellion against the tyrant Nero. Usually only a bust of the *Genius* is shown, only one of the Spanish issues likewise copies (and refutes) the Neronian type (Kunckel, 1974, 116, nos. 3–7); the Vespasianic type clearly exploits these emissions and their ideological implications.

[39] The birthday of the living emperor is not found in the *Arval Acta* after 69 (Henzen, 1874, 54), though the day was certainly celebrated in the state cult at large.

FIG. 7.2. Sestertius of Caligula
Notes: Obverse: Pietas seated; reverse: Caligula sacrificing at the dedication of the temple of Divus Augustus in AD 37.

FIG. 7.3. A: Sestertius of Tiberius, AD 22–23, showing the statue of Divus Augustus by the theatre of Marcellus, altar in front; B: As, *c.*AD 42, reverse: Diva Augusta

(*Fasti*) which had become foully sullied by the flattery of the times', as Tacitus says.[40] Vespasian and his Senate thereby reverted to the Augustan model, implicitly rejecting later developments in the formal definition of the imperial position as aberrations. The emperor was again first among equals.

The emperor's *Genius* returns, however, in the *Arval Acta* under Domitian, a mere fortnight after his accession.[41] So his

[40] Tac. *Hist.* 4. 40. 2: '*Tum sorte ducti, per quos redderentur bello rapta, quique aera legum vetustate delapsa noscerent figerentque et fastos adulatione temporum foedatos exonerarent modumque publicis impensis facerent*'.

[41] The Brothers sacrificed on the Capitol '*ob votorum [co]mmendandorum causa pro salute et incolumitate . . . Domitiani Aug(usti)*'; Scheid (1998, 131 l. 43 = *CIL* VI. 2060 l. 43); commentary by Scheid (1990, 344f.). That the sacrifice was in fact the first time the practice was revived by the Brothers

permission for this worship must have been almost immediate. This is the only instance of such a sacrifice in the *Acta* from his reign. It is a general problem that the much scantier number of ceremonies carried out by the Arval Brothers in this period, as opposed to the Julio-Claudian era, makes the activities of the college much less informative as a reflection of the state cult at large. There is, however, confirmation from elsewhere that Domitian's *Genius* did in fact receive state sacrifices during his reign.

With Domitian's death, a new dawn broke in the relationship between emperor and Senate; it is hardly a coincidence that our only literary source mentioning state worship of the emperor's *Genius* belongs to this time. The younger Pliny in his *Panegyric to Trajan* gives us a detailed portrayal of a good versus a bad emperor. After lauding Trajan's modesty in rejecting his own statues to be set up with those of the gods—unlike Domitian—the speaker continues:[42] 'With similar reverence, Caesar, you will not suffer public thanks for your benevolence to be offered to your *Genius*, but direct them to the godhead of Jupiter Best and Greatest; to him, you say, we owe whatever we owe you, and your benefactions are the gift of him who gave you to us'.

The notion of the emperor as Jupiter's viceregent on earth is particularly strong in this period, but this is not what concerns us here.[43] Pliny's didactic tone is, in spite of all humility, unmistakable, and he goes on to describe vast sacrifices offered to Domitian as further example of his impious *superbia*.[44] The sacrifices to Jupiter are paralleled, somewhat oddly, with state worship of the emperor's *Genius*, which by implication must have taken place under Domitian. Pliny's opposition to this worship does not fit very well with his main theme here of irreverence to the gods: worship of the *Genius* would of course

seems confirmed by the preceding entry from 14 Sept. 81, Domitian's *dies imperii*, where their sacrifices on the Capitol did *not* include the *Genius*, though this had apparently always been the case under Nero and his short-lived successors.

[42] Plin. *Pan.* 52. 6: '*Simili reverentia, Caesar, non apud genium tuum bonitati tuae gratias agi, sed apud numen Iovis optimi maximi pateris: illi debere nos quidquid tibi debeamus, illius quod bene facias, muneris esse qui te dedit*'. Tr. Radice, Loeb edn., adapted; Sauter (1934, 42); cf. (private worship by an *Aug. lib.*) Stat. *Silv.* 5. 1. 73ff.; 186ff.

[43] Fears (1981, 79ff.).

[44] See further p. 227f below.

in no way exclude worship of Jupiter. There was no question of an either-or, nor could there ever have been any aspect of competition between the two gods, as is clearly evident from the inferior ranking of the *Genius* in such ceremonies. But the point of the argument is not logical coherence on the theological level: allowing his own *Genius* to be worshipped in state ceremonies was irreconcilable with the *moderatio* required of an emperor by Pliny. His *Panegyric* holds up a mirror reflection of the ideal emperor from the point of view of a high-ranking senator. State worship of the emperor's *Genius* was unacceptable because it defined the high-born priests and other senators involved in such cult as servile *clientes* of the emperor.

Pliny's passage shows that after Domitian the ruling emperor's *Genius* was once again dropped from the state cult. This seems confirmed from the *Arval Acta* where there is no trace of such worship under Trajan, Hadrian, and Antoninus Pius. Although we possess few fragments of the *Arval Acta* from this period, and the Brothers appear to have performed only their own cult of Dea Dia and the new year vows, we may reasonably assume that Trajan's precedent was followed, and that the *Genius* of the ruling emperor did not receive state worship in this period.

It is, however, encountered again in a fragment of the *Arval Acta* from AD 176, thus, surprisingly, from the reign of the 'good' emperor Marcus.[45] The formula employed in the fragment may supply us with information as to when the god reappeared in the state cult; the sacrifice is, uniquely, recorded as *Genio imperatoris*. The use of the supreme military title suggests that the Senate reintroduced this worship in Marcus' absence, when the emperor fought his Germanic wars, and later dealt with the aftermath of Avidius Cassius' rebellion in the east; in fact, he was absent from Rome for almost eight years (169–76),[46] perhaps including the time of the sacrifice in the fragment (summer?). On the interpretation advanced here, it seems surprising that he should have allowed its reintroduction after the series of 'bad' emperors, who had formerly enjoyed such worship. But presumably, at this late stage, its

[45] Scheid (1998, 252 l. 7).
[46] Birley (1966, 268f.).

ideological sting had worn off: the emperor was by now in any case an unquestioned *dominus*.

The worship of the *Genius Augusti* is probably again evidenced in the *Acta* from the next of the 'bad' emperors, Commodus, but now simply carried on, we may presume, from the later reign of his father Marcus.[47] From the reign of Septimius Severus, no *Acta* are preserved, but the emperor's *Genius* was certainly cultivated by the Brothers under Caracalla (211–17), Severus Alexander (222–35), and Gordian III (238–44), after whose reign the Arval college apparently ceased to record their ceremonies on inscriptions.[48]

There is a further, albeit tenuous, argument for expanding this list of emperors. In the sacred grove of the college was a building, usually called in the inscriptions *tetrastylum*, where many of the Brothers' rites took place. The same construction, apparently, is called *Caesareum* or *aedes Caesarei* in the *Acta* from 81 and a slightly later year (Domitian), 183 (Commodus), 218 (Elagabalus), 224 (Severus Alexander), and 240 (Gordian III).[49] This alternative term Mommsen explained as caused by the sacrifices to the *Divi* performed there in the instances from 183, 218, and 224.[50] But for these ceremonies the term *aedes Divorum* or the like would have been more appropriate. On the occasion in 224, however, the sacrifices *ante Caesareum* also included the *Genius* of the ruling emperor; and in 240, under

[47] Henzen (1874, 112f.); Scheid (1990, 293f.; 1998, 265 and 272): AD 183 and 186, sacrifices '*pro salute Augusti* (186: *[. . .] in Cap[itolio . . .] . . . [Iovi o. m.] bovem marem, [Iunoni reginae vaccam, Minervae vaccam, Sa]luti vaccam, [Providentiae deorum vaccam, genio ipsius] taurum*.)' The restoration of the *Genius* seems likely from the ranking of the gods involved in the sacrifices; furthermore, the term *Caesareum* is found in the *Acta* from 183; see below.

[48] Henzen (1874, 210, Index) s.v. *Genius*; Gordian III: see n. 49 below.

[49] Henzen (1874, 20, 24, 148). AD 81 (Scheid (1998, 130 l. 15)): May rites to Dea Dia under Titus, but engraved under Domitian—the later year, with the same rites, is after 81, but before 86 (Scheid (1998, 139)); 218: under Macrinus, but engraved under Elagabal (Scheid (1998, 293 l. 4)); 240: Scheid (1998, 332 l. 16). It is not entirely certain that the two terms *tetrastylum* and *Caesareum*/*aedes Caesarei* do refer to the same building (*contra* Henzen (1874, XXIf.), but Scheid (1990, 113ff.) argues convincingly in favour of the idea). The discussion is, however, irrelevant in this context, since it hardly touches the proposition put forward here on the term *Caesareum*.

[50] Mommsen (1905, 278 = 'Über die römischen Ackerbrüder' (1870)), and in Henzen (1874, XXII n. 1), followed by Scheid (1990, 113ff.).

Gordian III, sacrifices were performed there to the *Genius* alone. It was rather this worship that determined the name. If so, since the building was named *Caesareum* in the entry from 218, under Macrinus, but engraved under Elagabalus, either of these emperors may be added to the list.[51]

Further confirmation comes from the coinage, whose depictions of the semi-nude *Genius* merit more attention. Under Trajan, Hadrian, and Antoninus Pius the type is only encountered as the *Genius populi Romani*; under Marcus the figure simply does not occur on the coinage. However, in Commodus' last years the youth reappears, labelled as the *Genius Augusti*, for the first time since Nero's issues.[52] A reaction, apparently, once again is visible in two early issues of Severus, with the reappearance of the *Genius populi Romani*. Significantly, they date from the early years of Severus' reign, when he acted the 'senatorial' emperor and the avenger of Pertinax, before he fell out with the Senate and, *inter alia*, had Commodus deified.[53] In Severus' later coinage, the type reappears on a few issues; the depictions are unlabelled, and hence ambiguous.[54] After these issues, the type disappears for generations. Since, presumably, the emperor's *Genius* was now habitually worshipped in the state cult, and the emperor was formally established as *dominus*, the issue was probably irrelevant, and over and done with. The emblematic representations and their connotations could, however, be reused, now no doubt as mere stereotyped symbols of *moderatio* versus *dominatio*. *Genius Augusti* is shown again on issues of Gallienus, an emperor who did much, in dress and court ceremonial, to further elevate the imperial position, and

[51] Henzen (1874, CCII. 4 = *CIL* VI. 2104. 4); date unknown, but before 27 May.

[52] The material is conveniently assembled by Kunckel (1974) in her catalogue (116ff.): Trajan: 129, M IV, nos. 1–2 (interpreted as the *Genius Aug.*; but the legend '*s.p.q.R. optimo principi*' rather suggests the *Genius p. R.*) = BMC III. 60, nos. 205–11; Hadrian: 116f. nos. 11–17; Commodus: 124, nos. 3–4, Taf. 4. 5 = BMC IV. 825, no. 645, pl. 109. 1; id., 742, nos. 288–90, pl. 98. 10–11 (*sestertii, denarii, aurei*, Rome, 190–1).

[53] Kunckel (1974, 117, nos. 18–19, Taf. 2. 6) = BMC V. 29, no. 59, pl. 6. 19; 34, no. 81, pl. 7. 15; Severus, and Senate: Dio (Xiph.) 75. 2. 1f.; 4. 1ff.; 7. 4ff.; Birley (1988, 104f.).

[54] Kunckel (1974, 123, nos. 14–17, Taf. 2. 7 = RIC IV. 1. 116, no. 190; 119, no. 219, pl. 6. 19; BMC V. 268, no. 564, pl. 42. 5; RIC IV. 1. 173, no. 599.

his immediate successors.[55] Again, the *Genius populi Romani* reappears on anonymous issues, probably issued by the Senate after the death of Aurelian, when, after a short interregnum, the Senate in fact chose his successor. The issues were few, and by now even this general symbolism was apparently worn out, for both *Genii* are commonly shown on the coinage under the Tetrarchy and in the fourth century.[56]

My overview gleaned from the coinage seems to fit the development traced above in the *Arval Acta* (though with gaps in both sequences), which can hardly be a coincidence.[57] The list of emperors, whose *Genius* was the object of state worship, includes Marcus, Severus Alexander, and Gordian III, and hence no longer only the 'bad' emperors. This suggests that the reintroduction of the god in, probably, Marcus' later years was final (probably, as suggested by the coinage, with a lapse in Severus' first years), and that henceforth the god was there to stay. His absence from the preserved *Acta* under some emperors after Commodus should therefore be mere coincidence. Only then, apparently, was the process completed by which the emperor's *Genius* took over the constitutional place and iconography of the *Genius populi Romani*, a development of which we may have seen the first trace already under Augustus.

The fact that Pliny's *Panegyric* is our only literary source that mentions the practice, and at that indirectly, may be an argument against according it such importance as I do here. Yet this is not a very good argument: all our literary sources represent more or less the point of view of high-ranking senators, and the more uncomfortable this cliental cult was to these senators, the more reason to pass it by. We may remember Dio's remark that Caligula early in his reign showed such admirable modesty that he rejected the proposal of state worship of his *Genius*, even causing his refusal to be published on a bronze tablet.[58] This passage was written at a time when the

[55] Kunckel (1974, 124, nos. 5–8, Taf. 4. 6–8).

[56] Anon.: Kunckel (1974, 117, nos. 20–2, Taf. 2. 8); later: id. 117ff.

[57] The coinage actually appears the more conservative medium: only in Nero's and Commodus' last years is the *Genius Augusti* depicted, though he had received state worship for years before. Note also that the god is absent from Domitian's coinage, where the state worship, however, seems assured.

[58] Dio 59. 4. 4.

practice had probably been revived once again, and it may likewise have a didactic point. Both Dio and Pliny mention the custom, not as in existence—for this there is no direct literary evidence—but negatively, for being rejected. If anything, this suggests that it was not because it was felt to be unimportant that our literary sources ignore the state worship of the emperor's *Genius*.

A further hint in this direction appears from summing up the history of the *Genius Augusti* in this context, as sketched out above. He was worshipped at least from the time of Claudius (Caligula is a possible first) to Vitellius, dropped under Vespasian, restored under Domitian, expelled again after his death (probably by Nerva), and finally and, it seems, permanently restored under Marcus. Apart perhaps from Claudius, this listing corresponds exactly, until Marcus at least, to the sequence of 'bad' emperors in the period, a characterization which depends exclusively on the senatorial, or senatorially biased, literary sources. This can hardly be fortuitous. There is of course far more to the story than the worship of their *Genii*, but the accordance between the two lists suggests that this aspect did indeed have an important role to play in it. The *Genius* phenomenon may have drowned in the abundance of juicy slanders against these emperors served by our literary sources. But often enough, the scandalous bits will have been a cloak for more substantial reasons behind the negative portrayals. Attacks on senatorial social pride and self-esteem, such as the servile *Genius* worship, was perhaps the strongest of such reasons, though rarely argued in any direct fashion. Again, what mattered most was too uncomfortable for mention.

CONCLUSION

In this chapter on the worship of the ruling emperor's *Genius* in the state cult of Rome, I have attempted to see its origins in the household cults as vitally important to its meaning and connotations. In doing so, I have claimed here an important development in the constitutional definition of what an emperor actually was, attempting to show that this process was far from carried through under Augustus. Despite the generally accepted claim to the contrary, Augustus' *Genius* was in fact never worshipped in the state cult. Such worship of the living emperor's *Genius* entered the state cult only later, and the decisive initiative may be ascribed to Claudius (Caligula here as elsewhere matters little). We have seen a development, or zigzag course back and forth, that only ended under Marcus or the Severans. The *Genius* of the emperor in the state cult has so far been almost completely overlooked, except for the reign of Augustus, to which the whole development sketched here has been ascribed. The reason for this neglect must be attributed to an almost exclusive dependence on the literary sources, where the emperor's *Genius* hardly plays a role. The *Arval Acta*, where he does, have till recent years been curiously ignored as a source on the constitutional and religious (no dichotomy intended here) history of the Roman state.

So it was only in the later second century that the formal constitutional definition of the emperor as absolute head of the state household was finally established. By then the opposite notion of the emperor as a fellow senator, first among equals, had for generations been dead in governing practice, if not in the bearing of the 'good' emperor towards top senators. In practical politics it may never have existed as anything but an ideological screen: Pliny regularly terms Trajan *dominus* in his correspondence with the emperor, and so, no doubt, did his peers. That, however, was their own business. How they termed the emperor, worshipped him on their own behalf, and no matter how sycophantic was their individual and even collective bearing towards him, this had no impact on the formal constitutional definitions (or niceties, we might be tempted to say). What seems strange, however, is how important these niceties were felt to be by high-ranking senators. *Clientes* in practice, they abhorred to be so in theory.

8

'In Every House'? The Emperor in the Roman Household

Private cult of the emperor, its form and its quantity, must be decisive for any general interpretation of emperor worship, especially so since scholars have usually claimed that the phenomenon was exclusively or overwhelmingly a public one, and from this conclusion have often questioned the 'sincerity' or 'true religiosity' of imperial cults. Such notions are in fact christianizing, but it should still be important to establish whether emperor worship was in fact predominantly to be found in the public or municipal sphere, or whether, as I suspect, this view merely reflects that almost all the attention of scholarship has hitherto focused exclusively on municipal worship and the state cult in Rome.[1] I shall begin by examining the most unequivocally 'private', in any sense of the word, branch of cultic life, that of the household cults, and the extent to which emperors had a presence in this sphere.

Unfortunately, the sources fail us almost completely in this field. This is hardly surprising, considering the nature of our evidence which overwhelmingly consists of texts and monuments created, indeed published, for the public eye to behold: mainly monumental stone inscriptions. Sources of this nature will of course be increasingly absent in relation to the degree of privacy, or lack of public exposure, of these cults. Private cults involved well-informed insiders who had little need of explanatory monuments to enlighten or impress outsiders, ancient or modern. Furthermore, the literary texts generally ignore life in the household during the empire. We would perhaps be better off, if we had comedies from this period, but none are preserved. As it is, our literary texts generally narrate only eccen-

[1] There is no general study on private emperor worship; for the few remarks on the subject in scholarly literature—almost exclusively of the 19th century only—see Santero (1983, 111 n. 3).

tric aberrations from the usual patterns which were well known and hence without interest to contemporary audiences. Many common practices therefore go largely unnoticed, and may force us to arguments *e silentio*. Even the archaeological finds, from which we might perhaps expect better treatment, cause considerable problems of methodology and interpretation, as we shall see shortly. The paucity of evidence forces us to group together evidence from the first two centuries AD in the attempt to form a picture; though this may appear a dubious exercise, we stand no chance whatsoever of tracing any chronological developments. The basic point, however, is that absence of evidence cannot be taken as evidence of absence, as has usually been assumed in the few remarks found on the subject in modern scholarship.

There is hardly any archaeological evidence of emperor worship in the *domus*. Mosaics and wall-paintings from private houses in Pompeii, Ostia, or other localities practically never contain any references to the emperor. In one of the few studies on the subject, this has been stressed by Bickerman who also found the absence of imperial portraits in private contexts revealing.[2] To him this absence suggested that the imperial cult and other imperial honours were confined to the public sphere, and were without interest to the private individual. The apparently widespread existence of *collegia* dedicated to worshipping the living emperor, treated below (chapter 9), may seem to render such a conclusion dubious. Before entering that discussion we should, however, examine whether Bickerman's claim of absence is in fact correct, and on what it is based.

The evidence does not actually confirm this absence. As I will shortly attempt to demonstrate, imperial honours in the household focused on the ruling emperor rather than on the *Divi*, as did private emperor worship in general (or indeed emperor worship in any context outside that of the state cult in Rome). If this was so, we could not in any case expect to encounter, for example, mosaics or wall-paintings depicting the emperor. The point is decisive, for the types of monuments leaving the clearest archaeological traces are exactly the more immobile and stationary ones, such as mosaics and wall-paintings, and

[2] Bickerman (1973, 3ff.).

not the more temporary ones. These more immobile types of finds were also the costliest to install, and their motives therefore generally had a more 'timeless' and general appeal; thus Pompeian wall-paintings usually depict scenes of fantasy architecture or mythology. Scenes from specific cults are practically only found in the paintings of *lararia*, depicting the household worship of *Genius* and *Lares*, which was of course a constant, 'timeless' factor in the life of the household. Other cultic scenes encountered in Pompeian wall-paintings are of a very generic, non-specific kind, mainly romantic rustic shrines set in landscapes of bucolic idyll.[3]

In Bickerman's argument, he rather revealingly points to modern parallels: 'Think of the portraits of Stalin, Hitler, and even of Nasser, in every shop, in every home of their respective subjects'.[4] However, portraits exactly like these in thousands of homes, reproductions of photographs or paintings, or more rarely portable miniature busts, would usually not leave behind the slightest trace in excavations centuries later. Since the Roman emperor could, likewise, pass away at any moment, we should expect supposed imperial portraits in private homes to have been of a similarly temporary and modest character, rather than large and costly wall or floor decorations which could have lost their relevance at any moment.

This theoretical reasoning receives support from a letter of Fronto to his imperial pupil Marcus Aurelius in the mid-second century:[5] 'You know how in all money-changer's bureaus, booths, bookstalls, eaves, porches, windows, anywhere and everywhere there are likenesses of you exposed to view, badly enough painted most of them to be sure, and modelled and carved in a plain, not to say sorry, style of art . . .'. The information is as unique as it is incidental, yet obviously sound: the addressee would surely have been in the know to see through any flattery or exaggeration on this point. Here is the obvious parallel to Bickerman's ubiquitous dictators. Fronto's

[3] Ling (1991, 157, 162 f. and *passim*).

[4] Bickerman (1973, 5).

[5] Front. *Ep. ad M. Caes.* 4. 12. 6 (Loeb edn., vol. i, p. 207): '*Scis ut in omnibus argentariis mensulis perguleis taberneis protecteis vestibulis fenestris usquequaque ubique imagines vestrae sint volgo propositae, male illae quidem pictae pleraeque et crassa, lutea immo, Minerva fictae scalptaeve* . . .'.

passage may, like the literary sources in general, only be relevant to conditions in the capital; yet the fortuitous survival of this bit of evidence should again caution us against concluding anything from apparent absence elsewhere.

The claim of imperial absence in the household thus rests on dubious assumptions. For instance, wooden panel paintings, apparently mentioned by Fronto, which were perhaps the cheapest and most easily disposable form of imperial portraits, would not be traceable in excavations, not even in Pompeii.

We may in this connection think also of sculptured imperial miniature portraits whose very size points to the house sphere; to what extent, however, they were employed in a cultic context or merely for decorative purposes, we cannot say. Two miniature busts of Augustus come from Herculaneum, but their exact provenance is unknown. That is in fact the case for all imperial miniature portraits from Italy (or anywhere else, for that matter). We possess relatively few such small-scale busts, but most of those preserved belong to the early empire.[6] Bearing in mind Fronto's remark, it is once again doubtful to conclude anything from their relative scarcity which must in any case be due partly to the fact that they were usually in economically valuable metals, such as bronze or the precious metals, marble being relatively intractable on such a small scale.

To return to the excavational evidence, it is true that few imperial portraits of any kind have been discovered in a private context. Yet, as has been pointed out by Simon Price, considering how few of the imperial portrait busts and statues in our museums have any identifiable provenance, even this basic argument is undermined.[7] However, several imperial portraits have actually come to light in private houses. A statue of Livia was unearthed in the Villa dei Misteri in Pompeii, and in another villa in the town a portrait of a young Julian prince (Marcellus?) had been tucked away in a back room, presumably after the youth had lost his political significance.[8] A life-size silver bust of Galba was found in the street immediately outside

[6] Schneider (1976); 7ff. for the Herculanean busts.

[7] Price (1984*a*, 119).

[8] Villa dei Mist.: Maiuri (1931, 223ff.) (the identification may be doubtful); prince: M. Hofter in *Kaiser Augustus und die verlorene Republik* (1988, 328f. with lit.) (for the type see Fittschen and Zanker, 1983, i. no. 19).

a grand house in Herculaneum, from which it had presumably been carried, before being dropped in panic, at the eruption of Vesuvius in 79.[9] A collection of imperial Julio-Claudian bronze portraits was found in the foundations of an apparently contemporary villa in Rome, and an inn (*caupona*) in Ostia has yielded a small marble bust of Commodus.[10] Even in death people could carry their imperial portraits with them: a marble bust of Septimius Severus was found at Isola Sacra, the ancient burial grounds of Ostia.[11] Furthermore, full-size imperial portrait sculptures have in half a dozen cases been discovered in villas in the Italian countryside;[12] the owners of these villas are, however, unknown, and since they may indeed have been emperors, this evidence is not so useful in this context.

Literary sources also furnish us with examples of imperial portraits in private houses, with or without cult. The younger Pliny possessed in one of his country houses a collection of statues of late emperors which he had inherited. Apparently to put the statues to some useful purpose he applied to the emperor Nerva for permission to add his statue to the group and transfer the statues to Tifernum, where he intended to build a temple for them. The application was shortly afterwards repeated to Trajan who had in the meantime succeeded Nerva. In both cases the request was granted, and the temple was eventually built.[13] Ovid, in his exile at Tomi on the Black Sea, received from a patron in Rome silver images of Augustus, Tiberius, and Livia. A few years later, with Augustus dead and the poet still in Tomi, busts of Tiberius' two sons Germanicus and Drusus had been added to the collection, and Ovid every

[9] The cuirassed bust, often wrongly described as of silvered bronze, is the only certain sculpture portrait of this emperor (more or less fantastic further identifications abound); M. R. Borriello in *Unter dem Vulkan* (1995, 170f.) (best depictions and highly competent description, but no refs.); Fabbricotti (1976, 74f.) with lit.

[10] Villa: Hill (1939, 401ff.): only Augustus and Nero (Fittschen and Zanker, 1983, i. no. 18) can be identified; the walls of the villa were in *opus reticulatum* (*NSc* (1880), 466), chronologically in accordance with the portraits; Commodus in *caupona*: R. Paribeni in *NSc* (1916), 417ff.; Calza (n.d.), no. 23.

[11] G. Ricci in *NSc* (1939), 59ff.; Calza (n.d.), no. 55.

[12] Neudecker (1988); for private provenances outside Italy see Price (1984*a*, 119) and also Bickerman (1973, 6).

[13] Plin. *Ep*. 10. 8; 3. 4; 4. 1; see p. 98 above.

morning sacrificed incense and prayed to the portraits.[14] Ovid's verbose and cringing verses on the subject were clearly caused by exceptional circumstances, his ardent desire to earn imperial pardon and return to the capital, but it does not necessarily follow that the same goes for his possession and worship of the images. A contemporary inscription from central Italy records that a knight bequeathed in his will five imperial silver images—probably of the same persons as in Ovid's sanctuary—to his home town.[15]

Tacitus (*Ann.* 4. 64) records an image of Tiberius in a senator's house in Rome; the information is not given with any implication that the placement was unusual, but merely because the portrait miraculously survived a devastating fire on the Caelian Hill. In connection with a case under the *lex maiestatis* in the first year of Tiberius, brought against a certain Falanius, a knight 'of moderate fortune', Tacitus mentions a statue of Augustus in a private garden, and it appears from Tiberius' verdict in the case that such statues of his predecessor were also to be found in houses.[16]

To move to the directly cultic presence of the emperor, the passage of Tacitus just quoted furnishes us with a vital piece of evidence, resulting from the historian's polemical purpose in demonstrating, not quite fairly, how Tiberius' enforcement of the *lex maiestatis* even crossed the threshold of the private house. Again, as in the case of Fronto, the information is as unique as it is fortuitous: one of the accusations brought against Falanius was that he had admitted a sexual pervert among 'Augustus' worshippers [*cultores*] who existed in all households in the form of associations [*in modum collegiorum*]' during the later years of Augustus.[17] Tacitus may exaggerate, and his

[14] Ov. *Ex Ponto* 2. 8; 4. 9. 105 ff. For Ovid and the *domus Augusta* see Millar (1993), rightly stressing Ovid as a 'rejected loyalist' rather than the aspects of distanced sarcasm or subtle opposition often attributed to the poet's relationship with the regime.

[15] *AE* 1978. 286 = Letta (1978) (from L'Aquila).

[16] Tac. *Ann.* 1. 73: '*Nec contra religiones fieri, quod effigies eius, ut alia numinum simulacra, venditionibus hortorum et domuum accedant*'. Cf. Dig. 48. 4. 5. 2: '*Idem Pontio rescripsit* [Marcianus] *non videri contra maiestatem fieri ob imagines Caesaris nondum consecratas venditas*'.

[17] Tac. *Ann.* 1. 73: '*Haud pigebit referre in Falanio et Rubrio, modicis equitibus Romanis, praetemptata crimina, ut quibus initiis, quanta Tiberii arte gravissimum exitium inrepserit . . . Falanio obiciebat accusator quod inter cultores*

statement may have relevance to the capital only, but the information serves no polemical purpose, and there is no reason basically to question his testimony. His wording, and indeed the explanatory information in itself, indicates that these imperial household associations were *not* common knowledge to Tacitus' contemporaries; it was apparently a phenomenon of the early empire which may originally have served as an inspirational backdrop to the establishment of imperial *collegia* proper outside the *domus*. Incidentally, though such cults could in principle have functioned without images, the existence of these domestic associations indicates that portraits of Augustus in some form or other must have been a common feature in private houses in the capital during these years. The statue of Augustus in Falanius' garden may thus have been the cult image of 'Augustus' worshippers'.

There is some literary evidence for the practice of placing images of the emperor or other benefactors—but never their *Genii*—among the other household gods in the *lararium*. The absence of the *Genius* in this connection was probably due to the circumstance that the figure would have implied a cliental relationship to a fellow man, something which would have been socially humiliating to persons of rank. It might have been expected that imperial images would have turned up in the undisturbed *lararia* of Pompeii where, in twenty-six instances, excavations have revealed statuettes of house gods *in situ*; but that is not the case.[18] As for the literary examples, I have already quoted the pathetic case of Ovid. Likewise, the courtier L. Vitellius, father of the later emperor, worshipped golden images of Claudius' powerful freedmen Narcissus and Pallas among his *lares*, and Marcus Aurelius honoured his teachers to the extent of inserting their golden portraits in his *lararium*. Suetonius presented Hadrian with a bronze statuette or miniature bust of Augustus as a child, and the emperor worshipped

Augusti, qui per omnis domos in modum collegiorum habebantur, Cassium quendam mimum corpore infamem adscivisset, quodque venditis hortis statuam Augusti simul mancipasset. Rubrio crimini dabatur violatum periurio numen Augusti'. The year is AD 15, but such widespread establishment of cult associations only since Augustus' death seems inconceivable, and Augustus is not styled *Divus* here, so the associations must date from his lifetime.

[18] Boyce (1937), index s.v. 'Statuettes'.

it between the *lares* of his bedchamber.[19] The Historia Augusta (*M. Ant. Phil.* 18. 6) states that the popularity of Marcus Aurelius was so immense that it was considered sacrilege not to have his image in one's house, if one had the means to afford it, and 'even in my time', as the author says, his statue was to be found among the household gods in many homes. The story is clearly nonsense in terms of specific information, but just might still reveal something about the practice in general, which is of course what matters here.

All the texts have one aspect in common: the instances are mentioned because they represent exceptions to the usual, presupposed pattern and thereby gain in interest. Ovid was desperate to be recalled. Vitellius' worship of the imperial freedmen is cited as an example of his servile *adulatio* and sycophancy: that a high-ranking senator, thrice consul and censor with Claudius, should have worshipped ex-slaves, and thereby socially submitted to them, was to Roman eyes a monstrous and ridiculous self-humiliation, and it is evidently this grotesque aspect which adds interest to the incident and causes it to receive attention. Exactly because Vitellius possessed images of the imperial freedmen in his *lararium*, one of Claudius must also have been present in it. But in this there would have been nothing startling, since Vitellius was socially far inferior to the emperor. The social submission involved would therefore have been natural in this instance, and hence it went without mention. The same applies to the anecdote of Marcus and his teachers, illustrating his singular affection for them, which caused him to worship someone so socially inferior to himself. Hadrian's worship of the child Augustus' image is of course mentioned by Suetonius from pride that the emperor valued his gift so highly. The stories in the Historia Augusta on portraits of Marcus in private houses are clearly presented because the notion of sacrilege in not possessing the emperor's image was startling, and—if the notorious source allows such a conclusion—because it was unusual to have portraits of an emperor in one's *lararium* long after his death (at least in the fourth century).

[19] Suet. *Vit.* 2. 5; HA *M. Ant. Phil.* 3. 5; Suet. *Aug.* 7. 1; another *lararium* story, bogus, is in HA *Sev. Al.* 29. 2.

Though what or whom to worship among his house gods was the choice of the *paterfamilias*, it seems that the focus in house cults was generally on the living emperor, and not on the dead ones. First, this was almost exclusively the case in private cult associations which may reasonably be taken as a rough indicator for non-official emperor worship in general. Secondly, the imperial libation before private banquets of the early empire, a subject to which I shall shortly return, was performed only to the living emperor. Thirdly, there is the common-sense argument: it seems difficult to find any general reason why private piety and interest should have been retrospective instead of concentrating on the emperor primarily responsible for contemporary prosperity. To imagine, for instance, Fronto's passage, quoted above, on the ubiquity of Marcus' portraits in Rome as dealing with images of *Divi* instead, would seem profoundly absurd. In fact, outside the exceptional context of the state cult in Rome and its offshoots in the army cults (see p. 341 below), there generally seems to have been little interest in the emperor once he was dead.

This predilection for present power-wielders could lead to problems when emperors changed, as illustrated by the case of the Baetican proconsul Granius Marcellus who was charged with *maiestas* for replacing the head of Augustus' statue with one of Tiberius shortly after his accession.[20] The statue presumably stood in Marcellus' home in Baetica—the head-swopping would have been inconceivable in a public space and the informer, Marcellus' quaestor, had had frequent access to the house. The main point is not that Marcellus was too stingy to commission a new statue, though of course he may have been, but that Augustus' portrait had simply lost relevance to him at the death of the emperor.

The absence of imperial portraits in Pompeian *lararia* shows at least that the practice of including the emperor among the house gods was not uniform. Yet the literary sources seem to indicate that the phenomenon was a common one, since all the instances mentioned in them and quoted above were exceptional in one way or the other. What we may surmise to have been the 'normal' case, the ruling emperor in the *lararium*, is

[20] Tac. *Ann.* 1. 74. 3; Katzoff (1971).

hardly ever mentioned (only in the abnormal case of Ovid), and this seems difficult to explain in any other way than that the practice was very common, and hence not interesting enough to be mentioned. It is for the very same reason that Roman house cult in general is so badly illuminated in the literary texts. Since these sources are preoccupied almost exclusively with conditions in Rome, it is possible that the inclusion of the emperor among the house gods was mainly practised in the capital only. Yet the widespread existence all over Italy of private cult associations dedicated to the emperor does not seem to indicate lack of interest or enthusiasm outside Rome and its higher echelons of society.

THE LIBATION TO THE EMPEROR

In one case worship of the emperor certainly entered the *domus*, not informally and on individual initiative only, but by decree of the Senate. After the conquest of Egypt in 30 BC the Senate decided, among other honours to young Caesar, that a libation should be poured to him at all banquets, public and private.[21] There is no evidence that the ritual was ever performed before public banquets. That would have collided with the anti-monarchical resistance to worshipping the living ruler in the state cult, and we may therefore surmise that the public ceremony was vetoed by young Caesar himself. As for private banquets, however, we possess a handful of sources indicating that the ritual was commonly performed in early imperial Italy. From all the sources—Ovid, Horace, and Petronius—it appears that the libation was performed in connection with ceremonies to the *lares* of the household. Horace evokes, in an ode addressed to Augustus, the longing of Italy for her Caesar during his absence in Gaul 16–13 BC; thus the farmer in his vineyard:[22]

On his own hillside each man spends the day, and weds his vines to waiting trees; thence gladly repairs to the feast, and at the second

[21] Cass. Dio 51. 19. 7: '. . . *καὶ ἐν τοῖϲ ϲυϲϲιτίοιϲ οὐχ ὅτι τοῖϲ κοινοῖϲ ἀλλὰ καὶ τοῖϲ ἰδίοιϲ πάντας αὐτῶι ϲπένδειν ἐκέλευϲαν*'. There was a precedent for this in the similar, but spontaneous, honour accorded to C. Marius *c.*101 BC (Val. Max. 8. 15. 7; Plut. *Mar.* 27. 9); see p. 51 above.

[22] Hor. *Carm.* 4. 5. 29ff. (tr. Bennett, Loeb edn., adapted): '*Condit quisque*

course invokes thee as a god. Thee with many a prayer, thee with pure wine poured from bowls, he worships; and mingles thy divinity [*numen*] with his household gods [*Lares*], like Greece mindful of Castor and great Hercules.

Ovid in his *Fasti* describes ceremonies to the family gods on the *Caristia*, 22 February, a festival for the family; after mentioning food offerings to the *lares*, the poet proceeds:[23]

And now, when dank night invites to slumber calm, fill high the wine-cup for the prayer and say, 'Hail to you! hail to thee, Father of thy Country, Caesar the Good!' and let good speech attend the pouring of wine.

Neither Horace nor Ovid of course allows us to conclude that the ceremony was commonly practised; both accounts may in this respect be dismissed as the flattery of 'court poetry'. Far more revealing is Petronius (*Satyricon* 60) where, between two courses at Trimalchio's dinner party, saffron-spouting cakes and fruits are brought onto the table. The guests assume this to be a divine honour, so they all rise and exclaim 'Good fortune to the emperor, Father of the Fatherland!' (*'Augusto patri patriae feliciter!'*). Three slaves then enter the room, and two of them place statuettes of the *lares* (i.e. of Trimalchio) on the table, while the third walks around holding a bowl (*patera*) full of wine, whilst exclaiming 'May the gods be propitious!' (*'dii propitii!'*).

In this instance we can exclude the possibility that the ritual is described merely or primarily to flatter the emperor,[24] and the instinctive and immediate reaction of the diners shows that the ceremony must have been generally established (it does not actually emerge from the passage whether the perfumed items were in fact intended for the emperor, or just perceived to be

diem collibus in suis, | et vitem viduas ducit ad arbores; | hinc ad vina redit laetus et alteris | te mensis adhibet deum; | | te multa prece, te prosequitur mero | defuso pateris, et Laribus tuum | miscet numen, uti Graecia Castoris | et magni memor Herculis.'

[23] Ov. *Fast.* 2. 633ff. (tr. Frazer & Goold, Loeb edn.): '*Iamque ubi suadebit placidos nox umida somnos, | larga precaturi sumite vina manu, | et "bene vos, bene te, patriae pater, optime Caesar!"| dicite suffuso sint bona verba mero.*'

[24] For he—Nero—is not otherwise mentioned in the preserved parts of the *Satyricon*. For commentary on the ritual see Slater (1986, 43), pointing out that the recipient of the libation must be Nero, not Augustus.

so by the guests). It should be noted that none of the texts describing the libation makes mention of a portrait of the emperor in connection with the ceremony. The rite could then not even in theory leave any traces in the archaeological material: yet another warning against concluding too much from a supposed absence of imperial images in private houses.

It has generally been supposed that the libation was performed to the *Genius* of the emperor rather than to himself, and this interpretation seems universally accepted in recent scholarship. Yet all our sources mention the libation as being performed to the emperor himself, in direct and god-like fashion. The idea of the *Genius* was first advanced by Mommsen who saw in Horace's ode, quoted above, an allusion to the compital cults of the emperor's *Genius* and *Lares*. Since this cult form was established only around 7 BC, whereas the ode was written in 14 or 13 BC, this view has rightly been abandoned, but strangely the *Genius* interpretation has stuck despite the fall of its premise.[25] Thus, in support of her similar interpretation of the imperial cult in Italy generally, Lily Ross Taylor quoted the libation as a certain instance of a cultic act performed to the emperor's *Genius* where the word itself was 'suppressed'.

Since Horace in his ode, which is addressed to Augustus, mentions his divinity—*tuum numen*—this concept has therefore normally been seen as synonymous with *'genius'* in this text at least; and alternatively, the interpretation *numen=genius* has been claimed to be confirmed by the very same passage, thereby making the whole argument neatly circular.[26] I will treat the concept of the emperor's *numen* and the passage of Horace elsewhere and there attempt to demonstrate that *numen* is not the same as *genius*, neither in the ode nor anywhere else.[27] Suffice it to say here that Horace in lines 32–3 unequivocally describes the worship as directed to Augustus himself (*'te . . . adhibet deum'*). There is thus no *Genius* present in any of these sources: they unanimously describe a libation to the emperor himself.

One source, however, a wall-painting from Pompeii, has

[25] Mommsen (1880, 107ff.); Fishwick (1991, ii. 1. 375f.) for exhaustive lit. and historiography.

[26] Fishwick (ibid.) is illustrative of this circularity.

[27] See p. 246f below.

frequently been marshalled in support of the libation being indeed performed to the *Genius*. In the garden of a private house in Pompeii (reg. IX. 9. 13) is a small niche, a *Lararium*, situated on the western wall, near the southern corner; to the right of this niche older scholars have described a painting which was destroyed many years ago.[28] To my knowledge no photograph or other reproduction of the fresco exists, and we therefore have nothing but short descriptions of the scene to rely on. It ought to go without saying that such a ghostly monument is inadmissible as evidence for anything. Yet, since it is still brought forward as an argument in recent scholarship,[29] I will for the sake of argument deal with it, and beg the reader's forgiveness for the much ado about nothing which follows. The fullest description of the fresco is due to Boyce, apparently based on autopsy in the early 1930s:

> On the l(eft) stands a tripod of unusual form, with a dark-coloured vessel upon it. The Genius, standing to the r(ight), pours a libation upon the tripod; he wears a wreath of leaves; the toga does not seem to be drawn over his head as usual, though the preservation of the painting is poor at this point; he holds no cornucopia. Behind and to the r(ight) stand two figures: in the first plane, a camillus; also wreathed, and carrying fruit in a shallow dish; above and farther r(ight), a popa, wreathed and carrying an ax. To the l(eft) of the Genius are two wreathed figures, apparently women, though it is impossible to be certain, for only the upper portions of their figures are preserved. On the l(eft) side of the niche there was not room for painted figures, but on the adjoining S(outh) wall the figure of the Genius appears again, clad in a white toga and pouring a libation upon a yellow cylindrical altar with a fire; he is unbearded, his flesh is reddish, in his l(eft) hand he holds a yellow cornucopia.

The *Genius* on the south wall was interpreted by Mau as the *Genius Augusti*, received into house cult in accordance with the decree of the Senate in 30 BC: for under this figure a grafitto, likewise lost, had carefully been incised with 9 cm. high letters: *EX S(enatus) C(onsulto)*—'By decree of the Senate'. The *Genius* was apparently not contemporary with the rest of the

[28] Mau in *RM* 5 (1890, 244); id. (1900, 253); Boyce (1937, no. 466) with lit.; nothing of note preserved when I visited the site some years ago.

[29] Thus by Fishwick (1991, ii. 1. 376); id. (1995, 25).

painting, but had been deliberately preserved when the wall was redecorated, to which phase the rest of the depictions belonged.

This attractive yet bold interpretation has been accepted by all later scholars. There are, however, problems, apart from the subsequent destruction of the painting. First, if Mau's interpretation be correct, the *Genius* as recipient of the libation in this instance would stand in opposition to all the literary sources, presented above. Secondly, nothing about the second '*Genius*', on the west wall, actually identifies the figure as a *Genius*: he apparently had neither the toga drawn over his head nor a cornucopia, the two distinctive features in the iconography of togate *Genii*. It therefore seems more natural to interpret the figure as the priest in the sacrificial scene depicted on the west wall. There would then only be a single *Genius* in the depiction, as usual in the *Lararium* paintings of Pompeii, namely that on the south wall.

To probe further, the sacrificial scene on the west wall clearly deviates from comparable Pompeian *Lararium* paintings. In these a sacrifice and the *Genius* and/or *Lares* of the *paterfamilias*, that is, the gods to whom the sacrifice is actually performed, are always depicted. Apparently that was not the case here: the so-called '*Genius*' must rather, as mentioned, have been the priest in the ceremony, and there was no trace whatsoever of the *Lares* in the painting. This must mean that the sacrifice was performed to the only god represented, namely the *Genius* on the south wall. If so, Mau's interpretation cannot stand: for the sacrificial attendant (*popa*) with his axe shows that a sanguinary sacrifice formed part of the ritual, whereas the libation to the emperor in the nature of things was bloodless. Even if this animal sacrifice was to some other god(s), such as the *Lares*, a connection between the priest's libation and the *Genius Augusti* seems difficult to sustain: our sources state that the imperial libation should be, and was, poured immediately before the meal, or in Petronius between two courses in the banquet. In the painting, however, the libation took place before the slaughter, or at least contemporaneously with it (as is usual in representations of Roman blood sacrifices where the libation was commonly used as an 'aperitif' to the god(s) before the immolation). Mau's interpretation is therefore acceptable only if the *Genius Augusti* and the cultic scene had no connection with each other—in which case there would not even be an imperial libation to write about.

If we are to accept that the figure on the south wall was indeed the *Genius Augusti*, it seems, I believe, more reasonable to interpret the fresco in the light of the compital cults. The owner of the house could have been a *magister vici* who established in his own garden a private cult of the *Genius Augusti* whom he had been wont to worship in his office.[30] The inscription *EX S. C.* would then refer to a senatorial decree which in 7 BC, or somewhat earlier, ordered or approved the reorganization of the compital cults in Rome and the inclusion of the *Genius Augusti* in them.[31] The interpretation may seem strained, but no more so than that of Mau, and it would solve the apparent conflict with the literary evidence: the painting had in fact nothing to do with the imperial libation.[32] Mau's interpretation, on the other hand, entails such problems that, even disregarding its blatant conflict with the literary sources, it must fall to Occam's razor: the theory simply does not fit with the fresco as described by Boyce. We are thus left with the literary sources, and their wording is unequivocal: the libation decreed by the Senate in 30 BC was to young Caesar himself, not to his *Genius*. In the light of the image of emperor worship that I have sketched in the preceding chapters, this should not surprise us; on the contrary, a centrally ordained libation to the *Genius Augusti* would have imposed on the proud and noble a cult form deeply humiliating to their social self-esteem.

30 For the compital cults in Pompeii see Spinazzola (1953, 169ff.).

31 For the probable existence of such a decree see p. 127 with n. 42 above.

32 It should be noted that the function of the house to which the garden belongs is unknown and therefore cannot assist in the discussion: a *hospitium* according to Mau, contra Sogliano in *NSc* (1891), 260.

9
Corporate Worship

Tacitus' statement (*Ann.* I. 73, quoted above p. 203), that worshippers of Augustus (*cultores Augusti*) were found in all the households of Rome is the only reference we have to such imperial worshippers within the *domus*, a fact which should caution us against claiming evidence of absence on the basis of absence of evidence. Inscriptions are, by their very nature, a public phenomenon; we therefore cannot expect Tacitus' *cultores Augusti* to turn up there. However, outside their own households, slaves and freedmen are often found to have established cultic associations—*cultores*—dedicated to the worship of a particular god, or group of gods.[1] These groupings have been almost totally overlooked in research. In most cases their object of worship was one of the 'old' gods; for instance, Silvanus is frequently encountered in this context, and though he played no part in the state cult, nor in the municipal cults of Italy, he appears to have been very popular indeed among persons of servile status.[2] However, in quite a few cases the associations chose as their object of worship the emperor and his *Lares*.[3] It is difficult to say whether and on what level there is any connection between these groupings and Tacitus' household *cultores*. Furthermore, it is uncertain how common such imperial *cultores* actually were, for the inscriptional evidence is hardly overwhelming.

As is evident from the inscriptions, *cultores*, whatever their object of worship, were practically always slaves or freedmen. I will argue that this form of cultic grouping, including the term *cultores*, was characteristic of the major Roman households; hence slaves and freedmen, when they established cultic

[1] Breccia (1910) for *cultores* in general.

[2] Dorcey (1992); for servile cults generally see Bömer (1981, i) and (1990, iii).

[3] Breccia (1910, 1296ff.) for the evidence (also *CIL* XI. 8098); the only (partial) modern study is Santero (1983).

associations outside their individual households, stuck to the form and terminology known to them from this context.

CULTORES PRIVATORUM

Some confirmation for this view comes indeed from the title of Tacitus' *cultores Augusti* within the households. Furthermore, the term *cultores* is the usual one in the inscriptional evidence—our only source in this field—for cultic household associations dedicated to worshipping the *Genius* and *Lares* of private individuals. Thus we find in the inscriptional evidence a dedication of unknown character (an altar?) set up to a private man by the 'worshippers of his *Lares*' (*cultores larum eius*), also a 'college of [worshippers of] Marcellinus' *Lares*' (*collegium larum Marcellini*),[4] and a burial place donated by a private man and his son to the 'worshippers of their *Lares*' (*larum suorum cultoribus*).[5]

The earliest datable instance of such *cultores* is from Rome, given in a funerary inscription (*CIL* VI. 10267): 'Hymnus Volusianus, Caesar Augustus' slave, . . . councillor of [the college of] the Volusian *Lares*' (*Hymnus Caesaris Aug(usti servus) Volusianus . . . decurio larum Volusianorum*). The inscription, of Augustan date, gives evidence of a large slave *collegium*, which (by legacy?) had become the property of the emperor, presumably because this branch of the *gens Volusia* became extinct; at least so runs Mommsen's commentary in his publication of the inscription (*CIL*). The size of the association is suggested by the fact that it had a governing body of *decuriones*, and its existence can even be traced to the Flavian age or later, since another funerary inscription mentioning the body was set up to a certain *T. Flavius Philetus* (*CIL* VI. 10266). In Mommsen's interpretation these inscriptions would appear as a somewhat astonishing illustration of the fidelity of these slaves towards their former house cult, after they had become members of

[4] M. Nonius Arrius Paulinus Aper: *CIL* V. 4340; IX. 2481.

[5] *CIL* XI. 8098; cf. V. 4440 (*colleg. larum*); outside Italy: *CIL* XII. 2677 (*cultores larum Sex. Antoni Mansueti et L. Valeri Rufini*: an association with two *patroni*, composed of slaves and freedmen of both, and hence not a household cult in the strict sense); *CIL* XIII. 1747 (*coll. larum dom(u) Iulian(a)*); *CIL* III. 4792.

another household (*domus*). Instead we may possibly see Hymnus as an individual gift to the emperor, but it seems more obvious to interpret both him and Philetus as having been members of the *collegium* even without having been owned by the Volusii: an example, then, of household cult expanding outside its strict sphere. Such a view receives support from the fact that at least the main branch of the *gens Volusia* did not become extinct in Augustus' day, but continued to flourish and hold the highest offices in Rome until the time of Domitian. During the early empire the family belonged to the absolute *crème de la crème* of senatorial aristocracy, and was closely involved with the imperial house. The burial grounds of the *familia* of the Volusii on Via Appia have furnished us with a great number of funerary inscriptions set up to their slaves and freedmen, two of whom are termed 'priest of the *Genius* of our [master] Lucius'—*sacerdos Geni L(uci) n(ostri)*.[6]

In a few instances these associations are actually named as *cultores* of a man's *Genius*,[7] though this form is less frequent than *cultores larum*; this probably reflects the fact that the *Genius* was a minor god in comparison with the household *Lares*, and it corresponds to the Augustan compital cults (which had clearly drawn inspiration from the sphere of household cult), where the *Genius Augusti* played a subordinate role in relation to the *Lares* and was in fact rarely mentioned in the altar inscriptions.[8] In one instance, the worship seems to have been accorded portraits of a private man: an inscription from Aesernia is evidence of a burial place donated 'to the college of the worshippers of Lucius Abullius Dexter's statues and shields'—'*collegio culto(rum) statuar(um) et clipeor(um) L. Abulli Dextri*'. On the analogy of the titles of imperial cult associations, such as 'worshippers of the emperor's images' (*cultores imaginum Augusti*), the portraits (the 'shields' were no doubt *imagines clipeatae*, busts placed on shields) probably

[6] *CIL* VI. 1833*a* (cf. *AE* 1983. 23) (Augustan); 1967 = 7366 (cf. 7283); Sinn (1991, no. 56) with Abb. 165 (Augustan); for the columbarium see M. Buonocore in *I Volusii Saturnini* (1982, 17–35).

[7] *CIL* IX. 6320: '. . . *nomine culto(rum) Geni Britti Cordi*'; II. 5157 (Noricum): '*Genio Anigemio* [possessive dative or adjective of Anigemius] *cultores eius v(otum) s(olvit) l(ibentes) m(erito)*'.

[8] See p. 125 f above.

represented Dexter himself; he belonged to the very top of Aesernia's aristocracy in the second century.[9]

The inscriptions mentioning these associations are very few indeed, but as mentioned above this follows from the fact that they belonged to or near the household sphere. However, though more frequently encountered than the household associations, it may be objected that the inscriptions naming imperial *cultores* are not very frequent either.

There are of course more criteria than that of public–private which determined the amount of inscriptional evidence available for these groupings. One of the most obvious is that of economic means. The inscriptions show that *cultores*, no matter who was the object of their worship, were practically always slaves or freedmen, and clearly of humble economic means; presumably such associations filled a need for members of these status groups, who were not affluent or influential enough to become *Augustales* or officials in the compital cult. This of course implies that they would leave behind far fewer sources, including inscriptions, which also required some means to erect. The very few inscriptions testifying to *cultores* of the house gods of private persons confirm this impression: they are either funerary or erected by the *patronus*, not by the worshippers themselves, and as we shall see, exterior assistance is also commonly to be detected in the inscriptions of the imperial *cultores*. We may further note that both groups of inscriptions, though few, are distributed all over Italy. These features do in fact suggest that such associations, whether of the household type dealt with above, or of the emperor, were quite common; almost completely ignored in scholarship, they certainly merit closer attention.

CULTORES OF THE EMPEROR

As mentioned above, household, or 'extended household' associations appear to have furnished an important background and source of inspiration to the private *cultores* dedicated to worship of the emperor (or to the cult of the 'real' gods, which

[9] *CIL* IX. 2654; Dexter's offices: IX. 2655, including (imperial) *flamen* (only imperial cult has flaminates attested in Aesernia); cf. IX. 2483 (*cul(tores?) Flaminiani*).

is indeed more common in the inscriptions). The designations of these imperial cult associations vary in part from *collegium* to *collegium*, as is to be expected from such apparently uncoordinated and spontaneously established enterprises. We find in the inscriptions—practically our only source—*cultores domus divinae* or *domus augustae* or *larum aug(ustorum)* or *imaginum domus augustae* or *larum et imaginum domus augustae* and so on; and, less frequently, *collegium*, such as in *collegium magnum larum Caesaris nostri* or *larum et imaginum dom(i)n(i) invicti Antonini Pii* and so on.[10] The words *cultores, imagines, domus,* and to a lesser degree *lares* are thus found again and again, and they point to origins in the sphere of household cults. Some of these associations clearly belonged to the imperial household, having only the emperor's slaves and freedmen as members, whereas others did not belong to a particular *domus*; it is worth noticing, however, that this distinction did not entail any difference in titulature.

Thus these associations seem to have ultimately originated in the household cults, whose members then continued to employ the vocabulary and form of organization to which they were accustomed, even after leaving their *domus* and establishing cultic groupings outside it. By the late first century, at least, it seems that this form of emperor worship was more commonly found outside the household than within it, since the main reason for Tacitus' explanatory remark on the *cultores Augusti* must be that such household groupings were no longer so ubiquitous in his day. Indeed, most of our inscriptions date from the second or early third century; this is, however, true for the epigraphical sources generally, so once again no argument of frequency can be based on this chronological distribution.

I shall deal with only a few examples here. From the reign of Augustus we possess only one certain example of imperial *cultores* in Italy. A relief-decorated altar from Nola, which has been almost completely overlooked, bears on its front the following inscription (*CIL* X. 1238): 'Sacred to Augustus. The people of Laurinium restored [the altar] with their own money the worshippers *d. d.* [?]'—*Augusto* | *sacrum.* | *Restituerunt* | *laurinienses* | *pecunia sua* | *cultores* | *d. d.* (Fig. 9.1). These

[10] Breccia (1910) for the material.

FIG. 9.1. Altar from Nola
Notes: A: front; B: left side of the altar, showing *victimarius* and victim, a bull. (Sketch by Anders J. B. Jørgensen after author's photographs.)

laurinienses appear to have been the inhabitants of a *pagus* or district of Nola's urban area. The final *d. d.* is rather problematic, and renders the structure of the text difficult to grasp. One suggestion has been to transcribe *d(onum) d(ederunt)*—'gave the gift'—and see *laurinienses cultores* as the single subject of the sentence;[11] however, it seems strange that the subject is in that case split up by *pecunia sua*. Another suggestion has been *d(ecreto) d(ecurion*um)—'by decree of the decuriones'(i.e. the town council of Nola).[12] But *cultores* are always private associations, and it is therefore difficult to see any reason for

[11] Ribezzo (1937); he rediscovered the altar after its publication in *CIL*, but by then it had been immured in a wall of the house, 88, Riviera di Chiaia in Naples, so that only the front was visible. Ribezzo therefore only dealt with the inscription. The altar has since been removed from the wall and now stands, with all sides visible, in the courtyard of the same house, where I have studied it. A plaster cast of the altar is exhibited in the Mus. della Civiltà Romana, Rome.

[12] Mommsen in *CIL*, *loc. cit.*

the passing of a decree, which would be unique in this connection (we should rather expect *l(ocus) d(atus) d(ecreto) d(ecurionum)*—'the site given by decree of the *decuriones*'—but this is not the case). It has not been taken into account that *cultores d. d.* is cut in a recess of the stone, showing that the earlier text on the space has been chiselled out. The rather confusing character of the inscription may be partially explained by this meddling with the text, which appears, however, not only contemporary with the rest of the inscription, but may even have been cut by the same hand.

We are, however, in any case still left with the problem of *d. d.* I would suggest the restoration *cultores d(omus) d(ivinae)*. If that is correct, this would be the earliest known occurrence of *domus divina* as a term for the imperial house, a form not otherwise encountered before the reign of Tiberius.[13] The altar restored by the Laurinienses would then appear to have been taken over and reused not long afterwards by the *cultores*, who presumably had the bottom text erased and their own title added instead to mark this. If so, this sequence of events would to some extent explain why they were in possession of such a relatively costly monument, unique among imperial *cultores*. We cannot know the reason for such a takeover, nor when and why the Laurinienses restored the monument in the first place. Augustus owned much land around Nola (both he and his father died there); the *cultores* may therefore have been imperial slaves and freedmen, in which case we would after all be dealing with a household cult, but once again we have no means of knowing.[14]

The crude reliefs of the altar are clearly of local workmanship. The left side of the block, rather badly preserved, shows a *victimarius*, who, mallet in hand, leads a bull by a rein.[15] Incidentally, the scene confirms that a bull was the appropriate

[13] *CIL* XIII. 4635 (Tiberian); Phaed. 5. 7. 38; A. B. West, *Corinth* 8. 2, no. 68 (AD 55); *CIL* VII. 11 (Flavian) appear to be the earliest datable examples.

[14] Points advanced by Ribezzo (1937, *passim*), too speculative; 11 ff. he argues that the cult was restored in 27 when and because Octavian became Augustus, but numerous other reasons can of course be imagined.

[15] The altar reliefs have never been published before, merely described by Mommsen in *CIL loc. cit.*; the sacrificial victim he described as a cow: '*minister vaccam ducens securim tenet*'. There can, however, be no doubt that the animal is in fact a bull; cf. my Fig. 9.1.

victim not only to the emperor's *Genius*, but also to himself. The altar's back and right side shows various cultic implements, sacrificial knife (*culter*), a cauldron (for boiling the inner organs of the victim), a wine-jar, dish (*patera*), and the sprinkler (*aspergillum*).

Later on, as the overall number of inscriptions grows, we also encounter more examples of the imperial *cultores*. From Rome itself a dedicatory inscription for a small temple (*aedicula*) to Claudius and the imperial *Lares* mentions an association of the imperial household—*collegium Augustianum maius castrense*.[16] Outside the imperial *familia* another, slightly later, urban Roman inscription runs (*CIL* VI. 481): 'To the Worshippers of the Images of the Imperial House the managers [of the college] in the second year: [names of the five managers] gave as a gift with their own money [this?] sculpture of Liberty Revived by Servius Galba Imperator Augustus'—*Imaginum domus aug(ustae) cultorib(us) signum Libertatis restitutae Ser(vi) Galbae imperatoris Aug(usti) curatores anni secundi* [the names of five freedmen, none imperial] *s(ua) p(ecunia) d(ono) d(ederunt)*. There follows the date of the dedication of the statue: 15 October AD 68. The association had then been established shortly before (*anni secundi*) under Nero, to whose worship it had obviously been dedicated; yet quickly and automatically it assumed the ideology of the new emperor, branding Nero as a tyrant. Two pairs out of the five *curatores* are freedmen of the same masters, which may indicate that the *collegium* represented a continuation of household cults.

In some instances, the involvement of imperial freedmen in these groupings gives us further clues as to the background of such cults, and the ways they could be influenced or controlled from above. An epitaph to an imperial freedman, T. Flavius Trophimus, names him as 'founder of the college of the masters' divine power, which is under the temple of Divus Claudius'—*constitutori collegi numinis dominorum quod* [sc. 'collegium', hardly '*numen*'] *est sup templo Divi Claudi* (*CIL* VI. 10251*a*). In the foundation of Divus Claudius' temple are still preserved a row of *tabernae*, where the association had its meeting place; presumably the members were, at least partially,

[16] *CIL* VI. 40415 = Gordon (1958, i, no. 90) = Smallwood (1967, no. 131).

local shopkeepers. The fact that the club was established in Flavian times—the *domini* referred to were presumably Vespasian and Titus—indicates that we are not dealing merely with matters within the imperial household, where establishment of such associations would presumably be unnecessary, since they were already in existence. Unfortunately this inscription is unique in giving us the name(s) of whoever established it. But the hand of an imperial freedman is clearly visible in other cases, such as *CIL* IX. 3887: 'The overseer Onesimus, the emperor's freedman, made [the temple?] for the images and *Lares* for the Worshippers of Fucinus'—*Onesimus Aug(usti) lib(ertus) proc(urator) fecit* [sc. '*aediculam*' or the like] *imaginibus et laribus cultoribus Fucini*. The freedman, as *procurator* still in the service of the emperor, has thus erected a cult building of some kind for the *cultores Fucini*, worshippers of a personification of the Fucine Lake. Though the grammar is somewhat confusing, the images and *Lares* named (undoubtedly those of the emperor) were evidently donated to the cult association together with the building, whereby the cult was apparently completely changed. It should be recalled that the new form of worship was that of Onesimus' own house cult, or at any rate very close to it in form. There is one other instance of an imperial freedman supporting a group of imperial *cultores* (*CIL* VI. 30955); though the evidence is scant indeed, these are almost the only cases where outside involvement is evident. The examples furnish an interesting and literal illustration of the transfer of traditional house cults outside the house sphere—from *paterfamilias* to *pater patriae*.

Many of these associations actually belonged, as mentioned, within the imperial household itself. Thus the longest and most important source among the relevant inscriptions also deals with an association within the imperial household; here too external influences are evident, in this case clearly on the initiative of the worshippers themselves. The inscription, from Ostia, is on a marble tablet found in secondary context and dated in its text to AD 205:[17]

Locus adsignatus a Callist[o] Aug(usti) lib(erto) proc(uratore) cultorib(us) larum et imaginum dominorum nostrorum invictissimorum

[17] *CIL* XIV. 4570; tr. Meiggs (1973, 333), adapted.

Augustor(um) praediorum Rusticelianorum ad sollemnes dies confrequentandos curante Maximiano Aug(usti) n(ostri) verna vilico eorundem praediorum, sicut litteris ab eodem Callisto emissis contine(n)tur, dedic(atus) kal(endis) Iunis Imp(eratore) Antonino Pio Felic(e) Aug(usto) (iterum) co(n)s(ule).

Exemplum libelli:
Callistus Maximiano. [L]ibellum datum mihi a cu[lt]oribus larum Aug(ustorum) at (*sic*) te misi. Opertuerat (*sic*) te in tam religi[os]am rem ipse (*sic*) etiam omne(m) solli[ci]tudine(m) adhibuisse, ut locus [o]lim consacratus confrequentetur pro salute domi[n]orum n(ostrorum) Aug(ustorum duorum), quod vel nu[nc e]tiam volentibus cultoribus [f]acere intervenire cura, ut s[in]e recrasti(nati)one (*sic*) mundetur.

This site was assigned by Callistus, the emperor's freedman and procurator, to the worshippers of the Lares and images of our invincible lords the emperors on the Rusticelian estate for the celebration of due occasions under the care of Maximianus, our emperor's slave from birth, steward of the estate, as is provided in the letter sent by the above-named Callistus; the site was dedicated on the 1st of June when the emperor Antoninus Pius Felix Augustus was consul for the second time.

Copy of the letter:
'Callistus to Maximianus. The letter handed to me by the worshippers of the imperial Lares I have sent to you. In such a matter where religious duty was so clearly involved, you should have shown every anxiety to see that the site which had been formerly consecrated should be used for celebrations for the welfare of our lord emperors. Now, though the worshippers express their wish to do it themselves, see that you take the matter in hand and have the place cleaned without delay.'

Uniquely among the inscriptions dealing with such *cultores*, this document has been properly published,[18] and I shall therefore limit myself to a few comments. Consisting of imperial slaves (and freedmen?) employed on an imperially owned estate (*praedii Rusticeliani*) and under the authority of an imperial slave (Maximianus), the association clearly did not have a *lex sacra* or other formalized regulations for its activity. Instead the *cultores* had engraved in stone and set up the permission granted by Callistus, imperial freedman and procurator in

[18] G. Calza in *NSc* (1921), 235–41; further lit. in *CIL loc. cit.*

charge of the estate, to use an area of its land for cultic ceremonies on imperial feast days. That this rather unimpressive document was apparently the most prestigious text the worshippers had to publish is revealing; the absence of more formal regulations, which may here be demonstrated *e silentio*, appears to have been typical of the *cultores*, for there is no trace in the inscriptions of any for these humble associations. It is certainly worthy of note that the request of the *cultores* is being taken seriously by Callistus. Nevertheless, his reply seems pretty much a somewhat clumsy version of a routine document from the administrative level below the imperial chancery, and yet this inscription is after all the longest text and most impressive monument we possess from such worshippers.[19]

In two instances from Rome inscriptions inform us of temples, financed by *cultores* or their *curatores*.[20] The oft-repeated assertion that there was no cult of the living emperor in Rome is proved absurd by these and other private monuments.[21] The distinction is simply wrong in the geographical terms usually employed in research; Rome was clearly crowded with cults dedicated to the living emperor (and cult of the *Divi* was no doubt much rarer). Only in constitutional terms can the case be argued: in *the state cult*, and only there, no direct divine worship of the emperor took place. The fact that the mistaken claim as to the absence of emperor worship in Rome has become so commonly accepted as to be quoted in virtually every handbook on the Roman empire without any doubt or opposition only goes to show the exclusivity with which scholarship has focused on public emperor worship and ignored private cults.

It may be time for a summing-up on the imperial *cultores*. Their form of organization appears to have originated in household cults, where such groupings were common, at least in Rome, in the early empire (Tac. *Ann.* 1. 73). Later on, when such groupings had apparently become more rare within the households, the form was established and flourishing outside this context. Our evidence is sparse, not because these associations were rare, but because their members were humble

[19] A similar, though fragmentary example is *CIL* VI. 455 (AD 168).

[20] *CIL* VI. 253; 958.

[21] e.g. *CIL* VI. 905 (AD 14–29); 961 (altar, AD 103–13); 218 (*aedicula* and *ara*, AD 202); 607 (*aedicula* to the *domus Augusta*).

people, slaves and freedmen of low social standing and limited economic means. These groupings were, as private cults generally, practically always dedicated to the living emperor, hardly ever to departed ones (*Divi*).[22] Whether these associations belonged to the imperial household, or were open to others than the emperor's *familia*, their titulature was more or less the same; hence membership of such a grouping ideologically speaking expressed the worshippers' membership of the emperor's *familia*.

However, the worship accorded the emperor in these associations was in form somewhat deviant from usual house cults of the *paterfamilias*, for the *cultores* never appear to have worshipped the emperor's *Genius*; since all heads of households received worship of their *Genius*, this was perhaps felt to constitute too small an honour. The worship was rather, in most cases, dedicated to his images, or to the imperial family at large (*domus augusta* or *divina*). The role of the imperial image in this connection sets these associations apart from *cultores* dedicated to the 'old' gods. With these, we never find them described or termed as worshippers of images: their title is regularly simply *cultores* plus the genitive of the name of the god. The prominent role of the *imagines* in the titulature of imperial *cultores* presumably reflects a theological difference between the emperor and the traditional gods. Whereas they were omnipresent, the emperor was not present at the ceremonies and sacrifices to him of his *cultores*; so his image functioned as his representative. Whatever divine worship was accorded the emperor in this connection, he was not then credited with the traditionally divine omnipresence.

OTHER CORPORATE WORSHIP

Associations worshipping the emperor included many other groupings than those named *cultores*. A revealing case of such private devotion involved one of Tacitus' *bêtes noires*, Tiberius' praetorian prefect Sejanus. In his last years 'people' in Rome habitually sacrificed to his images, according to Suetonius and

[22] To my knowledge there is only one instance from Italy of a collegiate cult dedicated to a *Divus* (Pertinax): *AE* 1971. 64 = Zevi (1971, 472 ff.).

Cassius Dio. The evidence is further supported by Tacitus; the historian describes how Sejanus gradually increased his power after concentrating the praetorian cohorts in one camp in AD 23:[23]

No sooner was the camp finished, than Sejanus began gradually to insinuate himself into the good graces of the soldiers, mixing with them, and addressing them by name. He chose his own Tribunes and centurions. He intrigued also for influence with the Senate, obtaining distinctions and provincial commands for his own creatures; while Tiberius looked so indulgently on his proceedings that he would often commend him as his partner in toil, not only in private talk, but also in the Senate, and before the people, and permitted his statues to be worshipped in the theatres, in the public squares, and at the head quarters of the legions.

The passage seems to imply active permission rather than just passive sufferance.[24] This permission was of stunning importance and impact: it effectively presented Sejanus as co-regent of the emperor, even to the legions. At this point, however, we are more concerned with the worship in the theatres and public squares, *per theatra et fora*. In describing the fire in Pompey's theatre the year before, Tacitus reports that Tiberius commended to the Senate Sejanus' efforts in containing the calamity. The senators responded by decreeing that Sejanus' statue should be erected in the theatre. This statue is indeed mentioned several times in our sources; its notoriety presumably stems from the fact that this singularly glorious placement had hitherto been reserved for images of gods and members of the imperial family and Romans of old. The words *per theatra* no doubt refer to this statue (the plural is rhetorical, to go with

[23] Suet. *Tib.* 65. 1; 48. 2; Dio 58. 4. 3 f.; 58. 8. 4; 58. 11. 2; cf. 58. 7. 2 (Sejanus sacrificing to himself); Tac. *Ann.* 3. 72. 4; 4. 7. 3; 4. 2. 2 f. (tr. G. G. Ramsay, adapted): '*Ut perfecta sunt castra, inrepere paulatim militares animos adeundo, appellando; simul centuriones ac tribunos ipse deligere. Neque senatorio ambitu abstinebat clientes suos honoribus aut provinciis ornandi, facili Tiberio atque ita prono, ut socium laborum non modo in sermonibus, sed apud patres et populum celebraret colique per theatra et fora effigies eius interque principia legionum sineret*'.

[24] *Sineret* can have both meanings; it stands, however, parallel to *celebraret*, and as for the *principia legionum*, Tiberius must surely have granted active permission—though not an order, for the legions of Syria (no doubt made cautious by their involvement with Cn. Piso in 19–20) did not place Sejanus' image there (Suet. *Tib.* 48. 2).

fora, but the permission of course gave a precedent for other theatres in Rome and outside).

It may indeed have been Sejanus' statue in the theatre of Pompey that triggered off a petition to Tiberius as to whether worship was to be permitted, since habitual worship was then, as the incident suggests, accorded the other statues, divine or imperial, in the theatre. Hence the worshippers, no matter who they were, must have felt considerable unease as to how to react to this new statue of a non-imperial personage. Sejanus' position was unique, and their uncertainty must have been general; their possible petition may therefore have wandered up through the capital's administrative system to be ultimately referred to the emperor himself. Tacitus probably, to judge from his passage, read Tiberius' reply, in which the emperor as a precedent may have referred to the already existing worship of Sejanus in the legionary sanctuaries; certainty is of course impossible, but Tacitus' frequent perusal of documentary evidence, such as the *acta senatus*, in his *Annals* is beyond doubt, and the possible background outlined here would appear to fit his description very well.

Another and perhaps more important question is who these 'people' were who worshipped the images of Sejanus and the imperial family *per theatra et fora* in the capital. Though such worship could be and no doubt was carried out by individuals, Tiberius' ruling must have been given to some corporate body (it is furthermore difficult to imagine any individual suicidal enough to stick out his neck in such a delicate matter). Indeed most worship in public was performed by corporate bodies, whatever their exact nature. On the other hand the worship was clearly of a private nature; nothing of the kind took place in the state cult. These groupings could have included our *cultores*, but their humble status would render such worship unimportant to the government, and indeed to Tacitus. Persons of higher rank seem to be implied, and there is no reason to exclude senators from such ceremonies of private worship; that might seem to account for the stir, even shock, of our sources in their mention of this worship.

The stir was not, however, caused by the fact that such worship was accorded to mortals, nor that it took place in the capital. It seems obvious why the worship of Sejanus' images is referred to in our literary sources whereas such worship of imperial images goes unmentioned: that was no doubt habitual and a matter of course, in Tiberius' day as well as later, when Tacitus and Cassius Dio wrote. Hence it was never mentioned as such (only Dio refers directly to it, and then only in connection with the corresponding honours to Sejanus' images); as usual our literary sources furnish us with the curious and exceptional rather than with what was 'natural' and common knowledge. The instance goes to show how very common indeed must have been such worship of the emperor, or his image, in Rome (and no doubt everywhere else). Furthermore, the very vague and general descriptions of the worshippers in our sources further underline this conclusion, even if we allow Suetonius' comment that it took place 'everywhere' to be a rhetorical exaggeration. Once again, speaking of the nature of our sources, it is salutary to note that without Sejanus we would have no mention of these forms of imperial worship, extremely common though they were—hence, indeed, the silence of our literary sources.

Theatra et fora, theatres and public squares, were the sites *par excellence* for the erection of imperial statues. Though the cult was private, this must therefore not be taken as indicating anything more than a formal and legal definition. Indeed, as the Sejanus story shows, these associations often performed their worship in public, something which was very often the case with private Roman worship in general.[25]

My interpretation of the Sejanus incident may seem to press the evidence unduly, but it is supported by what is in this connection probably the most revealing literary source altogether, Pliny's *Panegyric to Trajan* (and to Pliny's fellow senators). After lauding Trajan for not allowing state worship to be accorded to the emperor's *Genius*, a passage I have dealt with elsewhere (p. 191), Pliny goes on to describe private sacrifices to Domitian on the Capitol (*Pan.* 52. 7): 'Yet previously vast herds of victims were often stopped on the Capitoline Way and large numbers forced to turn aside, for that grim statue of a brutal tyrant was worshipped with as much blood as the human blood he himself shed'.

[25] Beard (1994, 732 f.).

The bitter invective clearly implies that these sacrifices had also been performed by senators, possibly even corporatively, though not in state sacrifice (*pro populo publico sumptu*). Apart from obvious rhetorical hyperbole, such as the understandable claim *post festum*, that people had been 'forced' to perform these rites (as usual after the fall of a 'bad' emperor, all blame is put on him only), Pliny's criticism only depends on the claim that the worship was accorded to a gruesome tyrant, who did not settle only for the blood of beasts. The practice of sacrificing to an emperor is not attacked as such: which clearly implies that these ceremonies were also performed under Trajan, by senators, that is, or else Pliny would hardly have hesitated to attack the phenomenon itself.[26] Only extreme or bizarre circumstances, such as the non-imperial case of Sejanus or the rhetorical presentation of Domitian as a *monstrum*, cause the mention of such sacrifices, though they evidently took place under 'good' as well as 'bad' emperors. The fact that Pliny's *Panegyric* is a piece of high rhetoric should not cause us to reject this information: his audience would know better than any whether his statement was factually wrong. It clearly was not.

PRIVATE MONEY, PUBLIC FAVOURS

The compital cults (p. 116ff. above) were strictly speaking private, yet under tight control from the public authorities in Rome and elsewhere in the townships of Italy where they existed. At least in Rome the officials, the *magistri vici*, of these

[26] A group of junior senators appear to be listed as members of a cultic college—*ordo sacerdotum domus Aug(ustae) Palat(inae)* within the imperial household, though open to members from outside it: *CIL* VI. 2010. The commentary of *CIL loc. cit.* and *PIR*, 1st edn., III, no. 558 identify the Vitrasius Pol(l)io in the list of senators (*clarissimi viri*) as T. Pomponius Proculus Vitrasius Pollio, cos. II 176; but the name is listed as the fifth among the senators, whereas a consul—let alone a cos II—should have been placed at the very top of the group. Hence Pomponius' son T. Fundanius Vitrasius Pollio (*PIR*, 1st edn., II, no. 395) seems a much likelier candidate. He is recorded as becoming *salius Palatinus* in 170, but is otherwise unknown; considering his relation to the imperial house—his mother was the cousin of both Marcus and his empress Faustina—this silence suggests that he died prematurely, and the inscription should then be dated to about 170, give or take a few years; it cannot pre-date 161 (col. b, l. 5: *Augg. [l.]*).

cults were very much a part of the public administrative system of the city, albeit they were not state-funded (and hence they were private in legal terms). This close relationship and co-operation with the public authorities the compital cults share with another private category of people, the *Augustales* or *seviri Augustales* (not to be confused with titles of municipal public priests, such as *flamen Augustalis*). The (*seviri*) *Augustales* were municipal corporate bodies, absent from Rome, but often involved in imperial honours locally in Italian townships.[27] The title of (*seviri*) *Augustales* appears all over Italy from the reign of Augustus onwards. It is difficult to know how and why these uniform titles came to spread all over Italy. There is no trace of control or manipulation from the capital behind this development, and it seems most plausible to explain the pattern as resulting from competitive emulation between townships.

The *Augustales* were strongly involved in emperor worship, as is also suggested by their very title. To give again only a few examples, their meeting hall in Herculaneum was dedicated to Augustus and was indeed an *Augusteum*, a temple of the emperor; similar temples are known from Misenum, Otricoli, and Ostia; and at Brundisium a newly appointed *Augustalis* responded by erecting an altar to Trajan.[28] Scholarship on the *Augustales* has indeed agreed unanimously that they had emperor worship as their main function and *raison d'être*. That seems to be wrong, however, for the *Augustales* were not officials or members of a priesthood, but of an order (*ordo*), the local parallel to the *ordo equester*, which was the second order, below that of senators, in Rome; the *Augustales* similarly formed the second order, below that of the local senators, the *decuriones*, in each township. But it follows from taking the *Augustales* as members of a local *ordo* that they therefore did not have any functions of office. To be *Augustalis* was neither an office nor a priesthood. Their appellation after the emperor was thus purely honorary.

The order consisted of local men who in spite of personal wealth were unable to enter the highest order, the *ordo*

[27] Abramenko (1993) with lit.

[28] Otricoli, Misenum, and generally: Dareggi (1982); Misenum: Castiglione Morelli (1991); Herculaneum: *AE* 1979. 169; Etienne (1988); Ostia: Meiggs (1973, 217ff.); Calza (1941); Brundisium: *CIL* IX. 39.

decurionum of their towns, typically because they were not free-born, but ex-slaves. The existence of this second order, though strictly outside the public sphere, since only *decuriones* could hold public office, enabled local townships to exploit the economic resources of such wealthy locals. And conversely, the order and its interplay with the *decuriones* and the strictly public sphere of a town enabled such men access to a prominent local position and public honours even though they strictly speaking formed only a private association: they had no claim on public expenditure, though typically the *decuriones* would honour them with, for example, statues paid for from public funds. The *Augustales* formed an important part of the structure of euergetism in their townships, as is clearly evident from the abundant number of inscriptions testifying to buildings and other benefactions financed by them. The fact that they were not priests should not be taken as implying that they were not frequently involved in worship or erection of statues or other honours to the emperor; the inscriptions show us that they often were, which is hardly surprising, considering their prominent local position and the vast number of inscriptions left behind by this affluent order. Many of the buildings, statues, games, and so on set up by local *Augustales* honoured the emperor, as was the case in general for public monuments and festivals in these townships; but most did not. The common interpretation of the *Augustales* as imperial priests thus rests on a misunderstanding of definitions, and is misleadingly narrow. That is one reason for not dealing with them here, but the main one is the sheer scale of the evidence. A comprehensive monograph is lacking and would be welcome, incorporating not only the large body of inscriptional evidence mentioning them, but also the growing number of their known assembly halls, temples, and other monuments identified in excavations. A reasonably thorough treatment is not possible here, and I shall therefore leave them out of account with the observation that their activities were strictly speaking those of a private college, but closely interrelated with the formal public sphere of Italian townships.[29]

[29] See Abramenko (1993) and my review of this work in *JRS* 84 (1994), 259.

Among dedicators setting up temples and altars directly to the emperor, or to members of his family, in god-like fashion, both freeborn and freedmen, imperial as well as private, are encountered in the inscriptions. On the other hand, dedications to the emperor's *Genius* are almost exclusively set up by freedmen. This goes for the inscriptions from the compital cults, whose *magistri* and *ministri* were predominantly freedmen and slaves (p. 118 above); this is of course a special case, because these cults in Rome, whence they spread to the rest of Italy, were established and controlled by Augustus himself. But the pattern is the same in other dedications to this divinity. The only exception is a series of honorary altars set up by members of the *equites singulares*, the mounted bodyguard of the emperor in their barracks on the occasion of their honourable discharge. The altars, fifteen in number and spanning the years 118–89, are each dedicated to a long list of different divinities of special relevance to the corps (*CIL* VI. 31138–52); on four of the altars the list includes the emperor's *Genius*. These dedicators were certainly freeborn, but the exception cannot carry much weight; the fact that they were recruited outside Italy is perhaps not very important in this connection, but they were lowly born, and clearly stood in a cliental relationship to the emperor; and the *Genius*, life force, of the emperor seems appropriate indeed for members of his bodyguard.

In all other cases, the dedicators in inscriptions to the *Genius Augusti* are either freedmen or slaves. Considering the enormous role ascribed to the *Genius* in scholarship on the imperial cult in Italy, it is salutary to note that such dedications are very few in number; indeed, outside the compital cults only a handful are known. Some of these were set up by imperial slaves or freedmen, and therefore belong to traditional household cults; others were put up by non-imperial persons of servile status, but apart from the dedications of the *equites singulares* none of these can be dated with any certainty after the reign of Tiberius (see App. 2). The rarity of dedications to the emperor's *Genius* presumably indicates that such worship, accorded any *paterfamilias* by his *familia* and in no way entailing divine status for him, was felt to constitute too 'little' an honour, as I have already indicated in connection with the absence of the *Genius Augusti* in the titulature of the imperial *cultores*.

CONCLUSION ON PRIVATE EMPEROR WORSHIP

Leaving aside the dedications of *Augustales*, the worship at the compita, and the cults of soldiers, we are left with a substantial number of private groupings, inside as well as outside the household, which were initiated from below, apparently without any intervention from the *body politic* of the state, or, as in the case of Sejanus, with the emperor only responding with formal permission. In practice this even goes for the apparent exception, namely the libation before private banquets decreed by the Senate to Octavian in 30 BC; for without positive response from below, the libation would certainly not have become established practice, and be encountered as such a century later in Petronius. I have attempted here to establish an image of such private cults as very common and widespread indeed, in the *domus*, in the streets, in public squares, in Rome itself (perhaps there in particular) as well as outside the capital.

In some instances, though very few, we find emperors responding to these phenomena. In the case of Sejanus, the reply was positive; more often, when not merely ignored, which appears indeed to have been the usual attitude of emperors, it was negative. Early in his reign, Tiberius forbade the setting up of his portraits without permission, and banned completely the erection of his portraits among the cult images of the gods, in other words, any formal divine worship to himself.[30] The injunction was apparently relevant only to the state cult in Rome. Thus statues could indeed receive informal worship irrespective of where they were placed. Tiberius' attitude to such private worship was clearly very different: with Sejanus at the height of his power, the emperor not only displayed complete tolerance towards such worship of himself, as usual, but amazingly gave explicit permission for the same honours to be performed to the images of Sejanus. It was only when the emperor began to fear the Praetorian Prefect that he banned sacrifices to himself—and, implicitly, to Sejanus.[31] Another troubled emperor, Claudius, distanced himself from his erratic

[30] Suet. *Tib*. 26. 1; see p. 143 above.

[31] Dio 58. 8. 4.

and worship-craving nephew Caligula by repeating such a ban.[32] Whether directed against public worship, as in most recorded cases, or private worship, as in a few extraordinary instances, such pious protestations should not be taken too seriously. The refusal of divine honours was formulaic, a touchstone enabling the emperor to flaunt his *moderatio*, and thereby calm down a nervous Senate. Indeed, the extraordinary circumstances behind the few instances where emperors took a stand against private worship of themselves indicate that the phenomenon was as common as it was permanent. We may rest assured that such refusals of sacrifices had very little or no effect whatsoever, and obviously no man was ever prosecuted for sacrificing to his emperor.

[32] Dio 60. 5. 4.

10

Numen Augustum

The concept of *numen*, 'divine force or power' or 'divinity', has played a large role in scholarship on Roman religion. Older scholars, such as Warde Fowler or James Frazer in *The Golden Bough*, saw the concept as central in the archaic or supposed 'primeval' stage of Roman religion. In their view, the experience of *numen*, impersonal, mysterious, and inexplicable forces of nature, constituted the oldest Roman ideas of deity; only later, under Greek influence, did these forces develop into the anthropomorphic Roman gods of historical times. The concept was frequently compared to and identified with the Polynesian concept of 'mana'.[1]

These views have been discarded by modern historians of religion, together with the notion that there ever was a genuinely Roman religion, uncontaminated by Greek influence; and for all we know, the anthropomorphic version of divinity may well have been the 'original' one.[2] The central role played by *numen* in studies of primeval Roman religion, and the protracted debates as to its nature and function in prehistorical times, have, as I see it, 'spilt over' into another aspect of research, dealing with the emperor's *numen*. On the immediate cognitive level—what is the emperor's *numen*?—a voluminous scholarly literature has grown up. To me the amount of discussion in this field seems to stand in contrast to the simplicity of the answer, which is in fact, as we shall see, clearly suggested in the ancient sources.

These sources, it is true, never ask and hence never answer the question. So scholars have continued the discussion on a purely philological and theological level. As we shall see, a more material or archaeological approach may supply a convincing answer. Thus we could ask what or whom the cult images in a cult to the emperor's *numen* actually represented. The noun *numen* is neuter, so it cannot be personified; and hence it could

[1] Warde Fowler (1911, *passim*, esp. 118ff.); Wagenvoort (1947, 73ff.); other lit. and survey in Pötscher (1978, 355ff.).

[2] Thus Pötscher (1978).

hardly have cult images. Either these images represented something else, or the cults were aniconic. Correspondingly, since the sex of the sacrificial victims should in Roman sacral tradition correspond to that of the god worshipped, could animals be sacrificed, or was the cult bloodless, employing only wine and incense? In the answer to these concrete questions we should, if the sources allow us, be able to get to the contemporary view of what the emperor's *numen* was, or what was its closest 'personifiable' translation.

The complicated discussions on the subject reflect the fact that *numen* is a very vague term, difficult to pin down in concrete terms. Rather than try to get behind or attempting to defeat this 'obstructive' vagueness, as previous studies have usually attempted, we could perhaps use it as a distinctive and defining tool in the investigation.

The basic meaning of the word *numen* is not in doubt. As any Latin dictionary will tell us, the word means 'divine power' or 'divinity'/'godhead'. It is impersonal (cf. its gender), but belongs to a god,[3] and is the force or power by which the god manifests himself in the world. Alternatively, but of course very close to this meaning, it could, at least in the imperial age, denote the deity himself, or herself, and thus be a synonym for '*deus*' (or '*dea*'), like 'divinity' or 'godhead' in English.[4]

NUMEN AUGUSTUM OR *AUGUSTI*

As for the *numen* of the emperor there is today considerable confusion as to what the word actually signifies. Older scholars saw it as in this context completely synonymous with *genius*;[5]

[3] Pötscher (1978) argues that it is not the property of gods only, referring to the fact that also the Senate and the *populus Romanus* could be credited with *numen*; the argument has a (too) strong theological or dogmatic flavour in its attempt to define divine nature, but it is also flawed: as collective entities, both the *Senatus* and the *populus Romanus* were indeed gods, cf. their personifications, the *Genius populi Romani* and (later) *Genius senatus*.

[4] The original meaning of the word is accepted by most scholars, ancient and modern, to be a 'nod', noun to *nuere*, as *flumen* to *fluere*. Cf. Festus (p. 108 L): '*Numen quasi nutus dei ac potestas*'; Varro, *Ling. Lat.* 7. 85: '*numen dicunt esse imperium*'.

[5] Pippidi (1931) states the case for this; also Taylor (1931, *passim*, e.g. 220); for other instances see Fishwick (1991, ii. 1. 377 n. 10).

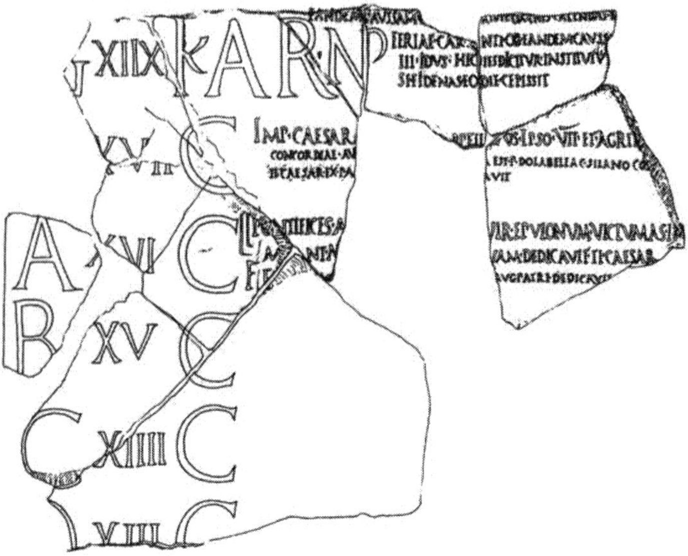

FIG. 10.1. The *Fasti Praenestini*
Note: Detail of the entries for January, that of the 17th is the lowest of the three shown.
Source: Drawing from Degrassi (1963), 114.

more recently, Fishwick has argued for its separate nature, though he still accepted that the word in some instances was used synonymously with *Genius*.[6] This view has effectively muddled up the picture and outline of the concept. Fishwick may of course be right that the question is as complex as he presents it, but his immense amount of detail and references, very useful, but not always of central relevance to the discussion, may indeed lead one to suspect the forest to have been lost in the trees in his version.

The question seems of great importance owing to an unfortunately fragmentary entry in the calendar from Praeneste, the *Fasti Praenestini*, for 17 January, (Fig. 10.1) in Mommsen's and Taylor's commonly accepted restoration, which is based on the existence of such altars in Narbo and Forum Clodii:[7]

[6] Fishwick (1969), restated, with exhaustive references, in id. (1991, ii. 1. 375 ff.); likewise Pötscher (1978).

[7] Degrassi (1963, 115, cf. 401) (=Ehrenberg and Jones, 1955, 46); Taylor (1937, 187 ff.); the *Fasti Praen.* were composed by Verrius Flaccus, for whom

XVI c(omitialis): Pontifices, a[ugures, XV vir(i) s(acris) f(aciundis), VII]vir(i) epulonum victumas in/m[ola]nt n[umini Augusti ad aram q]uam dedicavit Ti(berius) Caesar.

17 Jan., day of assembly [i.e. non-holiday]: [the four major priestly colleges of the Roman state] sacrificed victims to the *numen* of Augustus by the altar which Tiberius Caesar had dedicated.

The next line in the entry has been added by another hand after Tiberius became emperor in AD 14:

Fe[riae ex s(enatus) c(onsulto) q]u[od e(o) d(ie) Ti(berius) Caesar aram Divo] Aug(usto) patri dedicavit.

Holiday by decree of the Senate, because on this day Tiberius Caesar dedicated the altar to his father Divus Augustus.

Tiberius was adopted by Augustus in AD 4, and became sole heir two years later. The *Fasti* (minus the Tiberian additions) were probably engraved in AD 6, and Tiberius' dedication has been surmised to have taken place in AD 5 or 6.[8] It should no doubt be interpreted as an act of gratitude to Augustus for the adoption: 17 January was the date of Augustus' marriage to Livia Drusilla, mother of Tiberius, in 38 BC.[9] But the implications of this dedication go far beyond mere filial piety, for the worship centred upon the altar was a full-blown state cult, as is clearly evidenced by the participation of the four major priestly colleges of the Roman state. If the lines of the *Fasti* are correctly restored they therefore testify to a new and vital development in Augustus' position in the state system. Here we are dealing, not with what everybody may or may not have thought or felt or expressed in a private capacity, but with the strict formality of the 'constitution' of the Roman state. Hence the importance of what the emperor's *numen* actually was and signified.

To deserve credence, however, the extensive restorations must, at the very least, not conflict with the remnants actually preserved on the stone. As has in fact been noted by Degrassi

see now ed. R. Kaster of Suet. *Gramm.*; for municipal *Fasti* generally see Rüpke (1995).

[8] Engraved AD 6: Degrassi (1963, 141 f.); year of dedication: Pippidi (1933); Alföldi (1973, 43 f.); Torelli (1982, 63 ff.).

[9] *Fasti Verulani*: Degrassi (1963, 161).

and others who have, nevertheless, accepted the restorations, that is not the case here. The preserved left part of the letter interpreted as the decisive 'n' in *n[umini . . .]* looks decisively more like part of an 'm'; I have searched through all the n-forms in the *Fasti Praenestini*, and I have not been able to find a parallel to this supposed 'n': the sloping line of the letter's left half must, on the parallel evidence from the calendar, be an 'm'. The fact that the restoration has won general acceptance (presumably on the authority of Mommsen, Taylor, and Degrassi) and that no convincing alternatives have been suggested[10] makes no difference: it is mere guesswork, and even conflicts with what is preserved of the calendar entry. Lack of an alternative can never be a sufficient reason for accepting an extensive and unconvincing restoration. This is far from the only instance where the (over-)restorations of older scholars have done more damage than good, though they certainly cannot be blamed for the naïve credence accorded to their guesswork by later generations of scholars. In principle, restorations should never tell us anything we do not know already from unrestored sources. That is clearly not the case in this instance. The *ara numinis Augusti* in Rome is a ghost of modern scholarship. An honest approach is preferable: we cannot say with certainty, or even with likelihood, what was contained in the entry.[11]

The commonly accepted restoration may, however, receive

[10] Rejected only by Scott (1982, 438 ff.) who instead proposed '. . . *m[aior(es) provid(entiae) Aug(ustae/i) ad aram q]uam* . . .', but accepting the restorations of the Tiberian addition; his restoration has in turn been rejected by all scholars, thus Fishwick (1991, ii. 1. 378), rightly, since the *Ara Providentiae* now seems to have been dedicated on 26 June (year unknown), see Scheid (1998, 30 l. 55 ff.). Also, there is hardly room in the lacunae for the restorations, for Scott's abbreviations are not convincing. Worst of all, however, the altar would then be dedicated in the entry to the goddess Providentia Augusta, but in the Tiberian addition to Augustus himself, a problem simply ignored by Scott.

[11] A possible alternative, which is at least in accordance with the remnants on the stone, could e.g. be a dedication to *Mars Augustus Pater*. This would fit the lacunae, though the exact form of the name would to my knowledge be unique (as would a state altar to Augustus' *numen*); for *Mars Augustus* see e.g. Ehrenberg and Jones (1955, no. 43) (AD 6-7, Lepcis Magna); *pater* is commonly used with Mars; cf. also e. g. *Iano Patri Augusto*, Ehrenberg and Jones (1955, no. 43b) (=*ILS* 3320). But it it is hardly any use pursuing this game before new evidence turns up.

some support from the dedication a few years later of an *ara numini Augusti* in Narbo (AD 12), and an *ara numini Augusto* in Italian Forum Clodii (AD 18). The choice of cult object, centred on an altar, in these two separate places could perhaps be most easily explained as emulation of a cult in the capital. This argument is possible, though it cannot have any bearing on the restoration of the entry: for this was filled with reference to exactly these altars outside Rome, making, then, for circular reasoning. There are a few other Augustan instances of dedications to the imperial *numen*, but they are of little value in illuminating the supposed altar in Rome or the character of the concept.[12]

The altar in Narbo (*CIL* XII. 4333) has so far received almost all the attention,[13] despite the fact that the ritual centred on the altar is only summarily described: sacrifice of—unspecified—victims (*hostiae*) and a *supplicatio* of wine and incense. The *Genius* of the *paterfamilias* was usually worshipped with wine and incense in the house cult, and the identity of *numen* and *Genius* has been claimed on this basis.[14] But wine and incense were standard equipment in Roman sacrifices—thus generally offered to the gods as an 'aperitif' before blood sacrifices—and were always used in a *supplicatio* to a god. The argument is therefore based on lack of knowledge of Roman sacrificial procedures, and can be ignored—wine and incense are far too generic to settle anything. One other reason for the identification has been adduced, namely that the altar was dedicated on Augustus' birthday, and the birthday was the main festival of a man's *Genius*;[15] this also is far too generic a feature: Augustus' birthday was celebrated everywhere, *Genius* or no *Genius*.

The cult in Narbo was established as a mark of gratitude to Augustus, because he had settled disputes between the people and council (*decuriones*) of the city. What the problem was and

[12] *IRT* 324a, cf. Di Vita (1982, 558) (AD 11–12); *CIL* XI. 1161 (probably Augustan); *ILS* 158 = Ehrenberg and Jones (1955, no. 52) (Tiberian); Fishwick (1991, ii. 1. 378 f.).

[13] Champlin (1981); tr. and short comm. in Levick (1985, 119 f.); tr. (misleading) and further refs. in Sherk (1988, 7 ff.).

[14] Pippidi (1931, 106 ff.); Fishwick (1991, ii. 1. 379).

[15] Pippidi (1931, 83 ff., esp. 109).

what the emperor actually did is unknown, but this background undoubtedly goes far to explain the legal standing of the cult: it was not public (i.e. *pro populo publico sumptu*), since neither the magistrates nor the priests of Narbo, nor the *decuriones* as a body, had any part in the worship, nor was it paid for from the public funds of Narbo.[16] Instead the *populus* as a whole participated, and the cult was supervised, performed, and funded by a body of three knights (*e populo*, i.e. non-*decuriones*) and three freedmen. The cult must therefore, in terms of sacral law, be grouped under private worship (*sacra privata*), like for instance the compital cults. Even if the existence of a state altar to Augustus' *numen* in Rome should be accepted, it therefore appears that the cult in Narbo, so much shaped by local conditions, cannot in any case reflect a state altar of the capital beyond the basic choice of *numen* and altar for cult objects. Furthermore, the altar in Narbo took its regulations (*lex*) from the venerable old shrine of Diana on the Aventine in Rome. The regulations of this cult were indeed often applied to other shrines as a standard prototype.[17] But if the Narbo altar was set up in emulation of a homonymous altar in Rome, we might expect the *lex* to have been taken from this cult instead.

Far more revealing for the questions treated here, including the identity of our elusive *numen*, is the altar in Forum Clodii (*CIL* XI. 3303). The inscription telling us about it has never been examined in its entirety in the literature on *numen*.[18] Forum Clodii was a small and insignificant town in northern Etruria, north of Pisae. It was nearer to Rome than Narbo was, and not only in terms of geography. Whereas the form of the cult in Narbo was private and very much determined by local conditions, the unequivocally public cult by the altar in Forum Clodii should give us a truer reflection of the corresponding state cult in the capital, if indeed it ever existed. But the value of the inscription from Forum Clodii (AD 18) goes far beyond this observation. It deserves to be given in full:

[16] For these definitions, given by Festus, see p. 9 above.

[17] For the shrine of Diana see Syme (1956, 258 ff.) (= id., 1979, i. 308 ff.); regulations: Palmer (1974, 57 ff.).

[18] Brief commentary by Pippidi (1931, 107 ff.) on the aspects of the inscription which he took to confirm his theory of *numen* = *genius*.

Ti. Caesare tert. Germanico Caesare iter. cos.
Cn. Acceio Cn.f. Arn. Rufo Lutatio, T.Petillio P.f.Qui. IIvir.
decreta:
aediculam et statuas has, hostiam dedicationi. victimae natali Aug. VIII k.Octobr. duae, quae p(er)p(etuo)
inmolari adsueta[e] sunt, ad aram, quae numini Augusto dedic. est, VIIII et VIII k. Octobr.
inmolentur; item natali Ti. Caesaris perpetue acturi decuriones
et populus cenarent—quam inpensam Q. Cascell[i]o Labeone
in perpetuo pollicenti, ut gratiae agerentur munificentiae eius—eoque
natali ut quotannis vitulus inmolaretur.
et ut natalibus Augusti et Ti. Caesarum, prius quam ad vescendum
decuriones irent, thure et vino genii eorum ad epulandum ara
numinis Augusti invitarentur.
ara(m) numini Augusto pecunia nostra faciendam curavimus; ludos
ex idibus Augustis diebus sex p. n. faciendos curavimus.
natali Augustae mulsum et crustlum mulieribus vicanis ad
Bonam Deam pecunia nostra dedimus.
item dedicatione statuarum Caesarum et Augustae mulsum et crustla
pecunia nostra decurionib(us) et populo dedimus, perpetuoque eius die
dedicationis daturo[s] nos testati sumus, quem diem quo frequentior quod-
annis sit, servabimus VI idus Martias, qua die
Ti. Caesar pontif. maximus felicissime est creatus.

In the year when Tiberius Caesar for the third time and Germanicus Caesar for the second time were consuls and Cn. Acceius Rufus Lutatius and T. Petilius were duumvirs: Decrees: the temple and these statues, a sacrificial animal for the dedication [thereof]. On 23 and 24 September, on Augustus' birthday, 24 September, shall be sacrificed at the altar dedicated to the Augustan divinity the two animals that are usually sacrificed; moreover [that] the *decuriones* and the people shall hold a banquet on Tiberius Caesar's birthday, may he rule eternally, Q. Cascellius Labeo having promised to cover the cost of this indefinitely, so that he should be thanked for his generosity, and that on this birthday shall each year be sacrificed a bull calf; and that on both Augustus' and Tiberius' birthday their *genii* shall be invited with incense and wine to hold a feast on the altar for the Augustan divinity before the *decuriones* go to dine. We have had the altar for the Augustan divinity erected at our own expense. We have organized games for six days from 13 August at our own expense. On Augusta's birthday we have, at our own expense, distributed sweet wine and biscuits at [the statue of] Bona Dea to the women from the various town quarters. Moreover, at the dedication of the statues to the Caesars and Augusta we have distributed sweet wine and biscuits to the town council and to the people, and we have sworn always to do this on the anniversary of this dedication. We celebrate this, in order that for each year it may be better and better attended, on 10 March, on which date Tiberius Caesar was most auspiciously appointed *pontifex maximus*. (My translation)

The text was clearly composed of excerpts from several decrees of the local town council, confusingly bundled together out of grammatical context. This must account for the language of the text being somewhat clumsy in places, which causes confusion in the meaning of certain details. The inscription mentions in lines 4 and 17 the dedication of a cult building (*aedicula*) and statues of Tiberius, Augustus,[19] and Julia Augusta (=Livia), and it was clearly set up in close proximity to these monuments. Lines 4–12 apparently summarize, in a frustratingly abbreviated form, a decree of the *decuriones* ordering the establishment of the shrine and specifying the nature of its cult.[20] This cult seems to have been established already in Augustus' lifetime (and strangely its terminology or ritual were not updated to suit the new circumstances here four years after his death).[21] The decree then transferred it to the altar of the August *numen*[22] when it was decided to erect a temple and

[19] The *Caesares* could also be taken to be or include Germanicus and Drusus Minor, but they are otherwise not mentioned in the inscription, and Augustus and Tiberius are termed *Caesares* in l. 10.

[20] Evident from the use of the subjunctive in ll. 4–12, and from *ut* (depending on *decreverunt* or a similar verb in the text from which this was excerpted) in ll. 9 and 10.

[21] The text appears to reflect more or less verbatim the *lex sacra* of this older cult, for Augustus is not termed *Divus* nor Tiberius Augustus; note also the sacrificial victim of a bull-calf to Tiberius (see below).

[22] It seems most reasonable to take '*ad aram . . . dedic(ata) est*' in l. 5 adverbially to *inmolentur* rather than to '*inmolari adsuetae sunt*', partly because of the notable *vacat* between '*sunt*' and '*ad aram*' (presumably here reflecting a speech pause, as the comma in modern orthography), partly because the information of the sentence seems pointless if it referred only to an older, known cult at the altar without mentioning any changes in it.

statues in connection with the altar. It thus seems that the altar was of older date than the other monuments, and it had apparently been dedicated separately from these.[23] Nevertheless, since the altar was of relatively recent date,[24] and since only one cult is described in the inscription, altar and temple with statues must have constituted one unit.[25] The double dedication of one shrine certainly seems odd: either the temple and statues were not part of the original plan, which included only the altar, or—more likely—the explanation is simply linguistic bungling in the obviously strongly abbreviated summary of several—presumably two—decrees of the *decuriones*.[26] However, since altar, temple, and statues clearly belonged together, this is not of overriding importance.

We may now return to the more generally important question: what was actually worshipped in a cult of the emperor's *numen*? There is a basic and concrete line of reasoning which has not been pursued before in the literature on the subject. Since the gender of the word was neuter, the concept could hardly be personified, nor is it easy to see how it could receive sacrificial victims, since in Roman sacral law the sex of the victim should correspond to that of the god receiving the sacrifice. If the *numen* in this context meant the *Genius* we should expect the cult images in the shrine to represent the *Genii* of the persons worshipped. This was not the case in Forum Clodii: the statues clearly represented Augustus and Tiberius themselves, not their *Genii*. As for the sacrificial victims, we are only informed that a bull-calf (*vitulus*) was sacrificed on Tiberius' birthday, whereas the two victims for Augustus' birthday are unspecified. Since the cult described dates from Augustus'

[23] ll. 5–6: '*dedic(ata) est* (perfect tense) . . . *inmolentur* (present subjunctive with future sense)'.

[24] Alternatively the information of l. 13 (*ara(m) . . . curavimus*) would seem out of date and irrelevant in this connection.

[25] This seems evident also from l. 13 where '*aediculam*' and '*statuas*' must logically be implied with the altar, since '*pecunia . . . curavimus*' is equally relevant for all three items.

[26] Particularly l. 4: '*aediculam . . . dedicationi*' is strongly abbreviated (cf. Bormann's comm. in *CIL* ad loc.); likewise the lack of consequence in tense (present subjunctive (*inmolentur*), then imperfect subjunctive in the following verbs) seems linguistically sloppy (though there is no real difference in meaning between the two usages).

lifetime these victims must have been the corresponding older animals: bulls. Two full-grown animals for the father, a calf for the son would be appropriate for the usual correspondence between the god and his victim in Roman sacrifice. This of course implies that the victims were sacrificed to Augustus and Tiberius themselves; yet this seems the obvious interpretation. The neuter *numen* could not receive victims, since any animal is either male or female—at the very least we should expect steers, which were, however, still considered male, being sacrificed to infertile (but still male) gods. The emperor's *Genius*, it is true, also received bulls, but the cult images did not represent *Genii*.

The *Genii* of Augustus and Tiberius appear, however, in lines 10–12, where they are invited to eat on the altar on the imperial birthdays before the *decuriones* begin the sacrificial banquet. These lines are actually the only part of the inscription which has received comment in scholarship. The ritual has been claimed to prove both that *numen* and *Genius* were identical and that they were not.[27] In fact the ceremony can be used as argument for neither of these opposite views. The participation in ancient sacrifice of the god worshipped was of course deemed essential for the purpose of the ceremonies. Sacrifices constituted a concrete system of gift exchange essential to the functioning of human society; they were not merely empty rituals. In cults of 'normal', omnipresent gods their presence in the rituals constituted no problem. But the emperor was not omnipresent, a fact which was commonly recognized; hence probably the relative importance of the emperor's image in cults, a phenomenon which we have encountered elsewhere (see Chapter 9). Furthermore, the emperor's *numen* could not be personified and his images could not move; if the emperor's direct and active participation was required in the sacrificial banquet, the *Genius* was therefore the only candidate available. Like other 'normal' gods he could be omnipresent. The inscription from Forum Clodii is unique in furnishing us with such a detailed description of ceremonies in an imperial cult. It is therefore hardly possible to determine how typical was this

[27] Identical: Pippidi (1931, 107ff.); contra Taeger (1960, ii. 146) and taken by Fishwick (1991, ii. 1. 380) as decisive proof that *Numen* was *not* = *Genius*.

inclusion of the *Genius* in imperial rituals. But it is not, on the lines of the arguments above, very surprising in the *numen* cult of Forum Clodii. Furthermore, the *Genii* were invited on the emperor's birthdays, and a man's birthday was the main feast day for his *Genius*. The appearance of the *Genii* in this public cult may at first appear to conflict with my view, presented above, of the worship of a man's *Genius* as a servile phenomenon, degrading for the socially independent freeborn. But in a cult of the emperor's *numen*, a quality characteristic of the gods, it was explicitly formulated that the emperor was divine and not just a *paterfamilias*; this detail in the inscription would therefore be equivalent to a cult act to the *Genius* of a god, where social humiliation was presumably not relevant. The basic fact is that the cult was not dedicated to the *Genii*, which were thereby rendered socially harmless.

So much for the *Genii*. To return to the character of *numen* cult, it now appears from the Forum Clodii document that the phenomenon basically did not exist—a *numen* could not be worshipped—or rather that worshipping the emperor's divinity (*numen*) was simply synonymous with worshipping him directly, as a god.[28] This explanation has the great attraction of simplicity; and it is strongly supported by parallel evidence.

Let me begin with a passage by Suetonius (*Cal.* 22. 3), already quoted in my chapter 6 above, describing the cult established to Caligula's *numen*:[29]

He also set up a special temple to his own godhead [*numini suo*], with priests and with victims of the choicest kind. In this temple was a life-sized golden statue of the emperor, which was dressed each day in clothing such as he wore himself. The richest citizens used all their influence to secure the priesthoods of his cult and bid high for the honour.

Also in this case the cult image obviously represented the emperor himself, not his *Genius* (or a personified *numen*, however such a creature might look). Cult of the emperor's *numen* was—not only on the ritual level but also on the linguistic one—just a synonym for cult of the emperor as a god, as is

[28] To my knowledge, this interpretation has only been suggested by Toutain (1907, 53) who stated, without further arguments or discussion: 'Pour nous, le culte du numen impérial équivait pleinement au culte de l'empereur vivant.' Contra Pötscher (1978, 381). [29] Suet. *Cal.* 22. 3; see p. 150 above.

further borne out by Cassius Dio and Josephus: both mention the same temple as being dedicated to Caligula himself. A parallel example is furnished by the younger Pliny, who contrasts the senators' thankofferings to Jupiter's *numen* with those lately performed to Domitian's *Genius* (*Pan.* 52. 6):[30] 'With similar reverence, Caesar, you will not suffer public thanks for your benevolence to be offered to your *Genius*, but direct them to the godhead [*numen*] of Jupiter Best and Greatest . . .' The word '*numen*' is here no doubt used for stylistic reasons to provide a balance to '*Genius*'. But we know from innumerable other sources, notably the *Arval Acta*, that these state sacrifices were performed to Jupiter directly.[31] Similarly, the fact that the cult images by the altar to the Augustan *numen* in Forum Clodii represented the emperors themselves is not strange in the light of parallel evidence. We may note a dedication from Rome (*CIL* VI. 1192) to the *numen* of Attis; the reclining statue above the inscription clearly represents Attis himself.[32] An even better parallel is furnished by a dedication from Ostia (AD 160) to the *numen* of the *domus Augusta*, originally crowned by three busts in relief. Only the left one is preserved, representing Ceionius Commodus, who became emperor the year afterwards under the name of Lucius Verus; that makes it virtually certain that the two other busts will have represented Antoninus Pius, in centre position, and Marcus Aurelius as Caesar.[33] To return to Augustus, the same interpretation holds good for a passage of Horace, the interpretation of which has provoked perennial discussion (*Carm.* 4. 5. 31–6):

> . . . hinc ad vina redit laetus et alteris
> te mensis adhibet deum;
> te multa prece, te prosequitur mero
> defuso pateris, et Laribus tuum
> miscet numen uti Graecia Castoris
> et magni memor Herculis.

[30] Plin. *Pan.* 52. 6; see p. 191 above.

[31] Cf. further e.g. Mart. 9. 1. 6f.: '*dum voce supplex dumque ture placabit* | *matrona divae dulce Iuliae numen*'.

[32] Helbig, 4th edn. (1963, i, no. 1153) (E. Simon) with refs.

[33] Calza (n.d., no. 8 with refs. and Tav. V); the inscription '*Numini d[omus Augustae]*' is placed above a *tabula ansata* in relief with another inscription giving the titulature of Antoninus Pius in 160.

[From his field the farmer] gladly repairs to the feast, and at the second course invokes thee as a god. Thee with many a prayer, thee with pure wine poured from bowls, he worships; and mingles thy divinity [*numen*] with his household gods [*Lares*], like Greece mindful of Castor and great Hercules.

There is general agreement that the ceremony described is the libation decreed by the Senate to Octavian before banquets. The rite is generally interpreted as having been performed to the *Genius* of the emperor on the basis of this very passage, where *numen* is seen as synonymous with '*Genius*'. The libation was in fact to the emperor himself, as I have argued above.[34] Here we may merely note that the words of line 32 (*te mensis adhibet deum*) clearly point to direct cult—the words do not fit *Genius* cult, which in fact did not impute divinity to the person honoured, since all men had a *Genius*. This is entirely consistent with the mention of 'thy divinity' (*numen*) in line 35, and similarly the comparison with the deification in Greece of Castor and Hercules, likewise men who became gods, clearly points to direct cult: hence no *Genius*, but simply numinous Augustus himself. This interpretation of the (lack of) character of *numen* is even implicit in the restored entries of the *Fasti Praenestini*, accepted by all scholars who have nevertheless continued to argue for a more or less close connection between *Genius* and *numen*; to quote again the Tiberian addition after the main entry:

Fe[riae ex s(enatus) c(onsulto) q]u[od e(o) d(ie) Ti(berius) Caesar aram Divo] Aug(usto) patri dedicavit.

Holiday by decree of the Senate, because on this day Tiberius Caesar dedicated the altar to his father Divus Augustus.

That is, here the altar (and sacrifices) to the *numen* of Augustus is synonymous with it being dedicated to Augustus himself. Oddly, this has not been noted nor the consequences drawn in scholarly literature, presumably because of Lily Ross Taylor's theory that the word '*Genius*' was commonly 'suppressed' in the imperial cults of Roman Italy (see p. 77 ff above).

In fact, I know of no text, literary or epigraphical, where my rather banal interpretation does not make perfectly good sense.

[34] See p. 207 ff above.

The double meaning of the word *numen* as both 'god' and 'godhead' is thus no more puzzling than the same ambiguity of the word 'divinity' in English: the two meanings are actually very close to each other. This interpretation of *numen* also bears on the question of oaths by the name, *numen*, or *Genius* of the emperor (or any other being), an aspect I will unfortunately not be able to pursue here.[35]

So *numen* cult was merely a linguistic synonym for direct, godlike cult. The consequences of this observation for Tiberius' supposed state altar to his father's *numen* would be revolutionary. Cult images by the altar would have represented Augustus, and sacrifices would have been made to him directly. This means that such an altar would have enshrined Augustus as a state god in his lifetime, not only because *numen* was an unequivocally divine attribute, as argued by Fishwick and others, but because Augustus was then worshipped as a god of the Roman state while he was still alive. By contemporary standards such state cult would have turned the Roman state into a full-blown divine monarchy.

Rather than accept such a sweeping conclusion one should doubt, and even reject, the accepted restorations of the decisive lacunae in the entry of the *Fasti Praenestini*. No surviving sources mention such a revolutionary development in the Augustan settlement, despite the fact that it would have stood in complete and blatant contrast to everything else we know about Augustus' policy within the state cult.

Incidentally, whatever was actually commemorated in the entry of the *Fasti Praenestini* it seems that the Tiberian addition was based on a local misunderstanding. The *Fasti* were composed by Verrius Flaccus, house teacher of Augustus' heirs and hopes C. and L. Caesar, and therefore very close to the emperor himself.[36] The later additions to Flaccus' calendar were, on the other hand, composed locally without the benefit of his qualified information. Thus, on the basis of the only entry in their *Fasti* for 17 January, where the marriage of Augustus and Livia was not mentioned, the local authorities in Praeneste apparently assumed that the day was decreed a holi-

[35] But see p. 162 ff above.

[36] Suet. *Gramm*. 17; for comm. see ed. by R. Kaster.

day because of the event commemorated there, whatever that may have been. As is, however, evidenced by another calendar, the Tiberian *Fasti Verulani*, the real reason was the day's being the anniversary of Augustus' marriage to Livia, which fell on the same date. Such a senatorial decree turning the day into a holiday was perfectly natural when Tiberius became emperor, on which occasion his mother too was showered with honours.

The fact that we know of two altars to the imperial *numen* (though not with exactly the same title: *numen Augusti* in Narbo, but *numen Augustum* in Forum Clodii) from Augustus' last years may then be no more than a coincidence; it was not caused by emulation of a state monument in Rome. It seems, however, more likely than simple coincidence that some prototype or other actually did inspire the two monuments. There is in fact no good reason not to see the altar at Narbo as such a prototype. The disputes between the city council (*decuriones*) and people (*plebs*) of Narbo, whatever their nature, certainly required direct involvement from Augustus, and it may well be that the affair, as well as the city's honour to the emperor afterwards, was widely known. That the cult had some importance or fame is indicated by the fact that the Narbo inscription as we have it is not Augustan: it was re-ingraved in the second century.

That may be a weak argument. But we can indeed trace how the idea travelled from Narbo to Forum Clodii. The banquet to be held in the small Italian township on Tiberius' birthday was financed, the inscription tells us, by Q. Cascellius Labeo, who promised to cover the expense indefinitely, and was gratefully thanked by the town councillors. This Labeo was not a simple local character: his epitaph is known from Rome, and informs us that he had been chief engineer (*praefectus fabrum*) in the army. Cascellius was not from Rome, however. As indicated by his tribe-name as a Roman citizen (*Voltinia*), likewise known from his epitaph, he probably came from Gallia Narbonensis, and the name Cascellius is otherwise known only from this area, two of the other four inscriptions recording it coming from Narbo itself. Cascellius Labeo was clearly a wealthy and prestigious Roman knight; he had a connection with Forum Clodii—perhaps he owned property in the area—and it was probably on his suggestion, as well as with his money, that the town councillors of Forum Clodii established their altar. If so, Narbo was indeed the prototype.[37]

From wherever the councillors of Forum Clodii got the idea, their cult had its comical aspects. The fact that their town was very small and insignificant appears to be reflected in a surprising lack of sensitivity to more recent developments in Rome. The worship described in the Forum Clodii inscription was strangely outdated in AD 18: Augustus was not called *Divus* and apparently received bulls, whereas the proper victims to the *Divus* in the capital were steers. Though hardly unaware of the formal deification of the late emperor by the Roman Senate, the ritual consequences of this seem to have eluded the councillors of Forum Clodii, who continued to worship Augustus as emperor and Tiberius as heir.

[37] Demougin (1992, 623 f.) for Q. Cascellius Q(uinti) f(ilius) Vol(tinia tribu) Labeo; epitaph (Julio-Claudian): *CIL* VI. 3510.

11

A Parallel: C. Manlius, Caeretan 'Caesar'

Ever since its discovery in 1846 the so-called altar of C. Manlius has seemed one of the strangest of all imperial monuments, and most scholars have indeed interpreted it as such. The monument is perhaps best known for providing the standard example of an iconographical *topos* in Roman art, that of the ox sacrifice (Fig. 11.1).[1]

The altar, crowned by two volutes and hence of the most common type of Roman altars,[2] was unearthed in or by the theatre of Caere together with other pieces of sculpture; an admirable recent publication of the finds with transcripts of the contemporary records makes it appear very likely that the altar was found *in situ*, centrally located in the orchestra of the theatre.[3] In this connection it should also be noted that a fragmentary building inscription suggests that Manlius may have had the theatre erected.[4] The technical quality of the altar reliefs is very fine indeed, and the monument was probably produced in an urban Roman workshop.

The find spot, clearly a public place, and the iconography of the altar itself have caused most scholars to set it in relation to the imperial cult, and this view has long been commonly accepted. The interpretation does, however, entail problems, for the altar is not dedicated to an emperor. The inscription on

[1] Measurements: 0.98 (h.) × 0.75 (w.) × 0.6 (d.) m. Now in the Vatican (Museo Gregoriano profano); Helbig, 4th edn., i, no. 1058 (E. Simon); Taylor (1921); Ryberg (1955, 84ff. with fig. 39a–b); Torelli (1982, 16ff. with fig. I, 6–8); Fuchs *et al.* (1989, 89 ff.); Greek marble according to Torelli, of the same type as that of the *Fasti Caeretani*. I am not able to judge on identifications of marble types, but the marble certainly does not appear Lunensic.

[2] Hermann (1961, 11ff.).

[3] Fuchs *et al.* (1989, 29ff. and 89ff.); the rest of the sculptures from the 1846 excavation seem very appropriate for the theatre.

[4] *CIL* XI. 3621; Fuchs *et al.* (1989, 106, no. 21).

FIG. 11.1 The altar of C. Manlius
Notes: A: front; B: left side (the right repeats the motif); C: back; D: author's sketch from autopsy of the statuette held by the woman furthest to the left on C.

its front side reads (*CIL* XI. 3616): *C(aio) Manlio C(ai) f(ilio) cens(ori) perpet(uo) | clientes patrono* ('To Gaius Manlius, son of Gaius, *censor* for life, his *clientes* to their *patronus*'). Beneath the inscription and crowned by a garland spanning the width of the altar is depicted in high relief the slaying of a bull or steer (Fig. 11.1 A). The scene follows the standard pattern for the depiction of such sacrifices in Roman art: sacrificial butchers (*victimarii*) are in the process of felling the bull while the priest, to the right, is pouring the libation onto the sacrificial fire of an altar. In the background is shown a second layer of figures, a flautist (*tibicen*), a sacrificial attendant (*camillus*), a *victimarius* with the tray of *molae salsae,* and the head of a spectator. The scene is so very much a standard one that only the headline-like inscription can furnish us with more specific clues as to the exact nature of the cult depicted.

Moving to the rear side of the altar we encounter on the other hand a scene so specific that no obvious parallels are known (Fig. 11.1 C). On a high rock a woman, clearly a goddess, is seated on a throne; she is shown in three-quarter profile to the left, *capite velato*, and holding a *patera* in her left hand. To her left three women are standing on the ground; the one nearest to the rock is laying her hand on the knee of the goddess, apparently in a gesture of *proskynesis*. The woman furthest to the left is holding a statuette, but unfortunately the state of preservation makes it impossible to identify this figure with certainty—Ryberg saw it as a *Victoria*, Torelli as a *Lar*. Personal examination of this detail leads me to conclude that a *Victoria* is hardly possible (Fig. 11.1D).[5] To the left of the seated goddess, and roughly parallel to the women, stand three men in togas; the one in the middle has turned round to face right and has placed his right hand on the shoulder of the man facing left, a gesture which is watched by the third, younger man, who is standing by the rock. The whole scene has been the subject of much discussion, partly because it has no clear parallels in Roman art.

Each of the altar's short sides presents the same image, a *Lar* standing frontally on a piece of rock and holding a *patera* in his right and a *rhyton* in his left hand (Fig. 11.1 B), that is, in the standard scheme for the depiction of *Lares*, as encountered on

[5] One leg of the figure is preserved; this would seem to exclude Victoria, who is always depicted wearing an ankle-length chiton.

the compital altars and the *Lararia* of Pompeii.[6] On each side of the *Lares* is depicted a laurel tree: clearly the two laurels decreed by the Senate in 27 BC to be planted on either side of the door to Augustus' house. The trees are likewise shown next to the *Lares* on several of the compital altars.

These laurels have been decisive for the standard interpretation of the altar, since most scholars have taken them to signify that the *Lares* are those of the emperor, and that the cult scene on the altar front therefore depicts a sacrifice to the *Genius Augusti*. Taylor explained this motif on the grounds that Manlius' *clientes* were priests (*magistri*) in the imperial compital cult. Ryberg later recognized the problem of this interpretation, the lack of congruence between the pictorial motif and the inscription,[7] and she therefore suggested, hesitantly, that Manlius was a *sacerdos* in the imperial cult. Most recently, Torelli, who ignored the question of the *Lares* and their laurels, has suggested that the front scene depicts a sacrifice to Manlius' *Lar Genialis*. Although Torelli is, I believe, on the right track, his interpretation may be promptly dismissed: there is no evidence of a '*Lar Genialis*' in any source, and this notion must therefore count as a rather whimsical modern invention.[8]

Taylor's interpretation has been widely accepted, but raises serious problems. First, it seems odd if the altar's front side pays homage to the *clientes* rather than to Manlius by showing a cult which had nothing to do with him. Secondly, there were three or four *magistri vici* who functioned as priests in the compital cults, and this number also appears on most of the compital altars; the Manlius altar, however, in spite of compositional complexity and a large number of figures depicted on its front, shows only one priest in the ceremony and no sign of the *ministri vici*. As for Ryberg's modified version of the thesis, it is a weighty objection that the inscription does not name

[6] The closest parallel for these specific *Lares* is an altar from the Chigi collection, Ryberg (1955, 61 with fig. 32).

[7] So did Alföldi (1973, 34), who therefore concluded: '. . . zweifellos ein stadtrömisches Werk in sekundärer Verwendung'. On the basis of photographs he furthermore believed to see traces of an earlier inscription; neither I nor other scholars who have actually studied the altar by autopsy have discovered any trace of such reworking.

[8] The *Thesaurus Linguae Latinae* s.v. *lar*, s.v. *genialis* has no examples, nor does Torelli have any references.

Manlius' supposed priesthood in the imperial cult; furthermore, worship of the emperor's *Genius* and *Lares* outside the state cult in Rome now appears to have been the preserve of the lower status groups, slaves and freedmen, to which of course C. Manlius, *censor perpetuus*, did not belong.

The problem common to all the interpretations cited here is the apparent lack of concordance between the altar's iconography and its inscription. This has led all scholars to evaluate the one higher than the other, and hence to ignore one of them, as it happens always the inscription. The basic problem common to all interpretations is whether it is at all possible that the altar was not dedicated to whoever was actually worshipped on it. This problem has a more general relevance, for altars dedicated to the emperor would be bereft of informative value on the imperial cult if we cannot assume that they were used, or intended, for sacrifices to the emperor.

With regard to the Greek world, this problem of altar dedications has already been raised by Simon Price, who maintains that one cannot a priori accept correspondence between dedication and cult[9] (whether merely proclaimed as an intention or actually carried out). The discussion is certainly worthwhile. However, the great majority of altars are dedicated to traditional divinities, and it would be bizarre to maintain that altars dedicated to one god were usually, or commonly, used for sacrifices to another; there is no reason why the same should not apply to imperial altars. Furthermore, and decisively, to my knowledge no example is known where dedication and cult do not correspond (such as e.g. an altar dedicated to a male divinity, but where the victim depicted is female).

I have argued this point, partly because it is essential to any interpretation of imperial cults, and partly because the interpretations of the Manlius altar advanced so far must crumble, if these arguments are accepted. To Ryberg the *Lares* and their laurels were the conclusive argument for the altar's place within the imperial cult. However, laurel trees on either side of the *Lares* are extremely common in the paintings of Pompeian *Lararia*, where the *Lares* are those of the private household, often depicted with the *Genius* of the *paterfamilias*. The laurels

[9] Price (1984*a*, 216ff.).

have clearly been taken over from the iconography of the compital altars.[10] Nor should this be very surprising, for imperial symbols, or symbols of authority in general, are often found to have been taken over and used iconographically in social groups who had no rightful claim to them.[11] They have in this context become generic status symbols separated from their specific significance and symbolism. On the verbal level the same phenomenon is evidenced in a grafitto in a Pompeian *Lararium*, where the household *Lares* are termed *Lares augusti*, the sovereign title of the compital *Lares* after the reorganization of their cult in or about 7 BC.[12]

There is, then, no conflict between the altar's iconography and its inscription, and the altar may now be placed in its correct context: the *Lares* on its short sides are those of C. Manlius, and the sacrifice of a bull is, as the inscription says, to C. Manlius himself. In this connection Torelli's interpretation of the rear side is of considerable interest. He sees the scene as an illustration of the formulaic term *'in fidem clientelamque venire'*. The scene in his view therefore represents a *supplicatio* to *Fides*, who would then be the goddess on the rock; iconographically, this is quite possible. According to Torelli, the two men furthest to the right should be Manlius himself, who quite literally accepts a client *sub manu*, that is, under his authority. This idea is not entirely convincing, however: the technical term *sub manu* can, strictly speaking, refer only to a husband's power over his wife. The women to the left Torelli sees as the wife of Manlius and those of the *clientes*, who have received their new *Lares* and now worship *Fides*.

In the absence of comparable depictions no interpretation of

10 The laurels in Pompeian *lararia* have been noted by Alföldi (1973, 55f.), who followed Nilsson in seeing this as indicating that the emperor's *Genius* and *Lares* had substituted those of the *paterfamilias* in the household cults (for this idea see p. 123 above); also by Taylor (1921, 391 n. 4), whereby she as much as invalidated her own argument: 'It is unlikely that a private monument to Manlius' Genius and Lares familiares should have been adorned with scenes so closely analogous to those in vogue in the imperial cult at the time'. Also the placing of the *Lares* on the two short sides of the altar would seem to have been taken over from compital altars.

11 There is no monograph on this fascinating topic; for examples see Alföldi (1973, 56ff.) and Zanker (1987, *passim*).

12 Grafitto: Boyce (1937, no. 47); see p. 123 above.

the scene can be entirely convincing, but in the main Torelli's admirable attempt would appear to make sense, and it is well able to account for the many unique features and gestures in the scene. In any case the scene contains no clear imperial references whatsoever.

The priest on the altar's front has been emphasized, partly by the depth of the relief, and partly by the fact that the glances of the other participants in the ceremony are directed towards him. Ryberg and Torelli have interpreted this as indicating that the priest is Manlius himself, which would not accord very well with my interpretation nor with the altar's inscription. The argument is, however, not a strong one. Personal examination of the altar shows that the emphasis is not so strong as it may appear in some photographs—Ryberg's in particular. The priest is thus presented in no higher relief than the *victimarius* on the left, whose prominent position is clearly owing to his iconographical and ritual importance in the ceremony depicted. Furthermore, in Roman relief depictions of sacrifices the priest is actually always emphasized—for exactly the same reasons. The emphasis is therefore due to the fact that he is the most important person in the ritual. And lastly, if further arguments are called for, the man appointed to function as priest in this cultic society would naturally have been one of the most prominent and socially high-ranking members of Manlius' client body.

The date of the altar has been much debated, varying from Augustan to Claudian times.[13] Stylistic criteria are not conclusive, but Manlius' lack of *cognomen* in the inscription suggests the earlier dating. As emphasized by Torelli, this possibility receives strong support from another inscription from Caere (*CIL* XI. 3617), mentioning a certain *M(arcus) Manlius C(ai) f(ilius) Pollio*, likewise *censor perpetuus*, which shows his chronological proximity to the Manlius of the altar. The inscription furthermore designates Pollio as *tribunus militum a populo*, a title which belongs to the mid-Augustan period.[14]

[13] Taylor (1921): Augustan; Ryberg (1955): Tiberian; O. Brendel, *RM* 45 (1930), 204ff.: Claudian/Neronian.

[14] *CIL* XI. 3617; Torelli (1982, 19f.) (wrongly giving Pollio's *praenomen* as *C(aius)* and adding an unwarranted *C(ai) n(epos)* to his name); Nicolet (1967, 29ff.).

The names of the two Manlii strongly suggest that Pollio was the son of the altar's Manlius; alternatively, but less likely, the two men could have been brothers. In either case, Pollio's title makes it possible to assign a rough date to the altar. Torelli settled on about 10 BC, but the altar's laurels, apparently an iconographic loan from the compital cults, should perhaps give a *terminus post quem* of 7 BC, the main year of the Augustan re-establishment of these cults in Rome. However, considering Pollio's datable *floruit*, the altar can hardly be much later.[15]

To see the altar, and its cult, as dedicated to C. Manlius, as the inscription says, is an interpretation which has to my knowledge not been ventured before. This must simply be owing to the fact that the idea of divine worship of a human being, in particular a private man, has appeared too strange to believe. The same monotheistic notion has postponed for so long the realization that the ruling emperor did indeed receive divine worship in Italy; or it has underpinned the persistent claim that such cults, if they existed, were predominantly public, formal, and 'insincere'. However, as argued elsewhere here, the phenomenon was probably common even in republican Rome, though the nature of our sources will necessarily make it difficult to trace; indeed, the underlying notion is, anthropologically speaking, the 'normal' one, whereas its Judaeo-Christian rejection seems the more unusual phenomenon.

Though the Manlius altar appears unique, corresponding client or cult associations are indeed found in the inscriptional sources from Italy, and I have presented them in my preceding chapter. However, these associations normally consisted of slaves and freedmen, who worshipped the *paterfamilias*, his *Genius*, or his *Lares*. It is in this respect that the Manlius cult differs from the parallels shortly to be examined—for the worshippers of Manlius do not appear to have constituted such a household cult in the narrow sense of the term. The altar's inscription and images in fact show no indications of the worshippers being slaves or of servile origins,[16] and the altar was

[15] The altar is clearly not a funerary one, and Manlius must have been alive at the time of its erection: even apart from the find spot, the *Lares* had no place in the cult of the dead.

[16] Manlius is not called *dominus* or *noster*, and his worshippers do not describe themselves as *cultores* (practically always of servile status), which is

centrally located in a public theatre. As the inscriptional evidence shows, cult of a living man's *Genius* had the stigma of servile status or origins for the worshippers, and the freeborn thus avoided this form of worship. This may play a role in the fact that this particular cult was dedicated to Manlius himself, and not to his *Genius*, as one might have expected in connection with his *Lares*. On the other hand, however, the term *clientes* does not really suggest that the worshippers had much social status or pride to protect, but we should in any case avoid the common over-interpretation of seeing a *Genius* everywhere, whether he is mentioned or not. The altar was dedicated to Manlius himself, in divine fashion. The altar, with its location and splendid ornamentation, bears witness, in comparison with other preserved material, to exceptional affluence and social prestige in this cult association. The find spot, in a public place employed also for the erection of imperial statues, further stresses the prestige afforded to Manlius by this worship; it even makes it appear doubtful whether we are dealing here with a private or a public cult. But Manlius clearly had an exceptional standing in Caere, as we shall see. Hence, as in groupings dedicated to the worship of the emperor's images and *Lares*, the worshippers may have felt that a dedication to the *Genius*, that is the cult accorded every *paterfamilias* in his household, constituted too modest an honour, and hence for that reason have opted for the maximum divine honour.

The uniquely prestigious features of Manlius' altar can, I believe, be explained. Gaius Manlius and, as it seems, his son Pollio held a unique position in Caeretan society. This is borne out by their title of *censor perpetuus* in a municipal hierarchy where the office of *censor* was the highest attainable. The holding of this office for life is otherwise known only from the emperor Domitian's occupation of it in Rome. With their exceptionally high social standing the two Manlii would then have had *clientes* of higher rank and greater affluence than was possible for private persons in almost any other context. Their censorial office alone gave them the authority to remove

otherwise usual in such groupings (see p. 213ff. above). The word *clientes* certainly denotes low social standing in relation to the *patronus*, but not necessarily a servile status.

unwanted persons from the *ordo decurionum*, and it requires little effort to imagine the hold this would give them over the town's leading social groups. In my view, we have here the key to the apparent affluence and relatively high status of Manlius' *clientes*, though we unfortunately cannot say exactly who they were. The altar's inscription—*clientes patrono*—rather suggests that the cult was a private one, but we may now see why it was apparently so integrated in the public sphere of Caere as to render the dividing line between public and private somewhat academic. A comparable example may have been the sacrifices to Domitian which appear to have been performed by senators *en bloc*, but formally speaking still in their private capacity (see p. 227 f above).

In roughly the same period when Gaius Manlius presumably established his hold over Caere, Caesar Augustus ascended to absolute prominence in Rome. Though the background to the Caeretan story remains unknown, it cannot be without interest to note that the final collapse of oligarchic government in the capital was mirrored by a similar development in this small town of Tuscany.

12

'Heavenly Honours Decreed by the Senate': From Emperor to *Divus*

In the mid-second century, the historian Appian briefly characterized to his Greek audience how the Roman custom of deifying dead emperors had begun:[1]

> Octavian . . . decreed divine honours to his father [Caesar]. From this example the Romans now pay like honours to each emperor at his death if he has not reigned in a tyrannical manner or made himself odious, although at first they could not bear to call them kings even when alive.

Appian's words neatly sum up the apparent paradox of the phenomenon. When alive, all Roman emperors, without exception, carefully avoided divine status in the Roman constitution; after their death, several of them received the title of *Divus* and with it this very status, full-blown and apparently without any limitations whatsoever: state priests and state temples were decreed by the Roman senate for their worship. To Appian's outsider audience, this was puzzling: in the Greek-speaking world there was not much interest in kings and emperors after their deaths, nor was it obvious why there should be. In a system where honours to the emperor were triggered off by his immense power, just like honours to the old gods, the role of *Divi* seemed superfluous: kings and emperors were basically powerless once they had died, and even in Rome they were not generally credited with posthumous power. Characteristically, all ancient characterizations and full descriptions of the funerals and state deifications of emperors are in Greek; they are anthropological excursuses to an audience who lavished attention on their present emperor, and, not surprisingly, had little need for him when he was no longer emperor.

[1] App. *BC* 2. 148.

DIVUS: THE TERM AND THE CUSTOM

Wonder at the custom has generally been shared by modern scholars.[2] Few historians have in fact been able to take it seriously. The common response has been to down-play its importance: it has been rejected as a political formality devoid of religious significance, or any significance whatsoever. Even one of the latest specialist studies of the phenomenon begins on an apologetic note: 'The subject does not exactly belong to the central questions of Roman history, or history of religion'.[3] Yet whether imperial deification fits our mental categories, or the way we accordingly happen to structure our academic disciplines, is not really the point. What is more, significance on some level cannot be denied. Even the casual tourist in Rome can hardly fail to notice impressive remains of temples to the *Divi*, and may wonder at the enormous resources devoted to their honours by the Roman state; likewise, state art, both relief sculpture and coinage, conspicuously displays the ceremonial and ideology of the *Divi*. We are perfectly entitled to express wonder at this prominence, but there is no denying the importance of the phenomenon in contemporary terms.

To Appian, the custom of deifying dead emperors began with Caesar. That is a simplified view which is only half right. Caesar's case was a special one. His divine state honours were

[2] The best contributions on imperial funerals and apotheosis are, in my view: (*a*) Bickermann's classic study (1929), thought-provoking, though little short of manipulative as regards his dealings with the sources; this article, with its view of the procedure of deification as a kind of canonization, basically presupposed by all later studies, has set the agenda of the debate on the subject (a later version, basically restating his case is Bickerman (*sic*: he dropped the last 'n' in the USA) (1973)); (*b*) Kierdorf (1986*a*) who works completely within Bickermann's framework of 'canonization', but competently so; (*c*) Price (1987), asking the right questions, but depending too much on his predecessors for the answers, and still basically presupposing 'canonization'. The articles of Richard (in fact one article reprinted three times from 1966 to 1980) are concerned with details which I fail to find of central relevance, and add little of importance; Arce (1988) is highly valuable in collecting and presenting the archaeological evidence, though at times confused in argumentation.

[3] Kierdorf (1986*a*, 43): 'das Thema gehört nicht gerade zu den zentralen Fragen der römischen Geschichte oder Religionsgeschichte'; for *Divi* and the Greek world, see Price (1984*b*).

decreed by the Senate in his lifetime; true, they were not implemented before his death, but this was because he was murdered so soon after the passing of these decrees. Only the formation of the second triumvirate ensured his status as a state god. On the one hand, this status shed immense prestige on his heir, young Octavian, now *divi filius*; on the other hand, Caesar's case was an embarrassment to the later Augustan settlement and its stress on *moderatio*. So though Divus Julius was an unquestioned god of Rome, with state priest and public temple in the forum, he was, paradoxically, not the first in the line of *Divi*, as it was construed in the state cult of the empire. Caesar's cult under Augustus and later was what we may term 'self-contained'; only his priest and the cult personnel attached to his temple appear to have been involved in his state worship. The Arval Brothers, however, never sacrificed to Divus Julius; when they worshipped the list of *Divi*, it began with Divus Augustus, and this was presumably general for all the other colleges of state priesthoods too. A parallel was the cult of Magna Mater or Cybele; right from its beginning in the early second century BC, her state worship appears to have been confined to her temple on the Palatine. Such 'self-containment' of some cults of the Roman state reflects uneasiness in connection with them. The option was a practical one: in a deeply conservative cult system where outright abolition of unwanted or superfluous cults was out of the question, their isolation within the system was a way to accommodate such uneasiness. Though legally without question state cults—they must have functioned on behalf of the *populus Romanus*—these cults nevertheless in practical terms were only half part of the state system and the constitution.

The deification of Augustus after his death needs more than Caesar's precedent to explain it. After all, Caesar's precedent was generally *not* followed in the Augustan settlement, conspicuously and consciously. The creation of *Divi* has been seen as an inner contradiction in the state constitution of the early empire, where the emperor was, officially, first among equals.[4] But there is no contradiction. The undoubted power of Augustus could be a dangerous provocation if expressed openly

[4] Price (1987, 57).

and presented formally. At Augustus' death, however, his power vanished; as we shall see, this was hardly doubted by any contemporary. So there was then a much lesser provocation in the conferment of divine state honours; dead men were not dangerous (the main risk was rather the enhanced prestige shed on the successor by formal posthumous deification). There was no reason to maintain the fiction of the emperor as first among equals when he was no longer among the living.

We may furthermore point to a traditional aspect: death had traditionally elevated a person's status in Roman culture, and the dead generally possessed some vague form of divinity.[5] To some extent, this is explicable in the same terms as I have just argued as valid for an emperor: when men had left this world, its social hierarchy could no longer be threatened by questions of their status. Also, considering the exalted position of Augustus and later emperors in their lifetime, on the very brink of divinity, there was perhaps little alternative to state divinity after death, as argued by Price.

However, this explanation is too vaguely theoretical and it misses, I believe, the central point. Scholars have always seen the constitution of Rome, where the living emperor, though occupying an exalted position, did not receive state divinity, as the 'natural' model, and divine worship of the living emperor as the aberration craving explanation (note the cases of Caesar and Caligula). But this view, which is usually implicit in scholarly literature, basically rests on the notion of such worship as an absurd blasphemy towards the one and true God; it is patently christianizing. I have argued that divine worship of the ruling emperor of Rome was far from confined to sycophantic Greeks or rude barbarians recently brought under the sway of Rome. The phenomenon was found all over the Roman empire, including Italy and Rome itself; it was absent from one sphere only, namely the constitutional one of the state cult in Rome. This image rather suggests divine honours as one of the 'normal' responses to imperial power, and their absence from the state cult as the aberration, the exception in need of explanation.

[5] e.g. Plut. *Quaest. Rom.* 14; *Ep. Corneliae*, Nepos frg. 15: '*ubi mortua ero, parentabis mihi et invocabis deum parentem*' (much discussed, see Weinstock, 1971, 295 with lit. in n. 1); generally Bömer (1943); newer lit. can be collected from Scheid (1993).

The explanation seems banal—deceptively so—and has often been pointed out: Augustus maintained the fiction that Rome was no monarchy; hence he received no divine honours. This is true, but not comprehensive; some emperors rejected the notion of the principate, yet none of them, without exception, received divine state worship. I have already presented my explanation: the case of Caesar linked the formal divinity of a Roman ruler with his death. Based on the precedents of Hercules and Romulus, this had already been an uneasy problem in Caesar's case, and that was why he received the title of *Divus* in the last months of his life. *Divi* were always a subcategory of *Di*. But it was only later, as a consequence of the deifications of dead emperors with the title of *Divus*, that the word came to connote a lesser form of divinity (note e.g. Dio who regularly translates *Divus* by the Greek '*hērōs*'). Originally, in Varro's etymology, it had been the other way round: a *Divus* was a *Deus* who had always been divine, whereas men who attained divinity at their death were called by the more general term *Deus* (such as the *Di manes* and *Di parentes*) (p. 63 ff. above).

Scholars have not been able to answer the question of why Caesar was given the title of *Divus*, thus establishing the precedent followed in Augustus' case and hence for all later *Divi*; indeed, though it is important, the question has hardly been asked. Neither Hercules nor Romulus, Roman state gods who had once been men, ever bore such a title: it was obviously not necessary for the construction of a state divinity. But it was necessary in Caesar's case, because it emphatically spelt out that he was not a man who became god (in connection with his death), but a god unconnected with mortality; the use of the title should be seen as an attempt to circumvent any sinister connotations of Caesar's death in connection with this his crowning honour (see p. 67 above). Incidentally, however, his murder wrecked the scheme: henceforth also the title of *Divus*, though defined by Varro as an eternal god, would carry connotations of death. Scholars have certainly noted this for the later period, when the creation of *Divi* had become standard; note Vespasian's dying words 'Woe, I think I am becoming a god'—*Vae, puto deus fio*—or Caracalla's nasty (and untranslatable) wordplay when about to murder his brother, 'Let him be a *Divus* as long as he is not alive'—'*Sit Divus dum non sit vivus*' (not that there was any question of having Geta deified: *Divus* was simply synonymous with 'dead'). Thus Tertullian could categorically state: 'It is a curse to name the emperor a god before his apotheosis [i.e. death]'—'*Maledictum est ante apotheosin deum Caesarem nuncupari*'.[6] However, I submit that the notion was much older, though this has gone unnoticed; as mentioned, the problem was valid already in Caesar's case, and it constituted the fundamental reason why not only Augustus, but all later emperors, avoided state divinity, including the 'mad' ones, such as Caligula, who rejected the formal fiction of the principate. The notion of blasphemy was less relevant, and probably played no real role whatsoever. When, however, Augustus and later emperors actually did die, this fundamental barrier to state divinity simply went down. There was no longer any reason why not.

DIVUS AUGUSTUS: BACKGROUND

The idea that men of great prominence and virtue would receive a higher status in the afterlife than the 'normal' dead had been beautifully expressed, in a stoic garb, by Cicero in his, then as now, famous 'Scipio's Dream', which formed part of his treatise on the state. But the notion was much older, and ultimately depended on a view of the realm of the dead as a social mirror reflection of this world.[7] Persons of outstanding status and excellence in this world could hardly be expected to be mixed up indiscriminately with all the other dead in the next world. Cicero's version makes virtue, in the stoic sense, the prerequisite for entering heaven instead of the underworld. His 'Scipio's Dream' is basically a stoic appropriation of the notion, and his stress on virtue, rather than status and power, belongs to philosophy; so does the detailed formulation of the idea. Much older, as the notion was, than Cicero's famous

[6] Suet. *Vesp*. 23. 4; HA *Get*. 2; Tert. *Ap*. 34. 4; cf. Min. Fel. 21. 10.

[7] Cic. *Rep*. 6. 16; 6. 13; 24; already in Ennius, where Scipio Africanus is made to prophesy '*si fas endo plagas caelestum ascendere cuiquam est, | mi soli caeli maxima porta patet*' (Lact. *Div. Inst*. 1. 18. 11): Weinstock (1971, 294) who interprets these and similar texts as evidence that Scipio had a public cult—an example, I believe, of the common mistake of interpreting Roman (or Greek) religion on the basis of philosophical texts.

version, it was only this philosophical treatise which clearly formulated and described this realm of the Blessed. There is nothing strange in this; Roman (and Greek) views on the after-life, as expressed in cults of the dead, were vague and inconsistent, as was likewise the celestial theology formulated in divine worship. Ritual was the core of traditional pagan religion; theological and dogmatical speculation, on the other hand, belonged to the schools of philosophy.

Cicero's beautiful description is usually quoted in connection with the apotheosis of Augustus, and his ensuing state divinization after his death. But I wonder how relevant this elaborate philosophical construct really is to the question of imperial state deification. Poets and others in Augustus' lifetime certainly harped on the notion, predicting that Augustus would return to heaven whence he came. Anyone was free to predict this about anyone else they loved or respected, or to declare them divine.[8] Poets and prose writers could do it; likewise, individuals, cities, or the Senate on behalf of the Roman state could establish cults which did the same on a more continuous or permanent basis. However, poetry or even divine worship do not make gods in any absolute sense, but only in relation to the worshippers or poets making these proclamations. Such divinity was then relative—hence we may rather term it divine status—and unconcerned with absolute aspects. Indeed absolute aspects mattered little, whether in worship of the 'old' gods or the emperor. Speculation on these aspects belonged to philosophy; yet the extent to which divine cults and religious rites functioned and continued irrespective of philosophical ideas and dogmas in the Graeco-Roman world is illustrative—and should be taken seriously.[9] In Christianity philosophy and ritual are united in the same system, based ultimately on texts of absolute authority; it is christianizing to use philosophical texts as sources for traditional pagan religion. Instead this

[8] For a study of this imagery in love poetry, see Lieberg (1962).

[9] Liebeschuetz (1979, 31ff.); the classical example is Cicero who was an augur, though he had little faith in the rites performed by his priesthood, as expressed in his *De Divinatione*; but the relevance of 'faith' or 'belief' lay in philosophy, not in the workings of traditional ritual; for discussion of the irrelevance of 'belief' in the sphere of traditional Graeco-Roman cults see Price (1984*a*, 10f.).

sphere of activity was generally based on ritual action constructing a relative status system or hierarchy between honorand(s) and worshippers. In Cicero's 'Scipio's Dream', on the other hand, ascension, in absolute terms, to the stars is ordained by heaven independently of any religious rites or ideas men may hold on earth; in this cosmology earthly rites and procedures are utterly irrelevant and have no role to play.

Augustus' momentous and truly unique achievements made it incongruous that he would merely die and go where all others went (wherever that was). So it was obvious to credit him with divine origins and future, or to characterize him as a *deus praesens* while he lived. Modern scholars have seen a great difference between these two models, and meticulously gathered instances from the poets where Augustus is actually called *deus* or *numen*, as opposed to prophecies that he would merely return to heaven whence he came.[10] Again, this reflects a Christian preoccupation with the nature of divinity and theological speculation. In contemporary terms, however, the difference is not very important. Whether god or god-sent, Augustus was certainly not first among equals; in either case, he possessed a status far above that of other men. Whether it was expressed one way or the other mattered little; even terms such as *deus* or *divinus*, *sacer* and *numen* expressed, I believe, primarily status and power, not nature.[11] Augustus had burst out of the social structure of the republic, above which presided the gods.

Long before the death of Augustus, it was common knowledge that he would ascend to the stars at his death. What is surprising is that this knowledge was not confined to poets and others in Augustus' own circle, but was apparently shared by people on much lower social levels. Thus on a temple to Augustus' young sons Caius and Lucius Caesar in Campania the dedicator, a chief centurion, placed a poem, apparently of his own making (and certainly not among the masterpieces of Latin poetry):[12]

[10] e.g. Taylor (1931); Taeger (1960, 141 ff.).

[11] Contra Price (1984*b*), depending too much on philosophical sources; the article remains the only thorough discussion of basic terms such as *deus, divus*, and *theós* and their meaning.

[12] *CIL* X. 3757 (Acerrae) = *ILS* 137 with Taylor (1931, 224): '*Templum hoc*

May this temple, hallowed to the heirs, stand firm in their service,
since they carry the blissful name of Augustus:
thus may their father rejoice in the rule of his offspring;
for when time shall demand you as a god, Caesar,
and you shall return to your seat in heaven, whence
you will rule the world, may it be these who in your stead
hold sway here on earth and rule us by their felicitous vows.

The fact that this notion was apparently so obvious and widespread lends strong support to the view that divine honours were simply the 'natural' response to absolute power in antiquity.

It was also common knowledge that Jupiter himself would eventually receive the emperor in heaven.[13] The parallel between the king of gods and of men was the obvious one, and is extremely frequent in poetry and literature of the Augustan age, though all too easily obscured by the fact that Augustus, cautiously, rather stressed his links to other gods, primarily Apollo, in his lifetime.[14] Suetonius gives a long and interesting list of omens of Augustus' demise at the end of his life. When the emperor, a few months before his death, conducted the census in the Campus Martius,[15] 'an eagle flew several times about him and then going across to the temple [Agrippa's Pantheon] hard by, perched above the first letter of Agrippa's name [and of Augustus']. On noticing this, Augustus [withdrew from the ceremony, for] he declared that he should not be responsible for vows which he would never pay'.

sacratum her[edibus qui] | *quod ger[unt] Augusti nomen felix [illis]* | *remaneat, stirpis suae laetetur u[t regno]* | *parens; nam quom te, Caesar, tem[pus]* | *exposcet deum caeloque repetes sed[em, qua]* | *mundum reges, sint hei, tua quei sorte te[rrae]* | *huic imperent regantque nos felicibu[s]* | *voteis sueis.* | *L. Aurelius L. f. Pal. Rufu[s] primopilaris .[. . .]* | *XVI militans st[. . .]* | *imp. Caesaris [. . .]*'; cf. Price (1987, 76f.).

13 Ps.-Ov. *Cons. ad Liviam* 211ff.: '*Tu* [Augustus] *letum optasti, dis avertantibus omen,*| *Par tibi, si sinerent te tua fata mori.*| *Sed tibi debetur caelum, te fulmine pollens* | *accipiet cupidi regia magna Iovis*'. The date of the poem has been much discussed, see now Schoonhoven (1992, 22ff. with lit.); I find his dating of the poem to AD 54–5 unconvincing, and see no reason not to accept it as Augustan, for which see the convincing arguments of Fraschetti (1996, esp. 238f.); cf. Manil. *Astr.* 1. 799f.: '. . . *descendit caelo caelumque replebit* | *quod reget Augustus, socio per signa tonante*'.

14 Apollo: Zanker (1987, *passim*); Jupiter: e.g. Hor. *Carm.* 3. 5. 1ff.; Ov. *Trist.* 3. 35f.; *Fast.* 2. 131f.; Taeger (1960, 173); Zanker (1987, 313f.).

15 Suet. *Aug.* 97. 1, tr. Rolfe, Loeb edn. (adapted).

Apparently, then, the omen was immediately intelligible to all spectators; the eagle was of course Jupiter (or his messenger) coming to bring Augustus to heaven. The bird had of old been a symbol of apotheosis in East and West. In Greek mythology, there was of course the story of Zeus and Ganymede; and Zeus had raised his son Heracles to heaven. Jupiter's prominent role in connection with apotheosis is hardly surprising; the king of gods naturally decided who should enter heaven (furthermore, but probably less important, the sky, in which presided the gods, was his sphere).

Augustus might well ascend to heaven at his death, and become a god. I do not see this as the main aspect of his deification: the world was full of gods anyway. What mattered was that he became a god *of the Roman state*. This was decreed by the Senate on 17 September AD 14, and was constructed thereafter by state sacrifices to the new god of the *populus Romanus*. Modern scholarship has, I believe, consistently confused the two aspects, that of absolute and of relative divinity. This confusion reflects our christianizing preoccupation with the absolute aspect of divinity and its nature. Such questions were the subject of debate also in the ancient world, namely among philosophers, but it mattered little to the workings of pagan cults and religion. In a world with an infinite number of gods, divinity, or at least what made divinity worth cultivating, was always relative: not whether someone, emperor, beloved, or Jupiter, was a god, but *to whom* this was so.

Scholars have then, I believe, failed to distinguish between these different aspects, or rather taken it for granted that the aspect of absolute divinity was, as in Christianity, the important and decisive one. The senatorial decrees and the rites and sacrifices to *Divi* have, unwittingly, been seen merely as a reflection of the 'real' thing, that Augustus and later *Divi* actually and absolutely ascended to heaven, and so became gods. This view fails to take ritual seriously in its own right, as capable not only of reflecting, but of actually constructing social reality. Instead it presupposes the notion of belief as what must ultimately underpin a religious system. I shall return to this discussion in connection with analysis of Seneca's burlesque of the apotheosis of Claudius, the *Apocolocyntosis*, whose apparent irreverence to the whole institution of state deification has persistently puzzled modern scholars. First, however, we shall see what the sources actually tell us of the funeral and deification of Augustus and later emperors, who became *Divi*.

THE AUGUSTAN PRECEDENT

Dio preserves the lengthiest and most complete account of Augustus' funeral. A shorter version is given by Suetonius, who picks out measures particularly noteworthy or honorific, to fit his theme of Augustus' farewell as the culmination and epitome of a singularly successful reign. Suetonius of course had no reason to record all the appropriate procedures to his audience, who were familiar with them.[16] Dio, on the other hand, wrote for an outsider audience in the Greek-speaking world, and so his account purports to give a complete description of all the elements of this first imperial funeral. As we shall see, the difference in scope and purpose between the two accounts is important, though all too often ignored.[17]

The old emperor died at Nola on 19 August AD 14, and 'the body . . . was carried from Nola by the foremost men of each city in succession' (Dio). Suetonius adds that, because of the season, high summer, it was carried at night, and during the daytime was displayed in the basilica or temples of townships *en route*. At Bovillae, the equestrian order received the procession and took over the burden; they entered Rome with the corpse at night, and placed it in the vestibule of Augustus' house. The next day, according to Dio, the Senate met, with Tiberius presiding; Augustus' will was read, followed by four other documents of his: one on his own funeral, the *Res Gestae*, an account of the finances of the empire, and 'injunctions and commands for Tiberius and for the public'. Suetonius mentions only the first three items. The first of these contained 'detailed instructions regarding his funeral' (Dio), and presumably requested the Senate's permission for these procedures. Further glorifying honours were added by the Senate, such as

[16] More generally for Suetonius' method, see Wallace-Hadrill (1983, 14ff.).

[17] Dio 56. 31. 2ff. with a gap in the MSS; Suet. *Aug.* 100. 2ff.; Tac. *Ann.* 1. 7ff.

that the funerary cortège should pass through the Porta Triumphalis and be preceded by placards recording laws passed and peoples conquered by Augustus (Tacitus, *Ann.* 1. 8. 3). Suetonius gives a long list of these honours, though it is not clear which of them were actually passed or allowed by Tiberius (as mentioned, the biographer's main purpose is not to describe the funeral, but to stress the impressive honours as indicative of Augustus' glorious reign). They are, however, all concerned with the surroundings, rather than the content, of the funeral, which surely implies that the funeral procedures as such were decided already, namely, according to Augustus' own instructions.

The funeral itself is fully described by Dio:

> Then came his funeral. There was a couch made of ivory and gold and adorned with coverings of purple and gold. In it his body was hidden, in a coffin down below; but a wax image of him in triumphal garb was visible. This image was borne from the palace by the officials elected for the following year, and another of gold from the senate-house, and still another upon a triumphal chariot. Behind these came the images of his ancestors and of his deceased relatives (except that of Caesar, because he had been numbered among the demigods) and those of other Romans who had been prominent in any way, beginning with Romulus himself. An image of Pompey the Great was also seen, and all the nations he [Augustus] had acquired, each represented by a likeness which bore some local characteristic, appeared in the procession. After these followed all the other objects mentioned above. When the couch had been placed in full view on the rostra of the orators, Drusus read something from that place; and from the other rostra, that is the Julian, Tiberius delivered the . . . public address over the deceased, in pursuance of a decree . . .

Dio then gives a long version of Tiberius' speech, after which he continues:

> Such was the eulogy read by Tiberius. Afterwards the same men as before took up the couch and carried it through the triumphal gateway, according to a decree of the senate. Present and taking part in the funeral procession were the senate and the equestrian order, their wives, the pretorian guard, and practically all the others who were in the city at the time. When the body had been placed on the pyre in the Campus Martius, all the priests marched round it first; and then the knights, not only those belonging to the equestrian order but the others [i.e. cavalrymen] as well, and the infantry from the garrison ran

round it; and they cast upon it all the triumphal decorations that any of them had ever received from him for any deed of valour. Next the centurions took torches, conformably to a decree of the senate, and lighted the pyre from beneath. So it was consumed, and an eagle released from it flew aloft, appearing to bear his spirit to heaven. When these ceremonies had been performed, all the other people departed; but Livia remained on the spot for five days in company with the most prominent knights, and then gathered up his bones and placed them in his tomb.[18]

After the funeral, an ex-praetor by the name of Numerius Atticus stood forward and claimed under oath that he had seen the spirit of Augustus ascending to heaven. There was an obvious precedent for this, as Dio explicitly mentions. Romulus had suddenly disappeared from earth in a storm. Some suspected the senators of foul play; but Romulus soon afterwards appeared to the senator Julius Proculus, declaring that he had become a god and commanding the Romans to worship him with divine rites. This duly happened: Romulus became a state god under the name Quirinus. The parallel between Proculus and Atticus was close enough to be obvious, though it is not entirely clear whether Atticus actually witnessed Augustus' ascension at the funeral, or only slightly later after an apparition, as in the case of Romulus and Proculus. In the case of Romulus, his miraculous apparition convinced the Romans, so goes the story, that he had really become a god.

The award of a public funeral, itself an elaborate version of a traditional noble funeral, was no novelty; it had been decreed to several Romans before Caesar, with Sulla as a particularly prominent example.[19] Even in the empire, the distinction continued to be granted to prominent private citizens, so Augustus' funeral as such did not set him apart from other nobles. It differed in degree, not in kind, and I have here left out several details in the procedures, because they do not seem to have any relevance to the consecration of Augustus. There is one clear exception, however, namely the rite of the eagle, which according to Dio bore Augustus' spirit to heaven and so deified him; this had never been employed before. The detail is controversial, and I shall soon return to it.

On 17 September, apparently right after the funeral, the

[18] Dio 56. 34 and 42, tr. E. Cary. [19] Weinstock (1971, 348ff.).

Senate met and consecrated the late emperor: 'On that day heavenly honours were decreed to Divus Augustus' in the words of the state calendar.[20] These honours, which unequivocally turned Augustus into a Roman state god, consisted of three elements: the award of a new name to the departed emperor, who was henceforth called simply *Divus* Augustus; the decreeing of a state temple to the new god; the establishment of a priestly college, the *sodales Augustales*, and a *flamen* and *flaminica* (Germanicus and Livia) for his official worship.

Strictly speaking, the first of these honours was enough to turn Augustus into a state divinity; the other two, temple and priests, ensured, however, that his worship would be continuously honoured, and that his *memoria* would be eternal; they were an insurance against oblivion. The title of *Divus* had an obvious and direct precedent in that of Divus Julius, but Caesar had been a controversial figure, and there is more to the story, I believe; further interpretation of the title depends, however, on how we understand the procedures of state deification at large, so I shall postpone it. Suffice it to say here that Augustus' new celestial divinity was constructed as unequivocal; as with portraits of the other celestials, who were to be kept away from any ill-omened contact with death and its lower world underground, Augustus' image was not to be carried in funeral processions.[21]

[20] The exact date of the funeral is not specifically given; Levick (1976, 70) argues for 8 Sept. based on parallel evidence; Tac. *Ann.* 1. 10. 7 and Dio 56. 46. 1 imply that the meeting followed shortly after it. Calendar: Degrassi (1963, 510): *Fasti Oppiani, Amiternini* (version quoted here), *Antiates*: '*fer(iae) ex s(enatus) c(onsulto) q(uod) e(o) d(ie) Divo Augusto honores caelestes a senatu decreti*'.

[21] Price (1987, 80) argues, on the basis of legal rulings as to whether testamentary donations could be left to *Divi* as they could to other gods, that '*divi* both were and were not gods'. However, these rulings belong to the second century when the system had become routine from the great number of *Divi*, and the view is anachronistic when transferred to Augustus' case. The very fact that a legal decision was reached on the point only at such a late date argues against Price's view as characteristic of the first century. The only evidence that can perhaps be adduced in support of Price's case is the fact that mourning was decreed for senatorial women for a whole year after Augustus' demise (Dio 56. 43. 1; Price, 1987, 63 f.), which may seem to define it as death rather than ascension to the gods (but this could also be taken simply as a response to bereavement, which would be relevant in either case).

The *flamen* and *flaminica* of Augustus were modelled on the three *flamines maiores* to Jupiter, Mars, and Quirinus (who supplied the obvious precedent); also the *sodales* had an old and venerable precedent in the *sodales Titii*, supposedly established by Romulus to his co-regent Titus Tatius after his death. Likewise, the temple to Augustus was in no way set apart from the temples to other state gods; on the contrary, it was apparently modelled on the Capitoline temple of Jupiter. Also temples to later *Divi* were completely 'divine' in layout and design, as was indeed the temple to Divus Julius.[22] When, however, the number of *Divi* rose over time, it became impossible to grant a temple, *sodales*, and *flamines* to all of them. Some *Divi* never received a temple, others were installed in the temple of a close relative, and priesthoods were, from an early stage, bundled together, so that one *flamen* and each college of *sodales* dealt with several *Divi*.[23] Still, the temples to *Divi*, altogether perhaps fourteen in Rome, continued all through the first two centuries AD to be on a grand and impressive scale (p. 341–4 below); several are still prominent in the cityscape of Rome, and the continuous building programme of such temples clearly points to the great importance of the *Divi* (though at what level may be debatable; I shall return to this question).

Augustus and later *Divi* were then unequivocally removed from the world of mortals. Tacitus suggests some—subdued—opposition to the scheme: no honours were any longer reserved exclusively for the gods (I shall shortly return to his statement). It would, however, be wrong to see the deification as a symptom of religious crisis, or cynicism in relation to the traditional celestials. Little noticed by scholars, Divus Augustus and later *Divi* were meticulously placed in the hierarchy of the gods so as not to disturb it; the *Arval Acta* clearly show that the *Divi* ranked last among all gods worshipped by the Brothers (even

[22] Temple of Augustus: Fishwick (1990) and (1992); Price (1987, 78, with refs. n. 43 to temples of *Divi*) sees the temple of Divus Julius as the exception, since it 'incorporated the funerary altar erected over the pyre'. This seems to beg the question: if Divus Julius was a celestial god, his altar was not funerary.

[23] Already evident at the deification of Claudius, when the *sodales Augustales* became *sodales Augustales Claudiales* (Degrassi, 1947, 311 ff.); in the late 40s AD, the same man was *flamen* of both Divus Augustus and Diva Augusta (Hoffmann Lewis, 1955, 38).

below the living emperor's *Genius*, when this god became the object of sacrifices). There was evidently no question of rivalry, and the old gods had nothing to fear from the newcomer.[24]

'HE WANTED TO BE WORSHIPPED . . .'

A vital question remains. When and where was the detailed scheme of Augustus' deification established or thought out, and by whom? Clearly the funerary procedures were in place at Augustus' death; we have already noted that it was only left for the senators to think of further measures to add to his funerary honours, and that these measures were concerned only with the surroundings, not the contents, of the funeral. We know that the form of the funeral was not improvised for the occasion, something which would have been surprising in any case. Augustus had indeed left detailed instructions for his last journey on earth. Apparently nothing was left to coincidence, and Augustus requested the Senate's permission for the funeral to take place according to his *mandata*. In connection with the funeral Tacitus summarizes talk supposedly going around about the late ruler: first the positive verdicts on his life, then the negative ones. As part of the latter he makes a somewhat curious accusation:[25] 'No honours were any longer reserved for the gods, when he [Augustus] wanted to be worshipped with temples and cult images by *flamines* and priests'. Commentators have always taken this statement to refer to Augustus' lifetime policy in the field of imperial cults, and then hastened to protest his innocence: for Augustus had consistently refused this honour in Rome itself (in the Roman state cult, to be more precise) and ordained that Roma should be worshipped with him in provincial cults.[26] It is true that the criticism is weird

[24] Henzen (1874, *passim*).

[25] Tac. *Ann.* 1. 10. 5: '*Nihil deorum honoribus relictum, cum se templis et effigie numinum per flamines et sacerdotes coli vellet*'. Cf. for '*vellet*' Suet. *Aug.* 101. 4: '. . . *indicem rerum a se gestarum, quem* [Augustus] *vellet incidi in aeneis tabulis* . . .'; for '*effigie numinum*' Tac. *Ann.* 4. 37. 3: '*Ceterum ut semel recepisse veniam habuerit, ita per omnes provincias effigie numinum sacrari ambitiosum, superbum*'.

[26] Furneaux (1896, 197): 'vellet, used invidiously of mere permission . . .'; similarly Goodyear (1972, 166).

with reference to Augustus' lifetime; though it seems obvious that he enjoyed such honours when they were accorded to him in municipal and private cults, there was no need to encourage or even permit such worship: passive tolerance had been perfectly sufficient, very different from the strong 'wanted' (*vellet*) in Tacitus' remark.

An alternative interpretation, however, makes perfectly good sense. The words can instead be taken to refer to Augustus' desires for state deification as expressed in his directions for his funeral. The Senate's permission for these instructions was vital, because the funerary rites implied Augustus' deification. The rite of letting loose an eagle from his pyre certainly spelt out deification, and we shall later see that there is in fact no good reason for doubting this detail, though it has seemed so bizarre to modern scholars that they have commonly rejected it. One of the reasons why the meeting of the Senate before the funeral was taken up solely with the business of the funeral was then because Augustus requested the Senate to deify him after death, something which had never been done before (except in the myths of archaic Rome where this supposedly happened to Romulus: this could supply a precedent, but no blueprint or details for how it should actually be carried out in practice). Whatever criteria we employ in our interpretation, modern incredulity and (claimed) rationalism is the least fruitful to impute to the old emperor and his senators.

A closer look at Tacitus' words does indeed suggest that he is referring to Augustus' desire for posthumous state deification. One odd element is the phrase 'by *flamines* and priests'. *Flamines* were also priests (*sacerdotes*);[27] why two terms for the same concept? The actual arrangements of the worship of Divus Augustus suggest the answer: he received both a *flamen* and a college of priests, the *sodales Augustales*, for his worship. The words reflect this arrangement and consequently impute it to Augustus himself. To keep the criticism on a more general level—the accusation is after all Augustus' desire for divine honours, not the specific details in which it was expressed—'priests' was substituted for '*sodales*' (who were of course also

[27] Cf. Cic. *Leg.* 2. 8. 20: '*Divisque aliis [alii] sacerdotes, omnibus pontifices, singulis flamines sunto*'.

sacerdotes).[28] The plural of *flamines* rather than the singular is no problem: it is rhetorical, to go with *sacerdotes*, a stylistic feature frequently found in Tacitus.[29] Tacitus' phraseology in fact finds a close parallel in a passage of Suetonius about Tiberius, suggesting a common formula for the state worship of emperors (Suet. *Tib.* 26. 1):

> He forbade the decreeing of temples, *flamines* and priests to himself, and even the setting up of statues and images without his permission; and this he gave only with the understanding that they were not to be placed among the cult images of the gods, but among the adornments of the temples.

I have dealt with this passage elsewhere (p. 143 above) and argued that it refers to offers in the Senate of state divinity to Tiberius, more specifically temples, *flamen*, and *sodales*, that is, all the honours accorded to Augustus in 14: this then gave the full and ready-made formula of divine honours, now also offered to Augustus' successor whilst alive (neither the first nor the last time this was suggested). Suetonius' wording of the formula is exactly parallel to that of Tacitus: *templa*, *flamines*, *sacerdotes*, and even, in a much fuller formulation, the *effigie numinum*, cult statues as opposed to normal, ornamental images.

This interpretation of Tacitus' remark can also explain the seemingly odd context in which it is placed by the historian: '*nec domesticis abstinebatur*'—'nor were his domestic affairs spared' by his calumniators. This heading is followed by criticisms of how Augustus had in his youth abducted Livia from her then husband; how she had been a burden both to the state and to the house of the Caesars; how Augustus had acquiesced in the vulgar ostentation of his rich friends, such as Vedius Pollio; then comes the remark on his craving for divine honours; and finally how Augustus had adopted Tiberius in order that he would himself be remembered fondly when compared

28 The colleges of imperial *sodales* were frequently termed *sacerdotes* in Tacitus' day, thus *CIL* VI. 2189 (*sacerdotium Titialium Flavialium*); 1523 (*sacerdos Titialis Flavialis*); Wissowa (1912, 565 n. 4).

29 Thus *Ann.* 4. 2. 4: '*theatra et fora*' (see p. 225 above). There is also the possibility that *flamines* is collective for the *flamen* and the *flaminica*; but style should dictate the use of the plural in any case; cf. HA *Hadr.* 27. 3: '*et quinquennale certamen et flamines et sodales et multa alia*'.

to a successor so inferior. The listing plays subtly on the interplay between Augustus' domestic or family affairs and their damaging effect on the *res publica.* Again, if referring to Augustus' lifetime policy, the words on divine worship seem quite misplaced in this context. But referring to his posthumous honours of state temple, *flamen* and *sodales*, the context makes good sense, in a very Tacitean fashion. Elsewhere Tacitus lets Tiberius characterize the *sodales Augustales* (of whom the *flamen* was also a member) as the imperial family's own priesthood—'*proprium eius domus sacerdotium*' (*Ann.* 3. 64. 4). Now, the *sodales* were clearly a state priesthood, publicly funded. This is formality, but the reality as Tacitus saw it was very different: the blurring of distinctions between public and private, between the interests of one family and those of the state, the abuse of the state machinery for furthering personal desires—this constitutes a bitter, recurrent theme in Tacitus' *Annals*. So the state now had to support a priestly college which was in effect domestic. As a reference to Augustus' posthumous divinity the context of our passage is then not bizarre: it carries a subtly vicious point.

Tacitus may or may not be unfair in the calumnies he lists. However, the accusation that Augustus craved state divinity after death must simply be true in general terms. He would not have been deified unless he himself had wished this. But Tacitus' remark goes beyond this observation. It implies that Augustus knew and had planned the specific scheme adopted for his deification: the old emperor knew exactly what he wanted: temple, *flamen*, *sodales*. The remark is put into the mouth of Augustus' enemies, and we cannot be sure whether it reflects a mere suspicion that he had himself planned the details of his posthumous divinity, or whether it is a negative comment on what was factually true, as would be the case if Augustus specifically requested the honours from the Senate in his funerary instructions. The invective certainly seems more effective in the latter interpretation, whereas its specific allusion to the honours voted by the Senate in 14 appears rather superfluous if the butt of the criticism was only a general craving for worship after death. It was common knowledge that Augustus would be deified after death; but the precise measures adopted to achieve this in 14 cannot have been generally known beforehand.

The question is whether a specific request for deification was explicitly presented in Augustus' funerary instructions, or merely implied. My interpretation of Tacitus' remark can perhaps illuminate the point and purpose of the curious document known as Augustus' *Res Gestae.* A listing of the emperor's achievements and honours, it was read at the meeting of the Senate together with Augustus' other documents: his will, his funerary instructions, his account of the state of the empire and its finances; unlike these, the *Res Gestae* has come down to us, from inscriptional copies made and posted in Galatia. The document was obviously important to Augustus who, always prepared for his own death, revised and updated it at regular intervals during his life, the last time shortly before his demise. The point of the document is best approached from the context in which it was first presented, and for which it was presumably written: the first meeting of the Senate after Augustus' death.

It has been argued that not only the *Res Gestae* but also the documents that accompanied it should be seen not merely as supplements to Augustus' will, but as parts of it. Indeed, the argument continues, the order in which the texts were presented to the Senate corresponded to the normal structure of a Roman will; that of Augustus was in fact typical in principle, though unique in scope.[30] Most unusual, however, seems to be the *Res Gestae.* This document was read after the funerary instructions. Such instructions usually had a fixed structure, ending with requests to the heirs as to the upkeep of the tomb and their other obligations to the *memoria* of the deceased. If Augustus specifically requested his own deification, this would then have been the place for it. For what it is worth, Suetonius does not mention the rite of the eagle (to which I shall soon return). If this ritual did in fact take place at the funeral, this implies that the feature was contained in the instructions; I have already claimed that the senatorial motions summarized by Suetonius were concerned with the surroundings, not contents of the funeral, which suggests that these contents, which go unmentioned, were in place already, specified in the instructions.

Augustus' will may in principle have been typical in other

[30] Champlin (1989).

respects, but the *Res Gestae* had no clear or convincing precedent. The text has been compared to *elogia*, laudatory short biographies placed on statues of worthies; but these were written by others, and never kept in the first person, as is the case throughout the *Res Gestae.* Another parallel has been pointed out in the *laudatio funebris*, the biographical speeches of praise held over the corpse of dead people at their funerals; again, the first person would be absurd in this genre.

Seen as part of Augustus' will, in which he bequeathed large sums of money to the Roman people, and in the immediate context of the funerary instructions, the *Res Gestae* can be taken as the old emperor's argument, his *apologia*, for receiving his crowning honour, state divinity, which he had so modestly (or prudently) rejected throughout his lifetime. No text was ever more carefully composed or deliberately phrased. It is divided between accomplishments and benefactions interchanging with their rewards, honours accorded him by the Senate and people during his life. Significantly, the honours take up less than a third of the space accorded to the other categories, and the excessive honours are commonly mentioned for being rejected by the writer; taken as an account of achievements and benefactions versus honours, there is a clear deficit of the latter.

Years before, Augustus had humorously stated his case in a letter to Tiberius, when he told how he had voluntarily lost money at the gambling table: 'My kindness [*benignitas*] will carry me to heavenly glory'. The remark is a joke, but that explains little, and should not be used to dismiss it.[31] Without a serious and presupposed concept set off against the mildly self-mocking remark, it is not really funny at all. It was humorous to state the principle in connection with having sacrificed a few coins at the gaming table, and claim heavenly glory for the rather mundane quality of *benignitas*. The millions of sesterces, as well as Augustus' other benefactions and accomplishments as listed in the *Res Gestae*, that was the real thing, the principle humorously parodied in his remark. Now the reward should be

[31] Suet. *Aug.* 71. 3: '*benignitas mea me ad caelestem gloriam efferret*'; dismissed by Griffin (1984, 211 f.); Price (1984*a*, 114 f.) on jokes ('jokes are made precisely about those things that matter most'); Augustus' jokes: Yavetz (1990, 36 ff.).

forthcoming, and the account of honours made to balance with his unique achievements.

Only the Senate could grant this. We may now see why the *Res Gestae* had no real precursors or parallels in ancient literature: no man had ever before presented his own case for divinity after his death. And in this way we see how fitting it was for the *Res Gestae* to be inscribed in Augustus' temple at Ancyra in Galatia, from where we possess our fullest copy. In Rome Augustus of course had no public temple yet, and he requested that the document be engraved and set up outside his mausoleum; extracts from wills were commonly, it should be noted, copied in inscriptions placed on or by the tomb.

It was not left to Tiberius to present the argument for deification. Even in death Augustus planned to remain in control and argue his own case. In this way, the comparison to a *laudatio funebris* may not be completely wrong after all. Dio Cassius in his version of Tiberius' speech over Augustus' corpse lets him finish after a long-winded presentation of the late emperor's momentous achievements and benefactions (56. 41. 9):

> It was for all this, therefore, that you, with good reason, made him your leader and a father of the people [i.e. *pater patriae*], that you honoured him with many marks of esteem and with ever so many consulships, and that you finally made him a demigod [*hērōs*] and declared him to be immortal.

LATER FUNERALS

Apart from the—controversial—ascension of the eagle from his pyre, there was in strict principle little new in the rites of Augustus' funeral. It was modelled on traditional noble funerals, and though it was certainly the most splendid one to date, it differed in degree only, not in kind.[32] The pattern of

[32] Price (1987, 69f.); Weber (1936, 75ff.) and Richard (1980, 461ff.) have stressed the triumphal procession as a model for imperial and noble funerals; this is clearly true, but perhaps not very surprising: the triumph was the magnificent public procession *par excellence*, and particularly relevant for an *imperator*. I am, however, not convinced by the view of the procession as connoting triumph over death, which seems christianizing. Further Arce (1988, 35ff.).

Augustus' funeral was basically followed for later *Divi*, as is evident from two long descriptions of these ceremonies. One is an eyewitness account of Dio, apparently as good as complete, though preserved in a later source only, of the funeral of Pertinax in AD 193, presided over by the new emperor Septimius Severus. The other is given by Herodian in connection with Severus' death in AD 211, but purports to give a general description of the ceremonies to a provincial Greek audience.[33]

The use of a wax image as a stand-in for the corpse of the dead emperor figures prominently in these accounts. The image was, as we have seen, employed also at the funerals of Caesar and Augustus. Bickermann has made much of this aspect. In the cases of Pertinax and Severus, cremation had already taken place (Pertinax had been murdered months before the funeral, and Severus had died in York). However, on the basis of a passage in the Historia Augusta, briefly describing the interment of Antoninus Pius (who died in Rome), followed by his *funus*, Bickermann argued at length for a 'double funeral' of emperors in the second century; one 'normal' cremation and interment of the body in the tomb, followed by an elaborate cremation of a wax image, with release of an eagle. Bickermann explained the second ceremony as performing an illusion of an ascension in the flesh, as in the cases of Hercules and Romulus, since the wax image would melt away completely without leaving behind any mortal remains.[34]

This interpretation presupposes a concern with theological

[33] Pattern: see table in Price (1987, 60); Dio (Xiph.) 75. 4–5. 5; Herod. 4. 2. Price (1987, 61) argues convincingly that Pertinax' funeral followed the usual pattern, despite the peculiar circumstances in this case.

[34] Bickermann (1929) in Wlosok (1978, 86 ff.), followed by Kierdorf (1986*a*, 64 f.) (but contradicting himself 67); contra Vittinghoff (1936, 110 ff.); Weinstock (1971, 361). HA *M. Ant. Phil.* 7. 10 f. has been taken to suggest inhumation in the case of Antoninus Pius; the passage has aroused considerable debate (see Richard, 1980, 464 f.). Most of the literature on imperial funerals has concentrated on this theory of a 'double funeral'; Turcan (1958, 325 ff.), followed by Gros (1965–6, 477 ff.) and Richard (1980, 461 ff.), saw the custom of *funus imaginarium* furthered by the general transition from cremation to inhumation in the second century; further complications are inherent in the image proposed by Chantraine (1980, 71 ff.), followed by Kierdorf (1986*a*, 45). Price (1987, 96 f.) questions the notion of 'double funeral', a private ceremony of inhuming the corpse and a public one of cremating the image, and argues that cremation, of both corpse and image, continued to be employed in

aspects which smacks far more of Christianity than of Roman paganism. Elsewhere, pagan theology contained glaring theological inconsistencies, which were not felt to be a problem, simply because pagan religion was not very preoccupied with dogmas and theology (they were the preserve of philosophy); rites were what mattered, the rest was left to the gods. Also, there is no evidence to support Bickermann's decisive point, that the ascension should preferably or necessarily be in the flesh, nor anything to suggest embarrassment in connection with the gathering of the late emperor's ashes.[35] On the contrary: shortly after Augustus' funeral, his *flamen* and grandson Germanicus took to translating a Greek astronomical classic, the didactic poem *Phaenomena* by Aratos from Soli. When Germanicus came to Aratos' description of the star sign Capricorn which was Augustus' birth sign, he inserted two lines of his own making, with poetic licence portraying Capricorn as taking Augustus to heaven at the old emperor's funeral:[36] 'He

imperial funerals till Constantine; he draws atttention to the common depictions of the pyre, labelled *consecratio*, in the coinage through the second to early fourth centuries. The continued use of cremation in imperial funerals would, he rightly argues, have set them apart from those of *privati*, where inhumation became general during the second century. In any case, the method of disposing of the actual body of a dead emperor hardly matters much when the public ceremony was one of cremation, whether of image and body, or of image only. Inhumation of the body, on the other hand, has been claimed on the basis of the sarcophagus of Balbinus from the Praetextatus Catacombs. Price doubts the identification, but Balbinus was murdered and suffered *damnatio*, and so clearly did not receive an imperial funeral anyway. Personally, I fail to see the importance of the debate on 'double funeral': its relevance seems to depend entirely on Bickermann's unfounded theory of ascension in the flesh.

[35] Cf. Suet. *Aug.* 100. 4: '*Reliquias legerunt primores equestris ordinis . . . ac Mausoleo condiderunt*'.

[36] Germ. *Arat.* 558–60: '*hic, Auguste, tuum genitali corpore numen | attonitas inter gentis patriamque paventem | in caelum tulit et maternis reddidit astris*'. My translation of *genitali corpore* differs from those of Barton (1995) ('thanks to his body which engendered you'), A. le Boeuffle, ed. Budé (1975) ('qui avait pris corps sous son signe') and D. B. Gain (1976) ('on the body of this sign, under which you were born'); I prefer to take the words in the more obvious meaning as simply a separative ablative. For the Capricorn as Augustus' birth sign (born at night, thus his moon sign) see Barton (1995); for the idea that Tiberius and not Germanicus was the author (which I find unconvincing, albeit immaterial to my argument), see edn. of Gain (1976, 16ff.); cf. Vell. 2. 124. 3: '. . . *corpus eius humanis honoribus, numen divinis* . . .'.

was it, Augustus, who, leaving behind your engendered body, carried your divinity to heaven and, amidst the awe-struck peoples and our trembling nation, returned it to the mother stars'.

So Augustus' own state priest was not aware that mortal remains should have presented a theological problem. There is indeed a much simpler explanation for the use of an image. Wax statues have certainly been employed in royal funerary rites later, in the Renaissance and Baroque periods. For instance, the corpse of Elizabeth I was also hidden behind a wax image at her funeral in 1603.[37] The reason was not notions of ascension in the flesh, but simply its corruption. Elaborate state funerals, such as those of Elizabeth or of a Roman emperor, could not be improvised overnight. Preparations took time, during which the body would begin to rot and become unfit for display (the process could be delayed by evisceration, which was employed in Elizabeth's day).[38] There is no reason for suspecting anything else or more in the case of Roman emperors. Augustus' funeral took place about three weeks after his death, by which time the corpse must have been in a revolting state (it was high summer; Suetonius hints at the problem in saying that the body was carried from Nola to Rome during nights only *propter anni tempus*). Likewise, when 'every perfume and incense on earth and all the fruits and herbs and juices that are collected for their aroma are brought up and poured out in great heaps', as Herodian says in his description of the imperial pyre, this was not just because they smelt nice, but to quench what did not. So though Bickermann's theory of a double funeral as the usual procedure might be correct (though the one passage in the Historia Augusta is not impressive as evidence), decay of the flesh can easily account for it. Caesar's wax image may seem different, for he was cremated soon after his death. But the funeral was no doubt hurried

[37] Johnson (1974, 440), quoting contemporary description by Henry Chettle.

[38] Note e.g. the remark of Mary Tudor on her loss of Calais to the French in 1556, as reported by John Foxe in his *Acts and Monuments* (*Book of Martyrs*, 1st edn. 1563, numerous later edns., here quoted from ed. S. R. Cattley (1836–41), viii. 625): '. . . When I am dead and opened, you shall find Calais lying in my heart'.

through as an economized version of what Caesar had envisaged and planned; he too left directions for his own funeral, which presumably prescribed or envisaged elaborate ceremonial, and so specified the use of an image. Perversely, however, though presumably meant to hide corruption, the image was then employed by the Caesarians to display Caesar's horrid wounds to the angry mob.[39]

Herodian gives a puzzling description of the lying in state of the imperial image; for seven days, he claims, the illusion is maintained that the image represents, not a corpse, but the living emperor on his sick-bed: 'Each day the doctors come and go up to the couch, and each day they pretend to examine the patient and make an announcement that his condition is deteriorating'. Only on the seventh day is he declared dead, and the funeral ceremonies proceed. The description is strange indeed, but we need more than Herodian's interpretation to take it seriously. Herodian may well have misunderstood the rites; the fact that the senators and their wives, sitting by the image, were dressed in mourning, as Herodian says, does not suit the fiction that the image represented a living emperor; rather that it, as in other cases, simply functioned as a substitute for the corpse. The daily visits by the doctors make more sense as continued assurance that the patient was really dead.[40]

DEIFICATION, DAMNATION, AND DEVALUATION

In the age of Dio and Herodian the institution of state deification had long since become routine. Herodian cynically, or naïvely, comments: 'It is normal Roman practice to deify

[39] Suet. *Aug.* 100. 2; Herod. 4. 2. 8; for Caesar's funeral, probably 20 March 44, its problematic sources, and the image, see Weinstock (1971, 346ff. and 360f.); he suggests corruption of the body as the reason for the use of an image in imperial funerals (as does Price, 1987, 97), but despairs of an explanation in Caesar's case. A wooden image was carried on a bier at Sulla's splendid funeral (Plut. *Sulla* 38. 3).

[40] Herod. 4. 2. 3; Dio's description mentions a boy fanning the image to keep flies away 'as though it were really a person sleeping' (75. 4. 3); or, equally relevant, a corpse, we may add; the rite is also mentioned in *Cod. Iust.* 7. 6. 5 ('. . . *cadaver ventilare videntur*'); Weinstock (1971, 361 n. 2–3) is more speculative; Price (1987, 75f.) accepts and over-interprets Herodian's account.

emperors who die leaving behind them children as their successors'. Tiberius' warnings against cheapening the honours of Divus Augustus by bestowing them indiscriminately were in vain: even the first consecration after Augustus was to a person of little importance and achievement, Caligula's sister Drusilla. A generation later, Nero's dead baby daughter received the same honour. It is difficult to believe that such instances could ever have been taken seriously in their own right; for once the rather cynical explanation of political expediency and flattery (of the living emperor, that is) in connection with imperial cults seems appropriate. After Tiberius, all emperors who left behind an heir, and all empresses who predeceased their august husband, received state deification. So did numerous imperial children. Within these limits, deification became a conventional, even mechanical, response to imperial deaths.[41]

The practice of destroying all visible reminders of an emperor—his statues and his name in inscriptions—was clearly the opposite alternative to deification, showing any ruling emperor what the cost would be of ignoring senatorial opinion. First employed in Nero's case, it should not be confused with attempts to falsify or rewrite history, as known from modern dictatorships: the classic examples are the erasures of Trotsky from the foot of Lenin's pulpit, or the clumsy erasure of Dubcek—whose feet were forgotten in the process—from the group photograph of the Czechoslovak leadership in 1968. The Roman *damnatio* did not claim that a 'bad' emperor had never existed and ruled; the sheer number of inscriptions surviving with erasures of names, monuments which were apparently not completely destroyed or reused for other purposes, spell out the opposite point: the erasures were, and should be, visible as *exempla* or we might say 'anti-monuments' of damned rulers. Anonymity was to be their conspicuous punishment.

Tiberius and Caligula were in fact the only emperors who were neither appointed *Divi* nor consigned to oblivion at their deaths, and in both cases their ambiguous status clearly caused

[41] Herod. 4. 2. 1; Tiberius: Tac. *Ann.* 4. 37. 5: '*et vanescet Augusti honor, si promiscis adulationibus vulgatur*'; Drusilla: Barrett (1989, 86ff.); baby: Tac. *Ann.* 15. 23; routine: note e.g. Suet. *Dom.* 2. 3: Domitian bestowed on Titus '*nullo praeterquam consecrationis honore*'.

confusion at the time.[42] Later, however, there was no middle way: damnation or deification were the only options. This obviously came to devalue deification and make it routine; instead of being the unique and crowning reward, as in Augustus' case, it came to entail only the not necessarily very positive verdict of 'not guilty'.

CANONIZATION OR CREATION?

We are relatively well informed as to what actually took place at these ceremonies; but as for the meaning and theological implications of all this, numerous questions arise. First and foremost, was the late emperor made a god, or was his elevation to the sphere of the gods merely recognized by the Senate?

As for the early empire, the first century, the question seems settled. Two aspects have been taken as decisive by all modern scholars. First, the deifications were decreed by the Senate *after* the funeral, where the late emperor's soul left his corpse and ascended to heaven; and secondly, sworn eyewitness testimony of the ascension was admitted when the consecration was decreed, or so it is claimed. On the basis of these procedures, there is now agreement in scholarship that the Senate merely recognized a state of affairs. Indeed Simon Price, following Bickermann, compares the deliberations of the Senate to those of the Roman Catholic Church before recognizing a saint: 'The senate was not seen to create a deity arbitrarily; like the Roman Catholic Church deliberating about a candidate for canonisation, the senate was recognising a state of affairs.'[43]

The imperial funerals and consecrations from the mid-first century onwards are more controversial. In the case of Augustus the senatorial decree of consecration came after the funeral. We are ill-informed about later cases, but sworn evidence seems at some point to have been dropped from the proceedings. Furthermore, there is evidence that the decree, at least in some cases, came to precede the actual funeral. One of the latest

[42] Tiberius: Mattingly (1920, 37) (the imperial mint at Lyons apparently expected Tiberius to be deified in 37); Caligula: Barrett (1989, 177f.) (Caligula's name was sometimes chiselled out in inscriptions, sometimes not).

[43] Price (1984*b*, 83f.; 1987, 73 (quotation) and *passim*); Richard (1978, 1128); Bickermann (1929) in Wlosok (1978, 84), Arce (1988, *passim*).

studies has argued that this was already the case at Claudius' funeral. With greater certainty, the *Fasti Ostienses* show that Trajan's sister Marciana and the empress Faustina at their deaths in, respectively, AD 112 and 140 received the title *Diva* before their funerals.[44] It is doubtful if we can interpret this as evidence for a general change in procedure, for there is no other strong evidence. But in conjunction with the absence of the witness, this has been taken to reflect a real change. When a *Divus* or *Diva* could be deified before the funeral and ascension, this implies that the Senate, if it did not actually create gods, then at least took the ascension for granted beforehand: so Price concludes that 'religious tradition ceased to be relevant and the decision became more of a political formality'. Others have argued against such a view, and rejected the evidence of the *Fasti Ostienses* as impossible or exceptional: instead they claim that absolute ascension at the cremation, when the emperor's soul left his body, was and remained the *sine qua non* of deification; indeed, the biographer of Marcus Aurelius stresses the universal love for this *optimus princeps* by claiming that people and Senate united in declaring him a god before his funeral 'which was never done before or later', which may perhaps be taken to support this view (or at least confine the problem to Marcus' case only).[45]

The evidence of the *Fasti Ostienses* as to Marciana's and Faustina's deifications is, as we shall see (p. 301), irrefutable. What has, however, deadlocked the issue is the presupposition of both parties in this debate that the order of decree and funeral is such a decisive aspect; worse, this agreement basically rests on the assumption that the Senate, as in the procedure of canonization, merely recognized a state of affairs in the procedure of consecration. Then again, the interpretation of 'canonization' is taken as decisive to seeing the ceremonial as

[44] Claudius: Kierdorf (1986*a*, 62ff.) (see p. 299f below); Marciana and Faustina: Vidman (1982, 48; 64) (see p. 301 below).

[45] Vittinghoff (1936, 77ff.; 108ff.); Gros (1965–6, 477ff.); Richard (1980, 466f.); Kierdorf (1986*a*, 50); Price (1987, 91f.); contra Bickermann (1974); Temporini (1978, 219f.; 234ff.); Arce (1988, 131) (quoting, but misunderstanding Plut. *Quaest. Rom.* 14, which in fact quotes Varro, and is irrelevant to the *Divi*); Oliver (1949, 39); Scheid (1984, 121 n. 15); HA *M. Ant. Phil.* 18. 3 (see n. 69 below).

'sincere' in religious terms, as is explicitly made out in Price's comment on the later deifications. If anything, however, the conflicting evidence as to the order of senatorial decree and funeral suggests that this perhaps was not so important or decisive after all—a suggestion no scholar has cared to pursue, because the view of 'canonization' has simply been presupposed. It is, I believe, necessary to begin the examination all over again, based on the ancient sources. The attempt at interpretation must go back, beyond mechanical precedent, to the first and most significant imperial deification, that of Augustus.

If the commonly accepted interpretation of 'canonization' be correct, the state deification of Augustus would be in startling contrast to the outline offered above of the worship accorded him in his lifetime in Italy. There his exact nature, man or god, appears to have been without relevance to the establishment and workings of his cults, which merely formulated his status in the hierarchy of the world. We would in that case be dealing with an essential mental and theological difference between lifetime and posthumous cult. That is of course not impossible; indeed the common view on posthumous consecration in the early empire seems to receive some further support from the fact that Augustus was hardly ever termed *Deus* or *Divus* in his lifetime cults. Hence the posthumous name of *Divus* can reasonably be seen to entail a formulation of Augustus' nature, not of his status only.[46]

What should, however, invite scepticism is the rather disturbing similarity this view implies to central elements in Christian theology, as is clearly brought out by the comparison with canonization. In Christian dogma the exact nature of God—or, in Roman Catholicism, of saints—generally plays a central role, but this emphasis is very difficult to parallel in pagan Graeco-Roman cults (such deliberations belonged to philosophy). It would be surprising if the phenomenon of state deification of dead emperors was really the odd one out in this context.

The modern interpretation depends ultimately on three elements in the procedure of the deification of Augustus. They are

[46] For analysis of the terms *theós*, *deus*, and *divus* see Price (1984*b*) (see n. 11 above).

very much tangled up with one another in the argumentative construct, which in my view makes the overall interpretation of the procedure quite circular. First, there is the question of the eagle claimed by Dio to have been let loose from Augustus' pyre. Secondly, there is the use of sworn testimony of Augustus' ascension after his cremation. And thirdly, there is the fact that the Senate's decree of consecration was passed after Augustus' funeral, whereas in the second century, at least in the cases of Marciana and Faustina, it preceded the ceremony. I shall tackle them one by one here.

THE EAGLE

It is clear that the ceremony of letting loose an eagle from the imperial pyre was well established in Dio's day. For two reasons, it is now generally agreed that Dio's mention of this rite at Augustus' funeral is anachronistic, and that the custom only entered the ceremonial of imperial funerals at some later stage: first, the eagle rite, witnessed by all spectators, would make the use of a specific witness of Augustus' ascension superfluous; and, as one step further in the line of reasoning, the rite does not fit the established view that the Senate afterwards recognized, rather than created, a new divinity. Secondly, Suetonius does not mention the procedure in his (much shorter) account of Augustus' funeral.[47]

Augustus' own detailed directions for his funeral were read in the Senate before the ceremonies. *If* the eagle rite was in fact employed, it was presumably mentioned in this document, and the Senate's permission for the procedures to go ahead as specified would then have covered this detail too; or, alternatively, the Senate added it to the funerary procedures, though

[47] Dio 56. 42. 3 (p. 273 above); Bickermann (1929) in Wlosok (1978, 93 f. and *passim*); Vittinghoff (1936, 106–8); Richard (1980, 466); Kierdorf (1986*a*, 57); Price (1987, 95); Geyer (1965); Arce (1988, 131 ff.), depending on the common view of 'canonization', argues that an eagle was *never* employed but that the testimonies in connection with the funerals of Pertinax and Severus are 'symbolic', as are, he believes, representations in art; pictorial depictions could certainly be ambiguous: it is and was the strength of pictorial media that they can thus cater for different, even conflicting, needs and views. But it is no use interpreting written sources in the same manner: the testimonies of Dio and Herodian on these later funerals are utterly unambiguous as to the eagle rite.

this was not recorded by Suetonius. In either case the ascension was basically decreed in advance, and the Senate's later decree merely recognized that it had in fact taken place as scheduled, or simply specified the full ensuing honours of temple, *flamen*, and *sodales*; after all, the official calendar stated only that 'heavenly honours were decreed to Divus Augustus by the senate'. And so the procedural difference between the deification of Augustus and later of the *Divi*, or some *Divi*, where the decree preceded the funeral, would not have been very significant after all. So the usual view of 'canonization', which has made much of this difference and its theological implications, hangs on rejecting Dio's eagle as an anachronism.

Clearly Dio is often anachronistic, but mainly in his interpretations, not in his factual descriptions. Furthermore, his account in general seems reliable enough, and must ultimately depend on a contemporary description. There is no internal evidence to suggest that Dio, or his source, simply made up the eagle release. More decisively, the difference between the accounts of Dio and Suetonius can easily be accounted for. Dio, like Herodian, wrote for a Greek audience unacquainted with Roman customs in the remote capital. Dio, senator and consul in Rome, was of course not an outsider in the sense that Herodian was, but that is irrelevant in this connection—the audience of the two writers was the same. Suetonius, on the other hand, wrote for an urban Roman elite, who were familiar with the ceremonial employed at imperial funerals (of which Trajan's was still fresh in the memory when Suetonius' work was published).[48] Hence he mentions only the extraordinary items of singular honours and displays of grief, such as Augustus' receiving *two* funeral orations, one delivered by Tiberius before the temple of Divus Julius, the other by Drusus from the old Rostra; that he was carried on the shoulders of senators to his cremation place in the Campus Martius; that

[48] Kierdorf (1986*b*, 147–56) argues *e silentio* that Trajan never received the full state funeral. That is unconvincing: there is no reason why the standard ceremonies, which were common knowledge, should have been mentioned by our (few, late, and brief) sources; there is good reason to surmise that the standard rites simply drowned in Trajan's unique honour of a posthumous triumph. Trajan's deification does indeed suggest that he received the full funeral.

FIG. 12.1. Tiberian coinage in honour of Divus Augustus
Notes: A: As, AD 14–15, obverse: Divus Augustus with radiate crown, thunderbolt in front, star—emblem of celestial divinity—above his forehead. B: As, AD 34–36, obverse: Divus Augustus, reverse: eagle standing on a globe. C: As, AD 34–36. obverse like B, reverse: winged thunderbolt.

'there was even an ex-praetor who took oath that he had seen the form of the emperor, after he had been reduced to ashes, on its way to heaven'.[49] The eagle, on the other hand, was part of the stock set of rites employed in his own day too, and hence common knowledge to his audience.

Dio's account is, however, supported, I believe, by a contemporary source which has not been given its due in this connection. Tiberian bronze coinage celebrating the new *Divus*, depicts on the obverse the radiate head of Divus Augustus, and on the reverse an eagle on a globe, standing frontally with outspread wings and head raised heavenwards, as if about to soar aloft (hence it is hardly just a generic symbol of power, as claimed by Bickermann) (Fig 12.1.B). The same depiction is encountered in coinage of the second century, where it, like the even more common depictions of the imperial pyre, is labelled *consecratio*, and clearly embodies the notion of imperial

[49] Suet. *Aug.* 100. 4: *'nec defuit vir praetorius, qui se effigiem cremati euntem in caelum vidisse iuraret'*.

apotheosis. Another Tiberian type, contemporary with the eagle-reverse and clearly belonging to the same series, shows on its reverse instead a winged thunderbolt (Fig 12.1.C), again a specific reference to Augustus' ascension by (or as) Jupiter; the thunderbolt, though without wings, is also shown before the head of Augustus on coins issued shortly after his funeral (Fig. 12.1.A).[50]

The coin imagery suggests that an eagle was in fact employed at Augustus' funeral. The imagery of the eagle soaring aloft was easy to grasp for even the crudest spectator at Augustus' pyre. The Tiberian coin types with the ascending eagle and winged thunderbolt belong, it is true, to Tiberius' last years, but the renewed interest in Augustus' divinity and apotheosis displayed at this time is not difficult to explain. The temple of Divus Augustus was now finished, and its dedication was imminent. Tiberius left his island home of Capri to enter the capital and perform the ceremony, but he died beforehand in 37; the dedication was then only carried out by his successor Caligula, and celebrated on a magnificent sestertius type (Fig. 7.2).[51]

The eagle on Augustus' pyre demonstrates the extent to which earlier caution could now be thrown to the wind. Whatever risks may have been involved in harping on the parallel with the king of gods in Augustus' more official propaganda when he was alive, they had now been removed. The sinister correspondence between public divinization and death which the cases of Romulus and Caesar had—incidentally—established, could no longer hinder formal consecration.

[50] Tiberian coin series of Divus Augustus, eagle: BMC I. 142, nos. 155–6; RIC, 2nd edn., I. 82, cf. other issues 83 (winged thunderbolt on rev.), 70–1, 74–81; Schulten (1979, 23f.; 37 and *passim*) for later eagle coinage; Sutherland (1941) (type with eagle and type with winged thunderbolt die-linked); eagle type dismissed by Bickermann (1929) in Wlosok (1978, 91 n. 39); ignored by e.g. Kierdorf (1986*a*, 67) and by Price (1987, 95) who claims, wrongly, that the eagle in early imperial apotheosis scenes is confined to private art, particularly gems, only; for such depictions, see Megow (1987, 199f., 214f.) (Nero: probably posthumous). In state art, note also apotheosis of Titus on his arch in the Forum (Nash, 1961–2, i. 134).

[51] Suet. *Tib.* 74: pointless if the dedication was not imminent, and Tiberius did not intend to perform it; cf. Plin. *Nat. Hist.* 34. 18. 43; Caligula: Dio 59. 7. 1ff.

Contrary to most scholars, I see this development as the 'natural' consequence of the collapse of the republic; the fictional, though important, notion of Augustus as first among equals in the Roman state system was the aberration, not the omnipresent cults accorded Augustus in civic worship when he was alive. Incidentally, the posthumous consecration of Augustus further cemented the link between death and divinity in the Roman state, making divine honours to the living emperor in this context an even more dangerous notion. In fact, though several later emperors rejected the ideal of the emperor as a fellow senator, none of them, as we have seen, ever crossed this dangerous borderline between public and private worship in Rome.

If, however, an eagle did in fact carry Augustus' spirit to heaven in AD 14, Numerius Atticus' sworn testimony of the ascension seems strangely superfluous in the procedure of deification. His case in fact supplies the only potent argument against Dio's eagle, and so calls for further analysis.

THE WITNESS

The admission of sworn evidence to the ascension of Augustus is then decisive to the interpretation of 'canonization'. Our sources mention a witness after the funerals of Augustus in 14 and of Drusilla in 38; though scholars have taken the custom to have been employed all through the first century, there is in fact no later evidence. Indeed Seneca's satire of Claudius' deification, the *Apocolocyntosis*, clearly indicates that no witness was employed, for Seneca sarcastically refers the curious reader to the witness of Drusilla's ascension, who has lately also seen Claudius go to heaven. Having incurred so much ridicule for his earlier testimony, Drusilla's witness is, however, now afraid to speak up. If there had been a Claudian witness, Seneca would surely not have had recourse to this earlier testimony in his mockery of the custom (if it can be called thus on the basis of two incidents).[52]

[52] Augustus: Suet. *Aug.* 100. 4; Dio 56. 46. 2; Drusilla: Dio 59. 11. 4; Sen. *Ap.* 1. 2f., which scholars (e.g. Bickermann, 1929 (in Wlosok, 1978, 92) and Richard, 1980, 466) have, strangely, taken as evidence for a Claudian witness. Bickermann furthermore quotes Justin Mart. *Ap.* 1. 21. 3 as evidence, in spite

The fact that a witness stood forward in these two instances does not necessarily imply that this was of any importance to the process of deification. Indeed the evidence points to the contrary. When Livia became a *Diva* in 42, no witness seems to have been employed—she had been dead for thirteen years; yet there is no indication whatsoever that this constituted a problem. Furthermore, at Livia's death, her son Tiberius forbade the Senate to deify her on the grounds that she herself had not wished it.[53] If the Senate merely recognized a state of affairs, such an argument would have been oddly off the point.

Worse problems for the standard interpretation arise from the ascension of Augustus. Long before his death, poets, literature, and even inscriptions referred to his future—posthumous—elevation among the gods; the scheme was clearly general knowledge in his lifetime.[54] Augustus had indeed planned his own funeral in detail, and his subsequent deification was beyond doubt. But the emperor could hardly have mentioned the use of a witness in his specifications; if of any purpose at all, the testimony would have had to be spontaneous, at least officially so. We are therefore led to conclude that Augustus' achievements were enough, that is, that the meticulously prepared process of deification would have worked with or without a witness, who cannot therefore have been of decisive importance. We may of course adopt the cynical modern view that the witness, the ex-praetor Numerius Atticus, had been secured and bribed beforehand. Yet the fact that he was—afterwards—given one million sesterces by Augustus' grateful widow appears to contradict such a view.[55] By her donation, Livia laid his testimony open to cynical witticisms and ridicule. Unless we postulate an amazing degree of

of its obvious sarcasm, and even though Bickermann is well aware that Justin is not speaking of the custom in his own day, which makes his attack a safe one: amusement at the custom would have been shared by his audience, whether pagan or Christian (the *Ap.* is dedicated to Antoninus Pius). Scholars have in fact presupposed that the witness was employed all through the first century (e.g. Richard, 1980, 466; Price, 1987, 91); contra Kierdorf (1986*a*, 62f.).

[53] Tac. *Ann.* 5. 2. 1.

[54] Thus *CIL* X. 3757 with Taylor (1931, 224); Manil. *Astr.* 1. 799f.; Ps.-Ov. *Cons. ad Liviam* 211ff.; Price (1987, 76f.); p. 268f. above.

[55] Dio 56. 46. 2.

political ineptitude, her publicly declared gift must have sprung from genuine appreciation and gratitude for the testimony, which hence seems to have been spontaneous. And indeed, our sources suggest nothing else. Likewise, the ridicule Livia's gesture could have incurred was bearable and negligible, exactly because the testimony was *not* of any importance to the process of consecration.

The testimony of Drusilla's—unworthy—deification is mentioned with sarcasm and amusement,[56] and this incident appears to have discredited the behaviour. The several references to such testimony should therefore not lead us to attach much importance to it. On the contrary: the fact that ridicule was so obvious a reaction rather points to the structural unimportance of the phenomenon. Indeed, though scholars since Bickermann have seen the witness as part of the procedure of deification, even this view lacks any foundation whatsoever in the sources: neither Suetonius, Dio or Seneca claim that a witness was employed or used by the Senate when it passed its decree of deification—but merely that a senator stood forward and swore that he had seen the ascension. There is simply no evidence to suggest that this had any part to play in the deification procedures.

Yet we should still ask why these senators volunteered to give such evidence. Beyond personal motives and psychology, the explanation, as is indeed specifically mentioned by Dio, lies in the precedent of Julius Proculus and Romulus, and, I believe, in that only. With such a well-known and obvious precedent, described at length by Livy and Ovid, it would actually have been very difficult to avoid witnesses coming forward.[57] However, the discredit shed on the behaviour in the case of Drusilla prevented future occurrences of it. The fact that the tradition of testimony was dropped so quickly despite the splendid Romulean—and Augustan—precedent, spells out both the unease caused and the structural insignificance of the phenomenon.

[56] Sen. *Ap.* 1. 2f.; Dio 59. 11. 4, sarcastically detailed.

[57] Liv. 1. 16; Ov. *Fast.* 2. 481ff.; comparison Romulus–Augustus, ibid. 119ff.; cf. *Met.* 14. 806ff.; Price (1987, 74 with refs.).

THE CREATION OF A STATE GOD

I have argued above that an eagle was in fact let loose from the pyre at Augustus' funeral, as Dio says, and that the testimony of Numerius Atticus had no structural significance in the procedure of deification, indeed was not even part of it. If so, we must reject the idea that the Senate merely recognized, but did not create a god at the consecration of Augustus. The eagle, 'believed by the Romans to take the emperor's soul to heaven', as Herodian says, was after all placed in its cage and let loose from the pyre by human hands. The modern cynical attitude, rightly rejected by Price, has seen the ritual as deliberate fraud to fool the masses who would believe that they witnessed a miracle of divine intervention.[58] The cynicism inherent in this view may be credible; the alleged gullibility of the spectators surely is not. Furthermore, nothing in our sources suggests propagandistic trickery. Clearly everybody knew that the ceremonial was arranged by those left behind.

There is in fact no reason to suppose anything else, or more, than Herodian says. The bird of Jupiter was let loose from Augustus' pyre to take his worthy spirit to heaven. 'Thus was Pertinax made immortal', to quote Dio, and thus too Augustus. Human hands ensured that the late emperor's soul went to the gods instead of going underground to join the spirits of the dead. So the state of affairs, if so it was, recognized by the Senate on 17 September was brought about by men, ultimately by the Senate itself when it approved the eagle rite, whether this was contained in Augustus' directions for his funeral or added to them. And though it was Jupiter, or his representative, who performed the actual elevation, the king of gods was not given any choice in the matter. It is only to a monotheistic view that such a procedure is surprising, or even blasphemous. Unlike the Christian God, Jupiter, as well as patrons and emperors, was not all-powerful. If he received the honours and sacrificial gifts to which he was entitled, he was obliged to do the bidding of the Roman people, to return their honours with benefactions. To us the attitude may seem irreverent, but this

[58] Herod. 4. 2. 11; Price (1987, 56f.).

was basically how traditional Roman religion worked, or indeed any relationship between parties of unequal social standing.

Unlike the quaint oath of Numerius Atticus, the eagle rite was planned in advance and duly carried out. The procedure made the ascension of Augustus plain to see for all spectators. In other words, there was simply no need for a specific witness. The over-enthusiasm of Numerius Atticus was at best superfluous, at worst a positive embarrassment. No wonder imperial pleasure eventually made it clear that such testimony was not wanted.

THE SENATE'S DECREE

Only one difference may now remain between the first imperial deification and those of the second century. In Augustus' case, the senatorial decree recognizing the late emperor as a god of the Roman state came after the funeral; later it could precede the ceremony, as apparently in the case of Trajan's sister Marciana and the empress Faustina Maior.

Scholars have previously taken it for granted that the Augustan procedure was followed also at the deification of Claudius; in fact Bickermann strongly argued that Roman *ius divinum*, divine law, made any other order of events impossible: the decree of deification always had to follow, not precede, the ascension at the funeral.[59] This seems to presuppose Roman law as an entity granted to Romulus on Mount Sinai. Roman sacred law was in the hands of the Senate, which could always grant a dispensation if it was so inclined, for whatever reason.[60] In recent years, however, W. Kierdorf has re-examined the sources and argued that the senatorial decree already in Claudius' case preceded the funeral. Two sentences in Tacitus decidedly favour Kierdorf's view: 'Heavenly honours were

[59] Bickermann (1974, 363f.); his argument on the regulations of public mourning (*iustitium*) is in principle irrelevant to deification: all the instances he cites—Drusus Maior, C. Caesar, Germanicus—were 'normal' dead persons who were *not* deified. As a new custom state deification was presumably flexible and had to be constructed along the way during the early empire; before 14 there was simply no procedural precedent.

[60] Thus e.g. after the death of Augustus when Tiberius was formally absolved for having touched the body, something he was not allowed to do (perhaps as a *pontifex*): Dio 56. 31. 3.

decreed to Claudius and his funeral ceremony was celebrated in the same way as that of Divus Augustus, with Agrippina (Claudius' widow) emulating the magnificence of her great-grandmother Livia'. These words suggest that the funeral followed the decree; so they have been rejected as imprecise. A little later, Tacitus returns to the topic in connection with honours to Agrippina: 'Furthermore, two lictors were decreed by the senate, as well as a flaminate to Claudius, likewise a public funeral to Claudius, soon followed by his *consecratio*'. Again, the word order suggests the decree before the funeral. Scholars have, however, taken *consecratio* to mean the Senate's decree—the word can in its more general sense simply mean 'deification'. Though this was not really considered by Kierdorf, he appears right in rejecting such an interpretation: the word in its strict technical meaning, which makes better sense here, refers to the cultic instauration of the new god. Though Kierdorf was unable to explain the supposed change in procedure, he seems to have a case.[61]

However, his view, and Tacitus' wording, seemingly contrast with the clear information that the Augustan precedent was followed. Also, as Kierdorf notes, Dio in his version of Tiberius' funeral oration over Augustus makes the new emperor refer to his predecessor as already deified, though Dio was certainly well aware that the Senate's decree of divine honours to Augustus came only after the funeral. As with Dio's eagle, Kierdorf rejects this problem as an anachronism imported into the account by Dio (but this argument could also be used against Tacitus' wording). Again, Dio informs us that Caligula on his accession asked the Senate to deify Tiberius; the request came *before* the funeral (the Senate, however, procrastinated, and Caligula dropped the matter on his arrival in Rome with Tiberius' corpse); this too has been rejected.[62] Suetonius' short

[61] Kierdorf (1986a); Bickermann (1974); Tac. *Ann.* 12. 69. 4: '*Caelestesque honores Claudio decernuntur et funeris sollemne perinde ac Divo Augusto celebratur, aemulante Agrippina proaviae Liviae magnificentiam*'; 13. 2. 6: '*Decreti et a senatu duo lictores, flamonium Claudiale, simul Claudio censorium funus et mox consecratio*'.

[62] Augustan precedent followed: also Dio (Xiph.) 61. 35. 2; Tiberius' oration: Dio 56. 41. 9; Caligula and Tiberius: 59. 3. 7 (rejected by Bickermann, 1929 in Wlosok, 1978, 101 n. 78).

notices of Claudius' deification, on the other hand, may rather support the traditional view that funeral came first: 'and he was buried with the usual procession of emperors and placed in the number of the gods'; '[Nero] spoke the eulogy over Claudius and deified him, after he had been honoured with the most splendid funeral'.[63] Still presupposing that the order in procedure was of such decisive theological importance, Kierdorf's new theory effectively muddles up the picture.

There is more muddle. When Trajan's sister Marciana died in 112, the contemporary Ostian calendar (the *Fasti Ostienses*) stated that on 29 August 'Marciana Augusta died and was named Diva'; then went on to state that her daughter Matidia 'was named Augusta', and that 'Marciana Augusta was honoured with a public funeral' (the date is lost in the inscription).[64] This has been taken by scholars, following Bickermann's interpretation of the procedure as a 'canonization', as reflecting a momentous change in procedure (see p. 289). Bickermann himself argued that the formulation did not imply Marciana being declared a *Diva* by the Senate on the date of her death, that is, before her funeral, and that such a procedure was next to impossible. However, new fragments of the *Fasti Ostienses* which had already been found, but not yet published, when Bickermann wrote this, show unequivocally that such was indeed the procedure when the empress Faustina Maior died in 140: she was declared a *Diva* by the Senate before her funeral.[65] This settles the case for Marciana too. Another problem for Bickermann's idea of the ceremonial as a 'canonization' arises

[63] Suet. *Claud.* 45: '. . . *funeratusque est sollemni principum pompa et in numerum deorum relatus*'; Suet. *Ner.* 9: '. . . *Claudium apparatissimo funere elatum laudavit [et] consecravit*'. The phraseology could perhaps be pressed to refer to the formal *consecratio*, but not on the immediate level of understanding.

[64] Vidman (1982), 48: '*IIII K(alendas) Septembr(is): | [Marciana Aug]usta excessit Divaque cognominata | [. . . Mati]dia Augusta cognominata. III | [Marc]iana Augusta funere censorio | [elata est.]*'

[65] Vidman (1982, 49f.): '*X[- k. Nov.: Fausti]na Aug[usta excessit eodemq(ue) die a] | senatu Diva app[ellata et s(enatus) c(onsultum) fact]um funere censorio [eam efferendam.] | Ludi et circenses [delati sunt.—i]dus N[ov. Faustina Augusta funere] | censorio elata e[st. . .]*'. Even discarding all restorations there can hardly be any doubt as to the sequence between deification and funeral.

from a statement by Dio. A few months after the murder of the emperor Pertinax, his avenger Septimius Severus stood outside Rome with his army, ready to enter and topple the usurper Didius Julianus. The Senate, sensing which way events were going, declared Julianus a public enemy, hailed Severus emperor, and 'paid heroic honours to Pertinax' (as usual Dio translates *Divus* by '*hērōs*', also in their derivatives).[66] Only later, when Severus had entered Rome, did Pertinax receive his splendid funeral, with eagle ascension and all, of which Dio gave his eyewitness account. To avoid the problem, Bickermann claimed that the Senate before the funeral of Pertinax expressed only its desire to deify him.[67] This is fantasy: it runs counter to the wording of Dio who was in fact present at the Senate meeting.

If the reader is at this stage confused and fed up with the whole argument, this is exactly my point. Our sources simply do not support this modern notion of a rigid procedural sequence of decisive theological importance. If anything, the wording of the sources suggests that the ancient writers cared much less about these niceties than Bickermann and other modern scholars. However, if we drop the ingrained notion of 'canonization', all these difficulties disappear. Even in the case of Augustus, as I have argued, the late emperor had been elevated at the bidding of those left behind: the Senate in a decree approved the funerary rites, including the ascension of the eagle, and added further funerary honours.[68] So, on 17 September, after the funeral, the Senate simply formalized by a new decree what it had already decided before the funeral; the second decree furthermore specified the full set of honours, temple, and priests, to the new god of Rome. On this view, the

[66] Dio (Xiph.) 74. 17. 4: '*τῶι τε Περτίνακι ἡρωικὰς τιμὰς ἀπεδώκαμεν*'. Note also Kierdorf (1986*a*, 51).

[67] Bickermann (1974, 375).

[68] The passing of a decree before the funeral seems implied in Dio 56. 31. 2ff. (with a gap in the MS; the Senate's permission requested: 56. 32. 1) and clear from Suetonius (*Aug.* 100. 2f.) giving examples of additional honorary measures proposed in the Senate: the passing of at least some of them (cf. Tac. *Ann.* 1. 8. 3ff.) must presuppose a vote and a decree. Note also that decrees were passed at both the Senate meetings dealing with honours to the dead Germanicus in 19: *Tab. Siar.* fr. ii, col. b, ll. 18–21 (Crawford, 1996, no. 37).

sources make perfectly good sense, and so does Dio's version of Tiberius' funerary laudation, or Caligula's request to the Senate before Tiberius' funeral, or Dio's account of Pertinax' deification. Our authors can speak both as if deification followed and preceded the funeral, because this was actually the case: it was decided or permitted (by decree) beforehand, visually enacted by the ascension of the eagle, and then formally decreed and fully specified afterwards. Not that the order of events mattered in theological terms: the difference was only formal. The sequence of the procedures could be varied in points of detail, because the exact order of these details did not matter to the process of deification.

In that case, the procedure at Marciana's and Faustina's deifications need not concern us much: the discussion is not very important. Bearing this in mind, it may of course still be pursued. We may as well go for the simplest possible explanation.[69] Marciana and Faustina were certainly both *Divae* in the full sense. Yet the death of an emperor, we may argue, was of course very different. In the instances where he left behind an heir, and where deification was then appropriate, his death was followed by drawn-out, elaborate procedures. Considering the length of Pliny's *Panegyric*, performed for a rather banal occasion—his appointment to the consulate—we may safely assume elaborate and protracted verbosity on such important occasions as imperial deaths and accessions. For all this, one Senate meeting hardly sufficed. Indeed, after the death of Germanicus in 19, the Senate held two meetings.[70] This is strong evidence, for Germanicus was not deified: the two meetings were clearly held for purely practical purposes, because the amount of business, honours, speeches, and lamentations was too much for one meeting. Likewise when emperors died and were deified:

[69] Cf. HA *M. Ant. Phil.* 18. 3: '*Denique, priusquam funus conderetur, ut plerique dicunt, quod numquam antea factum fuerat neque postea, senatus populusque non divisis locis sed in una sede propitium deum dixit*'. Apart from any question as to the reliability of the source, it is not clear exactly what had never happened before or later: the deification—or acclamation, perhaps just one element in the full ritual—of an emperor before his funeral, or the Senate and people sitting together, or the combination of both features. I find the passage useless as evidence.

[70] *Tab. Siar.* fr. ii, col. b, ll. 18–21 (Crawford, 1996, no. 37).

we need no other reason than this purely practical one to explain why there were usually two meetings of the Senate. The procedure is clear at the death of Augustus: first a meeting dealing with his will and funerary arrangements (I have argued that it was actually here that the decision was taken to deify him); then the funeral, with its eagle rite, visual enactment of the deification; lastly another meeting, where the consecration, with temple, *flamen*, and priesthood, was formally voted and specified; the rest of the meeting was then devoted to the debate and mutual protestations of emperor and Senate.

The two-pronged procedure had one more advantage in cases of deification: tears and lamentations over the late emperor's death could be contained in the first meeting, the second one reserved for jubilation at the accession of the new emperor (the uneasy blend of joy and sorrow at Augustus' death was a theme to fit Tacitus).[71] Marciana's (or Faustina's) death, on the other hand, made no difference to the political situation. The senators lamented, voted her divine honours, and went home; there was no need to meet again.

As for Claudius, we cannot say for certain whether Tacitus or Suetonius is right in the sequence he suggests. But Tacitus seems the stronger candidate. His version is unequivocal; and since there would normally be two Senate meetings after an emperor's death, his version of just one meeting is the *lectio difficilior*. Indeed the particular circumstances of Claudius' death fit Tacitus' account in a rather cruel way, and make it likely that one meeting, before his funeral, would have sufficed: the late emperor's will was not read (its contents were inconvenient for Nero).[72] This would have saved time; and, judging from Tacitus' account of Nero's accession, the stage of senatorial lamentations over the unpopular late emperor should not have taken up too much time. Deification was speedily done with—the scheme was already there, ready-made, from the precedent of Augustus—so the senators could turn to what mattered: young Nero.

[71] Tac. *Ann.* 1.7ff.

[72] Tac. *Ann.* 12. 69. 5; Dio 61. 1; Levick (1990, 78 with n. 32).

THE IMAGERY OF APOTHEOSIS

The new ritual and imagery invented for Augustus' funeral and apotheosis had a tremendous impact. Such imagery could be understood by all spectators, even by those who were illiterate. Furthermore, it possessed the fruitful ambiguity of all visual language, and it could be, and was, varied and reshaped to incorporate and communicate all sorts of messages, connotations, and concepts. This same ambiguity, however, can be problematic for a modern interpretation: when is the imagery specific, giving a supposedly realistic reflection of actual ritual, and when is it symbolic, concerned more with ideology and connotations than with what people could actually see at imperial funerals?

The actual ritual of apotheosis at the funeral of an emperor involved the sending off of an eagle from his pyre to take his worthy soul to heaven. This is often shown in art: the eagle appears already on Tiberius' coinage in honour of *Divus* Augustus (Fig. 12.1.B), and recurs frequently on state emissions over the next centuries until Constantine. But the imagery of the coinage and public reliefs was far more varied than the increasingly emblematic eagle; apotheosis could be visually expressed in several ways. Thus it is frequently Eternity personified, Aeternitas, who on coins or reliefs carries an empress to her celestial dwelling (Fig. 12.2; cf. 12.3.B). This figure embodied two messages, overlapping in a suitably non-specific fashion. One obvious symbolic message was that of eternal life awaiting the emperor or his wife in heaven; the other promised eternal life in the memory of those left on earth, who by deifying the late majesty and establishing a permanent cult in his or her honour promised eternal remembrance: memory would never be allowed to die. The two notions of eternity flowed together in the figure of Aeternitas, and the suitably vague figure would not force a rigid choice between these versions of eternal life. In one other case the soul of the empress is shown carried by wind goddesses, *aurae*, a simpler and less ambiguous statement of the heavenly dwelling (Fig. 12.3.C).[73]

[73] Diva Faustina II, AD 176–80: Schulten (1979, 104, no. 263) (RIC 1697; BMC 1568).

FIG. 12.2. Relief panel depicting the apotheosis of the empress Sabina (d. AD 136)

Notes: The empress is carried to heaven from her pyre by the winged *Aeternitas*, Eternity, who holds as her attribute an eternally burning torch. The youth reclining by the foot of the pyre is a personification of the Field of Mars where imperial cremations took place; the identifying landmark, a monumental obelisk erected in the Field by Augustus, he once supported with his right hand has been destroyed. To the right the scenery is witnessed by the seated emperor Hadrian, husband of the deceased empress; the standing figure behind him has later been wrongly restored as a portrait of his successor Antoninus Pius. The much restored relief, now in the Palazzo dei Conservatori in Rome, was originally fitted on a monument (an arch?) in honour of Diva Sabina; another relief from the same monument depicts Hadrian delivering the funerary eulogy of his late wife.

And lastly, the emperor could travel to the sky on a horse-drawn carriage, a *quadriga*: with this means of transport Mars had already taken Romulus to the gods (cf. Fig. 12.3.D).[74] From the second century onwards the imperial pyre from which the ascension took place became a popular motif on the coinage in honour of *Divi* (Fig. 12.3.D). The imagery could be varied and recast without end to suit different needs or contexts; thus also in poetry: Germanicus in his translation-cum-additions of Aratos' astronomical classic the *Phaenomena* let Augustus be carried heavenwards by the late emperor's birth sign, the astrological Capricorn.[75]

All this, whether in visual imagery or in poetry, is symbolic language; unlike the eagle, specifically mentioned in our textual descriptions of imperial funerals, it is of course not to be taken literally. But sometimes we may be in doubt. The eagle was Jupiter's bird, or Jupiter himself, supremely suitable for the earthly monarch. It was less suitable for empresses: here we would expect the corresponding imagery of Juno, Jupiter's wife and queen. As the eagle was Jupiter's bird, so the peacock was Juno's. Thus a peacock carrying the empress to the sky is one of the motifs frequently found on the consecration coins of *Divae* (Fig. 12.3.G); or, alternatively, only the peacock is shown, standing, as an emblem of female apotheosis.

Here is a conflict between symbolic imagery and practicability in terms of actual ritual, for peacocks do not fly very well. Though a peacock on the funeral pyre would, with flames licking its tailfeathers, presumably be able to muster amazing flying ability, the bird would then merely perch on the nearest rooftop in rather unimpressive fashion. In other words, since the bird was in practice an unsuitable soul-carrier, the peacock imagery must be exclusively symbolic. However, the reality of the female version of the soul-carrying ritual is in fact also given by the images on coinage and other state art. The earliest known instance where we find a coin depiction of a bird carrying an empress to heaven, as opposed to merely showing it

[74] The *quadriga* is frequently shown on top of the pyre, Schulten (1979, *passim*); Mars: Ov. *Met.* 14. 819ff.

[75] Coinage: Schulten (1979); Germanicus: see p. 284f above.

C

A

B

D

E

F

G

H

FIG. 12.3. Examples of coins in honour of *Divi*

Notes: A: Sestertius of AD 34–36 in honour of Divus Augustus; obverse: statue of Divus Augustus on carriage drawn by four elephants, inscription *DIVO AUGUSTO S(enatus) P(opulus)Q(ue) R(omanus)*—'The Senate and people of Rome to Divus Augustus'. B: Sestertius, AD 140–61, of Diva Faustina Maior (d. 140); obverse: Diva Faustina; reverse: *Aeternitas* holding globe surmounted by Phoenix. C: Sestertius, AD 176–80, of Diva Faustina Minor (d. 176); obverse: Diva Faustina; reverse: Diva Faustina carried to heaven by wind goddesses. D: Sestertius, AD 180, of Divus Marcus (Aurelius) (d. 180); obverse: Divus Marcus; reverse: funerary pyre surmounted by a representation of the late emperor driving a *quadriga*, inscription *CONSECRATIO*—'deification'. E: Sestertius, AD 180, of Divus Marcus; reverse: Divus Marcus, carrying a sceptre and waving, carried to heaven on the back of an eagle holding a thunderbolt in his claws, inscription *CONSECRATIO*. F: Sestertius, AD 180, of Divus Marcus; reverse: eagle standing on garlanded altar, inscription *CONSECRATIO*. G: Sestertius, AD 176–80, of Diva Faustina Minor; reverse: Diva Faustina carried to heaven on the back of a peacock, inscription *CONSECRATIO*. H: Sestertius, AD 140–61, of Diva Faustina Maior; reverse: the temple of Diva Faustina with her cult statue in the *cella* (the temple is still standing, see Fig. 12.9), inscription *AETERNITAS*—'Eternity'. I: Sestertius, AD 161, of Divus Antoninus Pius (d. 161); obverse: Divus (Antoninus) Pius; reverse: honorary column surmounted by statue of Divus Pius, marking the spot of his cremation (the base of the column is still preserved, cf. Fig. 12.4), inscription *DIVO PIO*—'To Divus Pius'. J: Denarius, AD 140–61, of Diva Faustina Maior; reverse: star (symbol of celestial divinity and immortality), inscription *AETERNITAS*—'Eternity'. K: Nummus, struck in Alexandria AD 311, of Divus Galerius Maximianus (d. 311); obverse: Divus Galerius Maximianus; reverse: lighted and garlanded altar with eagle on front, inscription *AETERNAE MEMORIAE GAL(erii) MAXIMIANI*—'For the eternal memory of Galerius Maximianus'.

emblematically alone, actually involves an eagle.[76] This is supported by the best-known depiction of imperial apotheosis, the relief on the base of the honorary column marking the cremation spot of Antoninus Pius who died in 161 (Fig. 12.4). The late emperor is, uniquely, carried to the sky by a winged youth, Aion, limitless time, and thus a male equivalent of Aeternitas. With the emperor, on Aion's back, sits Antoninus' wife Faustina I who had in fact predeceased him by twenty years; presumably she makes the journey to earth to pick up her beloved husband. But on each side of the imperial couple is depicted an eagle, a discreet allusion to the factual ritual employed at such funerals. Exactly because an eagle is symbolically unsuitable for an empress, these depictions give us what amounts to proof that eagles, always great flyers, were also employed at the funerals of imperial women. The peacock, on the other hand, was symbolically suitable, indeed perfect as the female counterpart to the imperial eagle, but, alas, useless in more practical terms.

The imagery of the eagle of apotheosis appears in art shortly after the death of Augustus. I have already mentioned the Tiberian coinage in his honour (p. 293 above). The more specific scenery of the eagle carrying a deceased emperor on its back is first found on a cameo after Claudius' death in 54 (Fig. 12.5).[77] The motif was eagerly received at the private level, and copied or emulated by private people. Several relief-sculpted Roman epitaphs show their dead ascending to heaven on an eagle or, in the case of women, on a peacock.[78] This was obviously symbolic, but it clearly shows that the imagery was not an imperial monopoly, and that anyone was free to imagine and express the pious hope that their dear ones had gone to heaven to a new and blissful life. I illustrate here an example from Rome, now in Copenhagen (Fig. 12.6): a dead youth is shown sitting on an eagle flying upwards, with a lighted altar to the right, and a winged Amor showing the way to celestial bliss with his lighted torch. The depiction seems to copy closely

[76] Diva Sabina, AD 136–8: Schulten (1979, 79f., nos. 122ff.); *passim* for eagles and peacocks generally for *Divae*.

[77] Base of Antoninus: Hannestad (1986, 215ff.); cameo: Megow (1987, 199f. with Taf. 27, 1).

[78] Cumont (1917, 85ff.).

FIG. 12.4. Relief on the base of a column erected in honour of Antoninus Pius (d. AD 161)

Notes: Erected at the site of his cremation (and depicted on the coin Fig. 12.3.I). Antoninus is taken to heaven by a winged youth, Aion, god of limitless time (and thus a male variant of *Aeternitas*) and the Golden Age. Next to the late emperor his wife Faustina Maior, who had predeceased her husband by twenty years, briefly revisits earth to be at his side during the ascension. To the right sits Roma, Rome personified, saluting her late ruler, and to the left a personification of the Field of Mars, identified by the obelisk of Augustus' grand sundial (as originally on Fig. 12.2), marks the location where Antoninus' cremation and ascension took place. Presumably Aion will return to earth after delivering the imperial couple in heaven, to preside over the new Golden Age of Antoninus' sons and successors Marcus Aurelius (161–80) and Lucius Verus (161–9) who had the column erected (their dedicatory inscription is found on the other side of the base). The base now stands in the Vatican.

similar representations from the imperial iconography. The youth and eagle are shown in exactly the same fashion as Claudius and his eagle on the cameo depicting his apotheosis.

Such depictions must have existed also in connection with Augustus' deification. On the largest Roman cameo known, the *Grand Camée de France* in Paris, the old emperor is shown,

FIG. 12.5. Cameo cut in sardonyx showing the emperor Claudius riding an eagle and being crowned by a winged victory
Note: Probably made in connection with or slightly after Claudius' death and deification in AD 54. Bibliothèque Nationale, Paris.

with radiate crown and the rim of his toga drawn over his head, riding on the back of a youth dressed in Eastern costume, with baggy trousers and Phrygian cap on his head, and carrying a globe, symbol of world domination. The identification of the youth is highly controversial, but so far the most likely interpretation is that he is Iulus, the Eastern—Trojan—ancestor of the *gens Iulia* (Fig. 12.7).[79]

[79] *Grand Camée*: Megow (1987, 202ff. with Taf. 33), repeating H. Jucker's eccentric Claudian dating (the identification of Tiberius seems as certain as can be, hence the woman seated next to him must be Livia; both are clearly depicted as alive—on earth, not in heaven—hence a date between 14 and 29 should be unavoidable in terms of the iconography); cf. Jeppesen (1993).

FIG. 12.6. Private funerary relief, second century AD
Notes: Acquired in Rome and probably from Italy. A youth is carried to celestial bliss by an eagle, whilst Amor (presumably representing the love for the deceased of those left behind who commissioned the relief for his tomb) points the way to heaven with his ever-burning torch, the symbol of eternity. A lighted altar further stresses the piety and desire of those still living not to let the dead man's memory die. Second century AD. National Museum, Copenhagen.

Augustus' ascension by eagle is not known directly from any preserved monuments, but there is a most interesting piece of indirect evidence. A silver beaker from Herculaneum, presumably made for a fan of Homer, is decorated with a scene representing the apotheosis of the poet (Fig. 12.8).[80] The bard is seated, again in the same position as Claudius, on the back of an eagle; the bird is shown frontally, with outspread wings, and

[80] Measurements of beaker: diameter at rim: 14.7 cm., at base: 9.2 cm., height: 12.5 cm.; Pannuti (1984), thorough and useful, with Tav. I–IV; '*Le Collezioni . . . di Napoli*' i. 1 (1986, 210, no. 35); Cumont (1917, 78 f.).

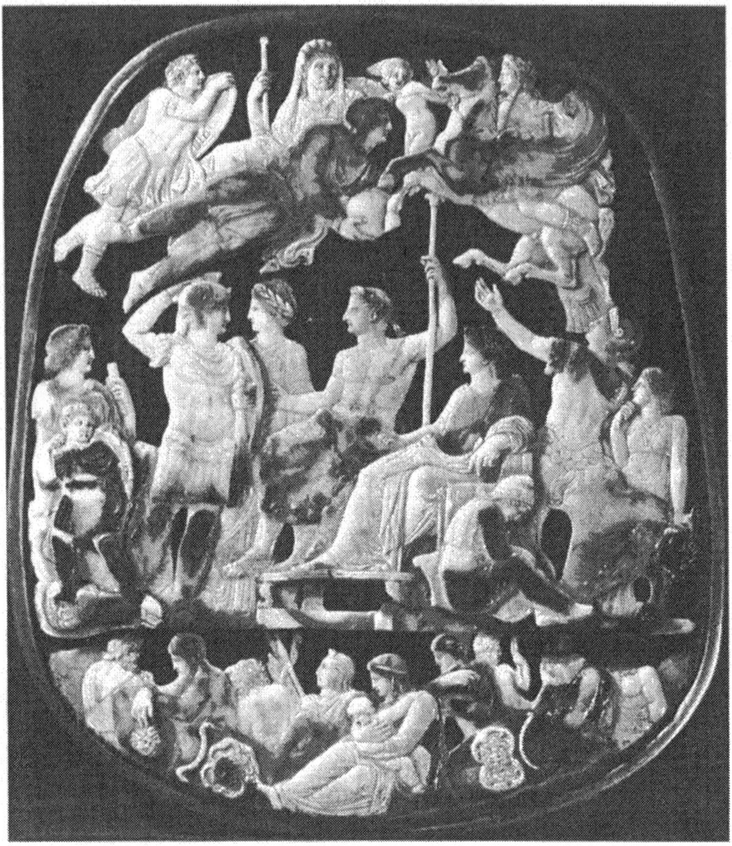

FIG. 12.7. Le Grand Camée de France, cut in sardonyx, AD 14–29
Notes: The emperor Tiberius and his mother Livia (seated) are shown in the centre among the living, whilst defeated and subject barbarians are relegated to the lowest plane. In heaven Divus Augustus, as usual wearing a radiate crown, occupies the central position like a guardian angel, seated on a youth in baggy, Eastern costume with a globe in his hands (perhaps Iulus, ancestor of the Julian family of Augustus and Tiberius). The globe, symbol of world domination, is held almost like a halo over the head of Tiberius, the ruling emperor, signalling a benevolent transference of power, presumably via the all-decisive adoption of Tiberius into the Julian family suggested by the figure of Iulus(?). Augustus is joined in heaven by, probably, Drusus Minor (d. AD 22) to the left and Germanicus (d. AD 19), riding a Pegasus, to the right. Neither of these were state gods, *Divi*, but could of course still, as could anybody, be represented in heaven in poetry or iconography. The winged Amor between the old emperor and Germanicus(?) suggests a strong emotional bond between the two. The identification of the other figures represented is highly controversial. Bibliothèque Nationale, Paris.

FIG. 12.8. Silver beaker from Herculaneum
Notes: Now in the Museo Nazionale, Napoli: the apotheosis of Homer, riding an eagle and flanked by personifications of his mourning 'children', the Iliad (in arms) and the Odyssey (with oar and cap). Line drawings by Anders J. B. Jørgensen.

gazing into the sky where it is about to go with its carriage. On each side of the bird sit two youthful figures. To the left a personification of the Iliad, shown as a young woman with weapons; to the right sits another young girl representing the Odyssey, with the oar of a ship in her hand (the poems are female because the words '*Ilias*' and '*Odusseia*' are both feminine in gender). The two poems are represented in gestures of mourning, the Odyssey wiping her eye, the Iliad more discreetly lowering her head. The beaker is Augustan or Tiberian: the scrollwork on which the figures act out the scenery forms a close parallel to such ornamentation in Augustan art, as for instance on the *Ara Pacis*.

There are further parallels, and details which in fact do not make much sense in connection with Homer—but would with Augustus. Thus Homer has the rim of his garment drawn over his head, as has Augustus on the *Grand Camée*. This is Roman, not Greek: it is a classic observation of difference between Greek and Roman divine ritual that Greeks sacrificed bareheaded in the liminal context of their encounter with the divine, whereas Roman sacrificers had the back of their heads covered with the rim of their togas. To continue, the armed *Ilias* figure is clearly reminiscent of Roma (the Odyssey could then have taken the place of a figure of, say, the *Genius populi Romani*, or perhaps a personification of the Campus Martius, where the cremation took place, as known from later depictions). Lastly, the composition on the beaker was seemingly not made originally for a circular surface, but for a flat rectangular surface, for the scrollwork ends slightly to the left and right of the two personified poems, with little attempt at combining the plants or making the decoration continuous around the beaker.

One by one, these arguments may be speculative and unconvincing; in combination, however, I think they make very good sense. The funeral of Augustus was the greatest and most spectacular show ever acted out in Rome, and people flocked from all over Italy to witness it. It is therefore not strange that the spectacle made a strong impression. Presumably, when a wealthy Homer lover in Herculaneum commissioned a piece of fine silverware, he then had this Augustan imagery copied and adapted, though only slightly, from an imperial monument, probably in Rome. A depiction created to honour the prince of men, the *princeps hominum*, was fittingly employed for the prince of poets, the *princeps poetarum*. Guests at this man's dinner table would not have missed the allusion.

All this is conjecture, not a statement of fact. The classic and still highly readable interpretation of the eagle-as-soul-carrier motif was given by Franz Cumont almost a century ago, and his view has been accepted in the short and rare comments of later scholars.[81] Cumont saw the Roman imagery as an import from the East, Syria to be precise, where the motif is commonly found, at least from the second century AD onwards. This view fitted well with Cumont's general view of the Orient as the great supplier of religious ideas and imagery to a merely passive and consuming Occident during the Roman empire: *ex oriente lux*. The late dating of the eagle rite in imperial funerals by modern scholars has indeed underpinned this view, whilst at the same time absolving 'rationalistic' historians from dealing with this seemingly irrational and senseless feature. The eagle rite could then safely be discarded as a late and bizarre aberration rather than a custom which can actually tell us something worth knowing about the Roman imperial system. Cumont, at least, was excused from explaining the feature in a Roman context, since his interest in the topic was exclusively confined to its role in Syria, and the Roman use of the imagery he therefore employed merely as a late source to illuminate the idea in Syria, its supposed country of origin. To Cumont, the ritual had been invented for the funerals of the Seleucid kings of Syria in the Hellenistic age; it was only because of this royal background that it was later copied, indeed aped, by unimaginative Roman emperors.

One basic fact remains, however. As also recognized by Cumont, we know nothing about Seleucid royal funerals, and the earliest known evidence for the rite is its employment at the funeral of Augustus, notwithstanding the unfounded rejection by some modern scholars. Furthermore, the Roman authorities would hardly have made direct use of a ritual which was explicitly and recognizably copied from funerals of the decadent Greek kings of Syria. On the present evidence, the ritual was in fact a Roman invention, thought out by Augustus, or the people who, with the Senate's approval, arranged his last rites. Where did the idea come from?

The eagle had had a long life as a divine symbol in East and West before Augustus' day. Its majestic flying ability and size automatically accorded it status as the king of birds, leading to

[81] Cumont (1917, 35ff., esp. 76ff.).

its connection with the king of gods, the Sun, Zeus, or Jupiter in different contexts.[82] In classical Greece it was employed as an image of success and progress, though not as a soul-carrier or in connection with apotheosis.[83] Later, in the Hellenistic age, this imagery gave it a place in funerary iconography as one among many symbols of the soul, presumably, flying to heaven at death (but, again, it is still never encountered as a soul-carrier).[84] Greek mythology also told tales which could, vaguely, fit into the imagery of imperial apotheosis. Zeus had taken his mortal son Heracles to heaven; and he had, in the shape of an eagle, abducted young Ganymede to his celestial dwelling. The last story may have played a role in developing the idea, though obviously not in any explicit fashion: Ganymede had been raped (implicitly in every sense of the word) from earth, because the king of gods was in love with him. This was obviously not appropriate for Augustus. Ganymede is in fact always shown held in the claws of the eagle, not sitting, voluntarily, on its back. The difference is not trifling: 'to dream of having an eagle sitting on the head of the dreamer signifies death, for the eagle always kills what he holds in his claws', the Greek dream-interpreter Artemidorus wrote in the second century AD.[85]

But there were more specific stories, developed and told during the lifetime of Augustus, to account for his stunning and divinely supported career. Suetonius gives a whole catalogue of them, and although he wrote a century after Augustus' death, such tales must have been most in vogue during the first emperor's lifetime, when his position was still a novelty craving explanation or reasoning. Jupiter, king of the gods, naturally features frequently in these stories, and his eagle in particular appears frequently. Already when the future Augustus was an

[82] Cumont (1917) is still fundamental for this.

[83] Thus Aristoph. *Av.* 978; id. *Eq.* 1012f.

[84] The earliest instance traceable is given in Diodorus' (17. 115) description of the funeral accorded Hephaistion by Alexander the Great in 323 BC: on his pyre were among other symbolic figures depicted eagles looking downwards on snakes (the soul about to leave the body?); among other symbols of (presumably) afterlife, eagles are depicted in a tomb in Marissa (Palestine) from the late third century BC: Cumont (1917, 52f.); Peters and Thiersch (1905), frontispiece and *passim*; Plato's soul was represented as an eagle on his tomb: *Anth. Graec.* 7. 62.

[85] Artemid. *On.* 2. 20 (p. 135 ed. Pack).

infant, his father dreamt that 'his son appeared in superhuman majesty, armed with the thunderbolt, sceptre and regal ornaments of Jupiter Optimus Maximus, wearing a radiate crown, and riding in a belaurelled chariot drawn by twelve dazzlingly white horses'.[86]

This story is particularly interesting, because it fits the imagery employed for Divus Augustus. His temple was modelled on that of Jupiter, and he was henceforth depicted with a radiate crown on his head, otherwise an emblem of the Sun (*Sol*), on coins and other images.[87] But there were other tales. When the future emperor as a boy 'was breakfasting in a grove at the fourth milestone on the Appian road, an eagle surprised him by snatching his bread from his hand, and after flying to a great height, equally to his surprise dropped gently down again and gave it back to him'.[88]

The boy was clearly destined for greatness; and the dainty imagery of the emperor as a fellow senator, first among equals, has no role to play in all this: the monarch of the gods destined him for a similar position among men. Sometimes the Jovean eagle could even be taken to stand for Augustus himself. When Tiberius was on Rhodes in quasi-exile, eagerly applying for a recall to Rome, 'an eagle, a bird never previously seen in the island, perched upon the roof of his house'; and a few days later Augustus' letter of recall arrived from Rome.[89] Most revealing of all such stories was the one of an eagle presaging Augustus' death and future divinity shortly before his death (quoted on p. 269 above). The story is particularly interesting, because the omen was immediately intelligible to all spectators, including Augustus himself: the eagle was Jupiter coming to take the old emperor to heaven. Why, then, did everybody immediately understand the omen, if we are to believe Suetonius' version? Presumably because the whole mythology of Augustus' future ascension to the gods and divinity at death had already been

[86] Suet. *Aug*. 94. 6, tr. Graves.

[87] Dream: Lorsch (1997); temple and Jupiter: Fishwick (1990) and (1992); coins: Schulten (1979); only from Nero onwards was the *corona radiata* also depicted on the head of the ruling emperor on some denominations.

[88] Suet. *Aug*. 94. 7, tr. Rolfe, Loeb edn. (adapted).

[89] Suet. *Tib*. 14. 4; the story can be traced back at least to Tiberius' reign: *Anth. Graec*. 9. 287.

shaped in Augustus' lifetime, namely by such stories as the ones given by Suetonius.

If so, the eagle rite at the funeral was suggested and largely shaped by these common and well-known stories. Political caution could at Augustus' death be thrown to the wind, and the obvious parallel and close relationship between the emperor and the king of the gods could now be expressed openly in public ceremonial. But it had been common knowledge long before. The eagle rite was a novelty developed for the occasion by uniting common Hellenistic imagery with aspects of the specific mythology developed around Augustus. Whatever the background, the new imagery was a stroke of genius: it was enthusiastically received and employed all over the empire, and reshaped and reused in other contexts, such as private funerary art. By the second century the imagery was so well known that it could even be presumed to enter people's dreams:[90]

> [To dream that] one is transported on an eagle is, on the one hand, an omen of death for kings and rich and noble people; for it is an old custom to paint and sculpt the dead on this social level as transported on eagles, and to honour them with such works of art. For poor people, on the other hand, it is a good omen: they will be lifted on high by wealthy people and gain great advantage, most often by way of a journey to foreign parts.

Two types of the imagery are here confounded by the dream-interpreter Artemidorus: 'to soar like an eagle in the sky' had already been a symbol of success and prosperity to Aristophanes and his contemporaries around 400 BC. But Artemidorus was, it seems, slightly wrong in taking the other imagery, that of death for kings and other grandees, as a very old usage. On present evidence it went back to AD 14 only, about a century and a half before Artemidorus' day. No new iconography can ever have been more successful: by the second century, the picture of a dead emperor or private person being carried by an eagle to the new abode in heaven was known to everybody in the cities of the Roman empire.

[90] Artemid. *On*. 2. 20 (p. 135–6 ed. Pack).

ABSOLUTE AND RELATIVE DIVINITY

As I have argued elsewhere, honours to the traditional gods as well as to the living emperor formulated their position, expressed a social hierarchy involving worshippers and the being worshipped. Formulation of this divine status was thus relative, and unconcerned with absolute aspects, such as the exact nature of the recipient of the honours. How does this view fit in with the making of a *Divus*?

Divi were certainly constructed and represented as ascending to heaven in an absolute sense. The eagle actually flew to heaven, and representations of the ascension in art depict this actual ascension. We are on tricky ground here, and may easily be misled by more or less conscious comparison with the ascension of Christ, as I believe scholars have generally been. But unlike the ascension of an emperor, no human actions were supposed to have constructed or brought about that of Christ. It was the Roman state who deified a *Divus*, by ritual action and, more importantly as I shall argue, by senatorial decree. As the emperor did actually ascend, he did become a god in an absolute sense. But this was hardly such a decisive or central aspect of the consecration rites as our Judaeo-Christian mentality would a priori have us believe. Bickermann (or Bickerman: he dropped the last 'n' in the USA) and his successors have stressed this absolute aspect. Bickermann, as mentioned, even saw the wax image of the late emperor employed at the funeral as fulfilling the function of illuding an ascension in the flesh, since no remains would be left of this image to suggest, uncomfortably, the emperor's mortality. This interpretation too is influenced by the ascension of Christ in the flesh.

True, Romulus and Hercules had also ascended in this fashion, leaving behind no mortal remains to suggest human frailty. The miracles demonstrated that they had returned to heaven whence they came, body and soul. A parallel case is that of Caesar. His ascension was not witnessed at the time of his funeral, but during the *Ludi Victoriae Caesaris* in July, a comet appeared in the sky. 'People' (Caesarians only, of course) believed it to be the soul of Caesar ascending to heaven. As with Romulus and Hercules, his case was, however, controversial.

There was in Hercules' case no Senate to declare him a god; so a miracle was needed instead. And Romulus, whose case, as we encounter it in Livy and Ovid, seems inspired by Caesar's, was unpopular among the senators; it was even rumoured that they had murdered him. Two miracles, of his corporeal disappearance and of his apparition to Julius Proculus, were needed as arguments to make the Senate recognize his divinity and make him a state god under the name of Quirinus. The Senate in 44 ignored the divinity it had conferred on Caesar in the last months of his lifetime. Another miracle, the comet, was necessary as argument for his adherents that the Senate was wrong: Caesar was a god, and should be recognized as such. Likewise, the ascension of Christ in the flesh gave proof that he was the son of God to a world which had scorned and rejected him. Without rejection or controversy, there was little need for such miracles.[91]

Miracles could not be arranged at will. More importantly, they were not necessary in Augustus' case: his apotheosis was not controversial. It was taken for granted even in his lifetime, and there was no doubt at his death that the Senate would deify him; there may have been critical voices, but they were subdued and uninfluential. Nor is there any evidence that supernatural proof or arguments were ever expected or arranged in connection with imperial apotheosis; I have already suggested a simpler reason for the use of a wax image, and the testimony of Numerius Atticus was apparently on his own initiative only (though it is of course not impossible that as well as merely following Romulean precedent, it was meant also to stifle any criticisms). The *Divi* received divine cult, which expressed their placement in heaven; and so they, as far as we know, did not receive funerary sacrifices at their tombs, as did 'normal' humans, whose spirits were imagined, however vaguely, to live on in the grave. Yet the ashes of Augustus, as of later *Divi*, were buried as were those of other humans, albeit in tombs of impressive size and splendour. Likewise, the tombstones of *Divi* gave their full names and earthly titulature, without the title of *Divus*.[92] The mortal remains of *Divi*, never placed in

[91] For later parallels, see Bickermann (1929) (in Wlosok, 1978, 97ff.); Caesar's comet: Weinstock (1971, 370ff.).

[92] *CIL* VI. 40375 (Vespasian); *CIL* VI. 40376 (Nerva); both: Hesberg and

their temples, were simply human; only their spirits were divine and ascended. There is thus no indication that the presence of these conspicuous tombs with their mortal remains and epitaphs were ever felt to constitute a theological problem. The Flavian *Divi* were apparently buried in Domitian's temple to their family, *gens* (*templum gentis Flaviae*), and, more revealingly, Trajan's ashes were placed in his column right opposite his divine temple.[93] This would only have emphasized the awkward problem of man or god—if it had indeed been felt to present a problem. But obviously it did not.

What really mattered, then, was apparently not that—or whether—the late emperor became a god in absolute terms (so what: the world was full of gods anyway), but that he became a god *of the Roman state*. Once again, we may argue that the aspect of relative divinity was the important one.[94] Even the absolute ascension of the eagle should be seen as a visual enactment of this decisive aspect: the procedure was indeed carried out by humans, acting with permission from the Senate and thus on behalf of the whole *populus Romanus*. The Senate was the highest state authority in the recognition or importation of Roman state gods, and had always been; it could confer divine honours on whomever it pleased.

Contemporary vocabulary used in connection with the deification supports this interpretation. Thus the state calendar stated under the date of 17 September AD 14, not simply that Augustus had become a god, but that 'on that day heavenly honours were decreed to Divus Augustus by the senate'.[95] This date clearly plays a more important role in the calendars than that of the actual ascension at the funeral, which I see as simply the visual enactment of deification. Likewise, the ascension

Panciera (1994, 142–7); *CIL* VI. 984 (= 31220) (Hadrian); 991 (L. Verus); 992 (Commodus). Epitaphs of deified empresses, however, name them as *Divae*, perhaps because of their less impressive earthly titulatures: *CIL* VI. 984 (= 31220) (Sabina); 987 (Faustina Maior).

[93] Flavians: Suet. *Dom.* 1. 1; Mart. 9. 20. 1 (the *Templum Gentis Flav.*, built on Domitian's birthplace, was not a temple for these *Divi*, but for the female personification of the *Gens*); Arce (1988, 78ff.); Trajan: Claridge (1993, 10ff. with refs.).

[94] Cf. e.g. Tert. *Ap.* 10. 3: '*sed nobis, inquitis, dei sunt*'; again at 13. 1, as the final argument envisaged by Tertullian after he has demonstrated that the pagan gods are not real gods.

[95] Degrassi (1963, 510).

at the funeral was in no way a prerequisite for deification; there is no evidence that Livia received a new funeral with ascension when Claudius had her deified in 42, thirteen years after her death. The same goes for other cases, such as Vespasian's daughter Domitilla, or Trajan's natural father; they had died years before the accession of their pious relatives, and were simply deified by decree, apparently without the construct of funerary ascension. The Senate had absolute authority to deify; there were no conditions or prerequisites beyond or above the pleasure of that body (though in practical terms it acted entirely according to the wishes of the ruling emperor).

We may note the words of a contemporary historian on Tiberius:[96] 'He consecrated his father [Augustus] not by imperial fiat but by divine worship [*religione*]; he did not simply call him, but made him a god.'

Employed by a Christian writer, this statement would imply severe criticism, but here it is used in a eulogy of Tiberius, with emphasis on his sincerity in deifying his father, and stressing that Augustus had not merely received the title of *Divus*, but also temple and cult. Another writer, addressing Tiberius, strikes the same theme in a rhetorical extravaganza with reference to Divus Julius and Divus Augustus in heaven:[97]

> My humility will have recourse to your good-will, all the more justly in that the divinity of the others [i.e. the 'old' gods] is assembled out of our conceptions, while yours, by an act of immediate faith, appears to equal the stars of your father and your grandfather, through whose extraordinary glow much glorious splendour has been brought to our rituals: for while we have received the other gods, we have contributed the Caesars.

Our other sources confirm this language: the late emperor was made a god by those left behind. The Senate and the Roman people made him their own god. This was what really mattered; the theological question, what happened in absolute terms, did not.

96 Vell. 2. 126. 1: '*Sacravit parentem suum Caesar non imperio, sed religione, non appellavit eum, sed fecit deum*'.

97 Val. Max. proem.: '. . . *mea parvitas eo iustius ad favorem tuum decucurrerit, quo cetera divinitas opinione colligitur, tua praesenti fide paterno avitoque sideri par videtur, quorum eximio fulgore multum caerimoniis nostris inclitae claritatis accessit: reliquos enim deos accepimus, Caesares dedimus*'.

SENECA'S *APOCOLOCYNTOSIS*

The model proposed here can, I believe, clarify several questions which have puzzled and preoccupied scholars. The first concerns what has always been seen as a prime source for imperial apotheosis: Seneca and his *Apocolocyntosis*.[98] The work has caused much unease among modern scholars; its blatant irreverence to a state god is surprising, even though we accept that it was meant only for a narrow court circle, and not for wider publication. So the purpose of the work has given rise to numerous theories and controversies. It has been seen as an attack on the institution of state deification. Others have argued that it is only the particular deification of the unworthy Claudius that is Seneca's target.[99] Another theory has, unconvincingly, taken the piece to be a covert attack on Claudius' strong-willed widow Agrippina, Nero's mother, who was state priestess (*flaminica*) of the new *Divus*. It has also been suggested that the piece may have circulated anonymously, though there is no evidence for this. It is furthermore difficult to imagine that the authorship could really have gone undetected for very long. Another view, which seems almost desperate, holds that the piece was written for the Saturnalia, where basically anything was allowed; that the piece was read at this festival is very possible,[100] but of course everything was not permitted even there (the living emperor Nero is flattered prodigiously in the piece). Common to all these interpretations is that they may to some extent reduce the basic problem, but they cannot make it go away. For instance, Claudius' deification conferred prestige not only on Agrippina, but on Nero, *Divi filius*, too; the new emperor, proclaimed in the satire as the inaugurator of a Golden Age, had not merely acquiesced in, but actively promoted the measure. So, presumably, had Seneca himself, the policy-maker behind the throne of the young prince. To us the problem seems a real one; the basic question is whether it was so to the ancients. Does Seneca in fact have the audacity

[98] See now the latest edition, Lund (1994).

[99] Price (1987, 87); Nauta (1987, 75); Versnel (1993, 110).

[100] Convincingly argued by Nauta (1987); cf. Versnel (1993) for the Saturnalian imagery within and outside the *Apocolocyntosis*.

in his piece 'to mock an official governmental act like a *consecratio*'?[101]

In the *Apocolocyntosis*, Claudius goes to heaven; in Roman terms, his absolute power as emperor made his candidacy a strong one. After all, great power was what characterized gods, and made them worth dealing with. There is no mention of the eagle, nor of any of the other elaborate rites of the funeral; even the senatorial decree of deification goes unnoticed. Claudius simply appears and demands entrance to the abode of the gods. Seneca's 'informant' is the witness who also saw Drusilla ascend (this historical episode is obviously the object of ridicule, as mentioned above): 'he is superintendent of the Appian Way, along which, as you know, both Divus Augustus and Tiberius Caesar went to join the gods' (*Ap.* 1. 2). Here is the first puzzle: Tiberius was actually never deified, though, like Claudius, he had a strong claim.[102] He had appeared too, and apparently been rejected by the celestians.

The gods are surprised and bewildered, and cannot even understand Claudius. Eventually he is recognized, however, and proceedings begin in the celestial Senate. The form has been taken to mirror the debate of the Roman Senate after Claudius' death, but with a difference: this debate is free.[103] There is, however, hardly any comment on the earthly procedure in this: it was simply a traditional feature in the genre of divine burlesques to portray the heavenly assembly as a squabbling Senate. Eventually, at the urging of Augustus, Claudius' application is rejected and he is hurled from heaven to the realm of the dead (where his punishment is actually not very strict). On the way down under, Claudius witnesses his own funeral procession and the merry-making caused by his death.

On the face of it, all this is inconsistent. Tiberius was never

[101] Eden (1984, 7), explaining the problem away by claiming that 'the governing class went through the motions of deifying Claudius' with no 'more sincere faith, or a deeper sense of self-importance, than they showed in their other attentions to the state religion'; cf. Nauta (1987, 75), adopting the cynical explanation of an 'insider' or court audience which could secretly mock its own public policy.

[102] Note e.g. Bickermann (1929) in Wlosok (1978, 101), speculative.

[103] Price (1987, 87f.).

deified, and Claudius goes to heaven before his own funeral, thus perhaps before he was actually consecrated by the Roman Senate (see p. 299 above) and certainly before he was sent heavenwards from his pyre by means of an eagle. However, there is no inconsistency. Seneca does, in briefly describing the funeral procession, harp mildly on the terrestrial procedure (*Ap*. 12. 1): 'And it was the most handsome affair imaginable, with no effort spared, so that you knew beyond doubt that it was a god being buried'.[104] But Seneca's piece is not about the relative deification of Claudius, the fact that the late emperor became a god of the Roman state; it is about the *absolute* divinity denied to Claudius at heaven's door.

This difference is puzzling to a modern audience, and it has persistently escaped the attention of scholars dealing with the *Apocolocyntosis*.[105] Surely, Claudius' state divinity must reflect his actual ascension to the realm of the gods. The notion, however, fails to recognize the role of the Senate by presupposing a christianizing view on ritual. Christian service and communion, with its miracle or symbolism of transubstantiation, is a ritual re-enactment of the word of God as contained in Scripture. The idea that ritual need not merely reflect more basic ideas and dogmas, but can in its own right construct social reality may be hard for us to grasp: in our societies rituals merely fulfil the function of reflecting tradition and cultural traits; in their own right, they are 'empty'. Pagan Graeco-Roman religion, however, was not based on holy texts of absolute authority, but on rites constructing social relationships and realities. The fact that the theology inherent in this system was rudimentary and often contained blatant logical

[104] *Ap*. 12. 1: '*Dum descendunt per viam Sacram interrogat Mercurius quid sibi velit ille concursus hominum, num Claudii funus esset; et erat omnium formosissimum et impensa cura, plane ut scires deum efferi: . . .*'.

[105] Note e.g. Kierdorf (1986*a*, 55) (extreme, but still representative): 'Bei Seneca wird Claudius anlässlich seines kurzen Aufenthalts im Götterhimmel ganz offiziel als *divus* bezeichnet, der Senatsbeschluss über die Divinisierung ist also schon vorausgesetzt; das Begräbnis dagegen findet erst etwas später statt, als der aus dem Himmel verwiesene Claudius auf dem Weg in die Unterwelt noch einmal die Erde passiert'; Nauta (1987, 75): '. . . Claudius had been solemnly deified—and his deification is the primary object of ridicule in the *Apocolocyntosis*!'; cf. id. 92 f.

contradictions merely goes to show that detailed theology was not really of importance in these systems. Rituals were what mattered, the rest was left to the gods (or to the endless, airy arguments of philosophy).

Seneca's *Apocolocyntosis* is essentially a burlesque philosophical, rather than religious, work. It harps on several notions from philosophy: the Stoic idea that the soul of the virtuous man will after death find his abode in heaven (and by this criterion, Claudius could not get in, power or no power); also on the Epicurean view of the gods as unconcerned with earthly matters (the bewilderment of the gods, when Claudius shows up: they do not even know who he is). Burlesques on the gods, as they were known in mythology and philosophical speculation, were of course an ancient literary *genre*; they had little or nothing to do with the rites and doings of pagan religion. And Seneca's satire has little or nothing to do with the actual consecration and worship of the new state god Divus Claudius. His ascension to heaven is his own doing. It has no connection with his ritual ascension at his funeral, nor with the decree of his deification, nor with the ever-repeated rites of his worship in state cult. Miriam Griffin in her book on Seneca concluded as to the *Apocolocyntosis*: 'The very title proclaims it a farce. Nothing here is sacred—except Nero'.[106] That is not true. The actual rites and rulings of the Roman state in making a god of Claudius are hardly touched upon in Seneca's burlesque. The references to them are few and circumspect, as in his remark on Claudius' funeral, and in the fact that the late emperor is actually termed *Divus* by his judges in heaven.[107] If anything this is a humorous clue that the Senate's deification of Claudius did not in the least depend on what the gods might or might not decide in heaven. It is only because we are so preoccupied with philosophical theology and dogma to the detriment of ritual and its constructive power that scholars have failed to realize what the *Apocolocyntosis* is actually about. The work gives us, I think, strong indications that this order of importance was exactly opposite in the pagan Roman mind.

106 Griffin (1976, 131).

107 Termed *Divus* by Hercules (9. 5) who supports his application; and by Augustus (10. 4) who opposes it.

Humans can, according to Seneca, elevate a man to heaven; only the gods, however, decide if he will actually be admitted. Yet there is (obviously) no intimation that the Senate, or Nero, acted wrongly (or even blasphemously) in the deification of Claudius; no suggestion that Claudius is not a real god of the Roman state, or that he should be expelled from the state pantheon, as he is expelled from heaven. Taken on our terms, however, Seneca's piece *does* suggest all these themes, and appears to be a dangerous exercise, even if (indeed because) its reading was confined to the court. But our terms are wrong here, preoccupied with the theological notion of divinity as an absolute. To the amusement of the audience, no doubt, Claudius does not make it. He does not gain divinity in the absolute sense. But absolute divinity did not matter much; it mattered so little that Seneca could, without risk, make it the theme of ribald satire. What mattered was the relative divinity, constructed by funerary rites (the eagle), senatorial decree, and sacrifices to the new god: the fact that Claudius had been declared a god of the Roman state and was worshipped as such. This, on the other hand, was serious, and not a subject for jokes. And so Seneca altogether avoids it. Contrary to what we might think, his jokes have few or no implications for Claudius' relative status in the state. Taken in this sense, the process of state deification was of course a 'political' phenomenon. But so was Roman state cult in general; Jupiter did not receive his incessant, sumptuous sacrifices because he was a god (among innumerable others), but because he was the foremost, most powerful god *of Rome*. The late emperor, Nero's father, was an unquestioned god of Rome. He had been elevated by Senate and successor, indeed sent to heaven; whether he was actually admitted was the gods' concern.

In terms of stoic philosophy, as presented by Cicero in 'Scipio's Dream', there is no denying that Seneca's piece is a symptom of outright cynicism in connection with the creation of *Divi*. Obviously virtue was not what gained access to the state pantheon (but maybe to the stars); being Nero's father was what counted. Even at this early date, 'routinization' and cynicism, as it seems, could hardly go any further than in the *Apocolocyntosis*; as we shall see, the feature is actually evident even in Augustus' case. Virtue or not, the prestige of having a father who had attained the culminating honour of state divinity was enormous. In this there was nothing new. Republican nobles who could boast a pedigree full of consuls similarly had little concern with whether their ancestors had been virtuous or not. It is misleading to stamp the *Apocolocyntosis* as merely an expression of supreme sarcasm. The philosophical notions of absolute divinity exploited by Seneca were simply not relevant to the relative godhead accorded to a Roman emperor by the Senate.

THE LIVING AND THE DEAD: *DIVI* AND DEATH

The very title '*Divus*' may, however, be adduced to support the claim that admittance to the Roman pantheon presupposed divinity in absolute terms, even if this was not the main point. Honours paid to the late and deified emperor were, after all, formulated as rendered to a god, not *as* to a god, as was generally the case with cults to the living emperor in Italy, where the theological question—man or god?—that has tormented scholarship for so long, was left open (because it did not matter).

Even so, however, we should not take the connotations of the terms *deus* and *divus* as mainly preoccupied with the question of absolute divinity, or the exact nature of the creature honoured, as is our 'god'. In the most important and religiously decisive sense *deus* and *divus* entailed an expression of status in relation to whoever employed the terms; so when granted as a state title, on behalf of the whole *populus Romanus*, the honour was immense, as opposed to such titles being used merely by individuals. Scholars have generally found it easier to accept that Caligula, who was mad anyway, craved divinity, than that Caesar, who is usually seen as a sensible man, actually became Divus Julius in his lifetime; so a strong branch of scholarship on Caesar has simply rejected or argued against our sources, though of unusually good quality and quantity. As argued elsewhere, if the title is seen primarily as an expression of status, unconcerned with theological aspects, the difficulty disappears.

The status entailed in the title of *Divus* was then, I believe, the decisive aspect. I have argued above (p. 63 ff.) that the word was chosen as the ultimate honour in Caesar's case because Varro's etymology had made it the highest one: *Divi* had always been gods, men who had become gods at death were termed *Di*. The notion of the ruler's mortality was a dangerous one, obviously to be avoided. The title of *Deus* would have had unfortunate connotations: it was only given to mortals after death, and would therefore have been extremely ill-omened for the living ruler. Varro's etymology was false, but that does not matter; it was apparently believed and it enabled senators to avoid such dangerous associations.

Status rather than nature, relative rather than absolute divinity: that goes too for the later use of the *Divus* title, as I have argued above in dealing with Seneca's *Apocolocyntosis*. There is in fact very little evidence that the titles '*deus*' or '*divus*' were avoided in connection with the living emperor because they were considered blasphemous. The avoidance rather depended on the incidental link established by the cases of Romulus and Caesar between these titles and the death of the emperor. Other ways of expressing the same status gap were available, and employed; slightly more vaguely, Claudius was termed *divinus princeps* by the Arval Brothers, and already Tiberius objected to the word *sacer* being applied to his labours and doings, a practice which became increasingly common as time passed.[108] By the later third and the fourth century the adjective, even in superlative, was the norm rather than the exception. Likewise, the formula DNMQE (*devotus/-i/-a numini maiestatique eius/eorum*)—'devoted to his/her/their divinity and majesty'—was standard in inscriptions to the emperor from the late second century onwards.[109]

At the death of Augustus, precedent alone would then have dictated the *Divus* title, though Caesar's case was a rather unfortunate one to harp back to. But there were stronger arguments. Augustus' death removed any obstacle to rewarding his benefactions with the crowning honour. However, not simply any form of posthumous deification would necessarily have constituted the honorific maximum required. The status of the dead was traditionally a very ambiguous one; in funerary cult,

108 Scheid (1998, 52f.); Suet. *Tib.* 27; Taeger (1960, *passim*).
109 DNMQE: Fishwick in *ZPE* 89 (1991), 197 n. 6 with lit.

primarily the *parentatio*, they were imagined, however vaguely, to lead an afterlife below ground, in their graves. Another and later notion, employed in Stoic philosophy, saw the reward for the virtuous to consist in ascension to heaven. In fact, the two views existed side by side in the early empire. The dead did also, however, possess a vague and impersonal divinity, as evidenced in their appellation as *Di manes* or, more rarely, *Di parentes*.[110] So any attempt to maximize the honours of the dead Augustus would have to avoid this ambiguity; first, by the title of *Divus*, as opposed to *Deus*; secondly by presenting Augustus as going unequivocally to heaven, as was thoroughly done by the rite of the eagle. This scheme to separate Augustus from the dead and avoid their ambiguous divinity was carried through emphatically. Hence a *Divus* shed all the earthly titulature, offices, names, and titles (except that of Augustus, originally a divine epithet) he had possessed while on earth; this titulature, as I have mentioned, was given only on the epitaphs over the mortal remains of *Divi* in imperial tombs. But Divus Augustus was simply that and no more: *pater patriae*, number of consulates, and so on were removed from his name.[111] *Divi* were thoroughly removed from this world. Hence also the ruling that the portraits of *Divi*, as well as of the other celestials, were not to be displayed in funeral processions, in spite of the fact that the portrait of Romulus, the obvious precedent, *was* in fact displayed in this context, even though he had become Quirinus after his ascension.[112] The absence of portraits of deified ancestors at imperial funerals obviously diminished the visual impact of the cortège. Yet the ban was necessary to spell out the message: Divus Augustus was a real god of Rome, not a dead man.

110 *Parentatio*: Scheid (1993); for the cult of the dead, see Bömer (1943); Gnoli and Vernant (1982).

111 Trajan, posthumously Divus Traianus Parthicus, may seem exceptional, but it was not an earthly title: his triumph over the Parthians was posthumous (a unique honour), hence when he was *Divus*: Kierdorf (1986*b*); Richard (1980, 463).

112 Dio 47. 19. 2; 56. 34. 2; 56. 46. 4; Price (1987, 79) interprets this as evidence of the problematic and ambiguous status of *Divi*; I fail to see why.

'WHO WILL WORSHIP SUCH A GOD? WHO WILL BELIEVE IN HIM?'

So far so good. However, the aspect of absolute divinity does apparently play a role in connection with the *Divi*. The concept of belief in absolute divinity, irrelevant in a relative status system, is never encountered in connection with worship of the living emperor. It is, however, in quite a few instances mentioned in connection with the *Divi*. We may note, for instance, Seneca's words on Augustus, held up as an ideal to the young emperor Nero: 'We believe him to be a god, but not because we are ordered to do so'. Likewise, Pliny's *Panegyric* contrasts Trajan's pious attitude to the cynical manipulations of earlier emperors: 'You gave your father [Nerva] his place among the stars with no thought of terrorizing your subjects, of bringing the gods into disrepute, or of gaining reflected glory, but simply because you thought he was a god'. And lastly, to return to Seneca's *Apocolocyntosis*, we can note Augustus' final argument in the heavenly Senate against admitting Claudius: 'Who will worship such a god? Who will believe in him? While you create gods of this sort nobody will believe that *you* are gods.'[113] These words ring familiar; they seem to fit religion, with belief as a core element, and even a touch of the notion of blasphemy, as we know it from Christianity. That calls for caution.

We never encounter such expressions of belief (or acceptance) in connection with cults of the living emperor; and only rarely in connection with those of the 'real' gods. When the notion is brought forward, it is always in philosophical writings, or with a distinct philosophical flavour.[114] In philosophy, where the notion belongs, there was of course a choice of schools and beliefs, and anything and everything could be debated. Yet the instances quoted above do not apparently

[113] Sen. *Clem.* 1. 10. 3: '*Deum esse non tamquam iussi credimus*'; Plin. *Pan.* 11. 2: '*Tu sideribus patrem intulisti non ad metum civium, non in contumeliam numinum, non in honorem tuum, sed quia deum credis*'. Sen. *Ap.* 11. 4: '*Hunc deum quis colet? Quis credet? Dum tales deos facitis, nemo vos deos esse credet*'.

[114] e.g. Hor. *Carm.* 3. 5. 1 ff.: '*Caelo Tonantem credidimus Iovem | regnare; praesens divus habebitur | Augustus adiectis Britannis | imperio gravibusque Persis*'.

belong to this *genre* (philosophical writings hardly ever debate the divinity of emperors, living or dead). In cultic life, given authority by the weight of tradition, the *mos maiorum*, rituals, primarily sacrifices, were what mattered. In this system of gift exchange, gods were cultivated simply because of their power, and out of that power were obliged to return the honours bestowed on them with benefactions. Imperial honours, whether cultic or not, functioned along the same lines. No sane person could, or did, doubt the enormous power of the ruling emperor. The same goes for worship of the 'old' gods, unless people rejected their very existence or connection with this world (as did the Epicureans). Even so, the force of the *mos maiorum* in a strongly traditionalistic society usually overrode philosophical scruples or doubts. In both cases, whether of gods or the living emperor, cult was the traditional way of dealing with highly superior power. Most Roman state gods had clearly defined core areas in which they wielded this absolute power—Mars in war, Ceres in agriculture, the living emperor in what we would, anachronistically, term the political sphere, Jupiter in several areas.

It was different with a *Divus*. It was never obvious what power, if any, an emperor possessed once he had left this world. In the *Apocolocyntosis*, it is a cruel theme that Claudius cannot grasp why his orders are not obeyed anymore, and nobody pays attention when he orders the execution of whoever displeases him. And there was never really any attempt to assign any areas of control to *Divi*. Nor would that have been an easy exercise: sky and earth were full of gods, specifically attending to all imaginable areas of human activity; all seats were taken already, so to speak. We may trace some notion of Divus Augustus interpreted as a guardian godhead for his ruling dynasty; but even this idea was never clearly or consequentially expressed. After Nero, last of the dynasty, even this role was less obvious, though the first emperor could still be thus employed later, as in an ideological sense the ancestor of any later *Augustus*. Later *Divi* would be even more unemployed in heaven; they might lend status and lustre to their descendants on the throne, but they were hardly ever credited with power. The question only arose when their portraits were damaged or their memories scorned. The fact that it arose at all illustrates the impotence of a *Divus*. It was not taken for granted that he could defend himself from attack or slander, though this was the position initially taken by Tiberius: '*Deorum iniuriae dis curae*' ('Insults to the gods are the gods' concern'). Later, however, such insults did come under the statute of *maiestas*, 'lese-majesty'.[115] Even when worshipped in state rites, their lack of power was obvious, and reflected on their status; Divus Augustus, in the sacrificial lists of the Arval Brothers, habitually ranks lowest of all gods mentioned (apart from other *Divi*), even lower than the *Genius* of the living emperor.[116]

In a system where the power of the recipient was a vital condition for worship to be worthwhile, *Divi* had a problem. The problem was of course not a new one, though the active creation of such impotent gods was. Over the centuries, numerous Roman state gods had been rendered obsolete and forgotten, either because their areas of influence were too small, or because they had been taken over by other divinities. They had either disappeared from the state cult, or sunk into obscurity, kept alive only by respect for the tradition, *mos maiorum*.

In the absence of power, only one thing could grant to *Divi* the divine status, for which they were neither qualified by this usual requirement nor by tradition, namely belief in their divinity. The absolute divinity claimed for *Divi* in the passages I have quoted above was emphasized only for lack of the real thing. It was, I believe, a symptom of crisis. Belief presupposes doubt, or its possibility: the more pious the protestations of belief, the more doubt on what really mattered, the power that traditionally entailed divine status, and hence on this very divine status itself.

As argued above, there was hardly any alternative to divine constitutional status when the ultimate honours were voted to late and lamented emperors by the Senate, considering the position, on the very brink or edge of divine status, they had occupied in life. And, as argued above, death had traditionally elevated a person's status in Roman culture. Furthermore, if it was basically the link between death and divinity that effectively

115 Tac. *Ann*. 1. 73. 5 with Goodyear (1981, ii. ad loc.); Levick (1976, 193 f.).

116 Henzen (1874, *passim*).

debarred the living emperor from outright state divinity, as I have argued here, death itself removed this hindrance. Yet, paradoxically, by then it was in a sense too late. The honours and worship accorded the *Divi* were devoid of religious content if the relationship was not, or it was unclear how it could be, a reciprocal one. Beyond the short-term dynastic relevance of a *Divus*, with Augustus as perhaps a partial exception, only precedent and the force of tradition would keep alive the worship of the *Divi*, as was the case for archaic and obscure state gods saved, on the brink of extinction, by Augustus' antiquarian reforms of the state cult.[117] As the number of *Divi* continually increased over the first two centuries AD, the problem was aggravated.

DIVUS AUGUSTUS AGAIN

This view of the cult of the *Divi* may seem harsh, and, it will be argued, fails to distinguish between the early period, primarily the case of Augustus, and later, when the system had become routine by overuse and the sheer number of *Divi*. But the problem, if so it was, was in fact evident very early.

Tiberius appears to have actively encouraged the cult of his father and predecessor. His position of course depended heavily on his adoption by Augustus. In a famous scene Tacitus portrays Tiberius' daughter-in-law, the elder Agrippina, bursting in on the emperor (in the palace?) while he is engaged in sacrifices to Divus Augustus; Tiberius should, she says, cease persecuting her and her children, the flesh and blood of the man he reveres with sacrifices (a vicious tirade, since Tiberius had entered Augustus' family only through adoption).[118]

Tiberius never dedicated the major temple to Divus Augustus in Rome, though its construction must have begun almost immediately after Augustus' death; that was left to Gaius. Some scholars have taken this to indicate that Tiberius did not care much about the honours to his predecessor.[119] The opposite is no doubt the case. There is evidence that the purpose of Tiberius' last journey from Capri, after having spent

117 Liebeschuetz (1979, 55ff.).

118 Tac. *Ann.* 4. 52. 3.

119 Thus Fishwick (1992).

eleven years on the island, was to enter Rome to dedicate the temple; at the approach of death, however, he despaired of the project and awaited the end at Misenum.[120] The long building phase of the temple should thus rather be taken as evidence that it was to be a particularly splendid building, with no expense spared; and so it appears indeed on the coins depicting it.[121]

More striking is the fact that Tiberius apparently did what he could to further the cult on the municipal level, striking because the authorities in Rome rarely interfered with the civic cults. Dio claims that after Augustus' death, shrines to the dead emperor were erected 'in many different places, some of the communities voluntarily building them and others unwillingly'. Later Dio, in describing Tiberius' publicly displayed reverence for Divus Augustus, writes: 'And in the case of the statues and the shrines which were being erected to Augustus, whether by communities or by private individuals, he either dedicated them himself or instructed one of the *pontifices* to do so'.[122] Dio is imprecise, and we cannot really exemplify his information. Tiberius certainly dedicated a precinct to Augustus at Nola, as well as the Capitol at Capua, but this was perhaps a special case, since the Nola temple was erected where Augustus had died.[123] In any case, Dio clearly suggests that there was so little enthusiasm outside Rome for the worship of the new *Divus* that it took pressure from Rome to get temples built. Likewise, Cyzicus was deprived of its freedom for assaulting Roman citizens and for neglecting to finish a temple to Divus Augustus (though the first charge may have been the decisive one, the mere mention of the second is still significant).[124] This information is striking; there are no examples whatsoever that municipal temples to the living emperor were ever erected under encouragement or pressure from Rome. That was clearly not necessary; at the most, the role of the emperor was a passive one, his permission being asked. So in the case of Nola, the

[120] Suet. *Tib.* 74: pointless if the dedication of the temple was not imminent, and Tiberius intended to do it; cf. Plin. *Nat. Hist.* 34. 18. 43.

[121] For the temple see Hänlein-Schäfer (1985, 113ff.) with all the literary sources; Fishwick (1992).

[122] Dio 56. 46. 3; 57. 10. 1.

[123] Tac. *Ann.* 4. 57; Dio 56. 46. 3; Hänlein-Schäfer (1985, 129f.).

[124] Tac. *Ann.* 4. 36. 2; Dio (Xiph.) 57. 24. 6; Suet. *Tib.* 37. 3.

only specific example we know of, we may ask whether the temple was erected primarily out of reverence for the dead emperor, or to receive the rare honour of a visit from the living ruler. The answer should be obvious, though it certainly does not imply that the cult of Divus Augustus was unimportant, only that the new god mattered little in his own right.

Dio was not very impressed with the supposed divinity of a *Divus* (his translation of the term is generally *hērōs*, a dead man); in his day few men were.[125] So we may doubt his testimony, especially since it refers to the period shortly after Augustus' death, when he and his achievements were still in fresh memory. But it is in fact borne out by parallel evidence. Thus, of the sixteen temples to Augustus known from Italy, seven are datable to his lifetime, and seven cannot be dated with any certainty; but only one, the temple at Nola, is certainly posthumous. The titles of municipal priesthoods present special problems, as argued in my chapter on municipal cults; there is evidence of some *flamines* certainly dedicated to Divus Augustus, since they date long after his death. They are very few, however, as they are to Divus Claudius; and there are no certain examples known for any later *Divi*. Statues were certainly set up to *Divi* by townships outside Rome, but they appear to date overwhelmingly from the period shortly after the death of the relevant emperor or empress. Such dedications then depended more on the successor or emperor husband of a particular *Divus* or *Diva* than on concern with their own eternal memory. We should also note that statues represent a one-off expense. Establishment of a public cult was a very different matter. Such cults were in principle meant to be continued forever, and would at the very least be awkward to abolish; and this type of institutionalized worship is then rarely encountered to *Divi* or *Divae* outside Rome.[126]

We may also point to emperor worship on the private level, which presumably reflects the lack of 'enthusiasm' for *Divi*.

[125] Also Herodian 7. 3. 5 has *hērōs* = *Divus*. Cf. Min. Fel. 21. 9: '. . . *et divi ceteri reges, qui consecrantur non ad fidem numinis, sed ad honorem emeritae potestatis*', essentially pointless if not true also in pagan eyes.

[126] For Ostia, which due to its proximity to Rome represents a partial exception to this pattern, see p. 89 above and for its flaminates to *Divi* see App. 3.

Very few cult associations were dedicated to the worship of *Divi* (and even those may, with one certain exception, actually have been established in the lifetime of the relevant emperor). Even more striking is the absence of *Divi*, including Augustus, from domestic cults, which appear to have been concerned exclusively with the living emperor. The case of Granius Marcellus, who exchanged the head of his statue of Augustus for that of Tiberius, may be exceptional in its crude bluntness; but what motivated his action evidently was not.[127] The pattern emerging is clear: the more private the cult, and hence free from influence or pressure from the Roman state cult, the more rarely do we encounter the *Divi*, and the more frequently is it the living emperor who is the object of veneration. People cared little about their emperors once these had left this world; and even when they did, the main, if indirect, target of their worship was usually the living emperor.

This is perhaps to be expected; what is surprising, however, is that this was apparently the case right from the beginning, even in the case of the first and greatest of emperors. Modern scholarship, depending far too much on the literary sources and their preoccupation with the state machinery in Rome, has conjured up an image of the imperial cult in Roman Italy as mainly preoccupied with the *Divi*, even to the point of denying that the living emperor ever received divine worship there. This image is manifestly false. It is only—partially—valid as regards Rome, not in geographical terms, as is usually made out, but in constitutional ones: the living emperor received only private worship in the capital. Conversely, the worship of *Divi* was almost exclusively confined to public cults, and perhaps even in this sphere not often encountered outside Rome.

DIVI IN THE ROMAN STATE CULT

The lack of local response to the cult of *Divi* in the capital is particularly striking, because the Roman state had an obvious medium by which it could, and did, disseminate such worship: the army.

[127] Associations: see p. 224 above; Marcellus: Tac. *Ann.* 1. 74. 3: see p. 206 above.

In the third century a Roman army unit, the *cohors XX Palmyrenorum*, was permanently stationed at the small town of Dura Europos by the empire's Syrian border with Parthia. The site was later abandoned and excavated between the world wars in a remarkable state of preservation. Among the finds was a cache of discarded administrative documents of the cohort, including fragments of its cultic calendar, the so-called *Feriale Duranum*. The text was written on a papyrus roll which had been worn to tatters from use. It can be dated to the reign of the last Severan emperor Severus Alexander (222–35).[128]

The *Feriale Duranum* contains a large number of rites, many of them celebrating events in the career of the ruling emperor. Some were marked by *supplicationes*, others by the sacrifice of a bull (*taurus*) to his *Genius*, as in the state cults in Rome.[129] The birthday of a surprising number of dead and deified emperors, eleven altogether in the preserved fragments, was also celebrated, again as in the state cult by the sacrifice of a steer (*bos mas*) to the relevant *Divus*. The *Divi* include not only the major ones such as Augustus, but also, for example, Claudius and Nerva, as well as Divus Julius (Caesar) who never appears in the *Arval Acta*. His cult had presumably been celebrated in the army without interruption from at least the reign of Augustus, and his appearance in the *Feriale* is good evidence that his reticent position in the Roman state cult did not apply in the army cults. *Divae* also feature in the calendar, though their birthdays were not marked by blood sacrifices, but by *supplicationes*, a lesser rite suggesting their minor importance. Among the *Divae* we find such characters as Trajan's sister

[128] Fink *et al.* (1940); Fishwick (1990, i. 3. 593 ff.).

[129] At least in the early empire there is good evidence of direct, divine worship of the emperor's image in the legionary headquarters, thus Tac. *Ann.* 4. 2. 3; Suet. *Tib.* 48. 2 (p. 225 above), and under Severus the quasi-military *cohortes vigilum* in Ostia seem to have worshipped the living rulers directly: see Gradel (1992, 46). It may be that the distinction between direct and indirect (*Genius*) worship was less clear or important in the legions than at the level of state cult and municipal worship, but the difference may also reflect a change of government policy towards the imperial cult of the army, with the strict state cult version being imposed on the army at some stage. In any case the soldiers would hardly have had any objections to direct emperor worship, and the rites to the *Genius* in the *Feriale Duranum* constitute strong evidence that the contents of the calendar had ultimately been decided in Rome.

Marciana, and Hadrian's mother-in-law Matidia (but not Livia, the first empress). There is even a *supplicatio* on the birthday of Germanicus who had died more than two centuries earlier, and never became a *Divus* (he had died in Syria which may partly explain the entry). The number of animal sacrifices (of oxen) in the calendar is stunning: whatever Roman soldiers had to put up with in the army, they got plenty of protein.

Obviously no Syrian soldiers in the early third century could have taken much of an interest in such characters as Claudius or Matidia. The document contains no Syrian references (discounting Germanicus, who died in the province), and totally reflects the state cult in Rome, so the text of the calendar was no doubt sent out and imposed from the capital. This renders it of great general importance, for the same must have been the case for all other army units of the time, all over the empire. To soldiers, the worship of the old (and new) *Divi* was a course in Roman imperial history (the edited version), and may have made sense as a symbol of their Romanness and its proud traditions—rightly so, since the calendar to such an extent reflected the state cult—as well as simply being an occasion for holidays and steaks. But in their own right the old *Divi* can have meant little to soldiers.

The calendar, imposed from Rome, must then count as representative for such army cult anywhere in the empire at this time. It clearly had a long tradition behind it, reflecting in the celebrations of the calendar layer upon layer of developments through a quarter millennium of Roman history. The *Feriale Duranum* should caution us against seeing worship of the *Divi* simply as an isolated feature of a narrow élite in Rome; as the document shows, their cult and their stories were spread all over the empire. The army cults were a school in history, not only for the soldiers involved, but presumably also for the local civilians among whom the units lived.

The cult of the army reflected the state cult in Rome to a surprising extent, but this connection was a one-way track only. The capital was and remained the place where such cults were voted, made, performed, and demolished. The *Divi* gradually through the first two centuries of the empire acquired a remarkable presence in the cityscape of Rome. Even today no visitor to the city can avoid noticing the impressive remains of

FIG. 12.9. Temple of Divus Antoninus and Diva Faustina
Notes: Little remains of such temples of the *Divi* once numerous in Rome. The best preserved of them is the temple of Faustina Maior (d. AD 140) in the Roman Forum. At the death of her husband Antoninus in 161, the temple was rededicated to both of them, as evidenced by the inscription above the front columns. Only the shell remains of the temple whose inside is taken up by a church constructed around 1600. The temple was depicted on Faustina's consecration coinage, see Fig. 12.3.H. Older excavation photo.

monuments set up by the Roman state in honour of the *Divi*: shattered ruins of Divus Claudius' gigantic temple complex, built under Vespasian; the column row of the Hadrianeum, now the former stock exchange; the temple of Divus Antoninus and Diva Faustina (Fig. 12.9); the Antonine *ustrina*, imperial cremation monuments; the massive mausoleums of Augustus and Hadrian.[130] Even more has perished, or remains unexcavated: the temple of Divus Augustus, painstakingly constructed over more than twenty years, and the probably most gigantic of

[130] For the remains see Nash (1961–2, i. 26f., 164, 243ff., 304, 450, 457ff., 512ff.; ii. 36f., 268ff., 501ff.).

all such sanctuaries, the temple of deified Trajan.[131] In state art, imperial apotheosis was evidently a favoured motif; to mention only the best-known example, we possess the relief-sculpted depiction of the ascension of Antoninus, accompanied by his wife Faustina, of vital dynastic importance, who had predeceased him by twenty years (Fig. 12.4). Likewise, imperial apotheosis and other types honouring *Divi* and *Divae* feature prominently in the coinage up to the fourth century.[132]

There is unfortunately no room to give detailed attention to the archaeological remains and temples of the *Divi* in Rome; but their mere prominence, and the immense resources devoted to their construction, must be beyond doubt. This may, on the face of it, seem to contradict my conclusions above. Yet the contradiction only appears because we are used to judging the significance of religious phenomena in terms of belief only; which level of interpretation certainly cannot account for the prominence of the *Divi* in the cityscape and state art of Rome.

The prominence of *Divi* and their cults in the public sphere and public squares of Rome, and to a much lesser extent elsewhere, as well as their almost complete absence from the private sphere is indeed explicable in other terms. The 'natural' response—divine honours—to imperial power was blocked, in the constitutional sphere of Rome, by its ominous connotations of death; so the cults of the *Divi*, as opposed to the living emperor, can be seen as an outlet for this response. That only explains the phenomenon in part, but it does suggest the full answer.

Even in establishing the cult of a *Divus* or *Diva*, the living emperor was, as I have suggested, a central figure. However, the divine status of *Divi* was in many cases left unaffected by the end of their dynastic importance. On the other hand, there are also several cases, all of the first century, of minor imperial relatives who became *Divi* in name only. There is thus no evidence that Vespasian's daughter and wife, who had died before his accession, were ever the object of cult, though they received the title of *Diva*; the same goes, more strikingly since here our evidence, with Pliny's *Panegyric*, is better, for Divus Traianus

131 Augustus: Fishwick (1992); Trajan: Claridge (1993, 20 with refs.); Packer (1994).

132 Antoninus: Hannestad (1986, 215ff.); coinage: Schulten (1979).

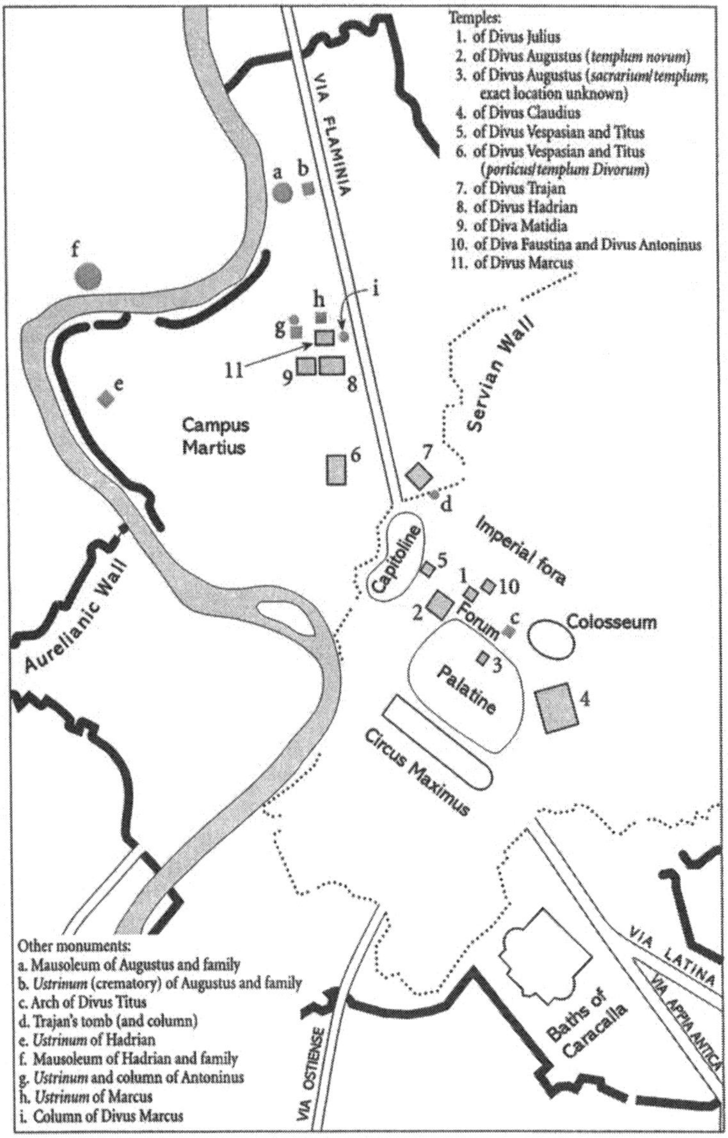

FIG. 12.10. Map of the centre of Rome *c.*AD 300, showing temples and other monuments of the *Divi* (excluding the temples of Divus Nerva, Diva Marciana, and Divus Pertinax, of unknown locations)

Pater, Trajan's natural father, or even for Domitian's infant son, a *Divus* known only from the coins. Apparently right from this date onwards, a gradation in honours could be employed, from state temple and priests down to the title of *Divus* only. Even earlier, Nero neglected to finish the temple to Divus Claudius, and even demolished what had been built, but that did not affect Claudius' status as state god (the *Arval Acta* even testify to his worship all through Nero's reign).[133]

There were, then, several classes of *Divi*: it was not a simple question of either-or. Some *Divi* only had the title, purely honorary, and never any state cult. Others had their own temple, their own *sodales*, and flamen (though all three elements were commonly shared by several *Divi*, typically grouped together according to their mutual family relations, or, in other words, by dynasties). These *Divi* with the full set of honours perpetuating their memory were the 'élite division' of the dead imperials, and they are the *Divi* encountered in the *Arval Acta*, for if the Arval college worshipped them, we may rest assured that so did the other grand priestly colleges of the state cult. Between these two extremes were further gradations: Divus Julius had his own temple and flamen, but no *sodales*, and the Arvals never worshipped him; his worship was 'self-contained' within the state cult, and presumably involved only the priest and personnel directly attached to his temple in the forum. Others could receive worship throughout the state cult without having a temple; this would be the case for several *Divi* while they waited for their sanctuary to be constructed. But in some cases, there were no plans to build one, or the plans were cancelled. This happened to Divus Claudius in Nero's reign; only Vespasian resuscitated the plan for his temple and saw it finished. Others like Lucius Verus never appear to have had a temple, not even a part in one as 'junior partner', like Livia in the temple of Augustus. *Divi* without a temple lived life dangerously: a physical sanctuary dedicated to them was the strongest guarantee that their memory would be kept alive. This was because cult without a temple could simply be allowed to lapse—no deliberate effort, merely negligence, was required to oust them from the state pantheon. A physical

133 Levick (1990, 187 with n. 1).

temple dedicated to them, however, had to be deliberately torn down or rededicated to another deity to oust them completely from memory.

We have no convincing evidence that the honour of deification was ever revoked, not even in cases from the extreme end of the scale, infant children of tyrants who later had their memory damned. But revoking the honour was never necessary. The gradations in several 'divisions' of *Divi* meant that the system was flexible enough to adapt and change without such crude measures, and in some cases, such as the minor Flavian relatives or Trajan's biological father, it was probably never even intended that these *Divi* should enter the state cult as such. In these cases the term *Divus* or *Diva* was apparently a mere title. *Divi* who were important enough to receive their own temple were usually important enough for such a monument and cult to fulfil its didactic point in the state cult, even in the longer run. There were exceptions, however, in the early period of the custom, when it was still in flux and tradition had not yet come to define its purpose and limits. Nero's baby daughter and his wife Poppaea received temples, but presumably these were not yet built when the emperor was toppled a few years after their deaths. Another instance involves the same emperor who grew up to regret, apparently, that his adoptive father Claudius had been deified. At least Suetonius claims that Nero 'neglected and revoked' Claudius' deification.[134] This is in fact the only time we encounter the notion of outrightly revoking the honour of state divinity. However, the information is slander, for the *Arval Acta* show that Divus Claudius in fact received state worship all through Nero's reign, though he tore down the half-finished temple of Claudius—a measure which would, as mentioned, certainly have made it easier to drop this god from the pantheon, by merely ignoring him.

The claim of outright de-deification is presumably made to shock Suetonius' audience, which is significant. *Divi* who turned out to be embarrassing or superfluous could simply be ignored; it was not necessary to dethrone them actively. Only the continuous performance of a cult, not a mere title, ensured the eternal memory of a *Divus*.

[134] Suet. *Claud.* 45.

Short-lived *Divi* can be seen as reflecting the excesses of a new system which had not yet settled enough to define its own purpose and boundaries clearly. To examine what was actually the point of state deification, we should now turn to the 'élite division' of *Divi*, those dead emperors and empresses whose cult was kept alive in the state cult reign after reign, sometimes for centuries. In 183 the Arvals worshipped sixteen *Divi*, and in 218 (and 224) the group had been expanded to encompass twenty dead emperors and empresses.[135] These numbers are surprisingly large. So is the number of *Divi* featuring in the *Feriale Duranum*, imposed from Rome: no soldiers on the Syrian frontier in the 220s could possibly have had much interest in, say, Divus Claudius or Diva Matidia. But then again, nor could Roman senators worshipping these characters in state cult in the same period. The message seems clear, and it is no doubt a didactic one: the honour of state divinity-cum-worship was forever.

The system of posthumous deification of virtuous emperors and their kin enabled Senate and emperor to turn the avoidance of lifetime state deification from a coincidence, or even a problem, as I have suggested for the early empire, into an advantage. By voting state divinity to dead emperors, the Senate didactically displayed to the ruling emperor, and empress, the reward awaiting them if they ruled and behaved according to the senatorial ideal. With the Roman obsession with *memoria*, the bait was an effective one, emphasizing the eternity of these honours: the memory of a dead emperor was ritually kept alive forever in the state cult. The point was eternally valid, long beyond the dynastic relevance of a particular *Divus* (or *Diva*); hence the very surprise we may feel at the state worship of obscure and outdated *Divi* well into the third century actually furnishes its own explanation. The ruling *princeps* had a more active role to play in this aspect of the delicate *pas de deux* between emperor and Senate. By lauding and honouring earlier *Divi*, mainly his father and predecessor, he could display, much more than mere filial piety and not only in words but in sumptuous buildings and ritual practice, his intentions to model himself on the senatorial ideal. When the

[135] Henzen (1874, 148); see further p. 355 below.

Senate at first refused to deify Hadrian after his death, and had to be strongly persuaded by his son and successor Antoninus before it acquiesced,[136] this was not merely due to petty malice against the old emperor: senators wanted his successor to be different (as he indeed turned out to be: the ideal senatorial emperor).

This primary function of imperial deifications only crystallized gradually from the much more erratic pattern of the early empire. In the early stages of the custom, during the first century, the honour had become more and more promiscuously and incidentally bestowed. Caligula's sister Drusilla, Nero's baby daughter, and several other *Divi* till the early second century were unimportant figures whose deifications carried no obvious didactic points. Indeed the supreme honour of state divinity seemed for much of this period to be heading towards steadily increasing devaluation, totally tied up in the immediate present and with no long-term relevance whatsoever. Gradually, however, time and dynastic change weeded out in this forest of early *Divi*, and engendered a system with clear didactic purpose. The system and its function, as outlined above, became fully fixed with the general conservative backlash of the adoptive emperors. Imperial children did not become *Divi* after Domitian (both Antoninus and Marcus had sons who died young); and not even Hadrian's adult, though short-lived, adoptive son Aelius Caesar received the honour. Likewise, the last woman to be deified without having been empress was Hadrian's mother-in-law Matidia in 119; and even she and Trajan's sister Marciana (died 112) received state temples, underlining that the deifications were to be taken seriously, and not merely a high-handed and costless hand-out of a fancy title, as in earlier honours to minor relatives. Significantly, their temples ensured their survival: both ladies, though never empresses, are in the *Feriale Duranum*. However, after Matidia till the early third century only emperors and empresses became *Divi* on departing this world. This limitation points to a more clear and steady purpose of apotheosis than in the first century. Emperors' dead babies and minor relatives had no obvious function to perform as 'role models'. But there was

[136] HA *Hadr.* 27; *Ant. Pius* 5. 1; Dio (Xiph.) 69. 2. 5; (Xiph.) 69. 23. 3.

always an emperor, and usually an empress, on the throne; and their well-behaved predecessors could fill the part.

This had then been much less obvious in the early stages of the system. There were apparently no protests in the Senate at the deification of Claudius (only sniggers at the funerary eulogy of the dead emperor read out by Nero).[137] Yet a leading figure in the new government, Seneca, could immediately afterwards in his cruel *Apocolocyntosis* present the new *Divus* as having been a horrendous failure as emperor—and many senators would have agreed, as in fact did Nero. Less than a century later, at the death of Hadrian, senators had a much clearer idea about the ultimate point of the exercise—and protested vehemently against deifying their late emperor.

The impressive monuments to the *Divi* in the city of Rome should then be interpreted as didactic showpieces, fundamentally in the same terms as for instance Pliny's *Panegyric to Trajan*. This interpretation can certainly explain the pattern of the cults of the *Divi* and their monuments, their prominence in the public cityscape of Rome, and to a much lesser extent in other cities and townships, and finally their striking absence from the private sphere. The monuments were decreed by the Senate for the eyes of the ruling emperor, and erected by him for the eyes of the Senate, and the cults of the *Divi*, in which the emperor participated on a footing with senatorial priests, continuously restated the points of didacticism and reassurance, which were thus the main props of the practice. Below and beyond the level of public ceremonial and display in the capital, constructing the relationship between the living emperor and the Senate, the *Divi* were then, unsurprisingly, far less significant.

PRESSURES ON THE OLD ORDER

If this interpretation is correct and comprehensive, the decisive, even if indirect, focus of the cults of the *Divi* in Rome was actually the ruling emperor—and the Senate. In situations of conflict between emperor and Senate, the system was, however, open to abuse, and as generally, the emperor held the strong

137 Tac. *Ann.* 13. 3. 1.

hand in the game, at least if he was able to ensure the succession. A decisive case, which points to the collapse of the system I have suggested above, was the deification of Commodus, ordered by Septimius Severus in 195. Commodus, who had been murdered two years previously, was everything an emperor should not be in the eyes of most senators; predictably, he suffered damnation of his memory immediately after his death.

However, having established his own position in 195, and in the knowledge that he possessed two sons to succeed him, Severus had Commodus deified, apparently in connection with his own fictitious adoption as the son of Marcus, Commodus' father, who had died fifteen years previously. The measure was obviously a symptom of Severus' falling-out with senatorial opinion, presumably because of widespread support in the body for his rival Clodius Albinus.[138] On the interpretation put forward here, the deification undermined the whole point and meaning of state deifications of late emperors. Though the practice had clearly become routine by the second century, it was not just an empty formality on the basis of mechanical precedent, as scholars have supposed. The function suggested here was of vital importance and relevance long after routine set in—indeed routine helped to define it more clearly—and state deifications still fulfilled that function perfectly under the Antonines. Commodus' deification, however, made a mockery of it.

By 195 there were further problems. In the late republic and early empire, status rather than divinity, or divine nature, had mattered most in traditional Roman cultic practice, and inner contradictions on the theological level, or with the arguments of philosophical schools, had not threatened these cults; to a surprising extent, religion functioned independently of philosophical squabbles, doubts, or satire (as in the case of Seneca's *Apocolocyntosis*). There is little room to trace the development here, but the contradictions with philosophy increasingly came to be felt as a problem; the rise of Christianity is merely the most conspicuous symptom of this. Though general developments on the mental, even only half- or even subconscious,

[138] Commodus: Dio (Xiph.) 76. 7. 4ff.; adoption and support for Albinus: Birley (1988, 117f. with refs.).

level of a whole age or its social élite are difficult to trace and explain in anything but the haziest terms, the third century did see concrete evidence of such rejection of traditional forms of worship in favour of new gods or ideas coupled with a somewhat more systematic theology than that of the old system.

Crisis in the traditional Roman state cult surfaced in the third century with revolutionary measures. About 220 Jupiter was, though not removed from the pantheon, deposed as the foremost god of Rome, a position he had held for more than seven centuries. The Syrian sun god Elagabalus took his place for a short time.[139] The young Syrian emperor Antoninus (later termed Elagabalus from his god) was hereditary priest of the deity in Syrian Emesa. The measure only lasted a couple of years till the emperor was murdered and his young cousin Severus Alexander, who also succeeded him in his hereditary priesthood, had to reinstate Jupiter and expel Elagabalus from the pantheon (his state temple was significantly rededicated to Jupiter Ultor, 'the Avenger'). However, the vicious blackening of young Antoninus' memory cannot overshadow a basic fact: such a development had simply been unthinkable in, say, the first century. The Syrian Antoninus was neither the first senator nor indeed emperor to hold unusual private views on religion; so had, for instance, Nero and Hadrian.[140] But their personal ideas had affected the state cult as little as had the views of senators in Cicero's day when several Roman nobles had accepted philosophical or religious ideas running counter to the state rites. At the most, personal favourites who were already part of the pantheon, such as Apollo under Augustus and Minerva under Domitian, could be favoured by 'their' emperors with temples and honours, though never supplanting Jupiter's formal place as the highest-ranking god in the state pantheon.

It is patently unhelpful to dismiss the Elagabalus episode as merely due to the personal eccentricity of a particular emperor.

[139] Herod. 5. 5. 7 (Elagabalus' name to precede those of the other gods invoked by officiating state priests); Dio (Xiph.) 80. 11. 1 (greater than Jupiter); HA *Elag.* 3. 4; 6. 7; 7. 4 (other gods as slaves and desire for monotheism); Frey (1989).

[140] Suet. *Ner.* 56: '*religionum . . . contemptor*'; Hadrian: Dio (Xiph) 69. 11. 3f.

What is more, henotheistic sun cults were popular and in another version later returned to the state pantheon; under the emperor Aurelian (270–5) a splendid temple was dedicated to Sol Invictus in Rome, and coins commonly depicted the god with the label '*Dominus imperii Romani*', 'Lord of the Roman empire', a slight to Jupiter which is at least comparable to the formal deposition of the old chief god under Elagabalus.[141] A later backlash, under Diocletian, reinstated Jupiter in his traditional role of unequivocal supremacy, stressed by the appellation of the senior emperor as 'Jovean'[142] (perhaps as much a declaration of the emperor's support for Jupiter as the other way round).

Such attempts at religious reform reveal at the very least dissatisfaction with the state cult in its established form within the governing élite. Some of those belonging to it embraced the idea of revolution rather than tradition, or the slow developments of the previous centuries. Others, the traditionalists, such as Diocletian or strong forces surrounding young Severus Alexander, wanted to turn the clock back and leave it there. The reforming attempts of Elagabalus and Aurelian failed, at least on the formal level (Sol Invictus came to have a strong influence on Christianity). The third attempt, of Constantine, succeeded in implanting a new system with a new God, Christianity, into the state cult, this time furthered by the establishment of a new capital, Constantinople; in Rome Christianity and the old state cult continued side by side till the end of the fourth century when the old cults were summarily banned.

It is difficult to state the role of the *Divi* and their cults in these developments. Already Tacitus in the early second century seems almost modern in his cynical neglect of the formal aspects of the Roman constitution, as constructed by senatorial decrees, laws, and religious rites, in favour of what 'really' mattered: the omnipotence of the *princeps*. Tacitus has little respect for the façade so meticulously constructed and upheld in the dealings between emperor and Senate. His masterpiece, the *Annals*, fails to indicate why the formal pro-

141 Halsberghe (1984, 2195ff.).
142 Liebeschuetz (1979, 237; 240ff.).

prieties continued for so long and clearly mattered so much to senators long after the historian's own day. Significantly, his neglect of the practice of deifying deceased emperors is almost total, contemptuously confined to three short sentences in connection with the deaths of Augustus and Claudius.

Tacitus showed his attitude indirectly, by silence. The practice of state deification was such a central aspect of imperial ideology and of the cultic system of the Roman constitution that it could not be criticized directly. But a contemporary of Tacitus, the Greek philosopher Plutarch, who knew Roman practice better than most of his countrymen, made his attitude clear. In his biography of Rome's founder Romulus, whose case furnished an obvious and frequently quoted precedent for deification of late emperors, Plutarch quotes the strange stories of the ancient king's corporeal disappearance from earth and subsequent divinity under the name of Quirinus. To Plutarch such tall tales of ascension in the flesh were not only untrustworthy, but also vulgar: what need could the soul possibly have for the body in celestial afterlife? Instead Plutarch argued for the philosophical notion, also presented by Cicero in 'Scipio's Dream', that the souls of virtuous humans would be rewarded with an abode in heaven:[143]

> We must not, therefore, violate nature by sending the bodies of good men with their souls to heaven [in such myths as that of Romulus], but implicitly believe that their virtues and their souls, in accordance with nature and divine justice, ascend from men to heroes, from heroes to demi-gods, after they have been made pure and holy, as in the final rites of initiation, and have freed themselves from mortality and sense, to gods, not by civic law, but in very truth and according to right reason, thus achieving the fairest and most blessed consummation.

Plutarch cautiously avoided stating explicitly what he was referring to in his digression, but the object of his criticism is nevertheless fairly obvious. As well as criticizing silly stories of bodies transposed to the dwellings of virtuous souls, he expressed his discomfort with the relative divinity, deification by decree of the Senate, granted to *Divi*. Nature and the divine

143 Plut. *Rom.* 28. 8 (tr. B. Perrin, Loeb edn.): '*οὐ νόμωι πόλεως*' ('not by civic law').

order of the universe would automatically reward deserving virtue: humans neither could nor should make gods. At the time when Plutarch wrote, the early second century, he cannot have had anything else in mind but contemporary practice in Rome. Like Christians and modern scholars who have attempted to present the procedure of deification as a kind of canonization, Plutarch disliked, on philosophical grounds, the idea that divinity could depend on its earthly worshippers. The version he preferred was the philosophical one of absolute divinity, reflecting a rational and well-ordered universe ruled by divine laws of reason and justice. This was the version Seneca had earlier exploited for laughs in his *Apocolocyntosis* (where this universe appears just as messy and ill-governed as the world of mortals), whilst prudently avoiding comments on the 'real' version of Claudius' deification by senatorial decree and public cult. Plutarch's cautious and indirect criticism, revealingly based on the old and harmless case of Romulus, is merely one example of a long tradition of philosophical criticisms of traditional cultic practices. But Plutarch's comment reveals that some pagans felt uncomfortable with the idea of deifying dead emperors by senatorial decree, although it was too dangerous to attack the custom directly.

Such scepticism was taken over and elaborated by Christian writers, to whom the idea was not merely wrong or questionable on philosophical grounds, but also supremely blasphemous. The inherent lack of logical and dogmatic coherence in the practice of state deification was viciously exploited by early Christian apologists. Their rhetorical techniques are revealing. An apologist of the Severan age comments on the custom:[144]

> But perhaps you imagine that men become gods after death; Romulus was made a god by the false oath of Proculus; Juba a god by the wishes of the Mauritanians; and so the other kings consecrated not because of belief in their divinity [*ad fidem numinis*] but in honour of their former power. In point of fact, they dislike the attribution of the name: they desire to remain men; they are afraid of becoming gods; old though they be, they would rather not.

The argument against belief in the divinity of the *Divi* would be pointless if not essentially correct. In ridiculing the custom

[144] Min. Fel. 21. 9f.

with philosophical arguments, the apologist, not surprisingly, avoids its real significance, for which I have argued above. The examples brought forward are revealingly weird: the ancient case of Romulus with the oath which Seneca and his contemporaries had already found ridiculous, by this age long dropped; and the deification of Juba by African barbarians. Contemporary practice, and even its obvious precedents of Divus Julius and Augustus, is characterized in vague, though unmistakable terms, no names or examples given. The caution evident here is general to the genre, but the attack on the system of imperial state deification is equally typical.[145]

The large number of *Divi* worshipped in state cult in the late second and early third centuries put increasing pressure on the system. The divine honours could be gradated from the mere title of *Divus* or *Diva* up to the full set of honours including temple and priests. Marcus Aurelius, deified in 180, was one of the last *Divi* to receive his own state temple. When the new emperor Elagabalus arrived in Rome from Syria in 218, five more *Divi* had been added to the pantheon: Pertinax, Commodus, Severus, Caracalla (fictitiously claimed as the father of both Elagabalus and his successor Alexander Severus), and probably Caracalla's mother Julia Domna. From the *Arval Acta* we know that the Brothers in 183 worshipped sixteen *Divi*, and this almost fits the number of *Divi* created minus the minor ones who had fallen in disgrace along with the emperor who had had them deified.[146] In 218 the number had risen to

[145] Cf. Tert. *Ap*. 10. 10; 13. 7f.; Justin Mart. *Ap*. 1. 21. 3.

[146] Last temples: p. 364 below. Henzen (1874, 148); Gilliam (1969); Fejfer (1992, 213); the lasting *Divi* till 183 should have been the ten emperors Augustus, Claudius, Vespasian, Titus, Nerva, Trajan, Hadrian, Antoninus, Marcus Aurelius, Lucius Verus; plus seven *Divae*: Livia, Marciana, Matidia, Plotina, Sabina, Faustina I, Faustina II. From 183 to 218 were added four emperors: Pertinax, Commodus, Severus, Caracalla, and the empress Julia Domna (see Fejfer, 1992). Apparently only the emperors were added between 183 and 218, so that Domna only had the title, and no cult. It is more of a problem to say who dropped out of the Arval list (which, it should be noted, only reflects the minimum number of 'major' *Divi*) before 183; I find Livia the strongest candidate, as also suggested by Bickerman (1974): no women received cult, as far as we know, as *Divae* under the Flavians; in 70 there was a revision of the public *Fasti* (Tac. *Hist*. 4. 40. 2), coins of Antoninus label the temple of Augustus and Livia merely as '*Templum Divi Augusti*', and she is absent from the *Feriale Duranum*, though the date of her birth, 30 January, is

twenty, the same number as in the next—and last—instance in the *Arval Acta* from 224.[147] Perhaps only the four new male *Divi* received worship by all the priestly colleges, with Julia Domna's divinity being merely titulary, or her cult confined to special occasions and worship by her own priest (no doubt shared with other *Divi*). This is perhaps not all that significant. We should not forget that the Arvals were only one among several colleges: all we can say is that *Divi* cultivated by them must have received worship across the board of the major state colleges. But already the cult of Divus Julius had been localized to his own temple and cult personnel, and never appears in the *Arval Acta* (nor do other 'self-contained' state cults such as that of Magna Mater).

COLLAPSE

Doubts about the system of deification must have been aggravated by the steadily increasing number of *Divi*, gods of little or no power. The decreasing influence of the Roman Senate, whose role and function was of decisive importance to the didactic point of deifying dead emperors and empresses, must have added even more pressure; and the deification of Commodus which made a mockery of this point cannot have helped. In the reign of Maximinus (235–8) the whole development appears to have come to a head in the state cult.

In 235 the last Severan emperor Severus Alexander had been murdered by his own troops, and the empire slided into the protracted crisis of the third century. The new emperor Maximinus was a soldier who spent his reign fighting the Germans at the Rhine border and never showed himself in Rome (as we shall see, this is quite significant to the story). The delicate role play between emperor and Senate, in which worship and creation of *Divi* was a prominent feature, can have cut little ice with him and his administration, engaged in a life-

preserved in the document. This is not to suggest that Livia lost her status as *Diva* or was expelled from her temple (the coins referred to show her in it, with Augustus), but merely that her cult became 'self-contained', i.e. her cult was no longer celebrated across the board of the state colleges, but only by the priests and personnel attached to the temple.

[147] Henzen (1874, 148).

and-death struggle to defend the empire against barbarian invasions. Money was needed for the army, and it was ruthlessly extorted:[148]

> But after Maximinus had reduced most of the distinguished families to penury, he then began to think it was an unimportant, insignificant activity and not enough to satisfy his desire. So he turned to the public treasury and began to expropriate any money in the city being collected for food supply and cash distribution to the common people, funds put aside for theatres and divine festivals, as well as dedications of temples, statues of the gods, and honours of Divi, and any ornamentation on public buildings or city decorations, or material that could be turned into coin was all melted down. That was what the people particularly resented; the appearance of a siege when there was no fighting and no one armed, caused public concern. Some of the lower classes turned to opposition and set a guard round the temples, prepared to be slaughtered and killed in front of the altars rather than see their country plundered. Throughout the cities and the provinces popular emotion rose to a high pitch at this point. The soldiers were not in favour of what was happening either, because their relatives and families bitterly upbraided them, alleging that it was their fault that Maximinus was acting in this way.

The historian Herodian who wrote this is often rhetorical and imprecise in his descriptions. But the plunderings of the gods in Rome seem carefully graduated. The gods were deprived of votive offerings, statues, and embellishments which could be melted down for coin; such objects were decorative and magnificent, but the actual cult did not depend on these surrounding trinkets, and was apparently carefully left enough to function. *Divi*, on the other hand, were robbed of their honours (*'timás'*), that is, as the word is commonly used, of their very worship; presumably the temple funds were expropriated, so the cults simply ceased to function. Till this point the *Divi* had been treated as full-scale gods in the state cult, even if they had commonly come to be regarded as second-class deities (as evident in the terminology of Dio and here of Herodian, terming them *'hērōes'*). Now this attitude surfaced in the formal aspects of the Roman state system, and the *Divi* were for the first time

[148] Herod. 7. 3. 5f. (tr. Whittaker, Loeb edn., adapted): '. . . *ναῶν τε ἀναθήματα θεῶν τε ἀγάλματα καὶ ἡρώων τιμάς, καὶ εἴ τις ἦν κόςμος δημοςίου ἔργου ἢ καλλώπιςμα πόλεως ἢ ὕλη νόμιςμα ποιῆςαι δυναμένη, πᾶν ἐχωνεύετο*'.

treated as lesser gods by the administration. There is no need to interpret the behaviour of Maximinus, or his agents, or indeed of the common people in Rome, as a symptom of religious crisis general to the whole state cult. The expropriations took place in a time of emergency when dire need made it imperative that everybody, including the gods, had to pay their share for the cause. In fact the reaction of the common people clearly suggests that the gods were taken very seriously indeed, and some people are portrayed as willing to die in their defence. Modern 'rationalistic' historians may find this difficult to accept and instead point to cuts in the corn dole or funds for festivals—*panem et circenses*—affecting the common people directly and materially.[149] Such a view presupposes that the man in the street cared for little but his own immediate material needs, and it rests on an unwarranted, if traditional, notion *ex eventu* that the Roman state cult was doomed. What is more, it ignores the explicit statement of Herodian's text.

The passage is strong evidence for the continued popular support of Rome's traditional gods at the time, and certainly cannot be adduced as evidence for the opposite conclusion. But the gradations or variations in the cuts of the public sector of divine worship are highly indicative. The *Divi* apparently suffered more than other gods. This cannot mean anything other than that they were perceived by strong elements in the government to be less important than the 'old' gods; they were basically powerless, and the risk of divine anger from their quarter was then negligible. In these emergency measures Maximinus or his agents merely took the consequence of what had always been reflected in the place of the *Divi* in the state cult: they were the lowest-ranking of all state gods.

Other evidence indicates that Herodian's information is sound. The last *Divus* who is recorded to have had *sodales* voted to him is Severus Alexander (222–35), and his deification probably occurred shortly after his death, at some point in Maximinus' reign. In 236 Maximinus' son Maximus was co-opted into the college of the *sodales Antoniniani*, the state priesthood dedicated to the worship of the Antonine *Divi*.

[149] Thus Whittaker in his Loeb edn. of Herodian (1970, 173 n. 3) and id. (1964, 359f.).

There is no later information, and the *sodales* of *Divi*, or their state *flamines*, are never heard of after this. Maximinus had indeed had Alexander murdered, and it would be obvious that cuts in the state cults would affect that of his predecessor. Our sources stress that Alexander's deification was voted by the Senate, and not promoted by an emperor;[150] this does indeed suggest that the Senate took the initiative and deified the much-loved (by senators) late emperor, also as a cautious expression of opposition to Maximinus, who was then not asked and indeed cannot have been pleased with the measure. In 238, at least, the Roman Senate progressed to open rebellion against the rapacious military emperor.

The *Arval Acta* appear to support the demise of the *Divi* in the state cult around this time. When the Arval Brothers performed lustration rites in the grove of Dea Dia in the later second and earlier third century, they sacrificed to a whole series of gods. The rites ended with sacrifices to the *Divi* outside the imperial temple (*Caesareum*) in the grove. This took place, in the preserved evidence, on two occasions in 183: in both instances sixteen *Divi* received offerings; then in 218, when the number of *Divi* had risen to twenty; then again in 224 where the *Genius* of the living emperor had been added to the ritual (ranked above the *Divi*, as usual).[151] However, in the last instance known, in 240, only the *Genius* received a victim, and there is no mention of any *Divi*.[152] This change could be taken to have been relevant only to the Arval college; but Herodian's passage indicates that the development was general to the state cult at large.

There is another piece of evidence that all, and not just some, state cults of *Divi* were indeed simply abolished. An inscription, found, copied, and lost in Rome in the late sixteenth century, gives a list of members of a priestly state college.[153]

[150] Alexander: HA *Sev. Al.* 63. 3f.; John Chrysostom. *In epistulam II ad Corinthios Homilia* 26. 4, for which see Usener (1902); Maximus co-opted: *CIL* VI. 1985, fragmentary *Fasti* of a college regularly convening in the temple of Antoninus and Faustina, hence almost certainly the *sodales Antoniniani*; see further n. 157 below.

[151] 183, 218, 224: Henzen (1874, 148).

[152] Scheid (1998, 332 l. 16).

[153] *CIL* VI. 1984.

A century ago it was beyond doubt identified as that of the *sodales Augustales Claudiales*,[154] the priesthood established in Augustus' honour after his death, and after the deification of Claudius in 54 also dedicated to his worship. The list gives the names of the holders of two particular seats (*decuriae*) in the college, numbers 27 and 28. Originally, in 14, the fixed number of *sodales* had been 21, plus four supernumerary seats given to members of the imperial family (Tiberius, Germanicus, Drusus Minor, and Claudius). The need to accord the honour to new members of the imperial family tended to slowly push up the number of seats, and in our list seat 27 was first filled in AD 51, when young Nero was co-opted as a member. Clearly an extra seat had to be created, because none of the ordinary ones was vacant at the time: membership was for life, so vacancies would occur only when a *sodalis* died. In 68 seat 27 had to be filled again, at Nero's death; his successor was not the new emperor Galba, who was already a member (Suet. *Galba* 8), but a senator. This man died in 92; his successor survived till 115; then another, for almost forty years, till 153; another till 161; another till 169; another till 202; another till 210; another till 225; another till 229; his successor died after only a year, for the seat was filled again in 230: and this is the ultimate entry in the list.[155]

To the right of the column for seat 27 is the corresponding list for seat 28. This seat was filled only intermittently, being the last one (or close to: within the periods when this seat was filled there may at times have been a seat 29, but that does not really concern us); for long periods there were only 27 members, and seat 28 did then not exist.The intermittent occurrence of this seat makes this list less illuminating; it was established for Titus Caesar in 71, left vacant at his death (his brother and successor as emperor, Domitian, was no doubt a member already), and only re-established in 197 to co-opt the prince Caracalla who later became emperor. When he died in 217 Caracalla was succeeded in the seat, as on the throne, by the new emperor Macrinus. At Macrinus' death in 218 the

154 Dessau in *Eph. Epigr.* III. 74–6, a lucid analysis.

155 230: Q. Petronius Melior, recorded as *sodalis Augustalis Claudialis* in *CIL* XI. 3367 = *ILS* 1180.

place was left vacant for a short time, then filled in 219 with a senator. And here ends the list for seat 28. Either the new emperor Antoninus (Elagabalus) did not join the college,[156] or other seats were vacant: his accession was a bloody one.

The inscription, probably on a marble tablet, would no doubt have formed part of a series listing the holders of all seats, but this list, probably the last in the series,[157] is the only one preserved, albeit only in a manuscript copy. The completeness of the text, also at the bottom of both the lists of seat-holders, strongly suggests that the tablet was complete (if worn in places), when found and copied. It is of course possible that the listing of the tablet was continued on another one now lost. But taken in conjunction with the absence of any later evidence for imperial *sodales*, and the words of Herodian, the inscription is strong evidence: the withdrawal of the honours for *Divi* between 236 and 238, presumably by simply expropriating the funds of such cults, finished the existence of at least the *sodales Augustales Claudiales*. This is a stunning conclusion, in every sense: if the college devoted to the first and greatest of emperors, the ideological ancestor of all later ones, was abolished through lack of funding, which *Divi* would have been safe? Presumably none; and in this light Maximinus' measures make better sense. Taking the funds of a few cults for some *Divi* could hardly have made much difference from a financial point of view. But expropriating the funds devoted to the worship of all the, at this point numerous, *Divi* would indeed have involved substantial sums. The measures of the emperor were ruthless: anything that could be spared was confiscated. And, unlike the other state gods, who 'only' had their votive offerings, images, and temple decorations plundered for coin,

156 The delay in filling the seat could perhaps be adduced in support: if Antoninus (Elagabalus) refused to join—which would have been unprecedented—the *sodales* may well have hesitated before filling it with someone else.

157 In 235 Maximinus would presumably have filled the seat of Severus Alexander, which may, however, have been established as seat 29 when Alexander became Caesar in 221. Maximinus' son Maximus would presumably also have received a seat, cf. the fragmentary *Fasti* (*CIL* VI. 1985) of the *sodales Antoniniani* (see n. 150 above), covering the period 213 to 236 (Maximus co-opted *supra numerum*); in this case, however, the bottom of the tablet is extremely fragmentary, and there is, tantalizingly, no saying if the list carried on beyond 236.

the very cults of the *Divi* could then be spared. An institution of more than 250 years' standing, on which pious old emperors had spent enormous sums and lavished much attention, was simply abolished in one go. As a prominent element in the relationship between the ruling emperor and the Senate, it could not be more fitting that these measures were carried out by the first emperor who never entered Rome. But there is no evidence whatsoever that the cults were ever restored: on the contrary, as we shall shortly see.

That something happened in the field at this time has gone unnoticed, for the language of deification continued long after this: words are cheap. However, exclusive preoccupation with the verbal or iconographic level will ignore imperial deification as a living ritual system, and not merely a set of ideological slogans and icons evoking a tradition which had now left the realm of living religion to join that of ideology. No wonder the result of such approaches, counting *Divi* merely from their appearance on coins or in panegyrics, will often leave imperial cult and apotheosis seeming lifeless, mechanical, superficial. The birthdays of many *Divi*, pagan and Christian, were celebrated through at least most of the fourth century, and probably beyond, by horse races in the Circus.[158] And some later emperors, though very few in the rest of the chaotic third century, would still have received splendid state funerals (with or without eagle rite). But this implies no more about any worship of them than do celebrations of the Queen's birthday or state funerals in modern times, and certainly cannot be taken to reflect any cults. Throughout the third and early fourth century new *Divi* and *Divae* keep appearing on the coinage after their deaths, though only briefly afterwards; and *Divi* could be praised and raised to the sky in panegyrics. These were emblematic expressions and displays of the *pietas* of the successor, but there is not a shred of good evidence after Maximinus that this imagery reflected any worship. One may look at what people say, or at what they do. By the latter criterion, the *Divi* had had their day and were spent as a force in divine worship.

The general development in the third century seriously

158 The Calendar of Philocalus, AD 354: Degrassi (1963, 237ff.); cf. Arnob. *Adv. Nat.* 1. 64. 2.

undermined the main point of the state cult of the *Divi*. Without the Senate as a vitally important partner of the ruling emperor, worship of the *Divi*, who unlike other gods were not powerful, lost its didactic function and became increasingly pointless. Without an emperor present in Rome, the Senate had lost its main audience for the cult; and an absent emperor could no longer, by participation in these cults with the—other—senatorial priests, demonstrate to the Senate his ambition to live up to senatorial ideals of how a *princeps* should rule and behave. But an emperor now had more pressing tasks than to please and reassure senators. Significantly, the attack on the cults of the *Divi* by Maximinus is recorded of the first emperor (excepting usurpers and the short-lived Macrinus in 217–18) who never entered Rome.

Also significantly, a restoration attempt is attributed to one of the last 'senatorial' emperors, Tacitus (275–6), who had indeed, uniquely in his day, been elected by the Senate; the armies of the empire had left the choice to the venerable body in Rome, an amazing decision showing that antiquarian nostalgia was not merely confined to a scribbling élite, but could be shared by supposedly rude soldiers too.[159] In any case the new emperor ordered, it is reported, that a temple be built for the *Divi* in Rome, but only the 'good' (that is, senatorial) emperors were to have a place in it.[160] The story suggests not so much a reform as a resuscitation of cults which had ceased to function. This is also implied by the cult proposed: the *Divi* would receive sacrificial cakes—that is, only bloodless offerings—on their birthdays and other feast days, such as New Year and the birthday of Rome. The project would in any case have taken

[159] The only other instance in the third century of emperors elected by the senate before they were proclaimed by soldiers or conspirators are the co-rulers Balbinus and Pupienus in 238 (Herod. 7. 10. 3 ff.). As it happens, the nostalgic deferral to the Senate in 238 and 275 reflected a 'constructed' past which had never really existed: before 238 all new emperors had been proclaimed or recognized by soldiers before receiving confirmation from the Senate. This also includes e.g. Nerva in 96, often wrongly taken to have been the Senate's sovereign choice, but in fact proclaimed in the palace.

[160] HA *Tac.* 9. 5: '*Divorum templum fieri iussit, in quo essent statuae principum bonorum, ita ut iisdem natalibus suis et Parilibus et kalendis Ianuariis et Votis libamina ponerentur*'. The author was, as is obvious throughout his work, obsessed with the concepts of *boni* versus *mali principes*.

care of cases such as Commodus and Caracalla whose deification had run counter to the didactic purpose of the whole exercise, and if not ensured its collapse, then probably helped to make it so sudden. But even the emperor Tacitus, or the nostalgic author of his biography, did not envisage a resuscitation of the old cults in their former splendour. The anecdote gains in credibility from being attributed to Tacitus of all emperors. At the very least, the project and its attribution shows that the author who penned it, probably in the later fourth century, understood the point of the old system well enough to refer the story to the perfect emperor for it.[161] However, the clock could not be turned back: the Senate's role was forever decisively diminished, and emperors could no longer reside permanently in Rome, too far away from the trouble spots of the empire. Tacitus ruled for only six months, and we hear no more of the scheme. It reflects little more than a dream about the good old days.

The great crisis of the third century also entailed an astonishing breakdown in the production of the historical sources—literary history writing, inscriptions—on which we depend. Thus the Arval Brothers in the 240s ceased to engrave their *Acta*, and this valuable source dried up forever. What we do know with reasonable likelihood is that no temple was constructed to a *Divus* in Rome after those of Marcus Aurelius (deified in 180) and Pertinax (deified in 193):[162] here the deification of Commodus indeed seems a decisive turning-point, undermining the custom from within at the same time as external development—of which Commodus' deification was an early symptom—put it under pressure from without. And the title of *Divus*, though found on commemorative coinage all through the third century and well into the fourth, turned into that only: a mere title. Thus it also appeared on coins commemorating Constantine who throughout his reign had supported the Christian church and was baptized on his deathbed.

161 Cf. the stories of another senatorial emperor and the *Divi*: HA *Sev. Al.* 28. 6; 29. 2.

162 Pertinax: Dio (Xiph.) 75. 4. 1; Marcus: F. de Caprariis in Steinby (1996, iii. 212), s.v. 'Marcus, *divus, templum*'; the information in HA *Carac.* 11. 6: '*Habet templum, habet Salios, habet sodales Antoninianos*' is partly nonsensical and presumably unreliable, a mere *topos*.

The title of *Divus* was now exactly what we must not generally take it to have been in the early empire, an epithet signifying little more than 'of blessed memory'. If we only look at the use of the title throughout the third and early fourth century, without considering its cultic reality or implications, we fail to realize what had actually changed, and it will seem most surprising that it could be used of Constantine and other Christian emperors, apparently without any obvious pagan connection or connotation attached to it.[163] But we may now see why: for a century before the death of Constantine the *Divi* had actually not been worshipped in the state cult. The development that turned the word '*Divus*' from an indication of true divinity, worshipped in cult, into merely an honorary title was a pagan, not a Christian one, and it had occurred long before Constantine's day. Thus in the 260s gold coinage of Gallienus in honour of Divus Augustus was inscribed '*Deo Augusto*'; the word '*Divus*' which was strictly his first name after 14 was not sufficiently honouring: it no longer suggested a 'real' god, with cults and all.[164] The word *Divus* eventually became so harmless that it could in medieval times commonly be used of saints, as a synonym for '*Sanctus*'. This process has come full circle in modern scholarship with the commonly accepted interpretation of the procedure of state deification as a 'canonization' like that of the Roman Catholic Church when recognizing a new saint.

The Roman state cult has frequently been seen as lifeless, mechanical, and fossilized during the empire, and without real importance for Roman history (unlike 'serious', that is, political, history of the period). If we do not take it seriously as cult, as ritual practice, this view will automatically turn out to be true. Rituals tend to appear pointless or silly to people who do not in one way or another participate in them. To attempt getting to the point of ancient pagan rites, it is perhaps most fruitful to ponder the meanings of modern rituals, which do not always or commonly conform to the views of their participants on any theological or verbal level. Church weddings, christenings, and funerals can be meaningful to people whether they

163 For the ambiguity of Constantine's consecration coins, catering for both pagan and Christian views, see Price (1987, 101 f.).

164 RIC V. 1 (Gallienus), nos. 1–2; Turcan (1978, 1011 f.).

believe in God or not, or accept the dogmas of their Church, or the dogmas reflected and expressed in the particular ritual. The relationship of modern secular people and society to traditional religious rites may make it easier for us than for previous generations to grasp that religion does not necessarily presuppose strict beliefs, or indeed belief at all, to function and be meaningful.

Rituals are staged symbolic expressions of concepts, feelings, or ideas which cannot be expressed adequately in mere verbal language. The cults of the *Divi* in their heyday fit such a characterization. Senators were obviously unable to criticize their ruling emperor openly, or direct him verbally as to how he ought to behave or not behave. Ritual language could continually state these points, as well as the participating emperor's answer to them, without causing offence.

Roman state cult was not fossilized. It did indeed change and develop during the empire, even if many modern observers find it hard to take seriously the actual main development, that of imperial deification, and even if it ultimately ended in failure. For two centuries after Augustus' reign hardly any new gods were accepted into the Roman state pantheon apart from the 'home-grown' *Divi*. Enormous resources were devoted to their conspicuous temples and magnificent cults. Imperial deifications were then the most visible and important aspect in the development of the state cult throughout this period. In this light the crisis and collapse of the cults of the *Divi* must have entailed crisis for the state cult at large, as well as vice versa. The most visible and splendid extension of the state worship for almost a quarter millennium could not simply be dropped without questions arising about the system as a whole. Seeing the substantial number of temples to *Divi* converted to other purposes or falling into decay must have filled all Christian hearts with joy—and others with further doubts than they had entertained when the traditional state cults and their gods had continuously marched on in their entirety. In this way, imperial deifications may eventually, in a negative fashion, have played a decisive role in European history. The most important question of ancient history is often phrased as to why it was Christianity which in the fourth century won over the Roman state, as if the old system was somehow just waiting to die at the appearance of a suitable successor. But neither Christianity nor any other religious system could have taken over as Roman state religion unless and until the old state cult began to crumble in crisis. The old world, not the new, seems the more obvious starting-point for investigating development and change.

The drastic measures of the emperor Maximinus between 236 and 238 were a response to an extreme situation, but they do suggest why Christian apologists singled out this particular institution for attack: this was one area where polemicists might get a pagan audience to listen. It seems in any case that the abolishments under Maximinus were permanent, for there is no sign whatsoever that the measures were ever repealed. Christians may not in themselves have been very significant as a political or religious force at the time, but the Roman government's treatment of them at various periods furnished a touchstone by which traditionalist forces in the ruling élite could demonstrate their respect towards the sacrificial principle of the old cults. Thus the emperor Decius in 249 unleashed the first persecution of Christians which covered, or was meant to cover, the whole empire; after a short break the policy was continued by one of his successors, Valerian (253–60), and taken up again by Diocletian (285–305).[165] Decius also, and significantly, paraded the male *Divi* from Augustus to Severus Alexander in a remarkable coin series, probably struck at Rome, defiantly professing loyalty to the traditional system in its, by now, probably most controversial aspect. The series seems even more stubbornly conservative in the context where state worship of these gods had ceased. However, these points should not be overstressed: the cult of the *Divi*, as evidenced in the *Feriale Duranum*, may well have continued in the army (the soldiers still required their meat), irrespective of what happened in Rome, and the primary audience of the coins could possibly have been troops stationed in Northern Italy.[166] Most, though not all, deified emperors from Augustus to Severus

[165] For these persecutions see Lane Fox (1986, *passim*, esp. 450ff.); for that of Decius: Rives (1999).

[166] RIC IV. 3 (Decius), nos. 77–100; Turcan (1978, 1009) for troops as audience; but Elks (1972) for a convincing reattribution of the series to the Rome mint from that of Milan.

Alexander, eleven altogether, are represented in the coin series, each with his own type: on the obverse his portrait with name in the dative, such as *Divo Augusto*, on the reverse an altar or an eagle standing with outspread wings and the legend *consecratio*, 'deification'.[167]

Early in his short reign Decius adopted an unprecedented measure to demonstrate loyalty to tradition by an edict ordering the inhabitants of the empire to sacrifice to the gods (significantly the requirement was as vague as that: the rite itself, not any specific recipients, was what the order was about). It is debated whether the order was from the outset targeted against the Christians, or whether it was simply the refusal of (some) Christians to comply which unleashed persecution on them. The latter view seems oddly academic to me: no emperor or his administration in the mid-third century could have been so utterly uninformed as to be unaware that Christians, or some of them, would be the only substantial group of the empire who would either refuse to comply or betray their beliefs (Jews were specifically exempt from the order). So I take it as obvious that the original edict was indeed from the outset targeted against the Christians, though they were not mentioned in it. The general request for sacrifice was then a quite clever way of isolating the Christians by stressing the one common feature—sacrifice—shared by practically all except Jews and Christians. Christian apologists exploited the common ground between themselves and their pagan audience in order to maximize the effect of their arguments against pagan customs; Decius similarly exploited the pagan common ground, sacrifice, shared by practically all pagans, in order to maximize support against the outsiders. Whatever view one may take of this discussion, the whole affair certainly developed into a persecution of Christianity; and as for later campaigns there can be no doubt that they were from the outset targeted against the Christians and their Churches.

[167] Decius' series of *antoniniani*: Augustus, Vespasian, Titus, Nerva, Trajan, Hadrian, Antoninus, Marcus, Commodus, Severus, Severus Alexander; the series can neither be taken as accurately reflecting the *Divi* in the state cult nor in the army cults: thus Divus Claudius is found in the *Feriale Duranum*, and in the state cult in at least 230 (and no doubt until Maximinus' cuts): *CIL* VI. 1984; XI. 3367 = *ILS* 1180 (*sodalis Augustalis Claudialis*).

Decius' measures against the Christians can be taken as yet another symptom that things were beginning to go wrong for the old order. Seen as measures to demonstrate loyalty to tradition, the centrally ordained persecutions of Christianity in the third century may presuppose that hostility or scepticism towards the old cultic traditions were now to be found within the governing élites themselves, far beyond the ranks of the Christians, and in circles too strong or influential to be attacked directly, unlike the Christians. But by singling out the Christians as a touchstone, Decius, Valerian, and later Diocletian in fact ensured that Christianity came to be perceived as an obvious camp for such scepticism; the traditionalist emperors by their own policy (which was otherwise remarkably ineffectual) advertised the Christian church as a logical alternative, so that oppositional elements of all kinds would now take an interest in the sect.

As it turned out, few policies can ever have failed more completely. This was not only because persecution was ineffectual: it depended on a rudimentary administrative apparatus and, decisively, on an élite, governing the provinces of the empire where the measures had to be implemented, whose members no longer unanimously shared the traditionalist sympathies of persecuting emperors, often irrespective of what they thought of the Christians as such. By their persecutions the traditionalists themselves constructed and nursed a relatively insignificant adversary into a formidable enemy.

CONCLUSION

The outline presented above has attempted to place state apotheosis of dead emperors in basically the same context as that of worship of the living ruler. By honouring, worshipping included, the ruling emperor, his subjects established with him a social contract mutually binding for both parties. This was the basic reason behind all honours, whether to gods, rulers, or patrons: by receiving such honours, the emperor was morally obliged to return benefactions, that is, to rule well. If he did so, he could eventually attain the ultimate honour: state divinity after death. Alternatively, if he broke the contract, his honours would be withdrawn and his memory condemned. This, and not an attempt to falsify history, was the main point behind damnation of his memory.

This contractual system functioned in the same way between patron and client, between gods and humans. The gods too could be punished for breach of contract. For instance, when national disasters, such as imperial deaths, occurred, the temples of the immortals were closed, by which measure they were deprived of worship. This was not just an 'empty' public rite. In some cases it could be carried further by spontaneous action from below; thus when the death of Germanicus was announced in Rome, 'the temples were stoned and the altars of the gods overturned'.[168] This was an extreme case. But the notion of *mutual* obligation and dependence was in fact built into the very core of the state cults. The gods were constantly enticed with promises of honours and threatened with having them diminished or withdrawn. For instance, at the New Year vows, performed by the consuls and by all the priestly colleges of the state, the chief gods of Rome on the Capitol were promised victims the next year if they fulfilled the demands made of them. In the republic these had been to keep and preserve the Roman state and keep it in vigour. During the empire, the vows were on behalf of the emperor and his family, giving the gods some victims and promising them further ones next year if they preserved the imperial family safe and sound. Thus the Arval Brothers on 3 January AD 81:[169]

The chairman [of the Arval college] C. Junius Tadius Mefitanus performed the vows for the welfare of the emperor Titus . . . and of Domitian Caesar . . . and of Julia Augusta and of their children, and after having sacrificed the animals promised by the chairman of the preceding year, he sacrificed to Jupiter Optimus Maximus two steers, to Juno Regina two cows, to Minerva two cows, to the public Welfare [*Salus*] two cows, promising [them the same] next year in the following words which were recited by L. Pompeius Celer: 'Jupiter Optimus Maximus, if emperor Titus . . . and Domitian Caesar . . . , of which two we hereby specifically make mention, will be alive and

[168] *Iustitium*: Vidman (1971); Germanicus: Suet. *Cal.* 5: '*quo defunctus est die, lapidata sunt templa, subversae deum arae, Lares a quibusdam familiares in publicum abiecti, partus coniugum expositi*'; cf. *Tab. Heb.* l. 55 (Crawford, 1996, no. 37); Versnel (n.d.).

[169] Scheid (1998, 126 l. 38 ff.).

their family be safe when the Roman people the next time shall arrive at the date of the 2nd January, and you till that date have preserved them safely from danger and they at that time will be in the same condition as that in which they are presently—if you grant us this good outcome of which we hereby specifically make mention, and you preserve them in the same or a better condition than the one in which they are presently; in return for your doing this, we promise that you will in the name of the college of the Arval Brothers receive [further] two steers with gilded horns.' [Followed by the same formula to Juno Regina, Minerva, and Salus Publica individually].

In this case the stick-and-carrot system failed: the emperor Titus died on 13 September. The gods did not keep their part of the bargain; and so they did not receive their victims—with gilded horns—the next 3 January.

The underdogs in these status relationships were thus no mere timid and defenceless creatures at the mercy of tyrannical caprice: the exercise of power worked both ways.

APPENDIX 1
DEDICATIONS FROM ITALY TO THE *GENIUS* OF LIVING NON-IMPERIALS

Funerary dedications, i. e. to the *Genius* of deceased men, which generally have another character (they are dedicated by close blood relatives of the deceased) are excluded; doubtful cases are, however, included.

CIL V.1868: Ixus l(ibertus) Genio domini v(otum) s(olvit) l(ibens) m(erito).

CIL V.2795: Genio dom(i)nor(um) (et) Cereri T(itus) Poblicius Crescens Laribus publicis dedit imagines argent(eas) duas testamento . . .

CIL V.5892: Gen(io) et [h]onori P(ubli) Tutili Callifontis . . . patr(oni) (centuriarum) XII coll(egi) aerar(i) c(oloniae) . . . M(ediolani) . . . et Iun(oni) Publiciae C(ai) f(iliae) Pomponiai . . . coniug(is) eius et Iun(oni) Tutiliae P(ubli) f(iliae) Pomponian(ae), constantii vivatis, L(ucius) Romatius Valerian(us) et Vocatia Valeria cum filis clientes.

CIL V.6502: Genio T(iti) Attilii Vibiani Clarus libert(us).

CIL V.6950: G(enio) C(ai) Enni Vibiani et Iun(oni) Lartid(iae) Priscinae M(arcus) Vibius Marcellus. (Possibly funerary, according to *CIL loc. cit.* found 'Taurinis in moenibus')

CIL V.6951: Genio M(arci) Isuni Proculi . . . patrono.

CIL V.7142: Genio M(arci) Cassii M(arcus) Satrius Vitulus h(onoris) c(ausa). ('Vitulus' could also be taken to mean a bull-calf, as a sacrificial victim to the *Genius*, instead of being Satrius' *cognomen*)

CIL V.7143: G(enio) Meropis n(ostri) Trophinus ser(vus).

CIL V.7468: Genio et honori L(uci) Pompei L(uci) f(ili) . . . Herenniani . . . collegium pastophorum Industriensium patrono ob merita.

CIL V.7469: Genio Q(uinti) Sertori Synergi Iunioris et Genio

Q(uinti) Sertori Severi patronorum c(ollegium) f(abrum) Ind(ustriensium).

CIL V.7470: Same text as preceding, but with 'c(ollegium) c(entonariorum)' as dedicator.

CIL V.7471: G(enio) Q(uinti) n(ostri) Moschus ser(vus).

CIL V.7505: Genio P(ubli) n(ostri) Thal[i]us, Thalio, Agathio lib(erti).

CIL V.7514: Genio Asiatici L(ucius) Ennius Secundus et . . . fili amico optimo. (Probably funerary: CIL *loc. cit.*: 'reperta dum ampliarentur moenia')

CIL V.7593: G(enio) L(uci) n(ostri), Iun(oni) Clivanae n(ostrae), Iun(oni) Annaeae n(ostrae) Vi[t]ellia Restituta.

CIL VI.257: Phoebus ser(vus) Genio ipsius d(onum) d(edit).

CIL VI.258: Genio Clodi Romani Hermes ser(vus) fec(it).

CIL VI.259: Genio Similis familia.

CIL VI.36754: Genio C(ai) Geruloni Ianuari Fortunatus decur(io) Gerulorum ser(vus).

CIL VI.30883: Genio M(arci) Livi Euni l(iberti) Olymphi fecit Livia Irene patrono.

CIL X.860: Genio L(uci) nostri Felix l(ibertus).

CIL X.861: Genio M(arci) n(ostri) et Laribus duo Diadumeni liberti.

CIL XI.356: [G]enio dom(i)nico Zoila vilic(us).

CIL XI.6806: Genio M(arci) n(ostri) Suavis et Tyrannus [l(iberti)].

AE 1990.51: Euaratus disp(ensator) magister Laribus et familiae de suo d(onum) d(edit) [Geni]o Galli n(ostri). (From Rome)

AE 1990.52: Genio Aucti n(ostri) Tropus l(ibertus). (From Rome)

APPENDIX 2
DEDICATIONS FROM ITALY TO THE *GENIUS AUGUSTI* UP TO AD 235

(excluding dedications by *magistri vici* or *ministri vici*, i. e. of the compital cults, see p. 118 above)

CIL VI.251: Genio Ti(beri) Caesaris Divi Augusti fili Augusti C(aius) Fulvius Chryses mag(ister) pagi Amentini Minor(is) donum dedit . . . (From Rome; date: AD 27)

CIL VI.252: Genio Imp(eratoris) Caesaris Nervae Traiani . . . Corinthus Caesaris n(ostri) Mettianus pedisecus rationis [vol]uptuariae collegio d(onum) d(edit). (From Rome; date: AD 103–17)

CIL VI.254: Genio ac Maiestati Imp(eratoris) Antonini Pii Felicis Augusti M(arcus) Aurelius Aurelianus devotissimus numini eius. (From Rome; date: the emperor is probably Elagabalus, thus 218–22)

CIL VI.31138–52: Dedications by the *equites singulares*, see p. 231 above.

CIL IX.2628: Genio Deivi Iuli parentis patriae quem s(enatus) p(opulus)q(ue) R(omanus) in deorum numerum rettulit. (From Aesernia; date: 44 BC or later (posthumous?))

CIL X.1561: Genio Caesarum Diognetus vilic(us) fec(it). (From Puteoli)

CIL XI.804: Apollini Genioque Augusti Caesaris sacrum L(ucius) Apusulenus L(uci) l(ibertus) Eros magister puteum puteal laurus d(e) p(ecunia) s(ua). (From Bononia; date: Augustan)

CIL XI.3076: Genio Augusti et Ti(beri) Caesaris, Iunoni Liviae Mystes l(ibertus). (From Falerii; date: AD 4–14)

CIL XI.8049: [. . . geni?]o Ti(beri) Caesar[is . . . / . . .]esius L(uci) f(ilius) [. . .]. (From Tuficum; but the restoration given here, from *CIL loc. cit.*, is totally uncertain)

CIL XIV.2349: Genio Germanici Auchenius. (From the Ager Albanus, near Castel Gandolfo; 'Germanicus' is perhaps, as suggested in CIL *loc. cit.*, the emperor Domitian, who had a villa there; but it may also merely be the name of a slave)

AE 1984.186: Porphyrus Aug(usti) lib(ertus) proc(urator) reg(ionum) Fal(ernae) et Stat(anae) [Aug(usti)?] n(ostri?) Geni[o] votum solvit. (From near Forum Popilii)

APPENDIX 3
TITLES OF MUNICIPAL PRIESTS OF EMPERORS IN ITALY FROM INSCRIPTIONAL SOURCES

(very doubtful cases are generally not included)

*: *Flamen* or *sacerdos* of more than one Divus.

of Divus Julius:
Flamen Iulianus: *CIL* V.2536.
Flamen Divi Iuli: *CIL* V.4384; 4459; IX.2598; *AE* 1975.353* (Firmum Picenum: *flamen Divi Augusti et Divi Iuli et Divi Claudi*).
Flamen Divi Caesaris perpetuus: *CIL* V.7478.

of Augustus (all datable to his lifetime, since undated instances can refer to any (Caesar) Augustus, i.e. the living emperor):
Sacerdos Caesaris: *CIL* V.4966 (could in principle also refer to Julius Caesar).
Augusti Caesaris sacerdos: *CIL* X.830 (date: 2 BC).
Augusti sacerdos: *CIL* X.837; 840; 943–4.
Flamen Caesaris Augusti: *CIL* X.947.
Flamen Augustalis: *CIL* IV.3882 (Augustan?); *CIL* XI.1421 (date: 4).
Flamen Aug(usti/-ustalis): *CIL* X.838.

of Divus Augustus:
Flamen Divi Augusti et Romae: *CIL* V.3936.
Flamen Romae et Divi Augusti: *CIL* X.131; 5393.
Flamen Divi Augusti: *CIL* V.4386; 5266 (date: after 98); 5267 (date: the holder evidenced in 65: Tac. *Ann.* 16.8); 6797* (date: after 117); 7605; *CIL* IX.3384–5; 5375; *CIL* X.1262; 1806; 4641; *CIL* XIV.2922 (date: 180–92); 2972 (date: 243); 2995 (date: 51–68); 3014; *AE* 1961.109 (Corfinium); *AE* 1975.349 (Aesernia); *AE* 1975.353* (see under Divus Julius).
Flamen Divi Augusti perpetuus: *CIL* V.7007 (date: after 79).
Sacerdos Divi Augusti: *CIL* V.4442(?); *CIL* X.945–6.

of Tiberius:
Flamen Tiberi Caesaris Augusti: *CIL* IX.652.
Flamen Tiberi Caesaris: Burnett *et al.* (1992) nos. 610–12 (Paestum, see p. 85 above).
Flamen Romae et Tiberi C[aesaris Augusti?]: *CIL* X.688 (could also refer to Claudius).

of Claudius:
No certain instances: Mommsen's restoration *ad loc.* of *CIL* X.1558 is pure fantasy; but see under Tiberius for a possible case.

of Divus Claudius:
Flamen Divi Claudi: *CIL* V.534–5 (date: 98–102); 875 (date: 105); 5126 (date: after 117); *CIL* XI.417; *AE* 1975.251 (Paestum); *AE* 1975.353* (see under Divus Julius).
Flamen Romae et Divi Claudi: *CIL* V.6431.

of Nero (as 'Augusti filius', AD 51–4: all refer to the same holder, see Mouritsen and Gradel (1991)):
Flamen Neronis Caesaris Augusti filii perpetuus: *CIL* IV.1185; 3884; 7992; 7995.

of Divus Vespasianus:
Flamen Divi Vespasiani: *CIL* V.6360; 6513* (*Flamen Divorum Vespasiani Traiani Hadriani perpetuus*); 6514* (*Flamen Divi Vespasiani et [Titi?]*; date: after 217); 6797* (see under Divus Augustus); 7021; *CIL* IX.2600; 2606; 2855; *CIL* X.413 add.; 5382; *CIL* XI.1447a (*flamen* in Ostia); *CIL* XIV.292; 298; 4641; 4664; *AE* 1934.232 (Aquileia); *AE* 1981.223 (near Aquinum); *AE* 1986.113 (Ostia); *AE* 1987.204 (Portus); *AE* 1988.182 (Ostia).
Flamen perpetuus Divi Vespasiani: *CIL* V.7458*.

of Divus Titus:
Flamen Divi Titi: *CIL* V.5239; 5667; 6514* (?; see under Divus Vespasianus); 6995; *CIL* XIV.400 (date: after 138); 4142 (date: 173); 4622; *AE* 1947.46 (from Carpiate, but probably *flamen* at Comum); *AE* 1988.184 (Ostia).

of Divus Nerva:
Flamen Divi Nervae: *CIL* XI.385–6; *AE* 1947.46 (from Carpiate, but probably *flamen* at Comum).
Flamen perpetuus Divi Nervae: *CIL* V.7458.

of Trajan(?):
Flamen perpetuus [Divi Vesp]asiani (et) Divi Nervae [(et?) Imperatoris Caesaris?] Traiani [Augusti?]: *CIL* V.7458.

of Divus Traianus:
Flamen Divi Traiani: *CIL* V.4368 (date: 117–38); 5126; 5312; 5908; 6513* (see under Divus Vespasianus); 6520; 6797* (see under Divus Augustus); 7375; *CIL* IX.2600; 2649; *CIL* X.4873; 5067.

of Hadrian(?):
Flamen Hadr(iani / -ianalis): *CIL* V.545 (if abbreviation should read '*Hadr(ianalis)*', Hadrian may possibly be a Divus at the time).

of Divus Hadrianus:
Flamen Divi Hadriani: *CIL* V.6513* (see under Divus Vespasianus); 8660; Pais, *Additamenta ad CIL V*.1227 (date after 161); *CIL* IX.1160 (date: 138–61); 2853; *CIL* XIV.353; 390–1 (date: 161–80); 4642.
Flamen perpetuus Divi Hadriani: *CIL* X.416.
Flamen Divi Hadriani perpetuus: *CIL* X.7507.

of Antoninus Pius(?):
Flamen Imperatoris [Antoni]ni Caesa[ris Aug(usti)]: *AE* 1975.257 (Paestum).

of Divus Antoninus:
Flamen Divi Antonini: *AE* 1988.201 (Ostia).

of Divus Marcus:
Flamen Divi Marci: *CIL* XIV.4671.
Flamen perpetuus Divi Marci Antonini: *AE* 1975.256 (Paestum).

of Divus Pertinax:
Flamen Divi Pertinacis: *CIL* XIV.4648; *AE* 1988.211* (*Flamen Divi Severi et Divi Pertinacis*; Ostia).

of Divus Severus:
Flamen Divi Severi: *CIL* XIV.373; *AE* 1988.211* (see under Divus Pertinax).

of Divus Antoninus Magnus (i.e. Caracalla):
Flamen Divi Magni Antonini: *CIL* XI.1230.

of all Divi:
Flamen Divorum omnium: *CIL* IX.5357; 5362–3; 5365; *CIL* XIV.444 (?: *flamen Divorum* [. . .]).

of 'Augustus' (i.e. the living emperor):
Flamen Caesaris Augusti: *CIL* IV.1180 (=*AE* 1949.9; date: 69–79).
Flamen Augustalis/Augusti: *CIL* V.2524; 3341; 7425 (date: 96–8); 7428; *CIL* IX.2648; 3434; 3437; 3522; 3613; 4686 (date: 184); 5441; *CIL* X.4868; 6766; *CIL* XI.2116; 3098 (date: 69–79); 6955 ('*flamen Aug(usti) beneficio Caesaris creatus*'; date: 62/3); *CIL* XIV.3500; 3590; *AE* 1980.417 (Sarsina); *AE* 1980.457–8 (Rusellae).
Sacerdos Augustalis/Augusti: *CIL* V.4950; 4960; *CIL* X.51; 6018.
Flamen Augustorum: *CIL* V.47.
Flamen Romae et Augusti: *CIL* V.3376; 3420; 3427; 5036; 5511; Pais, *Additamenta ad CIL V*.624; *CIL* XIV.373 (date: after 211); 400 (date: after 138); 4142 (date: 173); 4622 (date: after 81); *AE* 1955.168 (Ostia); *AE* 1955.169 (Ostia); *AE* 1988.201 (Ostia).
Flamen perpetuus Romae et Augusti: *CIL* XIV.4674/5.

BIBLIOGRAPHY

Abramenko, A., *Die munizipale Mittelschicht im kaiserzeitlichen Italien: zu einem neuen Verständnis von Sevirat und Augustalität* (1993).

Alföldi, A., 'Caesars Tragödie im Spiegel der Münzprägung des Jahres 44 v. Chr.', *Schweiz. Münzbl.*, 4, fascicle 13 (1953), 1–11.

—— Review of Gesche (1968), *Phoenix*, 24 (1970), 166–76.

—— 'Die zwei Lorbeerbäume des Augustus', *Antiquitas,* 14 (1973).

—— Review of Weinstock (1971), *Gnomon*, 47 (1975), 154–79.

Alföldy, G., 'Ein Tempel des Herrscherkultes in Comum', *Athenaeum,* 61 (1983), 362–73.

Amelung, W. (i (1903)–ii (1908)), and Lippold, G. (iii.1 (1936)–iii.2 (1956)), *Die Skulpturen des Vatikanischen Museums* (1903–56).

Anderson, M. L., 'A Proposal for a New Reconstruction of the Altar of the Vicomagistri', *BMGP* 5 (1984), 33–54.

Arce, J., *Funus imperatorum: Los funerales de los emperadores romanos* (1988).

Ausbüttel, F. M., *Untersuchungen zu den Vereinen im Westen des römischen Reiches* (1982).

Balsdon, J. P. V. D., *The Emperor Gaius* (1934).

—— Review of Dobesch (1966), *Gnomon*, 39 (1967), 150–6.

Barrett, A., *Caligula: The Corruption of Power* (1989).

Barton, T., 'Augustus and Capricorn: Astrological Polyvalency and Imperial Rhetoric', *JRS* 85 (1995), 33–51.

Beard, M., 'Religion' in *CAH*, 2nd edn. (1994), 729–68.

Bianchi, F., and Tucci, P. L., 'Alcuni esempi di riuso dell'antico nell'area del Circo Flaminio', *MEFR* 108/1 (1996), 27–82.

Bickerman, E., 'Consecratio', in den Boer (ed.) (1973), 1–37.

—— 'Die römische Kaiserapotheose', *Archiv für Religionswissenschaft* 27 (1929), 1–31 (reprinted in Wlosok (1978), 82–121).

—— 'Diva Augusta Marciana', *AJP* 95 (1974), 362–76.

Billows, R., 'The Religious Procession of the Ara Pacis Augustae: Augustus' *Supplicatio* in 13 BC', *JRA* 6 (1993), 80–92.

Birley, A., *Marcus Aurelius* (1966).

—— *The African Emperor—Septimius Severus* (1988).

BMC = Mattingly, H., *Coins of the Roman Empire in the British Museum* (1923–36).

Bömer, F., 'Ahnenkult und Ahnenglaube im alten Rom', *Beihefte zum Archiv für Religionswissenschaft*, Heft 1 (1943).

—— *Untersuchungen über die Religion der Sklaven in Griechenland und Rom*, i (2nd edn.) (1981)–ii (1960)–iii (2nd edn.) (1990)–iv (1963).

Boyce, G. K., 'Corpus of the Lararia of Pompeii', *MAAR* 14 (1937).

Braund, D., *Rome and the Friendly King: The Character of the Client Kingship* (1984).

Breccia, E., 'Cultores' in De Ruggiero, E., *Dizionario epigrafico di antichità romane* (1886–), ii.2 (1910), 1295–1317.

Bruneau, P., *Recherches sur les cultes hellénistiques à Délos* (1970).

Brunt, P. A., 'Lex de Imperio Vespasiani', *JRS* 67 (1977), 95–116.

—— 'The Fall of the Roman Republic and Related Essays' (1988).

Bulard, M., 'Peintures murales et mosaïques de Délos', *Monuments Piot*, 14 (1908).

—— 'Description des revètements peints a sujets religieux', *Expl. arch. de Délos*, 9 (1926).

Burnett, A., Amandry, M., and Ripollès, P. P., *Roman Provincial Coinage*, i (1992).

Calza, R., 'Ostia, Edificio degli Augustali', *NSc* (1941), 196–209.

—— 'Ritratti romani dal 160 circa alla metà del III secolo d. C.', *Scavi di Ostia*: I ritratti, parte II (n.d.) (*c.*1977).

Camodeca, G., *L'archivio Puteolano dei Sulpicii*, i (1992).

—— 'Tabulae Pompeianae Sulpiciorum (TPSulp.), Edizione critica dell'archivio puteolano dei Sulpicii', *Vetera*, 12 (1999).

Castagnoli, F., 'Su alcuni problemi topografici del Palatino', *RAL* 34 (1980), 332–47.

Castiglione Morelli, V. (ed.), *Il sacello degli Augustali a Miseno* (1991).

Champlin, E., 'Owners and Neighbours at Ligures Baebiani', *Chiron*, 11 (1981), 239–64.

—— 'The Testament of Augustus', *Rhein. Mus.* 132 (1989), 154–65.

Chantraine, H., '"Doppelbestattungen" römischer Kaiser', *Historia*, 29 (1980), 71–85.

Charlesworth, M. P., 'Some Observations on Ruler-Cult, especially in Rome', *HTR* 28 (1935), 5–44.

—— 'The Refusal of Divine Honours, an Augustan Formula', *PBSR* 15 (1939), 1–10.

Claridge, A., 'Hadrian's Column of Trajan', *JRA* 6 (1993), 5–22.

Crawford, M. (ed.), 'Roman Statutes', *BICS Supplement*, 64 (1996).

Cumont, F., *Études syriennes* (1917).

Dareggi, G., 'Il ciclo statuario della "basilica" di Otricoli. La fase giulio-claudia', *BdA*, 14 (1982), 1–36.

de Azevedo, M. Cagiano, *Le antichità di Villa Medici* (1951).

Degrassi, A., 'Fasti consulares et triumphales', *Inscriptiones Italiae*, 13.1 (1947).
—— 'Fasti anni Numani et Iuliani', *Inscriptiones Italiae*, 13.2 (1963).
dell'Orto, L. F. (ed.), *Ercolano 1738–1988. 250 anni di ricerca archeologica* (1988).
De Marchi, A., *Il culto privato di Roma antica*, i–iii (1896).
Demougin, S., *Prosopographie des chevaliers romains julio-claudiens* (1992).
den Boer, W. (ed.), 'Le Culte des souverains dans l'émpire romain', *Entretiens Hardt* 19 (1973).
Di Vita, A., 'Gli *Emporia* di Tripolitania dall'età di Massinissa a Diocleziano: un profilo storico-istituzionale', *ANRW* 2/10/2 (1982), 515–95.
Dobbins, J. J., 'The Altar in the Genius Augusti Sanctuary at Pompeii', *RM* 99 (1992), 251–63.
—— 'The Imperial Cult Building in the Forum at Pompeii', in Small (1996), 99–114.
Dobesch, G., *Caesars Apotheose zu Lebzeiten und sein Ringen um den Königstitel* (1966).
Dondin-Payre, M., 'Topographie et propagande gentilice: le compitum Acilium et l'origine des Acilii Glabriones', in *L'Urbs* (1987), 87–109.
Döpp, S. (ed.), *Karnevaleske Phänomene in antiken und nachchristlichen Kulturen und Literaturen* (1993).
Dorcey, P. F., *The Cult of Silvanus: A Study in Roman Folk Religion* (1992).
Eck, W., Caballos, A., and Fernandez, F., *Das senatus consultum de Cn. Pisone patre* (1996).
Eden, P. T., *Seneca: Apocolocyntosis* (1984).
Ehrenberg, V., and Jones, A. H. M., *Documents illustrating the Reigns of Augustus and Tiberius*, 2nd edn. (1955).
Elks, K. J. J., 'Reattribution of the Milan Coins of Trajan Decius to the Rome Mint', *NC* 12 (1972), 111–15.
Elsner, J., 'Cult and Sculpture: Sacrifice in the Ara Pacis Augustae', *JRS* 81 (1991), 50–61.
Eschebach, H., *Pompeji* (1978).
Etienne, R., *Le Culte impérial dans la péninsule ibérique* (1958).
—— 'A propos du *cosidetto* édifice des *Augustales* d'Herculanum', in dell'Orto (1988), 345–50.
Fabbricotti, E., *Galba* (1976).
Fears, J. R., 'The Cult of Jupiter and Roman Imperial Ideology', *ANRW* 2/17/1 (1981), 3–141.
Fejfer, J., '*Divus Caracalla* and *Diva Julia Domna*: A Note', *Acta Hyperborea*, 4 (1992), 207–19.

Fink, R. O., Hoey, A. S., and Snyder, W. F., 'The *Feriale Duranum*', *YCS* 7 (1940), 1–222.
Fiorelli, G., *Descrizione di Pompei* (1875).
Fishwick, D., 'Genius and Numen', *HTR* 62 (1969), 356–67.
—— 'The Name of the Demigod', *Historia*, 24 (1975), 624–8.
—— 'The Imperial Cult in the Latin West: Studies in the Ruler Cult of the Western Provinces of the Roman Empire', *EPRO*, 108: i. 1–2 (1987), i. 3 (1990), ii. 1 (1991).
—— 'Prudentius and the Cult of Divus Augustus', *Historia*, 39 (1990), 475–86.
—— 'On the Temple of Divus Augustus', *Phoenix*, 46, 3 (1992), 232–55.
—— 'The Inscription of Mamia again: The Cult of the *Genius Augusti* and the Temple of the Imperial Cult on the *Forum* of Pompeii', *Epigraphica*, 57 (1995), 17–38.
Fittschen, K., and Zanker, P., *Katalog der römischen Porträts in den Capitolinischen Museen und den anderen kommunalen Sammlungen der Stadt Rom*, i (1983)–ii (1985).
Fraenkel, E., *Plautinisches im Plautus* (1922).
—— *Elementi Plautini in Plauto* (1960).
Fraschetti, A., *Roma e il principe* (1990).
—— 'Indice analitico della *Consolatio ad Liviam Augustam de morte Drusi Neronis filii eius qui in Germania de morbo periit*', *MEFR* 108. 1 (1996), 191–239.
Frey, M., 'Untersuchungen zur Religion und zur Religionspolitik des Kaisers Elagabal', *Historia Einzelschriften*, 62 (1989).
Fröhlich, T., *Lararien- und Fassadenbilder in den Vesuvstädten. Untersuchungen zur 'volkstümlichen' pompeianischen Malerei* (1991).
Fuchs, M., Liverani, P., and Santoro, P., 'Il teatro e il ciclo statuario Giulio-Claudio', *Caere*, 2 (1989).
Furneaux, H., *The Annals of Tacitus*, ed. with intr. and notes by H. F., 2nd edn. (1896).
Galsterer, H., 'A Man, a Book, and a Method: Sir Ronald Syme's *Roman Revolution* after Fifty Years', in Raaflaub and Toher (1990), 1–20.
Garnsey, P., and Saller, R., *The Roman Empire: Economy, Society and Culture* (1987).
Geiger, F., 'De sacerdotibus Augustorum municipalibus' (Diss. Halle, 1913).
—— 'Sacra' in *RE* IA (1914), cols. 1656–64.
Gesche, H., *Die Vergottung Caesars* (1968).
—— *Caesar* (1976).
Geyer, U., 'Der Adlerflug im römischen Konsekrationszeremoniell', unpubl. thesis (Bonn, 1965).

Gilliam, J. F., 'On Divi under the Severi', *Hommages à Marcel Renard. Collection Latomus*, 102 (1969), 284–9.

Gnoli, G., and Vernant, J. P. (eds.), *La Mort les morts dans les sociétés anciennes* (1982).

Goodyear, F. R. D., *The Annals of Tacitus: Books 1–6*; ed. with a commentary by F. R. D. G., i (1972)–ii (1981).

Gordon, A. E., *Album of dated Latin Inscriptions* (1958–63).

Gordon, R., 'The Veil of Power: Emperors, Sacrificers and Benefactors', in North and Beard (1990), 199–231.

Gradel, I., 'Mamia's Dedication: Emperor and Genius. The Imperial Cult in Italy and the Genius Coloniae in Pompeii', *ARID* 20 (1992), 43–58.

——'Jupiter Latiaris and Human Blood: Fact or Fiction?', *Classica et Mediaevalia* 53 (2002), 235–53.

Griffin, J., 'Augustus and the Poets: "Caesar qui cogere posset"', in Millar and Segal (1984), 189–218.

Griffin, M., *Seneca: A Philosopher in Politics* (1976).

Gros, P., 'Rites funéraires et rites d'immortalité dans la liturgie de l'apothéose impériale', *AEHE*, 4th section (1965–6), 477–90.

Guarducci, M., 'Enea e Vesta', *RM* 78 (1971), 73–118.

Habicht, C., 'Die augusteische Zeit und das erste Jahrhundert nach Christi Geburt', in den Boer (1973), 39–99.

Halsberghe, G. H., 'Le Culte de Deus Sol Invictus à Rome au 3e siècle après J.C.', *ANRW* 2/17/4 (1984), 2181–201.

Hänlein-Schäfer, H., *Veneratio Augusti: Eine Studie zu den Tempeln des Ersten römischen Kaisers* (1985).

——'Die Ikonographie des Genius Augusti im Kompital- und Hauskult der frühen Kaiserzeit', in Small (1996), 73–98.

Hannestad, N., *Roman Art and Imperial Policy* (1986).

Hano, M., 'A l'Origine du culte impérial: les autels des Lares Augusti. Recherches sur les thèmes iconographiques et leur signification', *ANRW* 2/16/3 (1986), 2333–81.

Hanson, J. A., 'Plautus as a Source Book for Roman Religion', *TAPA* 90 (1959), 48–101.

Harmon, D. P., 'The Family Festivals of Rome', *ANRW* 2/16/2 (1978), 1592–1603.

Harvey, Jr., P. B., 'Historical Topicality in Plautus', *Classical World*, 79 (1985–6), 297–304.

Helbig, W., *Führer durch die öffentlichen Sammlungen klassischer Altertümer in Rom*, 4th edn., H. Speier (ed.) (1963–72).

Henzen, G., *Acta fratrum Arvalium quae supersunt* (1874), repr. 1967.

Herbert-Brown, G., *Ovid and the* Fasti*: A Historical Study* (1994).

Hermann, W., *Römische Götteraltäre* (1961).

Hesberg, H. von, and Panciera, S., *Das Mausoleum des Augustus: Der Bau und seine Inschriften* (1994).
Hill, D. K., 'A Cache of Bronze Portraits of the Julio-Claudians', *AJA* 43 (1939), 401–9.
Hoffman Lewis, M. W., 'The Official Priests of Rome under the Julio-Claudians', *Papers and Monographs of the American Academy in Rome*, 16 (1955).
Holland, K. A., 'The Shrine of the Lares Compitales', *TAPA* 68 (1937), 428–41.
Hölscher, T., 'Staatsdenkmal und Publikum', *Xenia—Konstanzer Althistorische Vorträge, Heft 9* (1984).
Hopkins, K., *Conquerors and Slaves* (1978).
Hülsen, C., 'Curia' in RE iv, cols. 1814–26 (1901).
Hurley, D. W., 'An Historical and Historiographical Commentary on Suetonius' *Life of C. Caligula*', *American Classical Studies*, 32 (1993).
Hurst, H., 'Nuovi scavi. nell'area di Santa Maria Antiqua', *Archeologia Laziale*, 9 (1988), 13–17.
'I Volusii Saturnini. Una famiglia romana della prima età imperiale' (various authors), *Archeologia: Materiali e problemi*, 6 (1982).
Jeppesen, K., 'Grand Camée de France: Sejanus Reconsidered and Confirmed', *RM* 100 (1993), 141–75.
Johnson, P., *Elizabeth I* (1974).
Kaiser Augustus und die verlorene Republik. Eine Ausstellung im Martin-Gropius-Bau, Berlin 7. Juni–14. August 1988 (1988).
Katzoff, R., 'Tacitus, *Annales* I,74: The Case of Granius Marcellus', *AJP* 92 (1971), 680–4.
Kienast, D., *Augustus: Prinzeps und Monarch* (1982).
Kierdorf, W., 'Funus und Consecratio. Zur Terminologie und Ablauf der römischen Kaiserapotheose', *Chiron*, 16 (1986*a*), 43–69.
—— 'Apotheose und postumer Triumph Trajans', *Tyche*, 1 (1986*b*), 147–56.
Kleiner, D. E. E., *Roman Sculpture* (1992).
Kockel, V., 'Archäologische Funde und Forschungen in den Vesuvstädten, II', *AA* (1986), 443–569.
Koeppel, G. M., 'Die "Ara Pietatis Augustae": Ein Geisterbau', *RM* 89 (1982), 453–5.
Kolbe, H.-G., 'Noch einmal Vesta auf dem Palatin', *RM* 73–4 (1966–7), 94–104.
Krause, M., 'Hostia', *RE* suppl. 5 (1931), cols. 236–82.
Kunckel, H., 'Der römische Genius', *RM* 20. Ergänzungsheft (Heidelberg, 1974).
Kuttner, A. L., *Dynasty and Empire in the Age of Augustus: The Case of the Boscoreale Cups* (1995).

Ladage, D., 'Städtische Priester- und Kultämter im Lateinischen Westen des Imperium Romanum zur Kaiserzeit' (Diss. Cologne, 1971).
Lane Fox, R., *Pagans and Christians* (1986).
Latte, K., *Römische Religionsgeschichte* (1960).
Le Collezioni del Museo Nazionale di Napoli, i.1 (1986).
Lefèvre, E., Stärk, E., and Vogt-Spira, G., *Plautus Barbarus: Sechs Kapitel zur Originalität des Plautus* (1991).
Letta, C., 'Le imagines Caesarum di un praefectus castrorum Aegypti e l'XI coorte pretoria', *Athenaeum*, n.s., 56 (1978), 3–19.
Levick, B., *Tiberius the Politician* (1976).
—— *The Government of the Roman Empire* (1985).
—— *Claudius* (1990).
Lieberg, G., *Puella Divina: Die Gestalt der göttlichen Geliebten bei Catul im Zusammenhang der antiken Dichtung* (1962).
Liebeschuetz, J. H. W. G., *Continuity and Change in Roman Religion* (1979).
Ling, R., *Roman Painting* (1991).
Lintott, A. W., *Violence in Republican Rome* (1968).
Lorsch, R. S., 'An *Omen* of *Divus Augustus*: Portent of Triumph or Divinity?' *Collection Latomus vol. 239, Studies in Latin Literature and Roman History VIII* (1997), 278–86.
Lowe, J. C. B., 'The *Virgo Callida* of Plautus, *Persa*', *CQ*, n.s., 39 (1989), 390–9.
Lund, A. A., *L. Annaeus Seneca: Apocolocyntosis Divi Claudii. Herausgegeben, übersetzt und kommentiert von A. A. L.* (1994).
L'Urbs. Espace urbain et histoire, various authors, *Collections de l'École Française de Rome* (1987).
McCrum, M., and Woodhead, A. G., *Select Documents of the Principates of the Flavian Emperors A.D. 68–96* (1961).
Maiuri, A., *La Villa dei Misteri* (1931).
—— *L'ultima fase edilizia di Pompei* (1942).
Marx, F., *Plautus Rudens. Text und Kommentar von F. M.* (1959).
Mattingly, H., 'Some Historical Roman Coins of the First Century A.D.', *JRS* 10 (1920), 37–41.
Mau, A., *Pompeji in Leben und Kunst* (1900).
Maxfield, V. A., *The military decorations of the Roman army* (1981).
Megow, W.-R., *Kameen von Augustus bis Alexander Severus* (1987).
Meiggs, R., *Roman Ostia*, 2nd edn. (1973).
Meyer, E., *Caesars Monarchie und das Prinzipat des Pompeius*, 3rd edn. (1963).
Millar, F., *A Study of Cassius Dio* (1964).

Millar, F., 'Ovid and the *Domus Augusta*: Rome seen from Tomoi', *JRS* 83 (1993), 1–17.
——and Segal, E. (eds.), *Caesar Augustus: Seven Aspects* (1984).
Momigliano, A., 'The Origins of Rome', *CAH* 7/2, 2nd edn. (1989), 52–112.
Mommsen, T., 'Die Litteraturbriefe des Horaz', *Hermes*, 15 (1880), 103–15 (=id., *Gesammelte Schriften* (1905–13) vii. 175–86).
——*Römisches Staatsrecht*, 3rd edn. (1887–8).
——*Reden und Aufsätze* (1905).
Moretti, G., *Ara Pacis Augustae*, i–ii (1948).
Mouritsen, H., 'Elections, Magistrates and Municipal Elite: Studies in Pompeian Epigraphy', *ARID*, suppl. 15 (1988).
——and Gradel, I., 'Nero in Pompeian Politics: *Edicta Munerum* and Imperial Flaminates in late Pompeii', *ZPE* 87 (1991), 145–56.
Musurillo, H., *The Acts of the Christian Martyrs: Introductions, texts, and translations by H. M.* (1972).
Muth, R., 'Römische Religio', *Serta philologica Aenipontana*, 7/8 (1961), 247–71.
——'Vom Wesen römischer "religio"', *ANRW* 2/16/1 (1978), 290–354.
Nash, E., *Pictorial Dictionary of Ancient Rome*, i–ii (1961–2).
Nauta, R. R., 'Seneca's *Apocolocyntosis* as Saturnalian literature', *Mnemosyne* 40 (1987), 69–96.
Neudecker, R., *Die Skulpturenausstattung römischer Villen in Italien* (1988).
Nicolet, C., 'Tribuni militum a populo', *MEFR* 79 (1967), 29 ff.
——*L'Inventaire du monde* (1988).
Niebling, G., 'Laribus Augustis magistri primi. Der Beginn des Compitalkultes der Lares und des Genius Augusti', *Historia*, 5 (1956), 303–31.
Nissen, H., *Pompeianische Studien zur Städtekunde des Altertums* (1877).
Nock, A. D., 'Religious Developments from the Close of the Republic to the Death of Nero', *CAH* 10 (1934), 465–511.
——*Essays on Religion and the Ancient World* (1972).
North, J. A., 'Praesens Divus', review of Weinstock (1971)), *JRS* 65 (1975), 171–7.
——'Conservatism and Change in Roman Religion', *PBSR* 44 (1976), 1–12.
——'Religion and Politics, from Republic to Principate', *JRS* 76 (1986), 251–8.
——'Religion in Republican Rome', *CAH* 7/2, 2nd edn. (1989), 573–624.

North, J. A., and Beard, M. (eds.), *Pagan Priests: Religion and Power in the Ancient World* (1990).
Ohr, K., 'Die Form der Basilika bei Vitruv', *BJb* 175 (1975), 113–27.
Oliver, J. H., 'The Divi of the Hadrianic Period', *HTR* 42 (1949), 35–40.
Orr, D. G., 'Roman Domestic Religion: The Evidence of the Household Shrines', *ANRW* 2/16/2 (1978), 1557–91.
Overbeck, J., and Mau, A., *Pompeji in seinen Gebäuden, Alterthümern und Kunstwerken*, 4th edn. (1884).
Packer, J. E., 'Trajan's Forum again: The Column and the Temple of Trajan in the Master Plan attributed to Apollodorus (?)', *JRA* 7 (1994), 163–82.
Palmer, R. E. A., *Roman Religion and Roman Empire: Five Essays* (1974).
——'Studies of the Northern Campus Martius in Ancient Rome', *Transactions of the American Philological Society*, 80, part 2 (1990).
Panciera, S., 'Due novità epigrafiche romane', *RAL* 23 (1968), 315–40.
——'Ancora tra epigrafia e topografia', in *L'Urbs* (1987), 61–86.
——'La collezione epigrafica dei Musei Capitolini', *Tituli*, 6 (1987).
Pannuti, U., 'L'apoteosi d'Omero. Vaso argenteo del Museo Nazionale di Napoli', *Accademia Nazionale dei Lincei: Monumenti Antichi. Serie miscellanea*, 3/2 (52 of the general series) (1984), 43–61.
Paris, R., *Dono Hartwig. Originali ricongiunti e copie tra Roma e Ann Arbor. Ipotesi per il Templum Gentis Flaviae* (1994).
Pescatori, G. Colucci, *Il Museo Irpino* (1975).
Peters, J. P., and Thiersch, H., *Painted Tombs in the Necropolis of Marissa* (1905).
Pfenner, H. H., and Yonan, E. A., 'Is a Science of Religion Possible?', *Journal of Religion*, 52 (1972), 107–33.
Pippidi, D. M., 'Le "Numen Augusti"', *REL* 9 (1931), 83–112.
——'La date de l'Ara numinis Augusti de Rome', *REL* 11 (1933), 435–56.
——'Recherches sur le culte impérial', n.d. (*c.*1939).
Platner, S. B., and Ashby, T., *A Topographical Dictionary of Ancient Rome* (1929).
Pollini, J., 'Studies in Augustan "Historical" Reliefs' (Ph.D. Berkeley, 1978); microfilm edn. Ann Arbor (1981).
Pötscher, W., 'Numen und Numen Augusti', *ANRW* 2/16/1 (1978), 355–92.
Price, S. R. F., *Rituals and Power: The Roman Imperial Cult in Asia Minor* (1984*a*).
——'Gods and Emperors: The Greek Language of the Roman Imperial Cult', *JHS* 104 (1984*b*), 79–95.

Price, S. R. F., 'The Consecration of Roman Emperors', in Price, S. R. F. and Cannadine, D. (eds.), *Rituals of Royalty: Power and Ceremonial in Traditional Societies* (1987), 56–105.

Raaflaub, K. A., and Toher, M. (eds.), *Between Republic and Empire: Interpretations of Augustus and his Principate* (1990).

Ribezzo, F., 'Il primissimo culto di Cesare Augusto', *Rivista indo-greco-italico di filologia, lingua, antichità*, 21 (1937), 1–25.

Richard, J.-C., 'Recherches sur certains aspects du culte impérial: les funerailles des empereurs romains aux deux premiers siècles de notre ère', *ANRW* 2/16/2 (1978), 1121–34 (practically repeated in *Klio*, 62 (1980), 461–71; orig. pub. in *Latomus* 25 (1966), 784–804).

Richardson, Jr., L., *Pompeii: An Architectural History* (1988).

Rives, J. B., 'The Decree of Decius and the Religion of Empire', *JRS* 89 (1999), 135–54.

Rizzo, G. E., *La base di Augusto* (1933).

Robert, L., 'Théophane de Mytilène à Constantinople', *CRAI* (1969), 42–64.

—— Bowersock, G. W., and Jones, C. P., *Le Martyre de Pionios prêtre de Smyrne* (1994).

Rüpke, J., *Kalender und Öffentlichkeit* (1995).

Ryberg, I. Scott, 'Rites of the State Religion in Roman Art', *MAAR* 22 (1955).

Sabbatini Tumolesi, P., 'Gladiatorum Paria', *Tituli*, 1 (1980).

Saller, R. P., *Personal Patronage under the Early Empire* (1982).

—— *Patriarchy, Property and Death in the Roman Family* (1994).

Santero, J. M., 'The "*Cultores Augusti*" and the Private Worship of the Roman Emperor', *Athenaeum*, 61 (1983), 111–25.

Sauter, F., 'Der römische Kaiserkult bei Martial und Statius', *Tübinger Beiträge zur Altertumswissenschaft*, XXI. Heft (1934).

Schäfer, T., *Imperii Insignia* (1989).

Scheid, J., 'Contraria facere: Renversements et déplacements dans les rites funeraires', *A.I.O.N., Sez. Archeologia e Storia Antica*, 6 (1984), 117–39.

—— *Religion et piété à Rome* (1985).

—— *Romulus et ses frères: le collège des Frères Arvales, modèle du culte public dans la Rome des empereurs* (1990).

—— 'Die Parentalien für die verstorbenen Caesaren als Modell für den römischen Totenkult', *Klio* 75 (1993), 188–201.

Scheid, J., 'Commentarii Fratrum Arvalium Qui Supersunt', *Roma Antica*, 4 (1998).

Schneider, B., *Studien zu den kleinformatigen Kaiserporträts von den Anfängen der Kaiserzeit bis ins dritte Jahrhundert* (1976).

Schoonhoven, H., *The Pseudo-Ovidian Ad Liviam de morte Drusi*

(Consolatio ad Liviam, Epicedium Drusi). A Critical Text with Introduction and Commentary (1992).
Schulten, P. N., *Die Typologie der römischen Konsekrationsprägungen* (1979).
Scott, K., *The Imperial Cult under the Flavians* (1936).
Scott, R. T., 'Providentia Aug.', *Historia*, 31 (1982), 436–59.
Sherk, R. K., *The Roman Empire: Augustus to Hadrian* (1988).
Shipp, G. P., 'Plautine Terms for Greek and Roman Things', *Glotta*, 34 (1955), 139–52.
Simpson, C. J., 'The Cult of the Emperor Gaius', *Latomus*, 40 (1981), 489–511.
Sinn, F., 'Die Grabdenkmäler 1: Reliefs Altäre Urnen' (Vatikanische Museen, Museo Gregoriano profano ex Lateranense: Katalog der Skulpturen I,1) (1991).
Slater, N. W., 'Satyricon 60.7: which Augustus?', *Liverpool Classical Monthly*, 11/3 (1986), 43.
Small, A. M. (ed.), *Subject and Ruler: The Cult of the Ruling Power in Classical Antiquity* (1996).
——'The Shrine of the Imperial Family in the Macellum at Pompeii', in Small (1996), 115–41.
Smallwood, E. M., *Documents Illustrating the Principates of Gaius Claudius & Nero* (1967).
Speidel, M. P., 'Commodus the God-emperor and the Army', *JRS* 83 (1993), 109–14.
Spinazzola, V., *Pompeii alla luce degli scavi nuovi di Via dell' Abbondanza (anni 1910–1923)* (1953).
Steinby, E. M. (ed.), *Lexicon topographicum urbis Romae*, i (1993)–ii (1995)–iii (1996).
Sutherland, C. H. V., 'Divus Augustus Pater: A Study in the *Aes* Coinage of Tiberius', *NC*, 6th series, 1 (1941), 97–116.
Syme, R., *The Roman Revolution* (1939).
——'Seianus on the Aventine', *Hermes*, 86 (1956), 257–66.
——*Roman Papers*, i–ii (1979)–iii (1984).
Taeger, F., *Charisma*, i (1957)–ii (1960).
Tamm, D., 'Ist der Castortempel das Vestibulum zu dem Palast des Caligula gewesen?' *Eranos*, 62 (1964), 146–69.
Taylor, L. R., 'The Worship of Augustus in Italy during His Lifetime', *TAPA* 51 (1920), 116–33.
—— 'The Altar of Manlius in the Lateran', *AJA* 25 (1921), 387–95.
——*The Divinity of the Roman Emperor* (1931).
——'Tiberius' *Ovatio* and the *Ara Numinis Augusti*', *AJP* 58 (1937), 185–93.

Temporini, H., *Die Frauen am Hofe Trajans: Ein Beitrag zur Stellung der Augustae im Prinzipat* (1978).
Torelli, M., *Typology & Structure of Roman Historical Reliefs* (1982).
Toutain, J., *Les Cultes païens dans l'empire romain*, i (1905)–ii (1907) (both vols. repr. 1967).
Treggiari, S., *Roman Freedmen during the late Republic* (1969).
Turcan, R., 'Origines et sens de l'inhumation à l'époque impériale', *REA* 60 (1958), 323–47.
——'Le Culte impérial au IIIe siècle', *ANRW* 2/16/2 (1978), 996–1084.
Unter dem Vulkan: Meisterwerke der Antike aus dem Archäologischen Nationalmuseum Neapel (Bonn Exhibition Catalogue, 1995).
Usener, H., 'Divus Alexander', *Rhein. Mus.*, 57 (1902), 71–3.
Versnel, H. S., *Triumphus: An Enquiry into the Origin, Development and Meaning of the Roman Triumph* (1970).
——'Two Carnivalesque Princes: Augustus and Claudius and the Ambiguity of Saturnalian Imagery', in Döpp (1993), 99–122.
——'Destruction, *Devotio* and Despair in a Situation of Anomy: The Mourning for Germanicus in Triple Perspective', *Perennitas. Studi in onore di Angelo Brelich* (Rome, n.d.), 541–618.
Vidman, L., 'Inferiae und Iustitium', *Klio*, 53 (1971), 209–12.
——*Fasti Ostienses*, 2nd edn. (1982).
Vittinghoff, F., 'Der Staatsfeind in der römischen Kaiserzeit' (Diss. Bonn, 1936).
Wagenvoort, H., *Roman Dynamism: Studies in Ancient Roman Thought, Language and Custom* (1947).
Wallace-Hadrill, A., 'Civilis Princeps: Between Citizen and King', *JRS* 72 (1982), 32–48.
——*Suetonius: The Scholar and his Caesars* (1983).
Warde Fowler, W., *Roman Ideas of Deity* (1911).
Wardle, D., 'Suetonius' Life of Caligula: A Commentary', *Collection Latomus* 225 (1994).
Weber, W., *Princeps. Studien zur Geschichte des Augustus I* (1936).
Weinstock, S., 'Victor and Invictus', *HTR* 50 (1957), 211–47.
——*Divus Julius* (1971).
Whaling, F. (ed.), *Contemporary Approaches to the Study of Religion* (1983).
Whittaker, C. R., 'The Revolt of Papirius Dionysius A. D. 190', *Historia*, 13 (1964), 348–69.
Wiseman, T. P., 'Conspicui postes tectaque digna deo: The Public Image of Aristocratic and Imperial Houses' in *L'Urbs* (1987), 393–413.
Wissowa, G., *Gesammelte Abhandlungen zur römischen Religions- und*

Stadtgeschichte (*Ergänzungsband zu des Verfassers 'Religion und Kultus der Römer'*) (1904).
——*Religion und Kultus der Römer*, 2nd edn. (1912), repr. 1971.
——'Neue Bruchstücke des römischen Festkalenders', *Hermes*, 58 (1923), 369–92.
Wlosok, A. (ed.), 'Römischer Kaiserkult', *Wege der Forschung*, 372 (1978).
Woytek, E., '*T. Maccius Plautus*, Persa. Einleitung, Text und Kommentar', *Österreichische Akademie der Wissenschaften, philosophisch-historische Klasse, Sitzungsberichte*, 385 (1982).
Yavetz, Z., 'The Personality of Augustus: Reflections on Syme's *Roman Revolution*', in Raaflaub and Toher (1990), 21–41.
Zanker, P., 'Der Larenaltar im Belvedere des Vatikans', *RM* 76 (1969), 205–18.
——'Über die Werkstätten augusteischer Larenaltäre und damit zusammenhängende Probleme der Interpretation', *BCAR* 82 (1970–1), 147–55.
——*Augustus und die Macht der Bilder* (1987).
——*The Power of Images in the Age of Augustus* (1988; English tr. of Zanker (1987)).
——*Pompeji: Stadtbild und Wohngeschmack* (1995).
Zevi, F., 'Miscellanea Ostiense, III. Il tempio del collegio dei "fabri tignuarii" e una dedica a Pertinace divinizzato', *RAL* 26 (1971), 449–79.
Ziolkowski, A., 'Was Agrippa's Pantheon the Temple of Mars in Campo?' *PBSR* 62 (1994), 261–77.

INDEX LOCORUM

INSCRIPTIONS AND PAPYRI

GENERAL INDEX